The Economics of Artificial Intelligence: Institutional Transformations and Implications for Capitalism

Preface

Dear Reader,

Welcoming you to "The Economics of Artificial Intelligence: Institutional Transformations and Implications for Capitalism." As you embark on this voyage through the pages of this book, I encourage you to investigate the profound changes that AI is catalysing in the realms of economics, society, and ethics. Certain epochs in human history stand out as turning points, where the convergence of innovation, technology, and human endeavour reshapes the course of our civilization. Certainly, the advent of Artificial Intelligence (AI) qualifies as one of these epochs. AI represents not only a technological advancement, but also a radical change in how we perceive and interact with the world.

I delve deeply into the core of this transformation in this book. With each page, you will gain a deeper understanding of how AI is redefining our economies, reshaping industries, and challenging the status quo. Our voyage is multifaceted, examining AI's impact on the very foundations of capitalism, the economic system that underpins a large portion of contemporary society. As you peruse through these pages, you will observe how AI, with its ability to process vast amounts of data and make complex decisions, is transforming not only industries but also the fundamental tenets upon which our economic systems are founded. From healthcare to finance and beyond, you will realise that this transformation offers limitless opportunities for optimisation, efficiency, and innovation. However, AI's history is not one of unbridled success. It is also a tale of difficult obstacles and moral conundrums. The rise of AI raises profound concerns regarding privacy, prejudice, job displacement, and income disparity. Our investigation invites you to contend with the consequences of a world dominated by artificial intelligence.

As the author, I intend to provide you with a thorough and thought-provoking guide to this complex terrain. I've compiled a variety of chapters, each of which is devoted to a specific aspect of the AI transformation. From economic planning to entrepreneurship, cyber security to international trade, I leave no stone untouched in our effort to provide a comprehensive overview of this new frontier. This book's structure allows for flexible navigation. You have the option of delving deeply into specific areas of interest or traversing the entire landscape chapter by chapter. Whether you are a scholar, policymaker, business leader, or just an inquisitive reader, you will find something of interest within these pages. As we embark on this exploration together, I encourage you to think critically, to engage with the ideas presented, and to imagine the future we are forging collectively. AI is more than just a technology; it is the canvas upon which we will paint the future of our societies and economies.

I am grateful to the brilliant minds who have contributed their insights to this effort, as well as to you, dear reader, for joining me on this journey. Together, we chart a course through the uncharted waters of the AI revolution, navigating towards a future in which the amalgamation of human and artificial intelligence propels us to new heights. This book will guide you through the intriguing world of artificial intelligence and its impact on our economies, societies, and very way of life.

Warm regards,
Saeed Mousa

Table of Contents

Introduction

The introduction of Artificial Intelligence (AI) is one of the most transformative chapters in the history of human progress. The emergence of artificial intelligence has ushered in a new era characterised by the fusion of human creativity and machine learning algorithms, with profound implications for our economies, societies, and institutions. This book, "The Economics of Artificial Intelligence: Institutional Transformations and Implications for Capitalism," is a voyage into the heart of AI's economic and ethical landscape.

As AI evolves, it is not only transforming industries, but also our economic systems and institutions. It is a force that, when strategically harnessed, can generate unprecedented benefits, such as optimising production and improving healthcare delivery. However, this transformative power also presents complex challenges, ranging from ethical dilemmas involving privacy and prejudice to economic disruptions and worries about income inequality.

Certain junctures in the grand tapestry of human history stand out as epochal moments that eternally alter the course of our journey. Unquestionably, the advent of Artificial Intelligence (AI) is one of these transformative chapters. It heralds in an era in which the marriage of human creativity and machine learning algorithms gives rise to a new paradigm, one with profound and far-reaching consequences for our economies, societies, and institutions. This book, titled "The Economics of Artificial Intelligence: Institutional Transformations and Implications for Capitalism," undertakes a comprehensive exploration of this fundamental shift, delving deep into AI's complex economic and ethical landscape.

The emergence and evolution of AI represent a convergence of human ingenuity and computational power that is unprecedented. With their ability to process enormous amounts of data, identify patterns, and make decisions, AI systems are redefining not only individual industries, but also the fundamental structure of our economic systems and the foundational principles upon which our institutions are founded. The ramifications of this transformation are profound and multifaceted, affecting nearly every aspect of our existence.

The strategic deployment of AI has the potential to yield numerous benefits. It can optimise production processes to make them more cost-effective and efficient. It can revolutionise the delivery of healthcare by improving diagnostics, treatment, and patient care. Nonetheless, alongside these extraordinary opportunities, AI's transformative power engenders complex challenges that cannot be ignored. As issues of privacy, bias, and accountability come to the forefront, ethical concerns loom enormous. In the meantime, economic disruptions are inevitable, raising urgent questions about job displacement, income inequality, and the very nature of work in an increasingly machine-driven world.

In this complex and rapidly-changing environment, navigating the intersection of AI and capitalism requires both keen insight and an in-depth comprehension of the forces at play. This book explores these forces comprehensively, providing a nuanced examination of how AI is reshaping the foundations of capitalism and the implications, both positive and negative, of this transformation.

In this book, we venture on a multidimensional journey, dissecting the profound effects of artificial intelligence on capitalism, one of the most influential economic ideologies of our time. With its emphasis on individual liberty, private property rights, and economic incentives, capitalism is a cornerstone of contemporary economic thought. Nonetheless, as AI continues its relentless march, it compels us to reconsider how these fundamental tenets correspond to the emergent AI-driven landscape.

Chapter 1: Institutional Transformations for AI Maximization

Our voyage begins with a deep dive into the need for institutional reform, which is driven by the revolutionary potential of AI-based innovation. Examining the far-reaching influence of institutional contexts on AI deployment, we shed light on the positive externalities that AI can generate for firms and society as a whole. Institutions play a central role in fostering efficient labour markets, facilitating training and education, and upgrading skills in the era of artificial intelligence.

Chapter 2: AI and the Evolution of Sectors, Firms, and Society

The second chapter explores the complex relationship between AI and the evolution of specific industries. We illustrate how AI is not only a technological instrument, but also a catalyst for sectoral evolution, influencing the formation, survival, and expansion of businesses. The concept of institutional complementarities takes centre stage, emphasising the interdependence between institutional norms and the development of AI.

Chapter 3: AI and the Future of Mass Production and Consumption

Within the pages of the third chapter, we venture on a journey to investigate the capacity of artificial intelligence to initiate a virtuous cycle between mass production and consumption. This chapter explores the role of institutions in activating this AI-based cycle while protecting values such as liberty, equality, privacy, and ethics.

Chapter 4: AI and Economic Planning

The fourth chapter explores the enticing possibility that AI could make central planning not only feasible but also efficient. We investigate the applicability of F.A. Hayek's assertion in the age of AI and analyse the delicate equilibrium between market forces and government intervention. Existing market structures are prompted to consider the potential applicability of AI-based centralised planning.

Chapter 5: Ownership, Power, and Coordination in the Age of AI

The fifth chapter investigates the command, coordination, and control dynamics in AI-driven economic planning. It sheds light on the fundamental impact of AI on industry-wide ownership concentration and provides glimpses of potential alternatives to centralised ownership models.

Chapter 6: AI and the Spectrum of Varieties of Capitalism

In the sixth chapter, we examine the co-evolution of AI and institutional forms, revealing their transformative effect across the spectrum of capitalist systems. Our investigation examines the potential reduction or proliferation of varieties of capitalism, providing insights into equilibrium shifts and potential "battle of systems" scenarios facilitated by artificial intelligence.

Chapter 7: AI and Economic Development and Innovation

In the AI era, Chapter 7 navigates the terrain of economic development and innovation. It examines the potential for AI to foster entrepreneurial capitalism, as well as its impact on innovation and the dissemination of innovative ideas. This chapter celebrates the role of entrepreneurs as economic ecosystem generators fueled by AI.

Chapter 8: AI and Human-Machine Interaction

The eighth chapter is devoted to the profound creative and innovative potential of AI-human interaction. We explore the transformative impact of AI on organisational routines and the evolving role of humans in creative functions. Our voyage investigates the implications of technological exploration and exploitation in AI-driven economic systems.

Chapter 9: AI and Market Regulation

Chapter 9 addresses the crucial question of how AI can help companies circumvent market regulations and promote market manipulation. It examines the urgent need for comprehensive regulation and the role of artificial intelligence as a complementary actor to the state. Our investigation extends to assessing the efficacy of extant antitrust norms, rules, and laws vis-à-vis AI-driven businesses.

Chapter 10: Ethics, Responsibility, and Governance in AI-Driven Economic Systems

The tenth chapter focuses on ethics, revealing the ethical implications of AI's ascension and their ripple effect on economic systems. We investigate the shared responsibility of firms and governments for governing AI-driven economic landscapes, as well as AI's potential to contribute to societal objectives and improve economic well-being.

Chapter 11: AI and Job Displacement

In Chapter 11, we navigate the turbulent waters of artificial intelligence's effects on employment and job displacement across multiple industries. Our investigation extends to the role that institutions must play in facilitating this transition and assisting displaced employees. As AI continues to ascend, we consider strategies for retraining and upskilling the workforce.

Chapter 12: AI and Income Inequality

The twelfth chapter explicates the complex relationship between AI adoption and income disparity. We delve deeply into the role that institutions must play in mitigating the negative effects of artificial intelligence on income distribution. Our path leads us to investigate potential policy interventions designed to address the widening income gap.

Chapter 13: AI and Intellectual Property Rights

The challenges of safeguarding intellectual property rights in an AI-driven economy are addressed in Chapter 13. We investigate the role that institutions must play to ensure equitable and effective intellectual property rights, and we consider potential reforms to adapt intellectual property laws to the unique characteristics of AI-generated content.

Chapter 14: AI and Cybersecurity

In the fourteenth chapter, cybersecurity vulnerabilities and threats associated with AI systems are highlighted. Our investigation focuses on the crucial role that institutions must play in developing comprehensive cybersecurity measures for AI applications. It includes potential regulations and standards required to safeguard AI systems against cyber hazards.

Chapter 15: AI and Environmental Sustainability

The potential of AI to contribute to environmental sustainability and renewable technologies is explored in Chapter 15. We investigate the role that institutions must play in fostering AI-driven climate change mitigation and resource management solutions. Our investigation reveals the difficulties and tradeoffs associated with balancing economic growth and environmental concerns in the age of artificial intelligence.

Chapter 16: AI and Consumer Behavior

In the sixteenth chapter, we examine the influence of AI on the decision-making processes and preferences of consumers. Our investigation focuses on the responsibility of institutions to safeguard consumer rights and privacy in AI-powered markets. In the age of AI, we explore the potential implications for advertising, personalised marketing, and consumer welfare.

Chapter 17: AI and Healthcare Economics

In Chapter 17, the transformative potential of AI in healthcare economics is highlighted. Our investigation focuses on the role that institutions must play to ensure equitable access to AI-based healthcare technologies. Within the realm of AI in healthcare economics, ethical and privacy concerns occupy centre stage.

Chapter 18: AI and Financial Markets

In Chapter 18, we examine the implications of AI for the efficacy and stability of financial markets. Our investigation extends to the role that institutions must play in regulating AI-based trading and investment algorithms, as well as evaluating the potential risks and challenges associated with AI-driven financial markets.

Chapter 19: AI and International Trade

The impact of AI on international trade patterns and competitiveness is explored in Chapter 19. Our investigation examines the role that institutions must play in defining trade policies and regulations pertaining to AI. It considers possible implications for global economic governance and cooperation in the age of artificial intelligence.

Chapter 20: AI and Economic Policy-making

The twentieth chapter examines the application of artificial intelligence in economic policy formulation and decision-making processes. The role that institutions must play in incorporating AI insights into policy design and evaluation is also investigated. It addresses potential obstacles and ethical considerations at the intersection of artificial intelligence and economic policymaking.

Chapter 21: AI and Capitalist Market Dynamics

Chapter 21 explores the effects of artificial intelligence on the dynamics of capitalist markets, including competition, market concentration, and market power. Our research examines the role institutions must play in the AI era to ensure fair and competitive markets. Faced with AI advancements, we consider potential ramifications for capitalism's efficacy and resilience.

Chapter 22: AI and Capital Allocation

The twenty-second chapter examines the impact of artificial intelligence on capital allocation in capitalist economies. Our research investigates the role that institutions must play to facilitate efficient capital allocation in AI-driven industries. It examines potential obstacles and considerations associated with maintaining a balanced and sustainable capital allocation system.

Chapter 23: AI and Entrepreneurial Capitalism

The opportunities and challenges that AI presents for entrepreneurial capitalism are outlined in Chapter 23. Our research examines the role that institutions must play in fostering innovation, entrepreneurship, and businesses in the era of artificial intelligence. It considers possible changes in the character and dynamics of entrepreneurial capitalism as a result of AI developments.

Chapter 24: AI and Market Disruption

We examine the disruptive potential of AI on existing market structures and established firms in Chapter 24. Our investigation includes the role that institutions must play in managing market disruptions and facilitating transitions in the AI era. We consider potential repercussions for capitalist economies and adaptation strategies to AI-driven market disruptions.

Chapter 25: AI and Capitalist Ideals

In Chapter 25, we conclude our odyssey by examining the compatibility of artificial intelligence with the fundamental principles of capitalism. In the context of AI-driven economic systems, we investigate the role that institutions must play in upholding and reconciling capitalist values. Our investigation delves into the debates and ethical considerations surrounding the intersection of AI and capitalist values.

As we embark on this expansive journey through the landscapes of AI and capitalism, I encourage you to delve deeply into each chapter, contemplate the questions posed, and seek solutions to the problems posed. The following pages provide a nuanced, exhaustive, and pertinent examination of a future in which AI and capitalism are intertwined. Collectively, they determine the fate of our economies, societies, and the world we leave to future generations.

Chapter 1: Institutional Transformations for AI Maximization

From transportation and healthcare to finance and entertainment, artificial intelligence (AI) is transforming many facets of our existence. Its potential to automate and optimise processes, generate insights, and create new products and services is enormous, as is its anticipated impact on productivity, growth, and competitiveness.

To realise this potential, however, requires more than technological advancements and business strategies. It also necessitates institutional changes that can facilitate, govern, and distribute the benefits of AI-based innovation in an equitable, sustainable, and accountable manner.

This chapter examines the necessity of institutional reform for AI-based radical innovation, the impact of institutional contexts on AI deployment and positive externalities for firms, and the role of institutions in efficient labour markets, training, education, and skill upgrading.

The first subtopic examines the challenges and opportunities of creating new institutions, regulations, and standards that can promote the development and diffusion of AI technologies that are consistent with human values, rights, and objectives. It discusses the tensions between innovation and regulation, competition and cooperation, national and global interests, as well as the implications for various stakeholders, such as businesses, employees, consumers, and governments.

The second sub-subject investigates how the institutional contexts in which businesses operate influence their AI strategies, practises, and outcomes, and how these can generate positive spillovers and externalities for other businesses, industries, and communities. It investigates the role of institutions in shaping the incentives, norms, and capabilities of firms to invest in artificial intelligence, collaborate with others, share data and knowledge, and align their interests with social and environmental objectives.

The third subtopic concentrates on the role of institutions in constructing labour markets that can adapt to the changing demands of AI-based economies, provide workers with adequate training, education, and skill upgrading, and guarantee social protection and inclusion for all. It discusses the difficulties of creating new forms of employment, skills, and work arrangements that enable workers to thrive in the AI era, as well as the potential of institutions to facilitate this transition while minimising the risks of job displacement, inequality, and social unrest.

This chapter seeks to provide a comprehensive and integrative view of the institutional transformations required to maximise the benefits and minimise the costs of AI-based innovation by addressing these subtopics. It draws on insights from a variety of disciplines, including economics, political science, sociology, and law, and invites readers to contemplate on the dynamic and complex nature of the AI revolution and the role of institutions in shaping its outcomes.

1.1.The need for institutional reform for radical AI-based innovation

Artificial intelligence (AI) is quickly evolving into a transformative technology with the potential to revolutionise how we live, work, and interact. Various industries, including healthcare, transportation, finance, and education, are being reshaped by AI-based innovations. However, with great power comes great responsibility, and the development and deployment of AI technologies pose significant ethical, legal, and social issues that require institutional reform to be addressed.

AI-based innovation is not a neutral force, but rather a socially and politically constructed process that reflects the values, interests, and power dynamics of different actors, necessitating institutional reform. Consequently, the difficulty of developing AI technologies that are consistent with human values, rights, and objectives necessitates the establishment of new institutions, regulations, and standards that can foster innovation while assuring accountability, transparency, and inclusivity.

This section of the chapter examines the need for institutional reform for radical AI-based innovation by discussing the challenges and opportunities of creating new institutions, regulations, and standards that can promote the development and diffusion of AI technologies that are consistent with human values, rights, and objectives. It discusses the tensions between innovation and regulation, competition and cooperation, national and global interests, as well as the implications for various stakeholders, such as businesses, employees, consumers, and governments.

Innovation vs. Regulation

Achieving a balance between innovation and regulation is one of the primary challenges of institutional reform for AI-based radical innovation. On the one hand, innovation is essential for economic growth, employment creation, and social welfare, and AI-based innovations have the potential to generate significant benefits in a number of fields, including healthcare, education, and environmental protection. On the other hand, innovation can generate negative externalities, such as privacy violations, discrimination, and job displacement, and AI-based innovations have the potential to exacerbate these negative impacts if they are not designed and implemented responsibly.

Consequently, the query arises: how can we promote innovation while also ensuring that it is conducted responsibly? The solution lies in developing a regulatory framework that both incentivizes innovation and ensures that AI-based technologies are developed and deployed in accordance with human values, rights, and objectives. Such a regulatory framework should be based on principles such as transparency, accountability, fairness, and inclusivity and involve a variety of stakeholders, including the government, industry, civil society, and academia.

Competition vs. Cooperation

Establishing a balance between cooperation and competition is a further challenge of institutional reform for radical AI-based innovation. On the one hand, innovation requires competition because it encourages firms to invest in R&D, develop new products, and enhance their performance. On the other hand, competition can generate negative externalities, such as market power, winner-take-all dynamics, and innovation lock-in, and AI-based innovations have the potential to exacerbate these negative effects if they are not subject to effective competition.

Consequently, the question arises: how can we simultaneously promote competition and ensure that AI-based innovations are subject to effective competition? The solution resides in establishing a regulatory framework that incentivizes competition and ensures AI-based technologies are subject to effective competition. Such a regulatory framework should be based on antitrust, interoperability, and open standards and involve a variety of stakeholders, including the government, industry, civil society, and academia.

National vs. Global Interests

Striking a balance between national and global interests is a further obstacle posed by institutional reform for radical AI-based innovation. On the one hand, national interests are essential for economic growth, employment creation, and social welfare, and AI-based innovations have the potential to generate substantial economic benefits for nations.

Given these potential advantages, it is evident that innovations based on AI have the potential to transform society as we know it. However, their implementation presents a number of obstacles that must be overcome if we are to maximise their potential while mitigating the risks they pose.

Institutional reform to support revolutionary AI-based innovation is one of the most pressing challenges. This requires the creation of new institutions, regulations, and standards that can promote the development and diffusion of AI technologies that are consistent with human values, rights, and objectives.

The current regulatory environment is ill-equipped to deal with the rapid velocity of technological change that we are currently experiencing. Many of the existing laws and regulations were created for a different era and are therefore obsolete and insufficient for addressing the challenges posed by AI-based innovation. Many of the current regulations, for instance, were designed to address the risks posed by industrial apparatus or toxic chemicals, and are therefore inadequate to address the unique risks posed by AI systems.

In addition, a number of tensions must be resolved in order to establish an institutional framework that can effectively support AI-based radical innovation. These include tensions between innovation and regulation, competition and cooperation, national and global interests, and the implications for various stakeholders, including businesses, employees, consumers, and governments.

The tension between innovation and regulation is one of the most significant. Innovation is essential for generating economic growth and enhancing societal well-being on the one hand. However, regulation is required to ensure that new technologies are developed and deployed in a manner that is safe, ethical, and consistent with societal values.

To resolve this conflict, we must establish an institutional framework that fosters innovation while mitigating the inherent risks of AI-based technologies. This may necessitate the development of new regulatory frameworks better adapted to address the unique risks posed by AI systems, such as bias, opacity, and unintended consequences. It may also entail the establishment of new institutions with the ability to provide guidance and oversight for the development and deployment of AI systems.

The tension between competition and cooperation is an additional issue that must be addressed. On the one hand, competition is essential for fostering innovation and enhancing productivity. Cooperation is required, however, to ensure that AI-based technologies are developed and deployed in a manner that is safe, ethical, and consistent with societal values.

To resolve this conflict, we must develop an institutional structure that promotes both competition and collaboration. This may necessitate the establishment of new institutions that can facilitate collaboration between various parties, such as businesses, researchers, and governments. It may also entail the development of new standards and best practises to ensure that diverse AI systems are interoperable and can collaborate in an ethical manner.

The conflict between national and international interests is a third tension that must be resolved. On the one hand, national interests are essential to a nation's ability to compete in the global economy and safeguard its citizens. Conversely, global cooperation is required to ensure that AI-based technologies are developed and implemented in a manner that is safe, ethical, and consistent with societal values.

To resolve this conflict, we must establish an institutional structure that serves both national and global interests. This may necessitate the creation of new international agreements and regulatory frameworks to ensure that countries can work together to resolve the risks posed by AI-based technologies.

Finally, we must consider the implications of AI-based innovation for a variety of stakeholders, including businesses, employees, consumers, and governments. AI-based technologies have the potential to disrupt numerous industries and sectors; therefore, it is crucial that the benefits of these technologies are distributed equitably throughout society.

To address these issues, we must develop an institutional framework designed to support the diverse interests of various stakeholders. This may entail implementing regulatory frameworks that ensure the accountability, transparency, and explainability of AI systems, in addition to safeguarding the privacy and security of individual data. It may also entail the establishment of new institutions and guidelines that promote the development of AI technologies that are consistent with human values, rights, and objectives.

In addition, institutional reform for AI-based radical innovation may entail the development of new approaches to intellectual property protection that strike a balance between innovation incentives and the need to make AI technologies accessible and affordable to all. This may involve the development of new legal frameworks for sharing and licencing data and algorithms, as well as the promotion of open-source AI initiatives.

In addition, institutional reform may involve the development of new training programmes and educational initiatives that prepare workers for the new jobs and skills demanded by the emerging economy propelled by artificial intelligence. This could involve investments in STEM education and training, as well as the development of programmes that teach workers the soft skills required to collaborate with and administer AI systems.

In conclusion, institutional reform for radical AI-based innovation may entail the development of new governance structures and international cooperation frameworks capable of managing the global effects of AI technologies. This could involve developing new norms and standards that promote responsible innovation and ensure that the benefits of AI are distributed equitably across all countries and societies, as well as establishing new multilateral institutions that facilitate international collaboration.

Overall, the need for institutional reform for radical AI-based innovation emphasises the significance of establishing new institutions, regulations, and standards that can promote the development and diffusion of AI technologies that are consistent with human values, rights, and objectives. This requires a collaborative effort between governments, businesses, academia, civil society, and other stakeholders, as well as a determination to experiment with new approaches and frameworks to tackle the complex challenges posed by artificial intelligence.

The impact of institutional contexts on AI deployment and positive externalities for firms

The impact of institutional contexts on AI deployment and positive externalities for firms is a complex and multifaceted topic that necessitates a nuanced comprehension of the factors that influence the development, adoption, and diffusion of AI technologies. Institutions play a crucial role in influencing the incentives, norms, and capabilities of firms to invest in artificial intelligence, collaborate with others, share data and knowledge, and align their interests with social and environmental objectives. In this chapter, we will investigate the various institutional contexts that influence the deployment of AI technologies, the positive externalities that AI can generate for firms, and the mechanisms by which these externalities can be leveraged for broader social and economic benefits.

Institutional contexts are the formal and informal rules, norms, and practises that regulate the behaviour of firms and other actors within a particular setting. These contexts can vary significantly across countries, regions, industries, and organisational structures, and can have a substantial effect on the development and deployment of AI technologies. Regulatory frameworks, intellectual property laws, data protection regulations, labour laws, education and training systems, and innovation policies are some of the most influential institutional factors on the deployment of artificial intelligence.

Regulatory frameworks are especially essential for the deployment of artificial intelligence because they can either facilitate or impede the development and spread of these technologies. There is a lack of clear and consistent regulatory frameworks for AI in a number of nations, which can generate uncertainty and discourage investment in these technologies. In contrast, unduly prescriptive or restrictive regulations can inhibit innovation and limit the potential benefits of AI. Consequently, it is essential for policymakers to establish a balance between providing a supportive regulatory environment for AI and ensuring that these technologies are developed and used in accordance with social and ethical values.

Intellectual property laws and data protection regulations are also essential for AI deployment, as they impact firms' access to and utilisation of data, algorithms, and other key inputs for AI development. In some nations, there is a lack of clarity regarding intellectual property rights for AI-generated content, which can present legal and business challenges for companies that develop or use these technologies. Data protection regulations also play a significant role in the deployment of artificial intelligence, as they can impact a company's ability to access and utilise large amounts of data for AI training and development. Policymakers must therefore design intellectual property and data protection regimes that strike a balance between the need to incentivize innovation and the need to safeguard individual privacy and data security.

Labour laws and education and training systems are also significant institutional factors that influence the deployment of AI. AI technologies are likely to have substantial effects on the nature of work and the skills required for various occupations. Therefore, policymakers must ensure that labour laws are adaptable enough to accommodate these changes and that education and training systems are equipped to equip workers with the skills they need to flourish in an AI-driven economy. This may necessitate substantial investments in continuous learning and reskilling programmes, as well as the creation of new educational models that incorporate AI and other emerging technologies into the curriculum.

Innovation policies are also crucial for the deployment of AI because they can encourage investment in R&D, promote collaboration between firms and other stakeholders, and establish innovation-friendly ecosystems. Numerous nations have enacted innovation policies that emphasise AI as a crucial investment and development area. These policies typically consist of a combination of funding support, tax incentives, and regulatory frameworks that are intended to foster AI innovation. However, the success of these policies is contingent on a number of variables, such as the quality of institutions, the availability of competent labour, the strength of intellectual property regimes, and the level of market competition.

In addition to these institutional factors, AI can also generate a variety of positive externalities for businesses and society as a whole. These externalities consist of increased productivity and efficiency, improved product quality and innovation, enhanced consumer experiences, and decreased environmental impact. For instance, businesses that implement AI technologies can benefit from increased accuracy and speed in data processing and analysis, allowing them to identify new growth and optimisation opportunities. This can result in increased productivity, cost savings, and higher quality products and services that satisfy the evolving needs of customers.

Moreover, AI can facilitate the development of previously impossible or prohibitively expensive products and services, such as personalised healthcare, autonomous vehicles, and smart energy systems. These innovations can create new markets, generate job opportunities, and enhance the well-being of individuals and communities as a whole. Using AI in healthcare, for instance, can improve patient outcomes by providing more accurate diagnoses, personalised treatments, and quicker drug discovery, while also reducing healthcare costs and increasing access to care.

Moreover, AI can contribute to environmental sustainability by allowing businesses to reduce waste, energy usage, and carbon emissions. For instance, AI can optimise supply chains, reduce transportation costs, and enhance resource allocation, resulting in a reduction in greenhouse gas emissions and a more effective use of natural resources. This can also assist businesses in complying with environmental regulations and enhancing their standing with consumers, investors, and other stakeholders.

The positive externalities of deploying AI are not limited to individual companies, but also extend to other companies and industries, generating a cascading effect of innovation and growth. For instance, a company's adoption of AI can generate new business opportunities for its suppliers, customers, and partners, resulting in increased economic activity and employment. Moreover, the diffusion of AI across industries can facilitate knowledge transfer, collaboration, and learning, resulting in more rapid and pervasive innovation.

However, the positive externalities of AI deployment are neither automatic nor uniformly distributed; rather, they are contingent on the institutional contexts within which firms operate. Specifically, the institutional contexts that support the development and diffusion of AI can also influence how its benefits and costs are distributed among various stakeholders. Consequently, it is essential to comprehend how institutional contexts influence the incentives, norms, and capabilities of firms to invest in AI, collaborate with others, and align their interests with social and environmental objectives.

Examining the experiences of various countries and regions is one method to evaluate the impact of institutional contexts on AI deployment and positive externalities for firms. Some nations, such as the United States, China, and Japan, have made substantial investments in artificial intelligence research and development and established institutional frameworks that encourage private sector investment and collaboration. These nations have also developed national AI strategies to promote innovation, economic development, and social welfare.

However, other nations have been less effective in deploying AI and reaping its benefits. This may be the result of a variety of institutional factors, such as deficient intellectual property rights, inadequate infrastructure, restricted access to capital, or a lack of skills and talent. In addition, some nations may encounter cultural or political obstacles to AI adoption, such as concerns regarding job displacement, privacy violations, or bias and discrimination in AI algorithms.

To promote the positive externalities of AI deployment and ensure that they are distributed equitably among various stakeholders, it is essential to address the institutional barriers and gaps that impede AI adoption and diffusion. This may involve a variety of policy interventions, including investments in education and training, support for research and development, establishment of legal and regulatory frameworks that strike a balance between innovation and social responsibility, and promotion of international cooperation and coordination.

In addition, institutional contexts can also influence the AI deployment strategies of businesses, especially in terms of how they approach collaborations and partnerships. In countries with stricter enforcement of intellectual property rights, for instance, firms may be more hesitant to share data or collaborate with other firms out of fear of potential legal disputes or loss of control over their proprietary information. In contrast, firms may be more likely to engage in joint ventures and knowledge-sharing initiatives to accelerate AI development and adoption in nations with more open innovation policies and collaborative cultures.

In addition to these country-level institutional factors, organisations are also subject to a variety of organisational and industry-level institutional pressures that can influence the deployment and outcomes of AI. For instance, institutional pressures such as social norms, cultural values, and industry standards can influence a company's decision to implement or invest in particular AI applications or technologies. Firms may also face pressure from investors, consumers, and employees, who may demand greater AI deployment transparency, accountability, and ethical considerations.

Despite these obstacles, AI can generate a number of positive externalities for businesses and society as a whole. These externalities consist of increased productivity and efficiency, improved product quality and innovation, and decreased costs and waste. AI technologies, for instance, can enable businesses to analyse large volumes of data in real time, identify patterns and insights, and make more informed decisions regarding production, logistics, marketing, and customer service. AI can also enhance the precision and accuracy of product design and testing, resulting in increased consumer satisfaction and loyalty. Additionally, AI can assist businesses in reducing energy consumption, carbon emissions, and other environmental impacts, thereby contributing to more sustainable and accountable business practises.

Additionally, AI can generate beneficial collateral effects for other businesses, industries, and communities. For instance, AI technologies can facilitate the sharing of data and knowledge, collaboration on R&D projects, and the formation of industry-wide standards and protocols. This can result in more efficient and effective supply chains, enhanced product quality and safety, and heightened innovation and competitiveness. AI can also have positive effects on employment and social inclusion, as it can create new job opportunities and enable individuals with disabilities or other work-related barriers to participate in the labour market.

In conclusion, the impact of institutional contexts on the deployment of artificial intelligence and positive externalities for firms is a complex and multifaceted issue that requires thorough consideration of a variety of factors at multiple levels of analysis. Institutional factors, such as legal frameworks, regulatory administrations, and cultural norms, can influence the AI strategies, practises, and outcomes of businesses, as well as facilitate or impede AI adoption and innovation. AI can also generate a number of positive externalities for businesses and society, such as increased productivity, innovation, and sustainability, as well as positive cascading effects for other businesses and communities.

The role of institutions in efficient labor markets, training, education, and skill upgrading

The role of institutions in constructing efficient labour markets that can adapt to the changing demands of AI-based economies, provide workers with adequate training, education, and skill upgrading, and ensure social protection and inclusion for all is essential for the sustainable development of 21st-century societies. The transformative effect of AI on labour markets and employment patterns has significant ramifications for the welfare of employees, businesses, and society as a whole. In this section, we will examine the challenges and opportunities of establishing institutions that can facilitate the transition to the AI era while mitigating the risks of job displacement, inequality, and social unrest.

The need to resolve the skills mismatch between labour demand and supply is one of the primary obstacles to constructing efficient labour markets in the AI era. Rapid advances in AI technologies are spawning new types of employment that require a unique set of skills and competencies. Complex problem-solving, critical thinking, creativity, people management, emotional intelligence, cognitive flexibility, and digital literacy are among the top 10 skills required for the occupations of the future, according to a report by the World Economic Forum (WEF) (2020). Nonetheless, a significant barrier to entry into the AI job market is created by the dearth of these skills among a large number of workers. This skills gap presents policymakers and institutions with a significant challenge, as they must find methods to provide workers with the necessary training, education, and skill upgrading to enable them to compete in AI-based economies.

To address the skills gap, institutions must play a more active role in providing workers with opportunities for lifelong learning that enable them to acquire the skills and competencies required for future employment. This requires the development of new forms of education and training that can adapt to the changing demands of the labour market and offer employees flexible and accessible learning pathways. Institutions can also support the development of new skills by investing in research and development that identifies the most important AI-era skills and designs training programmes to help employees acquire these skills.

Creating efficient labour markets in the era of AI is further complicated by the risk of job displacement and inequality. Despite the fact that AI technologies can create new types of employment, they can also displace many traditional positions that are susceptible to automation. According to a study by McKinsey, as many as 375 million employees may have to switch occupational categories and acquire new skills by 2030 (McKinsey, 2017). Displacement of workers can exacerbate inequality and social unrest, especially for low-skilled workers who may find it difficult to find new employment opportunities.

In order to resolve these issues, institutions must develop a comprehensive framework for social protection that can assist workers at risk of job loss. This entails the creation of new social safety nets that can provide income support, retraining, and upskilling opportunities for workers whose employment are automated away. Institutions can also play a crucial role in ensuring the equitable distribution of the benefits of AI technologies by developing new forms of taxation and redistribution that mitigate the negative effects of AI on inequality.

In addition, institutions can foster the development of new forms of employment and work arrangements that enable workers to thrive in the era of artificial intelligence. This requires the development of new forms of employment that provide employees with greater flexibility, autonomy, and control over their working conditions and hours. In addition, institutions can support the development of new types of work arrangements, such as teleworking and gig work, that enable workers to utilise their talents and competencies in novel ways.

In addition, institutions can play a significant role in shaping the development and deployment of AI in the labour market. For instance, they can establish regulations and standards for AI-based recruiting systems to prevent discrimination and bias against certain job applicants. They can also encourage the development of AI-enabled training and education programmes that help employees acquire the skills and knowledge necessary to adapt to the changing labour market demands. This can include reskilling and upskilling programmes, apprenticeships, and initiatives for lifelong learning that ensure workers remain competitive and productive in the era of artificial intelligence.

In addition, institutions can promote the adoption of AI-based technologies that can improve the safety, health, and well-being of workers, such as wearable devices that monitor employees' physical and mental health and prevent accidents and breakdowns. These technologies can enhance not only the working conditions of individual employees, but also the productivity and efficacy of the labour market as a whole.

Nonetheless, the deployment of AI-based technologies in the labour market raises concerns regarding job displacement, wage inequality, and social exclusion, particularly for workers in low-skilled and routine-based jobs. This emphasises the need for institutions to adopt policies and measures that can mitigate these risks and guarantee a fair and inclusive transition to the age of artificial intelligence. For instance, they can implement universal basic income programmes that serve as a safety net for workers whose livelihoods are eliminated by automation or other technological disruptions. In addition, they can promote collective bargaining and social dialogue between workers and employers to ensure that the benefits of AI-based productivity advances are distributed equitably to all stakeholders.

Chapter 2: AI and the Evolution of Sectors, Firms, and Society

Artificial intelligence (AI) is swiftly transforming the global economy, having profound effects on industries and sectors. Significant implications for employment, productivity, and innovation may result from the influence of AI on the evolution of specific industries, firm creation, survival, and development. The interdependence of institutional norms and AI evolution, as well as institutional complementarities, further affects the adaptability of economic systems to the AI age.

The response of specific industries to AI is complex and diverse, with some industries experiencing accelerated growth and others struggling to adapt. For instance, the healthcare industry has made significant strides in AI-based diagnostics, drug discovery, and personalised medicine, whereas the retail industry has encountered difficulties due to the rise of e-commerce and the automation of routine tasks. The impact of artificial intelligence on the labour market also differs by industry, with some sectors experiencing job displacement and others creating new employment opportunities.

Moreover, the evolution of businesses in response to AI is crucial to their survival and expansion. Companies that effectively integrate AI into their operations can increase their productivity, innovation, and competitiveness. AI-enabled customer service chatbots, for instance, can increase customer satisfaction while reducing costs, and AI-based predictive maintenance systems can prevent expensive equipment malfunctions. Conversely, businesses that fail to adapt to the AI era run the risk of falling behind their competitors and may struggle to survive in the long run.

The interdependence between institutional norms and AI evolution also plays a significant role in determining the economic impact of AI. Institutions, such as laws, regulations, and social norms, can both aid and hinder the development and adoption of artificial intelligence. For instance, institutions that safeguard intellectual property rights and encourage investment in research and development can stimulate AI innovation, whereas regulations that restrict AI's use can limit its potential benefits. In addition, institutions influence the distribution of AI's benefits across society, with some individuals and groups at risk of being left behind in the absence of adequate institutional support.

Institutional complementarities, or the degree to which various institutions reinforce one another, also affect the adaptability of economic systems to the AI age. Institutions that support continuous learning and skill upgrading, for instance, can assist workers in adapting to the shifting demands of the labour market, whereas institutions that provide social safety nets can assist workers displaced by AI. In addition, institutions that encourage innovation and entrepreneurship can facilitate the formation of new companies and the creation of new products and services.

Therefore, the impact of AI on the evolution of particular industries, companies, and society as a whole is substantial and complex, with potential implications for employment, productivity, and innovation. The interdependence of institutional norms and AI evolution, as well as institutional complementarities, further affects the adaptability of economic systems to the AI age. Understanding these dynamics is essential for policymakers, businesses, and individuals navigating the challenges and opportunities of the age of artificial intelligence.

The impact of AI on the evolution of specific sectors, firm creation, survival, and growth

This section discusses the effects of AI technology on numerous economic sectors, including healthcare, finance, manufacturing, and agriculture.

The evolution of AI has had a significant impact on the healthcare industry, particularly in medical research, diagnosis, and treatment. AI has the potential to transform the healthcare industry by increasing efficiency, decreasing costs, and enhancing patient outcomes. The acceleration of medical research is among the most significant contributions of AI to healthcare. AI can analyse immense quantities of medical data to identify potential treatments for previously unknown or undiscovered diseases and disorders. It can also aid in the creation of novel medications by identifying and predicting the efficacy of compounds. AI can also be used to recognise patterns in medical data that humans may have missed, which can lead to new medical breakthroughs and enhance patient care.

AI has the potential to enhance the accuracy and speed of diagnosis. AI can assist radiologists in detecting abnormalities in medical images such as X-rays and MRI imaging, for instance. AI algorithms can analyse medical images to detect potential cancerous lesions, enabling physicians to make more precise diagnoses. This technology can also be applied to the early detection of Alzheimer's disease, the prediction of cardiac disease, and the identification of genetic risk factors for certain conditions.

AI is also used to enhance treatment outcomes, in addition to its diagnostic applications. AI is capable of analysing patient data to generate personalised treatment plans that account for the patient's unique characteristics, such as age, heredity, and medical history. This technology can also be used to monitor patients' vital signs and notify physicians of potential complications before they become life-threatening. This can result in improved outcomes and decreased hospital stays and readmissions.

The application of AI in healthcare extends to the creation of medical devices. AI can be used to develop more precise, dependable, and efficient medical devices. For instance, AI algorithms can be used to enhance the accuracy of blood glucose monitors, which can save the lives of diabetic patients. AI can also be used to create medical devices capable of diagnosing and treating diseases in real time, such as implantable devices that monitor and regulate the heartbeat of patients with cardiac conditions.

The implementation of AI in healthcare is not, however, without obstacles. A major concern is the possibility of bias in AI algorithms, particularly in the diagnostic realm. The training of AI algorithms on biassed data sets can result in inaccurate and unjust outcomes. There are also concerns regarding data privacy and security, as healthcare information is sensitive and must be protected.

The cost of implementing AI in healthcare is a further significant obstacle. Although artificial intelligence has the potential to reduce costs over time, the initial investment can be costly. In addition, there is a dearth of qualified personnel capable of implementing and maintaining AI systems in healthcare.

Therefore, AI has the potential to transform the healthcare industry by increasing efficiency, decreasing costs, and enhancing patient outcomes. Utilising AI in medical research, diagnosis, treatment, and device creation can lead to new medical breakthroughs and enhanced patient care. However, the implementation of AI in healthcare is not without obstacles, and it is necessary to overcome these obstacles to guarantee the ethical and responsible use of AI in healthcare.

The financial sector also plays a significant role in the application of AI. As one of the most data-intensive industries, the financial sector is primed for AI adoption. AI has had a significant impact on the financial sector, transforming how financial institutions operate, make decisions, and interact with clients. This section will examine the impact of AI on the evolution of the financial sector, including firm formation, survival, and expansion.

The automation of previously human-performed tasks is one of the most significant effects of AI on the financial industry. This has enabled financial institutions to reduce expenses and improve efficiency. For instance, AI algorithms can analyse massive amounts of data in real-time and make trading decisions based on that data, which is impossible for a human trader. This has led to the development of algorithmic trading, in which computer algorithms rather than humans make trading decisions.

In the financial sector, AI has also been used to enhance fraud detection and prevention. Traditional fraud detection systems rely on rule-based systems in which specific fraud-detection principles are established. However, these systems have limited efficacy due to the constant evolution of fraudsters' strategies. On the other hand, AI-based fraud detection systems are capable of detecting anomalies in data and identifying patterns that would be difficult for a human to recognise.

Customer service is another area where AI has transformed the financial industry. AI-powered chatbots can handle routine customer questions and requests, allowing human customer service agents to focus on more complex duties. This has significantly reduced customer wait times and enabled financial institutions to provide support around the clock.

The application of AI to risk management has also had a transformative effect on the financial industry. Using artificial intelligence, financial institutions can analyse large volumes of data to identify potential risks and implement preventative measures to mitigate those risks. This has increased the accuracy of risk assessment and decreased the likelihood that financial institutions will make hazardous investments.

Additionally, AI has been utilised to enhance compliance in the financial sector. Financial institutions are required to adhere to a vast array of regulations, and failure to do so can result in hefty penalties and reputational harm. Large volumes of data can be analysed by AI-based compliance systems to ensure that financial institutions are in compliance with regulations and to identify potential compliance issues before they become a problem.

AI has resulted in the emergence of new financial technology (fintech) companies that are using AI to disrupt traditional financial institutions. Fintech companies use AI to provide innovative financial services that are speedier, cheaper, and more convenient than those offered by conventional financial institutions. This has increased competition in the financial industry, which has benefited consumers.

Nonetheless, the rise of fintech companies has also compelled traditional financial institutions to incorporate AI and other technologies in order to remain competitive. If financial institutions do not implement AI, they risk falling behind and losing market share to fintech firms.

In terms of a company's ability to identify prospective risks and take preventative measures to mitigate those risks, AI has been revolutionary. Financial institutions that have been slow to incorporate AI run the risk of falling behind their competitors and may face significant challenges in the future. AI has been transformative in terms of firm development by providing financial institutions with an abundance of data that can be used to identify new business opportunities. AI is capable of analysing large volumes of data to identify trends and patterns, enabling financial institutions to develop new products and services to satisfy their clients' evolving needs.

Therefore, it is evident that AI has had a profound effect on the financial sector. AI has enabled financial institutions to reduce costs, boost efficiencies, and improve client services. Nonetheless, the rise of fintech companies has also compelled traditional financial institutions to incorporate AI and other technologies in order to remain competitive.

Artificial intelligence has the potential to transform the manufacturing sector by increasing productivity, efficiency, and quality control. Utilising AI technologies in manufacturing can aid in streamlining processes, optimising production, and enhancing product quality, resulting in cost reductions and enhanced competitiveness.

Predictive maintenance is one area where AI is particularly beneficial in manufacturing. By analysing sensor and equipment data, AI algorithms can predict when maintenance will be necessary, allowing manufacturers to perform preventative maintenance and avoid costly unscheduled outage. Several major manufacturers, including GE and Siemens, have already employed this technology, resulting in significant cost savings.

Quality control is another area where AI is having an impact on manufacturing. AI algorithms can analyse product images and detect flaws that are not necessarily visible to the naked eye. This can help improve product quality and reduce waste, resulting in increased productivity and profits. AI can also be used to optimise inventory management, allowing manufacturers to reduce waste and increase productivity.

AI can also be applied to supply chain optimisation. AI can help manufacturers better comprehend the supply chain and make data-driven decisions by analysing data on inventory levels, shipping schedules, and other factors. This can result in supply chain cost savings and increased efficiency. AI can also be utilised to analyse production data and identify patterns and trends. This data can be utilised to optimise production processes and enhance product quality. Using AI, manufacturers can also create customised products and services for their consumers.

Nevertheless, the adoption of AI in manufacturing is not without its challenges. These obstacles include the need for substantial investments in data infrastructure and the possibility of job displacement as routine duties are automated.

Despite these obstacles, the advantages of AI in manufacturing are undeniable. By reducing costs, enhancing product quality, and boosting productivity, AI technologies can help manufacturers remain competitive in a globalising market. Manufacturers that effectively adopt and integrate AI technologies into their operations are likely to experience significant gains in terms of increased productivity, enhanced product quality, and decreased costs, as well as new growth and innovation opportunities.

In addition to the aforementioned advantages, AI can also assist manufacturers in improving production planning and scheduling. By analysing data on production rates, machine utilisation, and other factors, AI algorithms can assist manufacturers in optimising production schedules and decreasing the amount of time required to produce a product. This can result in a quicker time-to-market and a boost in competitiveness.

The development of digital siblings is another area where AI is influencing the manufacturing industry. Digital twins are digital representations of physical devices that can be used to simulate and optimise production processes. AI algorithms can help manufacturers identify potential bottlenecks and optimise the performance of machinery in real-time by analysing data from sensors and other sources.

AI can also enhance product design and engineering processes for manufacturers. By analysing customer feedback and other data, artificial intelligence algorithms can assist manufacturers in identifying areas for product improvement and developing new products that better meet customer requirements.

The adoption of AI in manufacturing is not, however, without obstacles. A significant investment in data infrastructure represents one of the greatest obstacles. To effectively use AI, manufacturers must be able to collect, store, and analyse large volumes of data. This can be a significant obstacle for smaller manufacturers who lack the capital to invest in the necessary infrastructure.

Another difficulty is the possibility of job displacement. As routine duties become increasingly automated, some workers may find themselves unemployed. However, AI has the potential to generate new employment opportunities, particularly in data analysis and machine learning.

Despite these obstacles, the advantages of AI in manufacturing are substantial. Manufacturers that effectively adopt and integrate AI technologies into their operations are likely to experience significant gains in terms of increased productivity, enhanced product quality, and decreased costs, as well as new growth and innovation opportunities.

The agricultural sector is one of the most essential sectors of the global economy, and AI has had a substantial impact on this industry. AI has the potential to revolutionise agriculture by increasing productivity, efficiency, and sustainability.

Precision cultivation is one of the most significant ways that AI is impacting agriculture. Utilising sensors, drones, and other technologies, precision agriculture collects data on crops, soil conditions, and other factors. Using AI algorithms, this data is then analysed to optimise crop yields, reduce waste, and enhance sustainability. Precision farming has the potential to increase crop yields by up to 30 percent, as well as reduce producers' water and fertiliser consumption, resulting in substantial cost savings.

The development of autonomous farming apparatus is a second area where AI is having an impact in agriculture. Autonomous agricultural equipment, such as tractors and harvesters, can navigate fields, avoid obstacles, and optimise operations using artificial intelligence algorithms. This technology has the potential to considerably reduce labour expenses and increase industry efficiency.

AI is also employed in agriculture to enhance crop quality. Images of crops can be analysed by AI algorithms to detect diseases and pests that are difficult to identify with the unaided eye. This can aid farmers in identifying and treating issues before they become prevalent, resulting in increased crop yields and quality.

Additionally, AI is being utilised in the agricultural sector to develop novel plant varieties with increased resistance to pests and diseases. AI algorithms can identify genetic markers associated with resistance to specific pests or diseases by analysing genetic data. This information can be used to develop more resistant plant varieties, resulting in increased yields and decreased pesticide use.

There are challenges associated with the adoption of AI in agriculture despite these advantages. The cost of implementing AI technologies is one of the major obstacles. Many small-scale producers may lack the financial means to invest in costly technologies, limiting their ability to reap the potential benefits of artificial intelligence.

Another difficulty is the requirement for data infrastructure. Effective AI algorithms require vast quantities of data, and many farmers may not have access to the data necessary for AI to be effective. This includes information regarding weather patterns, soil conditions, and other variables that can influence crop yields.

Lastly, there is the possibility of employment displacement due to the adoption of AI in agriculture. As routine duties become increasingly automated, some workers may find themselves unemployed. However, AI has the potential to generate new employment opportunities in fields such as data analysis and machine learning.

Despite these obstacles, the advantages of AI in agriculture are substantial. AI technologies have the potential to increase industry efficiency, decrease waste, and increase sustainability. As the global population increases, the demand for food will increase, and the agricultural industry will need to implement new technologies to keep up. Artificial intelligence will likely play a crucial role in the future of agriculture, ensuring that farmers can continue to meet the world's increasing food demands.

The interdependence of institutional norms and AI evolution

The interdependence of institutional norms and AI evolution is a complex and multifaceted topic that highlights the intricate connection between the evolution of AI technologies and the norms and values of the institutions in which they operate. Governments, regulatory authorities, and professional organisations play a crucial role in establishing the rules and guidelines that govern the development and application of AI technologies.

The establishment of regulations to ensure the development and use of AI technologies in a safe and ethical manner is one of the most essential responsibilities of institutions in relation to AI. For instance, governments may enact laws requiring businesses to adhere to particular ethical principles when developing and deploying AI systems. Similarly, professional associations may develop codes of conduct mandating that AI industry professionals adhere to particular ethical standards.

Institutional norms and values also significantly influence the development and evolution of AI technologies. Ethical considerations, for instance, may limit the development and deployment of AI technologies in certain domains. Through their norms and values, institutions may also influence how AI technologies are developed and deployed. For instance, an institution that places a high priority on privacy may require the development of AI technologies in a manner that protects the privacy of individuals.

Development of AI-powered decision-making systems is one of the most significant illustrations of the interdependence between institutional norms and AI evolution. These systems analyse vast quantities of data and make decisions based on the analysis using machine learning algorithms. Growing concern exists, however, that the decisions made by these systems may be biassed or unfair if the data used to educate them is biassed or if the algorithms used to analyse the data are flawed. This has led to demands for greater transparency and accountability in the development and deployment of decision-making systems powered by artificial intelligence.

The use of AI in healthcare is another instance of the interdependence between institutional norms and the evolution of AI. AI has the potential to enhance healthcare outcomes by enabling quicker and more accurate diagnoses, but there are ethical concerns regarding its use in this setting. Concerns exist, for instance, regarding the potential for AI to be used to deny care to vulnerable populations or to violate patient privacy. The norms and values of healthcare institutions have a significant impact on the development and deployment of AI technologies in this field.

The interdependence between institutional norms and the evolution of AI emphasises the need for a coordinated and collaborative approach to the development and deployment of AI technologies. The values and norms of the institutions within which AI operates, as well as the perspectives of stakeholders such as researchers, practitioners, and policymakers, should inform this approach. Institutions should collaborate to create guidelines and regulations that promote transparency, accountability, and ethical behaviour in the development and use of artificial intelligence (AI) technologies.

In conclusion, the interdependence between institutional norms and AI evolution is a crucial issue that must be carefully considered as AI technologies continue to develop and become more ingrained in our society. Institutions play a crucial role in shaping the development and deployment of AI technologies, and their norms and values must be considered to ensure that AI is developed and used in a secure, ethical, and equitable manner.

Institutional complementarities and their influence on economic systems

The development and deployment of artificial intelligence (AI) technologies have substantial consequences for economic systems and institutions. AI has been lauded in recent years as a transformative technology with the potential to alter how we live, work, and interact with one another. Nevertheless, the effect of AI on economic systems and institutions is contingent on the interaction between the technology and the institutional context in which it operates. This relationship can have a substantial effect on the adoption and diffusion of AI technologies, as well as their application within economic systems.

Institutional complementarities refer to the cohesion and uniformity of institutional arrangements within a given system. This may include formal institutions like laws and regulations, as well as informal institutions like social norms and values. Depending on how well they correlate with the capabilities and requirements of the technology, these institutional arrangements can either facilitate or impede the adoption and diffusion of new technologies such as artificial intelligence.

Influence on labour markets is one of the most significant ways institutional complementarities can effect the impact of AI on economic systems. AI has the potential to automate routine and repetitive duties, thereby increasing firms' productivity and decreasing their expenses. However, the adoption of AI technologies may also have significant employment ramifications, as it may result in the displacement of workers whose occupations are automated. The impact of artificial intelligence on labour markets is contingent on a variety of institutional factors, such as labour laws, regulations, and social safety nets.

In countries with robust labour protections and social safety nets, for instance, the adoption of AI may be less likely to result in pervasive job loss and inequality than in countries with weaker labour protections and social safety nets. By providing assistance to workers who are displaced by automation, robust labour protections and safety nets can help mitigate the negative effects of AI on employment. Moreover, robust labour protections can aid in ensuring that workers are treated fairly and that their rights are protected in the face of rapid technological change.

Nevertheless, AI's impact on labour markets is not limited to labour laws and social safety systems. Other institutional factors, such as the structure of the economy, the level of education and training of the workforce, and the availability of alternative employment opportunities, can also play a significant role in determining the impact of artificial intelligence on employment. For instance, if there is a shortage of skilled workers in a specific industry, the adoption of AI may increase employment by creating new positions that require the skills and knowledge of those workers.

The relationship between AI and innovation is a second instance of institutional complementarities in the context of AI. AI has the potential to drive innovation and create new industries, but this is contingent on complementary institutions such as intellectual property laws, research funding, and a qualified workforce. Institutions that foster innovation and entrepreneurship can foster an environment where artificial intelligence can flourish and contribute to economic development.

The impact of AI on innovation is not solely determined by the availability of complementary institutions. Other institutional factors, including the regulatory environment, the level of competition, and the degree of openness to foreign investment, can also play an important role in determining the impact of AI on innovation. A regulatory environment that is hostile to new technologies or that favours incumbent firms over new entrants, for instance, can hinder the adoption and diffusion of artificial intelligence and stifle innovation.

In addition, institutional complementarities are dynamic and subject to change over time. As technology evolves, institutions may be required to adapt and change in order to remain compatible with its capabilities and requirements. For instance, the development of AI may necessitate revisions to intellectual property laws to accommodate new forms of intellectual property created by AI, such as artwork or music generated by machines. Similarly, the use of AI in decision-making may necessitate modifications to regulatory frameworks to ensure the technology is utilised ethically and responsibly.

In addition to labour markets and innovation, institutional complementarities play an important role in the ethical and social implications of artificial intelligence. Concerns about the potential for bias, discrimination, and other negative outcomes are developing as AI becomes increasingly integrated into various facets of society, from healthcare to criminal justice. In order to address these concerns, institutions must develop and implement frameworks and standards for the ethical use of artificial intelligence, including issues such as accountability, transparency, and privacy.

The use of facial recognition technology illustrates the role of institutions in confronting the ethical implications of artificial intelligence. This technology has been extensively adopted by law enforcement and other industries, but its accuracy and potential for bias have raised concerns. Institutions such as governments and regulatory bodies must establish guidelines and regulations to safeguard the privacy rights of individuals and ensure the fair and impartial use of facial recognition technology.

In addition to the development and deployment of AI in healthcare, institutional complementarities are crucial in the development and deployment of AI in healthcare. AI has the potential to revolutionise healthcare by enhancing diagnosis, treatment, and outcomes, but it also raises concerns regarding patient privacy, data security, and decision-making bias. Hospitals, regulatory bodies, and professional organisations must collaborate to establish standards and guidelines for the ethical use of AI in healthcare, including data privacy, informed consent, and algorithm use in clinical decision-making.

Moreover, the connection between AI and institutional complementarities is not unidirectional. Additionally, institutions can influence the development and deployment of AI technologies. Institutions that prioritise environmental sustainability may, for instance, facilitate the development of AI technologies that promote renewable energy and reduce greenhouse gas emissions. Likewise, institutions that prioritise social equity may prioritise the development of artificial intelligence (AI) technologies that reduce inequality and promote social welfare.

AI and institutional complementarities have substantial effects on economic systems, social welfare, and ethical considerations. The relationship between technology and institutions is dynamic and complex, and the adoption and spread of artificial intelligence (AI) technologies hinge on a variety of institutional factors. A coherent and consistent institutional framework can facilitate the adoption and diffusion of AI technologies, ensuring that the technology's prospective benefits are realised while the negative impact on society is minimised. Institutions must therefore collaborate to develop and implement ethical and responsible frameworks for the development, deployment, and use of AI technologies.

Chapter 3: AI and the Future of Mass Production and Consumption

In recent years, Artificial Intelligence (AI) has been a significant transformative force, having a massive impact on production, consumption, and distribution, among other aspects of human existence. The implementation of artificial intelligence in mass production and consumption has resulted in a paradigm shift in the manufacturing and retail sectors, creating new growth and development opportunities. The combination of artificial intelligence with mass production and consumption has the potential to generate a virtuous circle in which increased production efficiency leads to decreased costs, increased consumption, and increased demand.

This chapter examines the potential for artificial intelligence to initiate a virtuous cycle between mass production and consumption, as well as the role of institutions in activating the AI-based virtuous circle while maintaining freedom, equality, privacy, and ethical values. The chapter will begin with an overview of the current state of mass production and consumption, then examine the potential benefits of AI in this context. We will then discuss the various difficulties and dangers associated with the use of artificial intelligence in mass production and consumption, including privacy concerns and ethical considerations.

The chapter will also examine the crucial role that institutions play in activating the AI-based virtuous circle while preserving individual rights and liberties, such as privacy, equality, and ethical values. We will investigate the role of governments, regulatory bodies, and professional organisations in establishing guidelines and regulations that promote the development and use of AI technologies in a safe and ethical manner.

This chapter aims to provide an in-depth analysis of the potential benefits and challenges associated with the integration of artificial intelligence in mass production and consumption, as well as the role of institutions in ensuring that the AI-based virtuous circle operates in a safe, ethical, and equitable manner.

The potential of AI to trigger a virtuous circle between mass production and consumption.

Artificial intelligence (AI) has the capacity to revolutionise the production and consumption of products and services. By automating and optimising production processes, AI can improve the efficiency, affordability, and environmental sustainability of mass production. Likewise, AI can assist consumers in making more informed purchasing decisions, thereby increasing demand for more sustainable and ethical products. This cycle of mass production and consumption has the potential to generate a more prosperous and sustainable economy for everyone.

For more than a century, mass production has been the foundation of modern economies. It has allowed us to produce goods in large quantities at a low price, making a diverse array of products affordable and accessible to the populace. However, industrial production has also been criticised for its negative effects on society and the environment. High levels of energy consumption, waste production, and pollution caused by mass production have contributed to environmental degradation and climate change. In addition, mass-produced standardised goods have been criticised for their lack of variety and for promoting a culture of consumerism that places a premium on quantity over quality.

AI has the potential to mitigate many of these criticisms of mass production by making it more efficient and environmentally friendly. Manufacturers can reduce energy consumption, refuse generation, and pollution by utilising AI to optimise production processes. AI can be used to optimise supply chain management, reduce inventory levels, and predict maintenance requirements, thereby reducing waste and energy consumption. AI can also be used to design and manufacture more environmentally sustainable products, such as those made from recycled materials or with less packaging.

In addition to enhancing the efficacy and sustainability of mass production, artificial intelligence can also increase demand for more sustainable and ethical products. By analysing consumer data, AI can assist businesses in comprehending consumer preferences and behaviour, enabling them to tailor their products and marketing strategies as necessary. This can aid businesses in promoting more sustainable and ethical products to consumers who are prepared to pay a premium for them. In this way, AI can help create a virtuous circle between mass production and consumption, where the more sustainable and ethical products are produced, the greater the demand for them, thereby driving further improvements in production processes and the creation of even more sustainable and ethical products.

Nevertheless, the use of AI in industrial production and consumption raises several concerns. One concern is that the increased efficiency and affordability of mass production made possible by artificial intelligence could lead to even higher levels of consumption, exacerbating environmental and social issues. Another concern is that the use of AI to tailor products and marketing strategies to individual consumers could increase consumerism and further separate consumers from the production process.

To address these issues, it is crucial that the development and use of artificial intelligence in mass production and consumption adhere to sustainability and moral conduct principles. This could include the development of guidelines and standards for the use of AI in these areas, as well as the participation of stakeholders such as consumers, environmental groups, and labour unions in the development and deployment of AI technologies. By ensuring that AI is developed and used in accordance with sustainability and ethical principles, we can ensure that

AI's potential to initiate a virtuous circle between mass production and consumption is realised to everyone's benefit.

AI's capacity to optimise the production process is an illustration of how it can contribute to this virtuous cycle. Analysing data from sensors and other sources, AI algorithms can identify inefficiencies in the manufacturing process and recommend improvements. This can ultimately result in increased productivity, decreased waste, and decreased costs. As production costs decline, businesses are able to reduce prices, making their products more accessible to consumers. This can result in a rise in demand, which can then drive additional production optimisation and cost reductions.

Through its capacity to personalise products and services, AI can also contribute to this virtuous cycle. Consumer data can be analysed by AI algorithms to determine individual preferences and then products and services can be tailored to suit those preferences. This can increase consumer satisfaction, which in turn can increase demand for more personalised goods and services. As the demand for personalised goods and services rises, businesses can invest more in AI-powered personalization, resulting in increased consumer satisfaction and demand.

There are, however, potential drawbacks to this virtuous circle. One concern is that the increased efficacy and decreased costs that AI can facilitate could result in the loss of jobs in certain industries. As production processes become increasingly automated and streamlined, it is possible that some occupations will become obsolete. If those who are displaced are unable to find new employment, economic inequality and social unrest may result.

A further concern is that AI-powered personalization may result in a "filter bubble" effect, in which individuals only receive information and products that reinforce their existing beliefs and preferences. This could result in a dearth of exposure to diverse perspectives and a consequent narrowing of worldviews.

To address these concerns, businesses and policymakers must adopt a proactive stance to ensure that the benefits of AI are distributed equitably and that any potential drawbacks are mitigated. This may involve investing in job training and education programmes for those who may be displaced by AI-powered automation, as well as promoting diversity and inclusion in the development of AI algorithms to ensure that they do not reinforce existing biases or exclusionary practises.

In the development of personalised products, AI has the potential to initiate a virtuous cycle between mass production and consumption. With the aid of AI, manufacturers are able to tailor their products to the specific requirements and preferences of individual consumers. By doing so, they can create a consumer base that is more engaged and therefore more likely to make repeat purchases.

For instance, clothing manufacturers can use AI algorithms to analyse consumer preferences, body measurements, and purchase history in order to create customised clothing designs. Using this information, they are able to create personalised products that are a perfect match for consumers and meet their unique style preferences. This personalised approach not only increases customer satisfaction, but also makes the manufacturer's business model more sustainable.

In addition, AI can aid in reducing waste and enhancing production's sustainability. Utilising predictive analytics, manufacturers are able to forecast demand and adjust production accordingly, thereby decreasing the likelihood of overproduction and waste. Moreover, AI can assist in optimising production processes, thereby reducing energy consumption and resource consumption.

It is essential to note, however, that the potential benefits of AI in creating a virtuous circle between mass production and consumption are accompanied by a number of risks and obstacles. The potential for AI to exacerbate existing inequalities in society is one of the primary concerns. For instance, personalised products may only be available to those who can afford them, resulting in further stratification of social strata.

In addition, the widespread implementation of AI in mass production and consumption raises concerns regarding the potential loss of employment and displacement of workers. As more manufacturing processes become automated, it is probable that a large number of positions will become obsolete. Especially in regions where manufacturing is a significant source of employment, this may result in social and economic unrest.

The potential for artificial intelligence to create a virtuous cycle between mass production and consumption is a complex and multifaceted topic that requires a comprehensive analysis of the various factors at play. In this section, we will delve deeply into this topic and investigate the potential impact of AI on the mass production and consumption relationship.

The optimisation of the production process is one of the most significant ways that AI can contribute to a virtuous circle between mass production and consumption. By analysing vast quantities of data on production processes and consumer behaviour, AI algorithms can identify areas for enhancement in the production process, resulting in increased efficiency and decreased waste. AI can be used to optimise supply chains, thereby reducing the amount of time and resources required to transport unprocessed materials and finished goods from one location to another.

In addition, AI can aid in the creation of new products that better satisfy the needs and preferences of consumers. By analysing consumer behaviour data, AI can identify patterns and trends that indicate the most popular and in-demand products. This information can then be used to develop new products with a greater likelihood of market success, resulting in increased sales and a more efficient use of resources.

In addition to optimising the production process and developing new products, artificial intelligence can also enhance the distribution and delivery processes. By analysing data on consumer behaviour, AI can identify patterns and trends in the most frequently purchased products and the most frequently visited retail locations. This data can then be used to optimise the distribution and delivery process, ensuring that products are delivered to the appropriate locations and times, thereby reducing wastage and increasing efficiency.

Through personalised marketing, AI can also contribute to a virtuous cycle between mass production and consumption. By analysing data on consumer behaviour and preferences, AI algorithms can create personalised marketing campaigns that are tailored to the individual requirements and interests of consumers. This can lead to increased sales and a more efficient use of resources, as companies can concentrate their marketing efforts on the products and services with the highest likelihood of market success.

Additionally, personalised marketing can enhance the consumer experience, resulting in greater customer satisfaction and loyalty. By tailoring marketing campaigns to the requirements and preferences of individual consumers, businesses can create a more personalised and engaging experience that is more likely to resonate with consumers and encourage repeat purchases.

Nonetheless, it is essential to recognise that there are potential risks associated with the use of AI in industrial production and consumption. The potential for AI algorithms to exacerbate market biases and inequalities is one of the most significant hazards. For instance, if AI algorithms are trained on data that reflects existing biases and inequalities in the market, these biases and inequalities may be perpetuated in their recommendations and decisions.

There are also concerns regarding the potential impact of AI on the labour market. As AI becomes more pervasive in mass production and consumption, there is a danger that it could replace human workers, resulting in job losses and increased inequality. It is essential to observe, however, that AI can also create new employment opportunities, particularly in data analysis and algorithm development.

In conclusion, the potential for AI to initiate a virtuous cycle between mass production and consumption is a complex and multifaceted topic requiring a comprehensive analysis of the various factors at play. While there are hazards associated with the use of AI in mass production and consumption, there are also significant opportunities for AI to increase efficiency, decrease waste, and create a more personalised and engaging consumer experience. To fully realise the potential of artificial intelligence in this field, it is necessary to develop regulations and guidelines that ensure AI is developed and used in a safe, ethical, and equitable manner. Additionally, it is essential to recognise the potential hazards associated with the use of artificial intelligence.

The role of institutions in activating the AI based virtuous circle while preserving freedom, equality, privacy, and ethical values

As artificial intelligence (AI) continues to advance and become more integrated into various sectors of society, it has become clear that institutions such as governments, regulatory bodies, and professional associations play a crucial role in shaping the development and application of AI technologies. In this context, an essential function of institutions is to activate the AI-based virtuous circle while preserving freedom, equality, privacy, and ethical values.

The AI virtuous circle refers to the notion that increased data availability and computational capacity can result in improved AI models and algorithms, which can then result in more accurate predictions and insights. This can generate more data and computing capacity, creating an improvement cycle that reinforces itself. By activating this virtuous circle, institutions can use AI to fuel innovation, boost efficiency, and improve the quality of life for individuals and society as a whole.

Despite the fact that the AI virtuous circle has the potential to bring about significant benefits, it also poses a number of challenges, particularly in terms of privacy, security, and ethical concerns. For instance, the collection and use of personal data by AI systems can raise privacy concerns, and the use of AI in decision-making processes can raise issues of impartiality and transparency.

To address these issues, institutions must actively shape the development and application of AI technologies. The establishment of regulations and guidelines that promote the ethical and responsible use of AI is an essential aspect of this role. Governments may, for instance, implement laws requiring companies to adhere to certain ethical principles when developing and deploying AI systems. Similarly, professional associations may develop codes of conduct mandating that AI industry professionals adhere to particular ethical standards.

In addition to establishing regulations and guidelines, institutions can play an important role in influencing the norms and values surrounding the use of artificial intelligence. For instance, institutions can promote a culture of responsible and ethical AI use by increasing awareness of the potential hazards and benefits of AI. This may involve providing individuals and organisations with educational and training opportunities, as well as engaging in public engagement and advocacy efforts.

In addition, institutions can promote the development and application of AI technologies in a manner that prioritises liberty and equality. Institutions can, for instance, work to ensure that AI systems do not reinforce or perpetuate prejudices or discrimination. This can include the development of AI models trained on diverse and representative data sets, as well as the monitoring and auditing of AI systems for potential biases.

Preserving privacy and security is another crucial aspect of institutions' role in activating the AI-based virtuous circle. When developing and deploying AI systems, institutions can establish regulations and guidelines mandating that companies implement stringent data protection and security measures. In addition, institutions can encourage the development and use of AI technologies that prioritise privacy and data security, such as machine learning algorithms that protect privacy.

In addition to establishing regulations and guidelines, institutions can play a crucial role in fostering and deploying AI technologies that promote freedom, equality, privacy, and ethical values. Institutions can foster innovation in the AI sector, for instance, by providing funding and resources for research and development, as well as by supporting firms and entrepreneurs in the field. By doing so, institutions can ensure that AI technologies are developed and deployed in a manner that advances the public welfare and addresses societal challenges.

In addition, institutions can play a significant role in ensuring that AI technologies are developed and deployed in an inclusive and equitable manner. This can be accomplished by promoting diversity and inclusion within the AI industry and ensuring that AI technologies are designed to satisfy the needs of a variety of user groups. To ensure that AI technologies do not perpetuate existing biases and inequalities, institutions may require the development and testing of AI technologies with the input of diverse stakeholders, including members of marginalised communities.

In the context of AI development and deployment, institutions must also be vigilant in safeguarding individual rights and liberties. This includes protecting the right to privacy and ensuring that AI technologies are not used for discriminatory purposes or to violate individual rights. Institutions can also play a role in ensuring that AI technologies are utilised in a transparent and accountable manner, with appropriate safeguards against abuse or misuse.

In addition, institutions can promote ethical considerations in the creation and deployment of AI technologies. This includes promoting values like impartiality, accountability, and transparency, and ensuring that AI technologies are developed and deployed in accordance with these values. Institutions can also support the development of ethical frameworks and guidelines for the development and use of artificial intelligence (AI) technologies, to ensure that these technologies are used for the greater good of society.

Institutions play a vital role in activating the AI-based virtuous circle while maintaining freedom, equality, privacy, and ethical values. AI has the potential to profoundly transform our society, and the rules and norms we establish around its development and use will determine whether its effects are positive or negative. In this section, we will discuss the specific ways in which institutions can contribute to the activation of the virtuous circle while ensuring that AI is developed and used in a manner consistent with our fundamental values.

First, institutions can establish regulations and guidelines that promote the ethical and socially responsible development and use of AI. Governments may, for instance, enact laws requiring companies to adhere to certain ethical principles when developing and deploying AI systems. Similarly, professional associations can create codes of conduct mandating that AI industry professionals adhere to certain ethical standards. These regulations and guidelines can ensure that artificial intelligence is developed and used in accordance with the principles of liberty, equality, privacy, and morality.

Institutions can also play a role in ensuring that AI is developed and utilised for the advantage of all members of society. This can be accomplished by promoting diversity in the creation and application of AI. For instance, institutions can promote the recruitment of diverse research and development teams, as well as initiatives that promote the use of AI in ways that benefit marginalised communities. Thus, institutions can ensure that the benefits of the virtuous circle are enjoyed by all members of society, not just a select few.

Thirdly, institutions can promote transparency and accountability in the creation and application of artificial intelligence. This can be accomplished by mandating companies and other organisations to disclose how they are utilising AI and its effects on society. Institutions can, for instance, compel businesses to report on how their AI systems are used to make decisions that affect individuals and communities. This can ensure that the virtuous circle is activated in accordance with our values, and that its benefits are shared by all.

Fourthly, institutions can encourage the creation of AI systems that protect personal privacy. This can be accomplished by requiring companies and other organisations to adhere to stringent data protection and privacy guidelines. Institutions can also support initiatives that encourage the development of artificial intelligence systems that employ privacy-enhancing technologies, such as federated learning and differential privacy. In this way, institutions can ensure that AI is developed and used in a manner that respects the privacy of individuals, a fundamental value in many societies.

Lastly, institutions can promote public awareness and education regarding the development and application of AI. By doing so, they can help ensure that the public is well-informed about the potential benefits and risks of AI, as well as develop public trust in the technology. This can be accomplished through public awareness campaigns, community outreach initiatives, and educational programmes that promote AI literacy.

As the use of artificial intelligence (AI) becomes more pervasive, the role of institutions in activating the AI-based virtuous circle while preserving freedom, equality, privacy, and ethical values will become increasingly crucial. In this section, we will explore the various ways in which institutions can promote the development of AI technologies while ensuring that they are developed and used in an ethical and equitable manner.

In order to activate the AI-based virtuous circle, one of the important roles of institutions is to promote research and development in the AI field. In addition to supporting startups and entrepreneurs working on AI-based projects, institutions can invest in research initiatives that seek to improve the accuracy and efficiency of AI technologies. By doing so, institutions can contribute to the development of an ecosystem that fosters innovation and promotes the creation of new AI technologies.

Despite the importance of promoting research and development, institutions must also ensure that these technologies are created and utilised in an ethical and equitable manner. The establishment of regulations and guidelines that govern the development and deployment of AI technologies is one method to achieve this goal. Governments may, for instance, enact laws requiring companies to adhere to certain ethical principles when developing and deploying AI systems. Similarly, professional associations can create codes of conduct mandating that AI industry professionals adhere to certain ethical standards.

Another essential function of institutions is to facilitate collaboration and knowledge-sharing between AI ecosystem stakeholders. Institutions can facilitate the sharing of data and knowledge among researchers, practitioners, and policymakers, thereby fostering a more interconnected and cohesive community. This can help to address some of the ethical concerns surrounding artificial intelligence, such as bias and privacy, by ensuring that stakeholders collaborate to address these concerns.

In addition, institutions can play a significant role in influencing the public discourse surrounding AI by educating the public about the benefits and risks of AI technologies. Institutions can collaborate with the media and other stakeholders to raise awareness of the potential of AI technologies, as well as the risks and difficulties associated with their use. Also, institutions can facilitate the development of AI technologies that are intended to promote liberty, equality, privacy, and ethical values. For instance, institutions can invest in the development of artificial intelligence (AI) technologies that promote equal access to healthcare or education or support environmental sustainability. By doing so, institutions can contribute to the development of an AI ecosystem that benefits society.

However, institutions must also ensure that AI technologies are not used to perpetuate existing social inequalities or to violate the privacy and freedom of individuals. This necessitates a careful balancing of interests, with institutions working to promote the development of AI technologies that advance the public welfare while protecting individual rights and liberties.

The creation of a regulatory framework to guarantee the development and deployment of AI in an ethical and secure manner is one of the most important responsibilities of institutions. Regulating the development and deployment of AI technologies will guarantee their openness and accountability. This requires, among other things, establishing standards for ethical and secure use, data privacy, and security. Additionally, regulations must ensure that AI-based systems are not designed to create or reinforce existing biases or discrimination.

In addition, institutions should establish and enforce codes of conduct that govern the ethical behaviour of AI industry participants. To ensure that these codes of conduct are founded on a solid understanding of the ethical implications of AI, they must be created in collaboration with ethics and philosophy experts.

Institutions must also promote openness and accountability in the creation and deployment of artificial intelligence. This means that organisations must provide explicit explanations of the reasoning behind AI system decisions and how those decisions were made. This can be accomplished through the creation of AI that is designed to provide explicit explanations of its decisions. Also, institutions must ensure that AI-based systems are accessible to everyone. This requires fostering equality in the creation and application of AI technologies. For instance, AI-based systems should be designed to meet the requirements of individuals with disabilities.

In the context of AI, institutions must play a crucial role in safeguarding privacy. This requires the establishment of regulations requiring organisations to acquire explicit consent from individuals prior to collecting or utilising their personal data. In addition, institutions must ensure that AI-based systems are designed to safeguard individual privacy. This can be accomplished through the use of technologies that protect privacy, such as differential privacy.

In conclusion, institutions play a crucial role in activating the AI-based virtuous circle while maintaining freedom, equality, privacy, and ethical values. To accomplish this, institutions must establish a regulatory framework that ensures the ethical and secure development and deployment of artificial intelligence. This necessitates establishing transparency, accountability, data privacy, and security standards. In addition to establishing codes of conduct, institutions must promote equality and privacy in the development and deployment of AI technologies. Institutions must ultimately collaborate to develop a framework that maximises the potential benefits of AI while mitigating its risks and negative effects.

Chapter 4: AI and Economic Planning

Artificial intelligence (AI) is rapidly altering many facets of our existence, including the economy. The potential for AI to revolutionise economic planning is a subject that is garnering increasing attention. In this chapter, we will examine the possibility that AI will make central planning feasible and efficient, as well as the relevance of Hayek's assertion in the era of AI and the market's superiority over the state in protecting individual liberty, privacy, and economic incentives.

Recent advances in AI have generated renewed interest in the concept of AI-based centralised planning, which has historically been associated with state control over the economy. With artificial intelligence's ability to process vast amounts of data and make predictions, it may be possible to develop a system that can coordinate economic activity more efficiently and effectively than traditional central planning. However, this raises significant concerns regarding the role of the state in the economy, the potential impact on individual freedom and privacy, and the capacity of AI-based planning to encourage innovation and entrepreneurship.

In exploring these questions, we will rely on the insights of economists like Friedrich Hayek, who argued that the market, not the state, is the best mechanism for coordinating economic activity and promoting individual liberty. We will examine the applicability of Hayek's ideas in the era of artificial intelligence and consider how they may inform our thinking about the potential benefits and risks of AI-based economic planning.

Finally, we will investigate the possibility of applying AI-based centralised planning to existing market structures. Could AI-based planning be used to supplement the market rather than supplant it? What would this entail for the current functioning of markets, and what would the ramifications be for economic efficiency, innovation, and personal liberty?

This chapter will provide a comprehensive overview of the potential of AI-based economic planning, along with its challenges and hazards. It will be of interest to economics and public policy scholars and practitioners.

The possibility of AI rendering central planning feasible and efficient

The possibility that artificial intelligence could make central planning feasible and effective has been a topic of interest and debate for decades. Central planning, the economic system in which the government regulates and manages all aspects of the economy, has been attempted in a variety of forms throughout history, with varying degrees of success. Recent advances in artificial intelligence (AI) technology have rekindled interest in AI's potential to make central planning a more viable and efficient option.

The government allocates resources and makes decisions on behalf of the entire economy under central planning. In a traditional economy, private enterprises and consumers would make these decisions based on the laws of supply and demand. However, central planning is frequently regarded as a more equitable and just system because it prioritises the requirements of the community as a whole over the profit motives of individual businesses.

The complexity of central planning has always been a challenge. The allocation and distribution of resources requires a comprehensive comprehension of the economy and the needs of the populace. Previously, this required vast quantities of data and the capacity to analyse it quickly and accurately. By analysing large quantities of data and making decisions based on that analysis, AI has the potential to significantly streamline this process.

Predictive analytics is one method that artificial intelligence can be used in central planning. Analysing historical data and using that information to predict future trends and outcomes is predictive analytics. This information can then be utilised to make allocation and distribution decisions. For instance, if predictive analytics indicate that a particular resource will be in short supply in the future, the government can take measures to increase production or discover alternative sources.

Optimisation algorithms are yet another method that AI can be utilised in central planning. The objective of optimisation algorithms is to determine the most effective method of allocating resources to accomplish a desired outcome. If the objective is to reduce traffic congestion in a city, for instance, optimisation algorithms can be used to determine the most efficient routes for public transport and the optimal locations for parking facilities.

Despite the prospective benefits of AI in central planning, its implementation raises concerns. One of the greatest concerns is the possibility of bias in decision-making algorithms. If the data used to train these algorithms is biassed, the AI may make decisions that are also biassed, resulting to unequal outcomes. In addition, there are concerns regarding the possibility of government overreach and the violation of individual liberties and privacy.

Moreover, AI could aid in monitoring and tracking the plan's progress, making adjustments and corrections easier along the road. By analysing data in real time, AI can provide decision-makers with valuable insights and assist them in identifying potential problems or improvement opportunities. This can result in more efficient and effective planning, leading to improved outcomes for all parties involved.

Also, it is important to observe that excessive reliance on AI for central planning carries with it potential risks. The potential for bias in algorithms used to analyse data and make decisions is one of the greatest dangers. If these algorithms are not carefully designed and tested, they may perpetuate existing biases and inequalities, resulting in unjust outcomes for certain groups of people.

Concerns also exist regarding the potential loss of human control and agency in a system that significantly relies on AI for decision-making. Despite the fact that AI can unquestionably provide valuable insights and aid decision-makers, it is essential to implement mechanisms to maintain human oversight and accountability.

Central planning has been a topic of discussion for decades, and the possibility of using AI to make central planning feasible and efficient is an intriguing one. The use of artificial intelligence in central planning has the potential to revolutionise the way economies are managed, allowing for more efficient resource allocation, increased productivity, and more equitable wealth distribution. However, a number of obstacles must be overcome before AI can be utilised effectively in central planning.

The complexity of the economic system is among the greatest obstacles. Numerous interdependencies exist between various economic sectors and industries. This complexity makes it difficult to construct precise economic models that can be used to make informed resource allocation decisions. However, AI has the potential to analyse enormous quantities of data, including economic data, and generate accurate models that can be used to make more informed resource allocation decisions.

Another difficulty is the possibility of bias in the decision-making data and algorithms. AI systems are only as effective as the data they are trained on, so if the data is biassed, so will be the system's decisions. This could contribute to unequal resource distribution and exacerbate existing inequalities. Consequently, it is essential to ensure that the data used to train AI systems is representative of the entire population and that the decision-making algorithms are transparent and accountable.

There are also concerns regarding the possibility that AI could be used to concentrate power in the hands of a few individuals or groups. The use of AI in central planning could lead to the control of resource allocation by a small group of individuals or corporations, resulting in the concentration of wealth and power. Consequently, it is essential to ensure that the use of artificial intelligence in central planning is transparent, accountable, and subject to democratic oversight.

In spite of these obstacles, the prospect of using AI to make central planning feasible and effective is thrilling. It has the potential to result in more efficient resource allocation, greater productivity, and a more equitable distribution of wealth. To realise this potential, it is necessary to address the aforementioned obstacles and ensure that the use of artificial intelligence in central planning is transparent, accountable, and subject to democratic oversight.

In addition, AI-based central planning can aid in addressing the problem of information asymmetry. In traditional market economies, information is not always distributed evenly, resulting in unequal market participant access to information. As a result, market failures and inefficiency may result, as certain individuals or organisations may enjoy an unjust advantage. AI, on the other hand, can access and analyse vast amounts of data from a variety of sources, including those that individuals and even governments may not have access to. This means that central planning based on AI can make more informed and equitable decisions because it has access to a much larger and more comprehensive reservoir of data.

It is essential to observe, however, that the implementation of AI-based central planning is not without obstacles. One of the primary concerns is the possibility of authority abuse. If a small group of individuals or a single entity controls the centralised AI system, there is a danger of corruption and manipulation for personal gain. Consequently, it is essential to implement checks and balances in order to prevent such abuses.

The complexity of the AI algorithms themselves is another obstacle. AI algorithms can be difficult to comprehend and interpret, making it challenging to ensure that they make ethical and impartial decisions. This is particularly essential when making decisions that could affect the lives of individuals or the overall functioning of the economy.

AI's ability to process vast amounts of data and recognise patterns that human planners may neglect is a potential advantage in central planning. AI could analyse, for instance, trends in consumer demand, resource availability, and production efficiency in order to optimise resource allocation and maximise the efficacy of production processes. This could result in improved decision-making, resource allocation, and productivity, all of which are essential components of central planning.

Another advantage of AI in central planning is its rapid adaptability to changing conditions. Traditional central planning systems can be sluggish and inflexible, making it challenging to adapt to fluctuating market conditions or unanticipated events. On the other hand, AI-powered systems can be designed to respond quickly to market shifts, supply chain disruptions, and other unforeseen occurrences. This could reduce the likelihood of shortages or waste, resulting in a more efficient use of resources and greater economic stability.

Nonetheless, the use of AI in central planning is not without potential hazards and obstacles. The potential for AI to make biassed or unfair judgements is a concern, especially if the data used to train the system is flawed or insufficient. This could lead to discrimination against certain groups or industries and undermine the equality and fairness principles that are frequently fundamental to central planning systems.

Another potential obstacle is the issue of openness and responsibility. In a conventional centralised planning system, decision-making is typically conducted in a transparent and accountable manner, with officials being liable for their decisions and accountable to the public. It may be more difficult to comprehend how decisions are made and to hold decision-makers accountable for their actions in the presence of AI-powered decision-making systems.

Moreover, there is the possibility that AI could displace human labour, especially in industries where routine or repetitive tasks are prevalent. This could have significant social and economic repercussions, especially if the benefits of AI are not distributed equitably throughout society.

To address these obstacles, it will be necessary to develop regulatory frameworks that assure the ethical and responsible use of artificial intelligence in central planning. This may include guidelines for data collection and analysis, transparency and accountability measures, and measures to resolve potential employment and social welfare impacts. Institutions such as governments, regulatory bodies, and professional associations will play a crucial role in developing and assuring the effective enforcement of these frameworks.

While the use of AI in central planning has the potential to increase efficiency and productivity, it also presents significant risks and obstacles. Consequently, it will be essential to develop regulatory frameworks that strike a balance between the potential benefits of artificial intelligence and the need to protect individual rights, promote equality, and guarantee transparency and accountability. By doing so, we can use AI to establish a more efficient and equitable society.

The relevance of Hayek's assertion in the age of AI and the superiority of the market over the state in protecting individual freedom, privacy, and economic incentives

Friedrich Hayek argued in his influential book, "The Road to Serfdom," that the market is superior to the state in preserving individual liberty, privacy, and economic incentives. Hayek's ideas have acquired renewed significance in the era of artificial intelligence (AI), as new technologies challenge traditional notions of privacy and individual autonomy. In this section, we will examine Hayek's ideas in light of the challenges posed by artificial intelligence and why they are still pertinent today.

Hayek's argument is predicated on the notion that the market is an order that arises spontaneously from the actions of individuals. Hayek argues that the market is superior to the state in preserving individual liberty because it permits people to make their own decisions about how to live their lives. In contrast, the state is inherently coercive and can readily become an instrument of oppression.

Hayek's argument that the market is preferable to the state is especially pertinent in the age of artificial intelligence. AI technologies have the potential to accumulate vast quantities of data on individuals and use that data to make life-altering decisions. For instance, AI algorithms can be used to determine if a job candidate is qualified for a specific position or if someone is likely to default on a loan. These decisions can have a substantial impact on the lives of individuals, and they pose significant concerns regarding privacy and individual autonomy.

Individual choice is one of the most significant advantages of the market over the government. Individuals are free to choose which goods to purchase, employment to accept, and investments to make in a market economy. The protection of individual autonomy and economic incentives is contingent upon the availability of this freedom of choice. When the government controls the economy, it restricts individual freedom and reduces their options. This can result in the state becoming an instrument of oppression rather than a defender of individual liberty.

Several sources pose a threat to the market in the age of artificial intelligence. The concentration of market power in the hands of a few large technology corporations is one of the greatest threats. These businesses have access to enormous amounts of data, which they can use to influence markets in their favour. This can lead to a situation in which competition is stifled and consumers have fewer options for purchasing products and services.

Utilising AI algorithms to make decisions about individuals poses another hazard to the market. These algorithms are frequently opaque, making it challenging for individuals to comprehend how they operate or to contest their decisions. This can result in individuals being denied opportunities or experiencing discrimination based on their nationality or gender.

Despite these obstacles, Hayek's ideas regarding the market's superiority over the state remain pertinent in the AI era. The market enables individuals to make decisions and safeguards their independence and economic incentives. It also promotes innovation and competition, both of which are necessary for economic growth and prosperity.

To ensure that the market remains a tool for protecting individual freedom and privacy in the era of artificial intelligence, it is essential to take measures to promote competition and ensure that individuals have access to information about how AI algorithms are used to make decisions about them. This may necessitate new regulations or policies that promote transparency and accountability in the application of artificial intelligence. Moreover, Hayek's assertion that the market is superior to the state in preserving individual liberty, privacy, and economic incentives is especially pertinent in the age of artificial intelligence. AI has the potential to significantly increase the amount of information that governments and corporations can collect about individuals, thereby increasing the risk of infringements on individual liberty and privacy. Consequently, it is crucial that appropriate safeguards be implemented to prevent the misuse of this information and to ensure that the rights of individuals are respected.

The market system provides a strong incentive for innovation and efficiency, which is one of its primary advantages. Businesses are always looking for ways to enhance their products and services in order to attract more consumers and increase profits. This competition promotes innovation, which results in increased efficiency and decreased costs. In contrast, state-controlled systems are frequently sluggish, bureaucratic, and resistant to change because there are few incentives to innovate or improve. In addition, the market system provides increased economic freedom and choice to individuals. Individuals in a market economy are free to choose which goods and services they wish to consume, and producers are free to offer a diverse array of products to satisfy their needs. This system enables individuals to pursue their own interests and allocate resources based on their own priorities, as opposed to the state dictating how resources should be utilised.

Ultimately, the market system affords higher privacy protection to individuals. Businesses must compete for customers in a market economy, and one way to do so is by safeguarding their customers' privacy. Companies that fail to do so run the risk of losing customers to rivals who are better equipped to safeguard customer privacy. State-controlled systems, on the other hand, may be less concerned with privacy protection because there is no competitive pressure to do so.

Hayek's assertion that the market is superior to the state in protecting individual freedom, privacy, and economic incentives remains highly relevant in the era of artificial intelligence. The market system provides strong incentives for innovation and efficiency, greater economic freedom and choice, and enhanced privacy protection for individuals. Therefore, it is crucial that we continue to promote and defend the market system so that these benefits are accessible to everyone. In addition, we must ensure that safeguards are in place to prevent the misuse of AI and to secure individual rights and liberties.

One of the most significant criticisms of Hayek's arguments in favour of free markets is that he ignores the ways in which markets can fail and the necessity of government intervention to resolve these failures. For instance, markets may be incapable of producing public benefits or adequately regulating externalities such as pollution. In such instances, government intervention may be necessary to guarantee that the benefits of economic activity are distributed fairly and efficiently. However, Hayek argued that the market is better equipped than the state to face these challenges. He argued that market participants have better information and incentives than government officials, and that the process of competition and innovation in markets is more effective at solving problems and improving economic outcomes than centralised government decision-making.

This argument has taken on new significance in the AI era. AI has the potential to increase economic efficiency and productivity, but it also raises significant concerns regarding privacy, security, and command. Some have argued that government intervention is required to ensure that artificial intelligence is used in a manner consistent with individual liberties and the public interest. However, Hayek's arguments imply that the market is better equipped than the state to resolve these challenges. In a free market, individuals are incentivized to develop and employ AI consistent with their own interests, while also considering the interests of others. The process of competition and innovation that occurs in markets is more effective than centralised decision-making by government officials in promoting the development of new technologies and practises that are consistent with individual rights and social welfare.

Moreover, the market is better suited than the government to safeguard individual liberty and privacy. Individuals are free to choose whether or not to participate in economic activity and to regulate how their personal information is used in a free market. In the name of safeguarding the public interest, government officials may be more likely to overreach and violate individual rights.

Even in the era of AI, Hayek's arguments in favour of free markets and against government intervention remain relevant. While government intervention may play a role in certain circumstances, such as addressing market failures or protecting individual rights, the market is better equipped to address these challenges and promote economic efficiency and innovation.

The market's reliance on a variety of information sources is another crucial factor in its favour. Hayek's theory of knowledge asserts that no individual or organisation can have access to all the necessary information to make the best decisions. Thus, central planning is destined to fail because it is founded on the fallacious premise that it is possible to know everything about an economy. In contrast, the decentralised structure of the market enables the collection of information from millions of individuals, resulting in more accurate and diverse data. This variety of data is essential for developing a dynamic and adaptable system that can rapidly adapt to changing conditions and requirements.

In contrast, AI systems in a centralised, government-run economy may be constrained by the availability of data, the algorithms used to process that data, and the quality of those algorithms. As a consequence, AI-based central planning may result in erroneous decisions due to a lack of diverse and comprehensive data. Moreover, centralised control of data raises privacy concerns, and the government may use the data to exert control over its citizens. Moreover, a market-based economy permits experimentation and innovation, which are essential for technological advancement. Hayek believed that individual liberty and competition result in experimentation, which leads to the discovery of new and more efficient methods of doing things. Entrepreneurs and innovators have the freedom to experiment and innovate in a market-based economy, resulting in the development of new technologies and industries. As described by economist Joseph Schumpeter, this process of creative destruction is essential for economic development.

In contrast, a state-controlled economy may impede experimentation and innovation because the government has little incentive to invest in new technologies and controls the means of production. This circumstance may result in the maintenance of the status quo and impede the development of innovative industries and technologies. The significance of economic incentives in driving innovation and progress is another crucial aspect of Hayek's argument. In a free market, businesses and individuals are incentivized to innovate and enhance their products or services to remain ahead of competitors and increase profits. This competition promotes efficiency, reduces costs, and results in the development of new and superior consumer goods.

When the government controls the economy, however, there is less incentive for innovation and progress. Politicians and bureaucrats make decisions based on political considerations rather than market demand, which can result in inefficient resource allocation and a lack of innovation. In addition, state-run industries frequently experience the "tragedy of the commons" problem, wherein no one is directly responsible for the success or failure of the industry, resulting in neglect and inefficiency. Some contend that the market's ability to safeguard individual liberty, privacy, and economic incentives may be diminished in the AI era. AI technologies can be used to collect and analyse enormous quantities of data about individuals, potentially violating their privacy and establishing a surveillance state. In addition, as AI becomes more advanced, it may automate an increasing number of jobs, resulting in substantial employment loss and economic disruption.

Hayek's assertion remains valid, as the market remains the best mechanism for assuring individual liberty and economic development. Even though AI may present new challenges, such as the need for new regulations to safeguard privacy and prevent the misuse of data, a free market still allows for innovation and competition that can propel the AI industry forward. Moreover, the automation of employment by AI can generate new opportunities and industries, just as the rise of the internet in the 1990s generated new opportunities and industries.

In conclusion, Hayek's claim that the market is superior to the state in preserving individual liberty, privacy, and economic incentives is still applicable in the age of artificial intelligence. Despite the fact that AI may present new challenges, such as privacy concerns and job automation, the free market remains the most effective mechanism for promoting innovation and progress. Instead of endeavouring to control or manage the industry, it is the government's responsibility to establish a regulatory framework that safeguards individual rights and prevents AI technology abuse.

The potential application of AI based centralized planning to part of existing market structures

Since quite some time, the use of artificial intelligence (AI) in centralised planning has been a topic of discussion. Centralised planning is an economic system in which decisions regarding the production and distribution of products and services are made by a central authority, such as a government agency, as opposed to the market. Centralised planning has advantages, such as the ability to allocate resources more efficiently and equitably, but it also has disadvantages, such as a lack of incentive for innovation and a propensity towards bureaucracy. However, markets are susceptible to market failures such as externalities and monopolies, despite their reputation for fostering innovation and competition. This section will investigate the potential application of AI-based centralised planning to extant market structures.

Prior to exploring the prospective applications of AI-based centralised planning, it is essential to comprehend how it operates. Utilising algorithms and machine learning, AI-based centralised planning makes decisions regarding the production and distribution of products and services. These algorithms are designed to consider multiple variables, including consumer demand, resource availability, and production costs. By analysing these variables, the algorithms are able to make efficient and fair decisions.

The healthcare sector is a prospective application of AI-based centralised planning. Patients, providers, insurers, and government agencies comprise a network of complex stakeholders in the healthcare industry, which is notoriously difficult to manage. However, through the use of AI-based centralised planning, it may be possible to increase the efficacy and equity of healthcare delivery. For instance, an AI-based centralised planning system could be used to allocate hospital beds and medical equipment more efficiently and fairly. In order to make decisions that benefit the greatest number of people, the system could take into account variables such as patient need, geographic location, and resource availability.

Transportation planning is a prospective application of AI-based centralised planning. Currently, the transportation industry faces a number of obstacles, including congestion, pollution, and safety concerns. It may be possible to address these challenges in a more efficient and equitable fashion using AI-based centralised planning. For instance, a centralised planning system based on AI could be utilised to manage traffic flow, optimise routes, and reduce emissions. The system could take into consideration traffic volume, road conditions, and environmental regulations in order to make decisions that benefit the environment and transportation system users.

It is essential to recognise that the potential implementation of AI-based centralised planning is not devoid of obstacles. The possibility of unintended consequences is among the greatest obstacles. An AI-based centralised planning system, for instance, could inadvertently create monopolies or impede innovation. There is also a risk of bias in the decision-making process, as the algorithms used in AI-based centralised planning are only as objective as the data on which they are based.

Some proponents of centralised AI planning argue that it could result in a more efficient allocation of resources and a reduction in inequality, but there are also a number of concerns that must be addressed. Under a centralised planning system, the potential for a lack of innovation and creativity is a significant concern. Without market incentives for innovation, it is possible that new product and technology development would be stifled. In addition, the possibility of bias and error in the AI planning algorithms could result in unintended consequences and negative outcomes.

Another issue is the absence of democratic accountability in a system of centralised planning. In a market economy, individuals have the ability to vote with their expenditures and choose which goods and services to purchase. In a centralised planning system, decisions are made by a small group of individuals or algorithms, which may result in a lack of responsiveness to the requirements and preferences of the larger population. In a centralised planning system, corruption and abuse of power are also possible.

Despite these concerns, there are still applications of AI-based centralised planning to extant market structures that have the potential to yield positive results. For instance, in the field of environmental regulation, AI-based planning could help allocate resources more efficiently and reduce pollution. In the healthcare industry, centralised planning could result in more efficient resource allocation and cost savings.

Optimising resource allocation is a further advantage of AI-based centralised planning. By analysing enormous amounts of data and employing sophisticated algorithms, AI is able to identify inefficiencies in existing market structures and recommend methods for more efficient resource allocation. This can result in enhanced productivity and economic expansion.

Moreover, AI can assist in mitigating the negative externalities associated with specific industries, such as pollution. By incorporating environmental considerations into the planning process, AI can assist in determining the most environmentally sustainable methods of resource allocation and encourage businesses to implement more environmentally friendly practises.

Nevertheless, the implementation of AI-based centralised planning presents numerous obstacles. One worry is that it could result in a loss of personal liberty and autonomy. Individuals may have limited control over their economic decisions in a centrally planned economy, where decisions are made by a central authority rather than the market. In addition, there is the possibility of government or corporate bias in the AI planning algorithms, which could result in unjust resource allocation.

Another difficulty is that AI may exacerbate existing social inequalities. If AI-based planning is not designed with equity and fairness in mind, it may exacerbate existing income, education, and resource access disparities. Despite these obstacles, AI-based centralised planning has the potential to mitigate some of the inefficiencies and externalities associated with current market structures. Nonetheless, it is essential that these systems be created with a focus on promoting equity, sustainability, and individual liberty, and after thorough consideration of their ethical and social implications.

Using AI-based centralised planning to improve extant market structures could have multiple benefits. The ability to optimise resource allocation, which is essential for attaining maximum efficiency and minimising waste, is one of the most significant advantages. Using data-driven algorithms, centralised planning systems can analyse market trends and consumer behaviour patterns, enabling more accurate supply and demand forecasting. In turn, this can assist businesses in making more informed decisions regarding production levels, pricing strategies, and inventory management, which can increase profitability and reduce costs.

Another advantage of centralised planning is its potential to increase market stability as a whole. In a free-market economy, supply and demand fluctuations can result in volatility, which can be detrimental to both businesses and consumers. By utilising AI-based planning tools, however, policymakers and businesses can better anticipate and respond to market changes, thereby reducing volatility and preventing economic recessions. Incorporating environmental considerations into decision-making processes, centralised planning can also assist with addressing externalities such as pollution and climate change.

Nevertheless, there are a number of potential disadvantages associated with AI-based centralised planning. The potential for government overreach and control is a significant concern. In a centralised planning system, policymakers and administrators would exert a great deal of influence over market decisions, which could stifle innovation and entrepreneurship. In addition, there is a risk that centralised planning could lead to a reduction in consumer choice, as algorithms rather than individuals make market decisions.

In addition, AI-based planning systems may perpetuate biases and discrimination, especially if they are founded on insufficient or biassed data. For instance, if AI systems are trained on historical data that reflects existing biases, they may perpetuate those biases in decision-making processes, resulting in unjust outcomes for certain groups. Consequently, it is crucial to ensure that AI-based planning systems are designed with diversity and inclusivity in mind, and that they are routinely audited to identify and rectify biases.

In conclusion, while there are potential benefits and drawbacks to utilising AI-based centralised planning in existing market structures, it is evident that the technology has the potential to revolutionise how markets operate. By optimising resource allocation, enhancing market stability, and addressing externalities, centralised planning systems can assist businesses and policymakers in making more informed decisions, which can ultimately benefit consumers and the economy as a whole. It is essential, however, to proceed with caution and ensure that these systems are designed and implemented in a manner that protects individual liberties and promotes diversity and inclusiveness.

Chapter 5: Ownership, Power, and Coordination in the Age of AI

The era of artificial intelligence (AI) has ushered in unprecedented changes to the ways in which we live, work, and conduct business. With the emergence of cutting-edge technologies such as machine learning, big data analytics, and robotics, AI has emerged as an increasingly significant economic development and competitiveness driver. As AI-based systems become more pervasive, however, queries about the power dynamics underlying these technological transformations are being raised.

This chapter will examine the intricate relationship between ownership, power, and coordination in the era of artificial intelligence. In particular, we will investigate the role of artificial intelligence in reshaping ownership concentration in various industries, as well as the potential alternatives to centralised ownership. We will also investigate the impact of the power dynamics inherent in AI-driven economic planning on coordination and control.

Particularly, we will investigate the command and control capabilities of AI-driven economic planning. We will examine how AI-based systems can be used to centralise decision-making and control, as well as the implications of such centralization for economic efficiency and social welfare. We will also investigate the potential dangers associated with centralised ownership, as well as potential alternatives for distributing ownership more widely throughout society.

This chapter aims to contribute to a greater comprehension of the intricate relationship between ownership, power, and coordination in the age of artificial intelligence. By examining how AI is reshaping the economy, we aim to shed light on the risks and opportunities associated with this disruptive technology.

The power of command, coordination, and control in AI-driven economic planning

In recent years, interest in the use of artificial intelligence (AI) for economic planning has increased. AI has the potential to transform economic planning, enabling for quicker and more effective decision-making. With this new power comes the possibility of centralised control and coordination, which poses questions about the distribution of power and ownership in society. In this section, we will investigate the command, coordination, and control capabilities in AI-driven economic planning, as well as their implications for ownership and governance structures.

AI has the potential to significantly increase command authority in economic planning. AI can provide planners with more accurate and timely information than was previously feasible by analysing large amounts of data. This can result in more effective decision-making because planners are better able to recognise and respond to altering economic conditions. Moreover, AI can automate many previously manual duties, freeing up resources for other endeavours.

Similarly, AI can also improve economic planning coordination. Planners can more easily coordinate the activities of various economic actors, such as businesses, individuals, and governments, using artificial intelligence. AI can help identify and propose solutions for supply chain bottlenecks, for instance. This can lead to increased economic efficiency and productivity.

Concerns regarding centralised control are also raised by the use of AI for economic planning. AI has the potential to concentrate power in a small group of planners or proprietors with access to the necessary data and resources to make decisions. This raises concerns regarding the distribution of power and property in society. Who is in charge of the AI systems? Who gains from their utilisation?

The concentration of power and proprietorship in AI-driven economic planning can have detrimental effects on society. It can result in a lack of accountability and transparency in decision-making, for starters. Planners and proprietors may make decisions that serve their own interests rather than those of society as a whole in the absence of adequate oversight. In addition, the concentration of power and ownership can reduce economic diversity and innovation. If a limited group of planners or owners controls the decision-making process, it may be less likely that they will consider alternative perspectives or approaches.

Alternative ownership structures are one potential solution to the issue of centralised control in AI-driven economic planning. As an alternative to centralised ownership, ownership could be dispersed among a larger group of economic actors, such as labourers or consumers. This could help ensure that decision-making is more democratic and transparent, and that more perspectives are considered.

In addition to command, coordination, and control, AI-driven economic planning has the potential to substantially alter the distribution of industry ownership. As AI becomes more pervasive and competent, ownership concentration among a small number of firms may increase. This is due to the fact that organisations with greater access to data, computing power, and AI technologies are better equipped to optimise production and obtain a competitive advantage over smaller organisations.

This trend towards ownership concentration has repercussions. In his book "Capital in the Twenty-First Century," economist Thomas Piketty contends that high levels of wealth concentration can cause economic and social instability, as well as a decline in democratic government. Furthermore, in a world where a small number of powerful AI-driven companies dominate entire industries, there may be concerns about their ability to influence government policies and regulations to their advantage, which could lead to a further consolidation of power.

In the era of AI, however, potential alternatives to centralised ownership may also emerge. Decentralised platforms and blockchain technologies, for instance, may facilitate increased peer-to-peer coordination and ownership, thereby reducing the need for centralised ownership and control. AI could also facilitate the development of new cooperative ownership models in which workers and stakeholders have a greater say in the administration and governance of businesses.

Possible bias and lack of diversity is a risk associated with the consolidation of command, coordination, and control in AI-driven economic planning. AI systems are only as objective as the training data and algorithms they employ. If the data utilised is biassed or inadequate, the AI system's decisions will reflect this bias.

Moreover, the concentration of authority in AI systems may result in a lack of decisional diversity. AI systems may be designed and maintained by a limited group of individuals with their own biases and perspectives, which may be reflected in the decision-making process of the system. This lack of diversity could result in decisions that reflect only the interests of a few individuals or groups, as opposed to those of the entire population. In addition, the power of command and control in AI-driven economic planning may contribute to accountability and transparency concerns. If the decision-making process is opaque and difficult for the public to comprehend, there may be little accountability for the AI system's decisions. As the decision-making process may be viewed as beyond the control of individuals or organisations, it may be difficult to hold them accountable for any negative outcomes resulting from AI-driven decisions.

There are concerns about the concentration of power and potential biases in the decision-making process, despite the fact that AI-driven economic planning has the potential to improve efficiency and coordination. Before implementing any technology on a large scale, the potential hazards and benefits must be thoroughly considered. The ability to optimise and coordinate complex systems at an unprecedented level of granularity is one of the principal benefits of AI-driven economic planning. By analysing enormous quantities of data in real-time, AI is able to provide insights and predictions that were previously inaccessible. This makes decision-making more efficient and effective, particularly in industries where multiple factors must be considered simultaneously.

Nonetheless, the power of AI-driven economic planning raises questions regarding who controls and benefits from these systems. Centralised planning can increase efficiency and coordination, but it also concentrates power in the hands of a small number of decision-makers. This concentration of power can result in inequity and restrict democratic participation. In addition, AI-driven economic planning necessitates vast quantities of data that can be utilised to extract value and extractive rent. Companies that own and control these datasets can acquire significant competitive advantages, resulting in a concentration of ownership and an increase in inequality.

The command, coordination, and control capabilities of AI-driven economic planning present both opportunities and challenges. Despite the fact that AI can optimise complex systems and enhance decision-making, the concentration of power and ownership can result in inequality and restrict democratic participation. It is crucial to consider these issues and find methods to balance the advantages of artificial intelligence with the need for democratic control and equitable distribution of power and resources.

The impact of AI on ownership concentration in all industries and potential alternatives to centralized ownership

The rise of AI and its integration into a growing number of industries have significantly altered how businesses operate. One of the most prominent effects of artificial intelligence is its effect on ownership concentration in various industries. This section will investigate how AI is affecting the concentration of ownership in industries, the potential repercussions of this trend, and possible alternatives to centralised ownership.

In numerous industries, such as healthcare, manufacturing, transportation, and finance, AI is facilitating the creation of economies of scale and scope. Due to their ability to use data and AI to optimise operations, production, and logistics, larger companies can outcompete smaller ones because of economies of scale and scope. These larger companies can then acquire lesser companies, thereby increasing the industry's concentration of ownership.

Increased ownership concentration raises concerns regarding market dominance, monopolies, and the impact on innovation and competition. In markets with concentrated ownership, firms can use their market power to set prices above what they would be in a competitive market, resulting in diminished consumer welfare. Additionally, ownership concentration can reduce incentives for innovation and investment in R&D, as firms face less pressure to innovate as a result of their market dominance.

AI is also altering the very nature of ownership. In the transportation industry, for instance, AI is making it simpler for businesses to automate their fleets, thereby reducing the need for individual car ownership. Instead, these businesses may adopt centralised fleet ownership, with individuals paying for access to the fleet. Similarly, the use of AI in the management of assets and investment portfolios is making it simpler for asset management companies to accumulate more funds and increase their ownership concentration in the finance industry.

A potential alternative to centralised ownership is platform cooperativism, a paradigm in which platform ownership is distributed among its users, who then have a say in how the platform operates. This model has been effective in the context of shared economy platforms such as ride-hailing and home-sharing. In these instances, users have a stake in the success of the platform and are incentivized to partake actively, resulting in improved outcomes for all parties.

The use of decentralised systems, such as blockchain technology, in which ownership is distributed across a network of participants, is an additional potential alternative to centralised ownership. This model may facilitate peer-to-peer transactions and reduce the need for centralised intermediaries, resulting in more decentralised ownership structures.

Consequently, the effects of AI on ownership concentration in various industries have far-reaching effects on the economy and society as a whole. The concentration of ownership can reduce competition, increase prices, and reduce innovation incentives. However, alternatives such as platform cooperativism and decentralised systems offer the possibility of more distributed ownership structures, which could result in more equitable and efficient outcomes.

A further alternative to centralised ownership is platform cooperativism, a decentralised form of ownership. In a platform cooperative model, ownership is distributed among the platform's consumers and workers, as opposed to being held by a small number of shareholders. This model permits a more democratic and equitable distribution of power and resources and has the potential to decrease economic inequality.

The concept of platform cooperativism is not new, but it has garnered renewed interest in recent years due to growing concerns about the power and influence of tech giants such as Amazon, Google, and Facebook. These businesses have been scrutinised for their monopolistic practises and the ways in which they profit from user data. This model is challenged by platform cooperativism, which is founded on the principles of collective ownership and democratic decision-making.

For instance, Lyft has been criticised for its treatment of drivers, who are classified as independent contractors as opposed to employees and therefore do not receive benefits or protections such as minimum wage laws. In response, a group of New York City Lyft drivers founded the Drivers Cooperative, a platform cooperative owned and operated by its members. The cooperative model permits greater control over working conditions and more equitable compensation.

Thus, it is evident that AI has a significant impact on ownership concentration across all industries and has the potential to exacerbate extant inequalities. However, there are alternatives to centralised ownership that provide a more democratic and equitable distribution of power and resources, such as worker-owned cooperatives and platform cooperativism. As AI continues to transform the economy, it is crucial to consider these alternative ownership models and investigate how they can be implemented to advance economic justice and social equity.

Chapter 6: AI and the Spectrum of Varieties of Capitalism

In recent years, the development of Artificial Intelligence (AI) has caused significant changes in the business and economics sectors. As a consequence, there has been a rise in interest in examining the connection between AI and the spectrum of capitalism. This chapter examines how the co-evolution of AI and institutional forms affects the spectrum of capitalism, the potential reduction or proliferation of varieties of capitalism and their equilibrium, and the emergence of disequilibria and a potential "battle of systems" due to AI.

Varieties of capitalism refer to the institutional differences that regulate economic activity in various nations. This includes labour market regulations, education and training systems, welfare administrations, corporate governance structures, and financial systems. In response to changes in the economic environment, these institutional arrangements are not immutable, but evolve over time. The co-evolution of AI and institutional forms generates new challenges and opportunities for various types of capitalism, which may result in alterations to the spectrum of capitalism.

One possible consequence of the co-evolution of artificial intelligence and institutional forms is the potential reduction or proliferation of varieties of capitalism and their equilibrium. Capitalism proliferates when new institutional forms arise in response to technological changes, such as the rise of artificial intelligence. These new institutional forms may not fit neatly into the existing categories of capitalism, resulting in the emergence of new types of capitalism. In contrast, the reduction of varieties of capitalism occurs when extant institutional forms converge in response to technological changes, such as the standardisation of AI technologies, thereby eroding the distinctions between various varieties of capitalism.

The co-evolution of AI and institutional forms may also result in the emergence of disequilibria and a potential "battle of systems" caused by AI. Different forms of capitalism have varying institutional structures that confer advantages and disadvantages on enterprises in various industries. The emergence of AI technologies may upset the existing equilibrium between various forms of capitalism and create new advantages and disadvantages for businesses in various industries. This may result in a "battle of systems" as various nations and corporations attempt to acclimatise to the new economic environment created by AI technologies.

This chapter seeks to examine the diverse ways in which AI and institutional forms co-evolve and influence the spectrum of capitalism's varieties. It will investigate the potential reduction or proliferation of varieties of capitalism and their equilibrium, as well as the emergence of disequilibria and potential "battle of systems" as a result of artificial intelligence. Through this analysis, we aim to shed light on how various nations and businesses can adapt to the AI-driven shift in the economic environment.

The impact of the co-evolution of AI and institutional forms on the spectrum of varieties of capitalism

It is anticipated that the co-evolution of AI and institutional forms will have a significant impact on the spectrum of capitalism. The spectrum of capitalism refers to the various institutional configurations and economic models that have arisen in various regions and countries around the globe. These institutional structures and economic models reflect the distinctive political, economic, and cultural characteristics of each region or nation.

By altering the manner in which economic activity is organised and coordinated, AI is likely to have a significant effect on the spectrum of capitalist forms. AI can improve the efficacy and efficiency of numerous economic processes, including production, distribution, and marketing. This could result in alterations to the institutional structures that support economic activity, including the responsibilities of firms, markets, and the state.

The emergence of novel forms of economic organisation is a possible consequence of the co-evolution of AI and institutional forms on the spectrum of capitalist varieties. AI could, for instance, facilitate the development of decentralised platforms that enable the coordination of economic activity across multiple agents without the need for a centralised coordinating authority. This may result in the emergence of new economic models that challenge the dominance of existing institutional structures.

Existing institutional forms may be reinforced as a result of the co-evolution of AI and institutional forms on the spectrum of capitalist variants. AI may enhance the efficacy and effectiveness of existing institutional forms, such as large corporations, by enabling them to manage production processes and supply chains more efficiently. This could further concentrate economic power in the hands of a few large corporations.

The co-evolution of AI and institutional forms has the potential to have various effects on the spectrum of capitalist varieties. Altering the comparative advantages of various institutional forms in diverse national contexts is one approach. For example, AI may make some institutional forms more efficient and competitive than others, thereby altering the optimal equilibrium between institutional forms in a given context.

In addition, AI may influence the distribution of economic activities across international borders. The development of artificial intelligence may lead to the concentration of certain economic activities in a few nations, while rendering others obsolete. This could result in a significant shift in the distribution of economic power and influence across the globe.

Moreover, the incorporation of AI into production processes may also affect the capital-labor relationship. Adoption of AI could lead to the substitution of labour with capital, resulting in a shift in the income and wealth distribution between capital and labour. This change may have substantial ramifications for the distribution of economic and political power among various institutional forms.

In addition, the co-evolution of AI and institutional forms may have an impact on the roles and powers of various actors within various institutional forms. For instance, the rise of artificial intelligence could increase the bargaining power of certain actors, such as platform proprietors, while decreasing the bargaining power of others, such as labour unions. This could lead to shifts in the power structure within various institutional forms.

The impact of the co-evolution of AI and institutional forms on the spectrum of forms of capitalism is a complex issue requiring in-depth examination. One of the most significant effects of artificial intelligence is the creation of new opportunities for businesses and entrepreneurs to develop and enhance their operations. The development of AI-powered technologies has resulted in an increase in the production of knowledge and is altering how businesses operate and compete. This occurrence is anticipated to result in substantial changes to the economy and a reorganisation of the institutional landscape.

AI is having an impact on the institutional structures of various economies, including liberal market economies, coordinated market economies, and mixed market economies. The use of AI technologies can enhance the performance of these institutions by increasing their efficiency and efficacy. AI technologies can also reduce production costs, increase the quality of goods and services, and boost a company's competitiveness. As a consequence, AI is transforming the institutional landscape of various economies and the way markets function.

In liberal market economies, AI is influencing how businesses operate and compete. Companies are able to optimise their operations, reduce costs, and enhance the quality of their products and services thanks to AI-driven technologies. These technologies also allow businesses to expand their market presence and increase their competitiveness. As a result, AI is anticipated to increase competition in liberal market economies and contribute to more efficient resource allocation.

In coordinated market economies, AI is influencing how businesses collaborate and coordinate their activities. To coordinate economic activities, these economies rely on robust social institutions, such as labour unions and employer associations. AI technologies can assist in augmenting the functionality of these institutions by boosting their efficacy and efficiency. For instance, AI can be used to improve supply chain management, reduce production costs, and enhance the quality of products and services. As a result, artificial intelligence is anticipated to increase the competitiveness of coordinated market economies and contribute to a more efficient allocation of resources.

AI is influencing the manner in which governments and businesses collaborate to accomplish their goals in mixed market economies. These economies rely on robust partnerships between the public and private sectors to foster economic growth and social welfare. AI technologies can enhance the functionality of these collaborations by increasing their efficiency and efficacy. AI can be used, for instance, to improve the delivery of public services, reduce production costs, and enhance the quality of products and services. AI is therefore anticipated to increase the competitiveness of mixed market economies and contribute to a more efficient allocation of resources.

In conclusion, the co-evolution of AI and institutional forms has had a significant effect on the spectrum of forms of capitalism. The use of AI technologies is altering how businesses operate and compete with one another, how they coordinate their activities and collaborate with one another, and how governments and businesses work together to achieve their objectives. As a result, artificial intelligence is anticipated to lead to a more efficient allocation of resources and increase the competitiveness of various economies.

The potential reduction or proliferation of varieties of capitalism and their equilibrium because of AI

The development and implementation of AI has the potential to diminish or expand the variety of capitalism and its equilibrium. This section will discuss the possible mechanisms that may result in these outcomes.

One potential effect of artificial intelligence is the homogenization of economic structures across countries and regions. With the increased availability of data and the development of AI technologies, businesses may find it simpler and less costly to operate in regions with comparable economic structures. This could result in a convergence of economic structures, in which countries adopt similar market-oriented policies and institutional forms in order to attract foreign investment and increase their competitiveness.

On the other hand, AI could also facilitate the spread of various forms of capitalism. With the ability to process vast quantities of data and automate duties, businesses may be able to operate more efficiently in a variety of institutional settings. This could contribute to the emergence of new forms of capitalism, in which firms are able to take advantage of distinctive institutional characteristics while maintaining high levels of efficiency and competitiveness.

The relationship between the impact of AI on the varieties of capitalism and their equilibrium and the regulatory environment is also close. Variable levels of regulation in various nations can either facilitate or impede the development and implementation of AI technologies. Countries with less stringent regulations may experience a greater proliferation of various types of capitalism, whereas countries with more stringent regulations may experience a decrease in the number of types of capitalism.

In addition, the role of the state influences the impact of AI on the variants of capitalism and their equilibrium. In some nations, the function of the state in shaping the economic system is central, whereas in others, it is limited. Depending on the institutional context, the development and implementation of AI may either strengthen or diminish the role of the state in shaping the economy.

In addition, the distribution of resources and authority is also related to the effect of AI on the various forms of capitalism and their equilibrium. The development and implementation of

AI may increase the concentration of resources and power in the hands of a few dominant firms, thereby reducing the variety of capitalism. Alternately, AI may facilitate the emergence of new businesses and industries, resulting in a proliferation of distinct forms of capitalism.

Thus, we can see that AI has a complex and multifaceted effect on the various forms of capitalism and their equilibrium. Numerous factors, such as the regulatory environment, the function of the state, and the distribution of resources and power, influence it. It is ultimately the responsibility of policymakers and other stakeholders to shape the institutional context in a way that maximises the benefits of AI while minimising its potential negative effects, despite the fact that AI has the potential to reduce or expand the varieties of capitalism.

AI's impact on the spectrum of forms of capitalism may also result in the emergence of entirely new forms of capitalism. Some experts contend that artificial intelligence could facilitate the emergence of a new form of capitalism known as "algorithmic capitalism." In this form, businesses and investors extensively rely on algorithms and data analysis rather than human intuition or judgement when making decisions. This may result in a transition from traditional market capitalism, in which individual investors make decisions based on their own personal interests and beliefs, to a more centralised form of decision-making that heavily relies on machine learning algorithms.

Nonetheless, the emergence of algorithmic capitalism may have unintended consequences. For instance, AI may exacerbate existing inequalities and power imbalances in society, as large corporations and wealthy individuals with access to the most advanced AI technologies will have a substantial competitive advantage over smaller businesses and those with less wealth. In addition, AI may enable certain industries to be dominated by a handful of large actors, thereby reducing competition and innovation in those sectors.

The emergence of new models of ownership and governance is a potential outcome of AI's impact on the spectrum of forms of capitalism. According to some experts, AI could facilitate new forms of decentralised ownership, such as blockchain-based systems, which could challenge traditional models of centralised ownership and control. For instance, blockchain-based systems could facilitate decentralised and democratic decision-making, where each participant has a say in the direction of the organisation, as opposed to decisions being made by a small group of executives or shareholders.

Nonetheless, the emergence of new models of ownership and governance presents obstacles. For instance, it may be difficult to establish distinct lines of accountability and responsibility in decentralised systems, which may result in confusion and inefficiency. In addition, it may be difficult to reconcile the diverse interests and priorities of the various participants in a decentralised system, which could result in conflicts and stalemate.

In this regard, AI is likely to have a substantial effect on the spectrum of capitalism's varieties. It could contribute to the proliferation of new forms of capitalism and the emergence of new models of ownership and administration. Nonetheless, it could exacerbate existing inequalities and power imbalances, reduce competition and innovation in certain sectors, and pose difficulties in establishing clear lines of accountability and responsibility. As AI continues to evolve, policymakers and business leaders will need to carefully consider these potential outcomes and devise strategies to mitigate any negative outcomes while maximising the potential benefits.

The impact of AI on the spectrum of varieties of capitalism is multidimensional and has the potential to both reduce and expand the number of existing varieties. On the one hand, AI has the potential to reduce the number of types of capitalism, as it may result in the convergence of economic institutions and practises across nations. This could occur because AI technology can generate efficiencies in production and supply chains, which could lead to the emergence of similar business models and industrial structures across economies. Additionally, the use of AI in financial markets could contribute to the proliferation of similar financial instruments and regulatory practises across nations.

On the other hand, AI may also contribute to the proliferation of variants of capitalism, as it enables the development of new and innovative economic institutions and practises. AI could, for instance, facilitate the creation of previously impossible business models, such as those that rely heavily on data analysis or automation. Different nations may employ these new business models in various ways, resulting in the emergence of new forms of capitalism.

AI may also influence the equilibrium of different forms of capitalism. Varieties of capitalism are frequently predicated on a delicate balance between various institutional factors, including labor-market institutions, financial-market institutions, and corporate governance. By altering the relative importance of various institutional factors, AI has the potential to upset this equilibrium. For instance, the use of AI in production may lead to a larger reliance on capital over labour, which could shift the power balance in favour of capital owners and diminish the bargaining power of labour.

Moreover, the impact of AI on the equilibrium of various types of capitalism may vary by country and region. This is because the impact of AI on institutional factors may vary based on the economic and social structures of various countries. For example, the use of AI in production may have a greater impact on countries with a long history of manufacturing, whereas the use of AI in financial markets may have a greater impact on countries with a significant financial sector.

The potential reduction or proliferation of capitalism due to AI could also result in a "battle of systems" between various economic models. In a world where AI is driving economic change, countries may attempt to safeguard their existing economic models or promote their preferred model. This could result in heightened tensions and competition among nations, and even geopolitical conflict.

In conclusion, the influence of AI on the spectrum of forms of capitalism is complex and multidimensional. AI has the potential to both reduce and increase the number of extant varieties of capitalism, as well as disrupt the equilibrium between existing variants. Furthermore, the impact of AI on the spectrum of varieties of capitalism may vary across countries and regions, leading to the possibility of a "battle of systems" between various economic models. Therefore, policymakers and academics must carefully consider the implications of AI for the future of capitalism and the world economy.

The emergence of disequilibria and potential "battle of systems" because of AI

The co-evolution of artificial intelligence and institutional forms could result in the emergence of disequilibria and a potential "battle of systems" between various forms of capitalism. The impact of artificial intelligence on the institutional forms that underpin various forms of capitalism is likely to be unequal, which could result in divergent economic outcomes across nations. Countries may employ incompatible approaches to AI-driven economic development, which could result in a potential conflict between various forms of capitalism.

The use of AI to automate work processes and reduce labour costs could lead to conflict. This could intensify the competition between nations to attract investment in automated production processes. Countries with strong technological capabilities and advanced educational systems may have a comparative advantage in this type of competition, which could contribute to a polarisation of economic outcomes across nations. Countries with weaker technological capabilities and less developed educational systems may find it difficult to acclimatise to this new environment, which could exacerbate existing inequalities between various forms of capitalism.

Utilising AI to manage and coordinate economic activity is another potential source of conflict. This may result in a concentration of economic power in the hands of those who control the algorithms and platforms underlying AI-driven economic coordination. In some forms of capitalism, this concentration of power may be regarded as a threat to individual freedom and autonomy, which could lead to a backlash against AI-driven economic growth. In other varieties of capitalism, the concentration of power may be regarded as a source of efficiency and innovation, which could result in divergent approaches to the development of AI-driven economic systems across nations.

The emergence of AI is likely to have profound effects on the evolution of various forms of capitalism over time. While some nations may benefit from the development of AI-driven economic systems, others may find it difficult to acclimatise to this new environment, which could lead to a conflict between various forms of capitalism. In the end, the effect of artificial intelligence on the global economy will depend on a complex interplay of technological, social, and political factors that are difficult to predict with absolute precision.

Diverse societies' cultural and ideological values are an additional aspect of the prospective "battle of systems" caused by the emergence of artificial intelligence. The adoption and implementation of artificial intelligence in economic and social systems can be influenced by cultural and ideological factors, which can have varying effects on the development of AI. This can result in the emergence of different AI-driven capitalism models in different regions of the globe, which could further complicate global economic relations and international cooperation.

In addition, the emergence of AI may present new opportunities for certain actors to acquire power and influence within the global economic system. For instance, companies and nations that adopt AI early may be able to obtain a competitive advantage over others, thereby consolidating their position and power in the global economy. This could result in increased economic inequality and possibly even geopolitical tensions between various nations and regions. Also, the potential for AI to automate employment and disrupt traditional industries could exacerbate existing economic and social inequalities, particularly for marginalised or vulnerable groups. As certain industries and professions become increasingly automated, those unable to retrain or adapt to new roles may encounter unemployment or underemployment, resulting in heightened inequality and social unrest.

To mitigate these potential risks and ensure that the development and implementation of artificial intelligence is conducted in a manner that promotes social and economic equity, policymakers and stakeholders will need to carefully consider the ethical and societal implications of AI. This could include investing in education and training programmes to ensure that workers can adapt to new roles, establishing regulations to protect privacy and prevent the abuse of power by AI systems, and promoting international cooperation and collaboration to ensure that the development of AI is transparent and accountable.

Consequently, the advent of AI has the potential to profoundly transform the global economic system, creating both new opportunities and risks for various actors. By carefully considering the potential implications of AI and taking steps to mitigate potential risks, policymakers and stakeholders can ensure that the development and implementation of AI is conducted in a manner that promotes social and economic equity while advancing global economic growth and development. As AI continues to evolve and influence the institutional forms and economic structures of various nations, disequilibria may emerge. This is due to the fact that the co-evolution of AI and institutional forms can result in shifts in the distribution of power, resources, and economic opportunities across various actors and sectors.

One of the potential outcomes of this process is the potential emergence of a "battle of systems" as actors and nations with diverse institutional arrangements and economic models compete for dominance and influence in the global economy. Countries with more centralised and state-led economic models, for instance, may be more likely to adopt AI-driven economic planning and obtain a potential efficiency and productivity advantage. On the other hand, countries with more decentralised and market-oriented models may be hesitant to adopt AI-driven planning, resulting in a potential competitive disadvantage. In addition, the emergence of AI may exacerbate existing tensions and conflicts between various economic models and ideologies. As AI technologies create new challenges and opportunities for both models, the tension between the more individualistic and market-oriented Anglo-Saxon model of capitalism and the more communitarian and state-led Rhine model of capitalism may intensify. This could contribute to a further polarisation between different economic systems and the ideological fragmentation of the global economy. To mitigate the potential emergence of disequilibria and the "battle of systems" caused by artificial intelligence, it is crucial to foster greater dialogue and cooperation between various nations and economic actors. This could include the creation of international frameworks and standards for the ethical use of artificial intelligence in economic planning, as well as efforts to promote the development of more inclusive and participatory institutional arrangements that can better incorporate the needs and interests of various stakeholders.

As AI technologies continue to advance, the potential for global economic disequilibria to emerge grows. This could result in a "battle of systems" as various nations, regions, or even businesses adopt diverse strategies for AI-driven economic development. The rise of China as a global leader in artificial intelligence and U.S. efforts to maintain its technological dominance have already strained the global economy. The unequal distribution of AI capabilities across industries and countries could be a potential source of disequilibrium. It is probable that AI-driven industries, such as technology, finance, and healthcare, will experience rapid expansion and a concentration of wealth and power. Meanwhile, traditional industries such as manufacturing and agriculture may struggle to adjust to AI and experience a loss of competitiveness. This could potentially lead to significant economic and social inequality and destabilise the global economy. AI's potential to disrupt established institutional arrangements, such as labour markets, social welfare systems, and intellectual property regimes, is another potential source of disequilibria. AI technologies such as automation and machine learning could displace human labour, resulting in job losses, stagnant wages, and social unrest. Moreover, AI-driven innovations may pose a threat to existing intellectual property regimes and result in the emergence of new forms of digital monopolies.

In response to these challenges, various nations or regions may employ distinct AI-driven economic development strategies, resulting in a "battle of systems." Some countries may, for instance, prioritise state-led investments in AI research and development and promote centralised planning and control of AI-driven industries. Others may employ a market-oriented strategy and concentrate on fostering innovation via private sector investments and entrepreneurship. These contradictory strategies may result in divergent economic outcomes and exacerbate geopolitical tensions. To address these issues and prevent the emergence of disequilibria and the "battle of systems," global cooperation and coordination on AI governance and regulation are essential. This may involve establishing international standards and norms for AI development, ensuring equitable distribution of AI benefits, and addressing the potential negative effects of AI on labour markets and social welfare systems. Moreover, it is essential to promote diversity and inclusion in the development and deployment of AI technologies in order to ensure that the benefits of AI are widely distributed throughout society.

The co-evolution of AI and institutional forms has the potential to affect the spectrum of capitalism's varieties. It can result in the reduction or proliferation of various forms of capitalism and their equilibrium, as well as the emergence of disequilibria and a potential "battle of systems." AI can bring about substantial benefits and efficiencies, but it can also challenge existing institutional structures and their underlying principles, such as personal liberty, privacy, and economic incentives.

As AI continues to shape and transform various sectors of the economy, policymakers, academics, and practitioners must carefully consider the potential effects on the existing institutional arrangements and their long-term viability. In addition, the rise of AI may necessitate the development of new institutional forms and frameworks that are more aligned with its benefits and challenges. Clearly, the intersection of AI and institutional forms is a complex and evolving topic that necessitates multidisciplinary perspectives and collaboration. By combining insights from economics, political science, sociology, and technology, we can gain a better understanding of the potential effects of artificial intelligence on the spectrum of capitalism and develop strategies that can leverage the benefits of AI while protecting individual freedom, privacy, and economic incentives.

Ultimately, as AI continues to advance and become more pervasive in our lives, it is crucial that our institutional structures evolve and adapt to these changes in a manner that is beneficial to society as a whole. Only through collaboration and careful analysis can we guarantee that the co-evolution of artificial intelligence and institutional forms will result in positive outcomes for all.

Chapter 7: AI and Economic Development and Innovation

The economic landscape is being swiftly transformed by Artificial Intelligence (AI). AI not only revolutionises production processes and creates new business models, but also alters the way entrepreneurs and innovators approach economic development. The potential impact of AI on economic growth and innovation has piqued the interest of policymakers, academics, and business executives.

This chapter examines the potential of artificial intelligence to nurture entrepreneurial capitalism or state capitalism, the impact of AI on innovation and the dissemination of innovative ideas, and the role of entrepreneurs in an AI-driven economic system. These topics are crucial for comprehending the potential benefits and hazards associated with the application of AI in economic development and innovation.

This chapter's first section will investigate how AI can support entrepreneurial capitalism, where market forces and competition drive economic growth and innovation. AI can provide entrepreneurs with new tools and resources for identifying market opportunities, developing new products and services, and improving production process efficiency. AI can however also support state capitalism, in which governments control economic activity and investment decisions. Government use of AI can increase state intervention in the economy and diminish the role of private enterprise.

The second section will examine the impact of artificial intelligence on innovation and the dissemination of innovative ideas. AI has the potential to accelerate the rate of innovation by automating previously resource- and time-intensive tasks. However, the use of AI in innovation can also contribute to the concentration of innovation in the hands of a few large companies, thereby limiting competition and the spread of innovative ideas.

In the third and final section, the function of entrepreneurs in an AI-driven economic system will be discussed. AI can provide new opportunities for innovation and development for entrepreneurs, but it can also present new challenges. Entrepreneurs will be required to adjust to the ever-changing AI landscape and acquire new skills and knowledge in order to reap the potential benefits of AI.

Therefore, the application of AI in economic development and innovation has the potential to revolutionise our approach to these fields. AI can provide new opportunities for growth and innovation, but it also poses significant risks, such as diminished competition and increased government intervention. Entrepreneurs, policymakers, and business executives must collaborate to maximise the potential benefits of artificial intelligence while minimising its deployment risks.

The potential for AI to foster entrepreneurial capitalism or state capitalism

The rapid development of artificial intelligence (AI) has the potential to have a substantial effect on the economic system, particularly in terms of nurturing entrepreneurial capitalism or state capitalism. These two economic systems differ in their approach to ownership, innovation, and overall economic development, and the impact of AI in these areas may result in the ascendance of one or the other.

On the one hand, AI may encourage entrepreneurial capitalism, which is characterised by a free market system with an emphasis on private ownership, innovation, and competition. Using AI, businesses can increase their efficiency and productivity, resulting in increased profitability and expansion opportunities. AI-powered data analytics, for instance, can assist businesses in making more informed decisions and identifying new market opportunities, whereas AI-powered automation can expedite production and reduce costs. In addition, AI has the potential to encourage innovation, a key driver of entrepreneurial capitalism. By automating mundane and repetitive duties, artificial intelligence can free up human resources for more creative and innovative endeavours. This can then lead to the creation of new products and services that can disrupt existing markets and create new growth opportunities.

AI could also contribute to the rise of state capitalism, which is characterised by the centralization of economic power within the state. In this system, the government controls and directs the growth of critical industries and plays a more active role in the economy. In China, for example, the government has made substantial investments in AI and is employing it to boost economic growth and competitiveness. This has resulted in the development of large-scale state-owned AI companies, such as Baidu and Tencent, which dominate the Chinese technology sector.

As the state exerts increased control over economic activity, state capitalism may be effective in fostering rapid economic growth and development, but it may also result in the suppression of individual liberties and entrepreneurship. Consequently, the potential impact of AI on the economic system is not predetermined, and its development can follow a variety of paths contingent on the prevailing social, political, and institutional factors. In determining whether AI leads to the rise of entrepreneurial capitalism or state capitalism, the role of policymakers and business leaders in moulding its development will be crucial.

Consequently, the potential for AI to foster either entrepreneurial or state capitalism is substantial. Utilising AI can increase efficiency and productivity, resulting in greater profitability and expansion opportunities for businesses. AI may also contribute to the centralization of economic power in the hands of the state, thereby stifling individual liberties and entrepreneurship. The future of artificial intelligence and its impact on economic development and innovation will be contingent on a number of factors, including the political and institutional context, policy decisions, and the actions of entrepreneurs and businesses.

AI's capacity to reduce the costs of starting and operating a business is a potential means by which it can encourage entrepreneurial capitalism. Many mundane and time-consuming duties can be automated by AI-powered tools, allowing entrepreneurs to focus on higher-level strategic decisions. AI can assist with market research, consumer segmentation, and personalised marketing, allowing startups to target their products more effectively. Additionally, AI can assist with financial forecasting and risk assessment, lowering the entry barriers for new businesses.

Moreover, AI can facilitate entrepreneurs' access to capital. AI is able to identify promising businesses with a high likelihood of success by analysing vast amounts of data. In turn, this can attract investors seeking to maximise their returns. AI can also be used to create more efficient and transparent financial markets, making it easier and cheaper for entrepreneurs to raise capital.

Concerns also exist regarding the potential for AI to promote state capitalism. State capitalism is an economic system in which the government exerts substantial control over the means of production and the distribution of resources. AI has the potential to bolster state authority by providing governments with new surveillance and social control tools. AI can be used to monitor citizen activities, predict their behaviour, and identify dissenters, for example. This may result in a further erosion of civil liberties and personal autonomy.

In addition, AI can exacerbate existing inequality and power concentration. Large corporations and governments can gain significant advantages from their ability to collect and analyse massive amounts of data, giving them an unfair advantage over smaller businesses and individuals. This could lead to a situation where a small number of powerful entities control the majority of economic resources and political authority, resulting in a form of state capitalism.

Consequently, the potential impact of artificial intelligence on economic systems is complex and multifaceted. It has the potential to both encourage entrepreneurial capitalism and reinforce state capitalism and the concentration of power. Policymakers must be cognizant of these potential repercussions and take measures to ensure that the benefits of artificial intelligence are distributed fairly and equitably.

The prospective impact of AI on economic development and innovation is thus substantial. It has the potential to foster entrepreneurial capitalism by reducing the costs of establishing and operating a business, but it also has the potential to strengthen state capitalism and the concentration of power. In order to ensure that the benefits of AI are distributed fairly and equitably, the role of policymakers in guiding the development and deployment of AI is crucial.

The advancement of artificial intelligence (AI) has the potential to have a substantial impact on the economic systems of the globe. The debate over whether AI will foster entrepreneurial capitalism or state capitalism is one of the most important in this discipline. This chapter will explore the potential for AI to influence the economic landscape in either direction, the impact of AI on innovation and the dissemination of innovative ideas, and the role of entrepreneurs in an AI-driven economic system.

On the one hand, AI has the potential to foster entrepreneurial capitalism by providing entrepreneurs with the tools and resources necessary to innovate and create new enterprises. AI can, for instance, assist entrepreneurs in analysing vast quantities of data and identifying new business opportunities. Additionally, it can automate mundane duties and free up time for entrepreneurs to focus on more strategic tasks. In addition, AI can facilitate the creation of new markets, boost competition, and reduce entry barriers, all of which can foster entrepreneurial capitalism. Moreover, AI can be utilised by the state to reinforce state capitalism by consolidating power and control within the government's hands. For instance, governments can use AI to monitor and regulate the economy, which could limit the autonomy of business owners and impede competition. Moreover, governments can use AI to create and manage large-scale infrastructure initiatives, which may inhibit innovation and creativity.

The impact of AI on innovation and the dissemination of innovative ideas is another crucial consideration. AI can assist entrepreneurs in developing new products and services by identifying novel concepts. Additionally, it can facilitate cross-industry and cross-geographic collaboration and the exchange of knowledge. However, the concentration of AI resources in certain regions or industries may distort the distribution of innovative ideas. This could contribute to a situation in which a small number of companies or regions dominate innovation, leaving others in the dust.

A critical area of concern is also the role of entrepreneurs in an AI-driven economic system. Entrepreneurs are indispensable for the creation of new businesses and the development of innovative concepts. The widespread implementation of AI could however disrupt the traditional role of entrepreneurs in the economy. For instance, AI could automate a significant proportion of the mundane duties that entrepreneurs currently perform, such as market research and financial analysis. This could make it easier for non-entrepreneurs to establish businesses, but it could also decrease the number of entrepreneurs in the economy.

The potential effects of AI on the economic system are evidently complex and multifarious. AI has the potential to foster entrepreneurial capitalism by providing entrepreneurs with the tools and resources they need to innovate and launch new enterprises. However, it could also be used to strengthen state capitalism by consolidating authority and control in the hands of the government. Important considerations also include the influence of AI on innovation and the dissemination of innovative ideas. Lastly, the function of entrepreneurs in an AI-driven economic system is a major concern. It is still unknown how these various factors will interact and shape the economic landscape in the coming years.

The impact of AI on innovation and the distribution of innovative ideas

The development of artificial intelligence (AI) has the potential to have a significant impact on the global economic systems. One of the central debates in this discipline is whether artificial intelligence will foster entrepreneurial or state capitalism. This chapter examines the potential for AI to influence the economic landscape in either direction, the impact of AI on innovation and the dissemination of innovative ideas, and the role of entrepreneurs in an AI-driven economic system.

On the one hand, AI has the potential to encourage entrepreneurial capitalism by equipping entrepreneurs with the means to innovate and establish new businesses. AI can assist entrepreneurs in analysing large quantities of data and identifying new business opportunities, for instance. It can also automate mundane duties, freeing up time for business owners to focus on more strategic endeavours. In addition, AI can facilitate the creation of new markets, increase competition, and reduce entry barriers, all of which can encourage entrepreneurial capitalism.

AI can also be utilised by the state to strengthen state capitalism by consolidating power and control in the hands of the government. For instance, governments can use AI to monitor and regulate the economy, which could restrict the independence of entrepreneurs and impede competition. In addition, governments can use AI to design and manage massive infrastructure projects, which could impede innovation and creativity. The impact of AI on innovation and the dissemination of innovative ideas is an additional essential factor to consider. AI can assist entrepreneurs in identifying innovative concepts and creating new goods and services. It can also facilitate cross-industry and cross-geographic collaboration and knowledge sharing. Nonetheless, the concentration of AI resources in particular regions or industries may distort the distribution of novel concepts. This could result in a few companies or regions dominating innovation, while others fall behind.

Concerns also surround the function of entrepreneurs in an AI-driven economic system. Entrepreneurs are essential to the formation of new enterprises and the conception of novel concepts. However, widespread AI adoption may alter the traditional function of entrepreneurs in the economy. For instance, AI could automate many of the mundane tasks presently performed by entrepreneurs, such as market research and financial analysis. This may make it simpler for non-entrepreneurs to launch new enterprises, but it may also reduce the number of entrepreneurs in the economy. Clearly, the potential effects of AI on the economy are complex and multifaceted. AI has the potential to promote entrepreneurial capitalism by equipping entrepreneurs with the means to innovate and establish new enterprises. However, it could also be used to strengthen state capitalism by consolidating government power and control. The influence of AI on innovation and the dissemination of innovative ideas is another crucial factor to consider. The function of entrepreneurs in an AI-driven economic system is a significant area of concern. In the coming years, it remains to be seen how these various factors will interact and influence the economic landscape.

In addition to the previously mentioned points, it is essential to consider the potential disadvantages of AI in innovation and the dissemination of innovative ideas. One concern is that AI may exacerbate existing prejudices and inequalities, especially if the data sets used to train AI algorithms are biassed. This could lead to the development and distribution of AI-powered products and services that do not suit the needs or preferences of specific demographic groups.

Another concern is that AI could lead to a concentration of innovation and the absorption of economic benefits by a handful of large corporations. As artificial intelligence and related technologies become increasingly important innovation drivers, firms with the resources to invest in these areas are likely to acquire a competitive advantage over smaller, less-funded firms. This could lead to a concentration of innovation in specific sectors or geographic locations, as well as the formation of winner-take-all markets that leave many businesses and individuals behind.

AI could facilitate the democratisation of innovation and the dissemination of innovative ideas. Tools and platforms powered by AI could assist in lowering the entry barriers for innovators, especially in disciplines that traditionally require a high level of technical expertise. AI-powered design software, for instance, could assist non-experts in creating complex products or prototypes, whereas AI-powered marketplaces could connect inventors with potential consumers or investors.

AI could also contribute to the acceleration of innovation by enabling researchers and inventors to collaborate more effectively and efficiently. Tools and platforms enabled by AI could facilitate the sharing of ideas and knowledge across disciplines and geographies, allowing for more rapid advancement in fields such as healthcare, energy, and transportation.

The impact of artificial intelligence on innovation and the dissemination of innovative ideas is likely to be complex and multifaceted. While there are unquestionably potential drawbacks to the expanding use of AI in these fields, there are also significant opportunities for AI to facilitate entrepreneurship and innovation, and to help ensure that the benefits of these activities are shared more broadly. AI's ability to recognise patterns and predict outcomes is one of its primary advantages in innovation. Algorithms capable of machine learning can analyse enormous amounts of data and identify patterns that humans may be unable to recognise. This can aid companies in identifying potential new products, markets, and growth opportunities. In addition, AI can be utilised to simulate various scenarios and evaluate new concepts before investing significant time and resources in their development. This can help to reduce risk and assure more efficient resource allocation.

AI can also improve the collaborative innovation process. Teams can collaborate more effectively with the assistance of AI-powered tools by automating routine tasks and streamlining communication. This can free up more time for creative pondering and brainstorming, leading to the generation of more original ideas. AI-powered collaboration tools can also help break down departmental silos and foster cross-functional collaboration, resulting in a more unified approach to innovation.

However, there are also concerns that AI could contribute to a concentration of innovation among a small number of firms or individuals. This is due to the fact that the development and implementation of AI technology requires substantial financial resources, technical expertise, and access to vast datasets. This may give established businesses and individuals an advantage over smaller, less well-funded competitors, resulting in a concentration of power and innovation among a small number of key actors. In addition, there are concerns that the application of AI to innovation may exacerbate existing disparities. This is due to the fact that AI-powered systems are only as effective as the data they are trained on, and biassed training data can lead to biassed results. Thus, if the data used to train AI systems is biassed, the innovation that results may also be biassed. Consequently, it is essential to ensure that artificial intelligence is developed and implemented in a transparent and accountable manner that takes into consideration the ethical and social implications of its use.

Clearly, AI has the potential to revolutionise innovation by providing fresh insights and development opportunities. There are, however, hazards associated with the use of AI in innovation, such as the concentration of power and innovation within a small number of companies or individuals and the potential for AI to exacerbate existing inequalities. Consequently, it is crucial to approach the development and implementation of AI in innovation with caution, ensuring that it is developed and utilised in a transparent, accountable, and responsible manner.

AI is transforming innovation and collaboration. AI is revolutionising the innovation process because it can process massive quantities of data and recognise patterns. AI can assist in identifying new opportunities, optimising existing processes, and accelerating and enhancing the innovation process.

The development of new products and services is a significant way in which AI influences innovation. AI algorithms can identify patterns and insights from enormous amounts of data, enabling the development of previously impossible products and services. AI-powered medical devices, for instance, can diagnose diseases and provide personalised treatment plans, whereas AI-powered applications can provide customer support and enhance customer experiences. AI also influences the dissemination of novel concepts. Historically, large corporations with the resources to develop and distribute new concepts have driven innovation. With the advent of AI, however, lesser businesses and startups can now compete with larger corporations in the innovation space. Platforms and marketplaces propelled by artificial intelligence enable smaller businesses to reach larger audiences and compete on a more level playing field.

Open innovation platforms, which use AI to connect businesses, entrepreneurs, and individuals with innovative ideas, are one example. These platforms allow businesses to access a larger pool of ideas and talent, which can stimulate innovation and promote development. Using the expertise of data scientists from around the globe, Kaggle, a platform that hosts data science competitions, has helped businesses solve complex data problems.

The impact of AI on innovation is not wholly positive, however. AI has the potential to stimulate innovation, but it can also stifle it by generating a feedback cycle that reinforces existing biases and perspectives. For instance, AI algorithms may be trained on biassed data sets, which can perpetuate biased results. In addition, the innovative use of AI raises ethical concerns regarding privacy, security, and control. Concerns about data privacy and security are raised by the possibility that AI-powered products and services will accumulate vast quantities of personal data. Moreover, the application of AI to innovation raises questions regarding who governs the innovation process and who benefits from it.

Thus, AI is transforming the innovation process, facilitating the creation of new products and services and altering the dissemination of innovative ideas. AI has the potential to promote innovation, but it also has the potential to reinforce biases and inequalities and raise ethical concerns. As AI continues to advance, it will be crucial for policymakers and businesses to carefully consider AI's impact on innovation and work to ensure that it is beneficial to society as a whole.

The role of entrepreneurs in an AI-driven economic system

Various industries, such as manufacturing, healthcare, finance, and transportation, have been transformed by the emergence of artificial intelligence (AI). AI-powered systems can aid in automating mundane duties, enhancing decision-making processes, and boosting productivity. In this context, entrepreneurs play a crucial role in leveraging AI to drive economic expansion and innovation. This section examines the position of entrepreneurs in an AI-driven economic system, as well as the opportunities and challenges they may face.

Initially, AI can be used by entrepreneurs to develop new business models, products, and services. AI can assist business owners in identifying market trends, consumer preferences, and untapped opportunities. Entrepreneurs can use AI-powered systems to analyse vast quantities of data, develop predictive models, and generate business strategy-informing insights. AI can be used, for instance, to create chatbots, virtual assistants, and personalised recommendations that improve consumer experiences and engagement.

Second, entrepreneurs can use AI to optimise and enhance their business operations. AI can assist business owners in automating mundane duties, reducing costs, and increasing productivity. Such applications include inventory management, quality control, and supply chain optimisation. AI can also assist business owners in making informed decisions by providing real-time data on business performance, consumer behaviour, and market trends.

Nonetheless, the adoption of AI presents numerous obstacles for entrepreneurs. An important obstacle is the high cost of AI development and implementation. AI-driven systems necessitate substantial investments in hardware, software, and personnel. Accessing these resources may be difficult for entrepreneurs, especially if they operate in a highly competitive market or encounter financial constraints.

AI can also produce a winner-take-all economy that favours large corporations over small enterprises. In order to train algorithms and increase precision, AI-powered systems require vast amounts of data. Therefore, large corporations with greater access to data and resources may have a competitive advantage over small businesses. This can result in the concentration of market power and the displacement of small and medium-sized businesses (SMEs) from the market.

To address these challenges, policymakers can devise initiatives to encourage entrepreneur adoption of AI. These initiatives may include funding for AI research and development, training programmes for entrepreneurs and small and medium-sized businesses, and policies that support the growth of AI ecosystems. Policymakers may, for instance, establish innovation clusters that bring together entrepreneurs, researchers, and investors to collaborate on AI-driven projects.

Entrepreneurs play a crucial role in driving innovation, developing new business models, and increasing efficiency in an AI-driven economic system. However, incorporating AI presents numerous obstacles for entrepreneurs, including high costs and market concentration. Policymakers can play a crucial role in addressing these challenges by devising initiatives that promote AI adoption and support the growth of AI ecosystems.

The function of entrepreneurs in an economy driven by artificial intelligence is a topic of great interest and significance. While artificial intelligence has the potential to transform the business landscape, entrepreneurs will play a crucial role in spurring innovation and creating new opportunities. This section will examine the role of entrepreneurs in an AI-driven economy, as well as the challenges and opportunities they may confront.

In an AI-driven economy, staying ahead of the trajectory is one of the most significant challenges for entrepreneurs. Entrepreneurs will need to be able to rapidly adapt to new developments in AI technologies if they wish to remain competitive. Consequently, entrepreneurs will need to be adept at identifying emergent trends and technologies and incorporating them swiftly into their business strategies.

Entrepreneurs must also be able to navigate the complex legal and regulatory landscape surrounding artificial intelligence. Governments and regulatory agencies are debating how to regulate artificial intelligence as its prevalence in the business world increases. Entrepreneurs must understand the legal and regulatory frameworks of their respective industries and be able to effectively navigate them. Entrepreneurs in an AI-driven economy must also strike a balance between automation and human expertise. While AI can automate many duties and procedures, human input and expertise will still be required. Entrepreneurs must be able to determine which duties and processes can be automated and which require human intervention, and then structure their businesses accordingly. Nonetheless, the prospective advantages of AI for entrepreneurs are substantial. Entrepreneurs can make more informed decisions and identify new growth opportunities with the help of AI technologies. For instance, analytics powered by AI can aid entrepreneurs in better understanding their consumers and targeting their marketing efforts. AI can also be used to optimise business processes, reduce expenses, and increase overall productivity.

In addition, AI can assist entrepreneurs in overcoming some of the traditional obstacles to entry in a variety of industries. Using AI-powered manufacturing and 3D printing, for instance, entrepreneurs can create custom products more quickly and at a lower cost than with conventional manufacturing techniques. This can balance the playing field for smaller, more nimble businesses that lack the resources to compete with larger, more established firms.

In an AI-driven economy, entrepreneurs will be responsible for driving innovation and creativity. AI can automate a variety of duties, but it cannot replace human ingenuity and creativity. Entrepreneurs must be able to identify new opportunities, develop innovative products and services, and create new business models that leverage AI technologies. Entrepreneurs play a crucial role in shaping innovation and driving economic development in an AI-driven economic system. Entrepreneurs are well-positioned to capitalise on these opportunities and drive the next wave of economic development, given the potential for AI to transform industries and create new markets.

One of the primary benefits of artificial intelligence is its ability to automate repetitive tasks and facilitate quicker decision-making processes. This can assist entrepreneurs in streamlining their operations and focusing on high-value duties like product development, market research, and customer engagement. By utilising AI-powered tools and technologies, entrepreneurs can increase their productivity, decrease their expenses, and strengthen their competitive advantage. Also, AI can assist entrepreneurs in identifying previously overlooked business opportunities and potential markets. For instance, AI-powered data analytics tools can assist entrepreneurs in identifying patterns and trends in customer behaviour, allowing them to develop more targeted marketing strategies and tailor their products to suit the needs of specific customer segments.

In addition, AI can aid entrepreneurs in making better decisions by providing them with more accurate and timely information. By utilising AI-powered predictive analytics and forecasting tools, business owners can gain insights into market trends, customer preferences, and other variables that can impact business operations. This can enable them to make more informed decisions and effectively mitigate risks.

The function of entrepreneurs in an AI-driven economic system does not, however, come without obstacles. One of the primary concerns is the possibility that AI will displace humans and cause employment losses. This could have a significant impact on the labour market and the economy as a whole, particularly if the displaced employees lack the necessary skills and training to adapt to the changing job market. In addition, the growing reliance on AI and automation may contribute to the concentration of economic power in the hands of a few large corporations. This could make it more difficult for small businesses and entrepreneurs to compete on the market, reducing innovation and economic development.

To address these challenges, policymakers and business leaders must devise policies and strategies that promote an AI-driven economic system that is more inclusive and sustainable. This could entail investing in education and training programmes to assist employees in acquiring the skills necessary for success in the digital economy. It may also entail fostering competition and innovation by supporting small and medium-sized businesses and fostering an entrepreneurial spirit.

As demonstrated, entrepreneurs play a crucial role in propelling innovation, growth, and economic development in an AI-driven economy. Entrepreneurs can increase their efficacy, identify new business opportunities, and make better-informed decisions by utilising AI-powered tools and technologies. To ensure that the benefits of AI are distributed more equitably throughout society, policymakers and business leaders must resolve the challenges posed by artificial intelligence (AI) and automation, such as job displacement and economic concentration.

The co-evolution of artificial intelligence and capitalism presents both opportunities and challenges for economic development and innovation. The institutional environment, as well as the design and implementation of policies and regulations that encourage competition, innovation, and entrepreneurship, determine whether AI has the potential to foster entrepreneurial capitalism or state capitalism. AI has the potential to reduce entry barriers for new entrants and disrupt existing business models, but it can also lead to the concentration of power and influence in the hands of a few dominant actors, stifling innovation and competition.

AI has a multifaceted effect on innovation and the dissemination of innovative ideas, as it can both facilitate and hinder innovation. AI has the potential to accelerate the rate of innovation, reduce costs, and improve the quality of goods and services, but it also has the potential to displace workers and exacerbate income inequality. Moreover, the distribution of innovative ideas is affected by a variety of factors, such as intellectual property rights, access to funding and resources, and network effects, among others. Entrepreneurs play a crucial role in an AI-driven economic system, as they are the agents of change and innovation in any economic system. While AI can automate certain duties and lower entry barriers, it cannot replace entrepreneurs' creativity, vision, and willingness to take risks. Therefore, enterprises must embrace AI as a tool for enhancing their competitive advantage and developing new business models.

Overall, the impact of AI on economic development and innovation is complex and multifaceted, and its potential to promote or inhibit capitalism, innovation, and entrepreneurship depends on a number of institutional, technological, and social factors. To maximise the benefits of artificial intelligence and minimise its negative effects, policymakers and stakeholders must design and implement policies and regulations that promote competition, innovation, and entrepreneurship, while also ensuring that the benefits of AI are widely distributed and its ethical and social implications are adequately addressed.

Chapter 8: AI and Human-Machine Interaction

The advent of Artificial Intelligence (AI) has revolutionised how we live and work, with far-reaching implications for many facets of human existence. Creativity and innovation stimulation is one of the key areas where AI has shown tremendous promise. This chapter examines the potential for AI-human interaction to foster creativity and innovation, the impact of AI on organisational routines and the role of humans in creative functions, and the implications for exploring and exploiting technological opportunities in economic systems in the age of AI.

Interaction between AI and humans has the potential to foster creativity and innovation; this is a thrilling frontier with vast potential. AI systems can augment human creativity by generating new ideas and facilitating the exploration of uncharted territories. Through the analysis of immense amounts of data and the capacity to recognise patterns and correlations, AI is able to unearth hidden connections and provide insightful suggestions that can inspire and enhance human creativity. By collaborating with AI, humans can utilise these capabilities to press the boundaries of innovation and make advancements in a variety of fields.

However, it is impossible to ignore the impact of AI on organisational routines and the role of humans in creative functions. As AI systems become more advanced, they have the potential to automate routine tasks, freeing up human resources and allowing people to concentrate on more creative and complex endeavours. This transition in the division of labour between humans and AI requires a reevaluation of the traditional concepts of work and creativity. AI can help generate ideas and provide creative input, but the human element is essential for critical thinking, intuition, and the ability to navigate ambiguity. In order to maximise the potential for innovation, it is necessary to comprehend the relationship between AI and human creativity.

Furthermore, the AI era has significant implications for the investigation and exploitation of technological opportunities in economic systems. AI can enhance exploration by rapidly scanning vast amounts of data, identifying emerging trends, and predicting future preferences and requirements. This can enable businesses and individuals to capitalise on new opportunities and create innovative solutions. On the other hand, increased reliance on AI can also lead to exploitation, where existing knowledge and established practises are utilised for efficiency and optimisation, potentially impeding exploration and the pursuit of disruptive innovations. In the AI era, it is essential to strike a balance between exploration and exploitation to foster continuous innovation and sustainable economic growth.

In this chapter, we will analyse the potential for AI-human interaction to foster creativity and innovation, examine the changing role of humans in creative functions within organisations, and discuss the ramifications of exploring and exploiting technological opportunities within economic systems. We intend to provide valuable insights and perspectives on how AI is reshaping the creative and innovative landscape and its effect on economic systems through a comprehensive analysis of the current landscape and emerging trends.

The potential for AI-human interaction to foster creativity and innovation

The potential for AI-human interaction to foster creativity and innovation is a fascinating and burgeoning field with great future promise. AI systems are capable of augmenting human creativity by generating novel ideas and assisting in the exploration of uncharted territories. This section will explore the various facets of AI-human interaction and its potential to foster innovation and creativity.

AI's ability to analyse vast quantities of data and extract meaningful insights is one of its primary contributions to fostering creativity. Through the use of sophisticated algorithms and machine learning techniques, AI systems can process and interpret data at a rate and on a scale that exceeds that of humans. This ability enables AI to recognise patterns, correlations, and trends that humans may overlook, thereby providing novel perspectives and stimulating new creative avenues. AI systems can also assist with ideation and idea generation. By employing complex algorithms, AI can generate a vast array of ideas, combinations, and possibilities that humans can further investigate. This collaborative approach between humans and AI can result in the convergence of diverse perspectives and the synthesis of ideas, thereby stimulating innovative thought.

Moreover, AI can serve as a catalyst for innovation by automating mundane and repetitive duties, thereby enabling human resources to focus on more complex and creative endeavours. AI systems enable individuals to devote their time and energy to problem-solving, critical thinking, and the exploration of novel ideas by performing routine duties. This change in the division of labour enables a more efficient use of human creativity, thereby releasing new potential for innovative advancements. In addition, AI can enhance the creative process by providing inspiration and feedback. AI systems are capable of analysing vast archives of extant creative works, such as art, literature, music, and design, in order to identify patterns, themes, and styles. This analysis can provide human creators with valuable insights and references, inspiring them and influencing their creative output. In addition, AI systems can provide feedback and suggestions in real-time during the creative process, facilitating the refinement and iteration of ideas.

Despite the fact that AI can be a highly effective instrument for fostering creativity and innovation, it cannot replace human creativity. The human element, which includes emotional intelligence, intuition, and the capacity to think abstractly and metaphorically, is still indispensable to the creative process. AI systems are designed to enhance human creativity by providing support, insights, and efficacy, but the essence of creativity resides in human minds. In addition to enhancing human creativity, AI-human interaction has the potential to foster innovation by facilitating collaboration and knowledge sharing. AI systems can serve as intelligent assistants, facilitating the connection of individuals with pertinent expertise, resources, and networks. AI can recommend potential collaborators and provide access to pertinent information and tools by analysing data and identifying connections. This collaborative environment fosters innovation by bringing diverse perspectives and expertise together, resulting in the cross-pollination of ideas and the emergence of novel solutions.

Moreover, the concept of serendipity can contribute to innovation through AI-human interaction. Serendipity, which is frequently defined as a fortunate accident or unanticipated discovery, has played a significant role in the development of numerous ground-breaking innovations. By analysing vast quantities of data and identifying connections between seemingly unrelated information, AI systems can facilitate serendipitous encounters. AI can inspire innovative advancements by exposing individuals to unexpected patterns, insights, and opportunities.

Ethical and responsible use of AI systems is an additional vital aspect of AI-human interaction for fostering innovation. As AI becomes more incorporated into creative and innovative processes, it is crucial to consider the ethical implications of issues like privacy, bias, and transparency. The design and implementation of AI systems should be guided by ethical considerations to ensure that they respect individual rights, uphold fairness, and promote inclusivity. AI can support a more inclusive and diverse innovation ecosystem by addressing these ethical challenges.

It is essential to observe that AI's influence on innovation and creativity is not limited to particular industries or domains. AI has the potential to spur innovation in numerous industries, such as healthcare, finance, manufacturing, and entertainment. In healthcare, for instance, AI can aid in medical research, drug discovery, and personalised treatment plans, resulting in advancements in patient care. In finance, artificial intelligence algorithms can improve trading strategies, risk assessment, and fraud detection, resulting in more secure and efficient financial systems. These examples illustrate the vast potential of AI to foster innovation in a variety of industries and fields. Furthermore, it is worthwhile to investigate the impact of AI on the dissemination of innovative ideas. AI systems can democratise access to knowledge and ideas by facilitating the sharing and exhibition of individuals' creative works. Powered by AI algorithms, online platforms can curate and recommend innovative content, exposing a larger audience to diverse ideas and nurturing collaboration. This broader dissemination of innovative ideas can inspire others, ignite new collaborations, and advance society as a whole.

The ability of AI systems to augment human capabilities and provide new avenues for ideation and problem-solving underpins the potential for AI-human interaction to promote creativity and innovation. AI algorithms are capable of analysing enormous quantities of data, identifying patterns, and generating insights that humans may not have considered. By leveraging the computational power and data processing capabilities of artificial intelligence, individuals can gain new perspectives, uncover hidden connections, and investigate innovative solutions to difficult problems. AI has demonstrated promising potential in the field of generative AI. AI that can generate new and original content, such as music, art, and writing, is known as generative AI. By acquiring knowledge from extensive datasets, AI models can generate novel compositions that exceed the creative limits of humans. This synergy between human input and AI-generated suggestions can inspire artists, musicians, and writers to investigate uncharted territory and create groundbreaking works.

In addition, it is essential to consider the impact of AI on organisational routines and the role of humans in creative functions. AI systems can automate mundane and repetitive duties, allowing humans to concentrate on higher-level creative thinking and innovation. By delegating mundane tasks to artificial intelligence, individuals can devote more time and cognitive resources to exploring new ideas, experimenting with various approaches, and engaging in critical thinking. This symbiotic relationship between AI and humans can result in more productive and efficient creative processes. Also, AI can facilitate the discovery and exploitation of technological opportunities within economic systems. The analysis of market trends, consumer preferences, and technological advancements by AI algorithms provides businesses with valuable insights for identifying untapped opportunities. Businesses can make data-driven decisions regarding resource allocation, product development, and market entry by leveraging AI-driven analytics. This proactive approach to technological exploration can stimulate innovation, boost competitiveness, and stimulate economic growth.

Nonetheless, it is essential to recognise the potential difficulties and limitations of AI-human interaction in fostering creativity and innovation. One difficulty is the possibility of overreliance on AI systems, which could impede human creativity and innovation if people become overly reliant on AI-generated suggestions. It is essential to strike a balance between AI assistance and human ingenuity in order to preserve the distinct creative capacities of humans. Additionally, ethical considerations regarding the impact of AI on innovation must be addressed. As AI systems impact the dissemination of innovative ideas, it is crucial to ensure equity, inclusivity, and equal participation opportunities. AI algorithms should be designed and trained to reduce bias and increase diversity of viewpoints. Additionally, issues of intellectual property, ownership, and attribution must be addressed with care to ensure proper recognition and compensation for human creativity within an AI-driven ecosystem.

The potential for AI-human interaction to stimulate creativity and innovation is substantial. The computational power, data analysis capabilities, and generative abilities of AI can enhance human creativity, facilitate the exploration of new ideas, and improve the dissemination of innovative content. To ensure that AI systems support human creativity without overshadowing or stifling it, a delicate balance must be established. By navigating ethical considerations and leveraging the collaborative potential of AI-human interaction, we can open up new frontiers for creativity and innovation.

The impact of AI on organizational routines and the role of humans in creative functions

The influence of artificial intelligence (AI) on organisational routines and the role of humans in creative functions is a dynamic and evolving field of study. As AI technologies continue to advance, they have the potential to revolutionise how organisations function and how humans participate in creative processes.

AI is capable of automating mundane and repetitious tasks, freeing up human resources for more complex and creative endeavours. By delegating mundane tasks to AI systems, organisations can streamline operations, increase productivity, and free up employees to focus on higher-order creative thinking and problem-solving. This shift in organisational routines can have profound effects on the structure of work and the manner in which individuals contribute to creative functions within their roles.

Human capabilities enhancement is a significant aspect of AI's impact on organisational processes. AI systems can assist humans with idea generation, data analysis, and making well-informed decisions. For instance, analytics tools powered by AI can process large datasets and extract meaningful insights, providing employees with valuable information to inform their creative processes. In addition to generating suggestions, recommendations, and alternative solutions, AI algorithms can stimulate human creativity and broaden the scope of possibilities.

Moreover, AI can improve organisational collaboration and collective intelligence. Over geographical boundaries, AI technologies facilitate real-time communication, knowledge sharing, and collaborative problem-solving. Through platforms and tools enabled by AI, employees can leverage collective expertise, gain access to pertinent data, and engage in collaborative innovation. As a result, problem-solving can benefit from increased creativity and a broader range of perspectives, as individuals from various backgrounds and areas of expertise can contribute their own unique insights. However, the incorporation of AI into organisational processes also presents obstacles and necessitates careful consideration. The potential disruption of established routines and work processes is a difficulty. Organisations must manage the transition to AI-enabled routines with care, ensuring that employees are adequately trained and supported in their efforts to adapt to new methods of working. Change management strategies, employee reskilling programmes, and effective communication are essential for facilitating a seamless transition and minimising potential resistance.

Moreover, despite advancements in AI, humans continue to play a crucial role in creative functions. Human creativity comprises a vast array of cognitive abilities, including abstract reasoning, intuition, emotional intelligence, and the capacity to navigate intricate social and cultural contexts. Although AI can supplement and support these capabilities, it is the distinct human perspective and creative insight that drive innovation and produce ground-breaking ideas. In addition, ethical concerns arise when analysing the influence of AI on organisational routines and the role of humans in creative functions. Organisations must navigate ethical issues associated with data privacy, algorithmic bias, and the responsible application of AI technologies. It is essential to ensure transparency, impartiality, and accountability in the design, deployment, and decision-making processes of AI systems in order to uphold ethical standards and prevent possible biases from influencing creative outcomes. As AI technologies continue to advance swiftly, the impact of AI on organisational routines and the role of humans in creative functions is an area of increasing interest and research. Organisations are investigating how AI can revolutionise their routines, boost their productivity, and open up new creative avenues.

A component of this effect is the automation of routine duties by artificial intelligence. AI-enabled systems can efficiently handle repetitive and mundane duties, allowing humans to concentrate on more complex and creative tasks. This automation can lead to increased efficiency, decreased errors, and time savings, freeing up employees' energy and cognitive resources for more innovative and strategic endeavours. AI can also enhance human creativity by providing intelligent assistance and improving decision-making processes. For instance, AI algorithms can analyse vast quantities of data and generate insights and recommendations that humans may have missed. This collaborative interaction between humans and AI can increase the creative potential by combining the AI's strengths in data processing and pattern recognition with human expertise, intuition, and contextual awareness.

Moreover, the role of humans in creative processes extends beyond the generation of ideas. Empathy, emotional intelligence, and social awareness are essential cognitive abilities for creative problem-solving possessed by humans. AI can assist with data analysis, generate suggestions, and provide inspiration, but the interpretive and evaluative aspects of creativity frequently require human judgement and a profound comprehension of social, cultural, and ethical contexts. Nevertheless, the incorporation of AI into organisational processes also raises significant concerns. The potential disruption of established work processes and employee roles is a challenge. Organisations must carefully manage this transition by providing employees with adequate training and support, nurturing a culture of continuous learning, and ensuring clear communication regarding the purpose and benefits of AI integration. Additionally, the use of AI for creative functions has ethical implications. Concerns such as algorithmic bias, data privacy, and transparency must be considered by businesses. Ensuring impartiality, accountability, and unbiased decision-making in AI systems is essential for preserving trust and preventing unintended consequences that may affect the distribution of innovative ideas.

Recent research has cast light on AI's potential to revolutionise organisational processes and creative functions. For instance, Brynjolfsson and McAfee's research examines the business implications of AI and emphasises the importance of augmenting rather than replacing human capabilities. Another study by Miao, Zhu, and Li investigates the application of AI to innovative business models, highlighting the need for organisations to adapt their routines in order to effectively leverage AI's potential. In addition, Zhou and Jiao investigate the future of work in the context of artificial intelligence and present the perspectives of Chinese entrepreneurs and managers on how AI is shaping creative functions. Their research emphasises the significance of human adaptability, inter-disciplinary collaboration, and ongoing learning for the successful integration of AI into creative processes.

In the era of AI, routines and processes within organisations are undergoing significant changes. Various aspects of organisational operations, including decision-making, data analysis, and automation, are integrating AI technologies. In the context of creative functions, this integration has both direct and indirect effects on organisational protocols.

By automating repetitive duties and augmenting human capabilities, AI has the potential to streamline and optimise current organisational processes. With AI algorithms analysing vast amounts of data, businesses can make more informed decisions, recognise patterns, and generate previously unattainable insights. This improves the effectiveness and efficiency of routine processes, freeing up human resources for higher-level duties. Moreover, AI-enabled technologies have the potential to contribute to the organisational creative process. AI systems are not inherently inventive, but they can help generate original ideas, provide inspiration, and facilitate the ideation process. For instance, AI algorithms can analyse immense amounts of data from various sources, such as customer preferences, market trends, and historical records, in order to identify potential areas for innovation and creative problem-solving.

However, the impact of AI on organisational creativity is not without obstacles. As AI undertakes more creative tasks, it is possible that the role of humans in creative functions will diminish. As AI systems rely on existing data and patterns to generate ideas, some argue that the use of AI in creative processes may contribute to a loss of originality. In AI-driven creative processes, the human element of intuition, imagination, and emotional intelligence may be neglected or undervalued.

To address these challenges, organisations must establish a balance between leveraging AI technologies for efficiency and creativity and recognising human creativity's unique contributions. Collaboration between humans and artificial intelligence (AI) systems, also known as "augmented creativity," has tremendous potential. It entails integrating AI tools into the creative workflow, with humans providing context, domain expertise, and critical evaluation of AI-generated ideas.

Organisations must cultivate a culture that embraces AI as a complement to human creativity, rather than as a replacement for it. This requires the creation of spaces for human-AI interaction, the promotion of interdisciplinary collaboration, and the provision of AI-literacy and creativity-enhancing training and development opportunities for employees. The influence of AI on organisational routines and the role of humans in creative functions is a dynamic and intricate phenomenon. It is essential to recognise the complementary responsibilities of humans and AI systems, despite the fact that AI has the potential to improve routine processes and contribute to creative endeavours. By adopting augmented creativity, organisations can leverage the power of artificial intelligence while preserving and fostering human creativity to drive innovation and success.

Implications for exploration and exploitation of technological opportunities in economic systems in the age of AI

In the era of artificial intelligence, technological opportunities abound, and their exploration and exploitation have substantial effects on economic systems. AI technologies have the potential to revolutionise industries, upend conventional business structures, and open up new growth and innovation avenues. Exploration and exploitation of these technological opportunities are crucial to the formation and success of economic systems. This section explores the implications of artificial intelligence for the investigation and exploitation of technological opportunities in economic systems, highlighting recent research findings and providing a thorough understanding of the topic.

1. Exploration of Technological Opportunities

Exploration refers to the search for new technological possibilities, novel concepts, and innovative solutions. AI has the potential to facilitate exploration by enabling organisations to process massive amounts of data, recognise patterns, and uncover hidden insights. Here are some important ramifications and research findings regarding the exploration of technological opportunities:

- Improved Data Analysis: AI algorithms can analyse large-scale datasets, including structured and unstructured data, to glean insightful information. This enables organisations to identify emerging trends, consumer preferences, and market opportunities that would have otherwise escaped their notice.

- Technology Scan: Tools propelled by AI can monitor and scan technological developments, scientific literature, patents, and industry reports to identify new technologies and their potential applications. This enables organisations to remain apprised of cutting-edge research and implement emerging technologies in their operations.

- Collaborative Innovation: Artificial intelligence systems can facilitate collaboration and open innovation by connecting individuals and organisations with complementary expertise and promoting knowledge sharing. Using AI-powered platforms, organisations can engage in crowdsourcing, open-source collaborations, and collaborative problem-solving to investigate technological opportunities collectively.

2. Exploitation of Technological Opportunities

Exploitation is the utilisation and commercialization of technological opportunities to create tangible goods, services, or processes. AI technologies provide numerous avenues for capitalising on technological opportunities, resulting in enhanced efficiency, productivity, and competitiveness. The following research findings and implications cast light on the utilisation of technological opportunities:

- Process Optimisation: Artificial intelligence can optimise operational processes by automating routine duties, increasing efficiency, and decreasing costs. Algorithms capable of machine learning can analyse historical data, identify inefficiencies, and recommend process enhancements, resulting in enhanced resource utilisation and productivity.

- Personalization and Customer Experience: Artificial intelligence enables businesses to provide personalised products and services by analysing customer data, preferences, and behaviour. Personalization improves the consumer experience, increases customer loyalty, and generates market competitive advantages.

- Agile Business Models: AI-driven technologies enable organisations to rapidly adapt to shifting market dynamics and customer demands. By incorporating AI into business model innovation, businesses can develop new revenue streams, investigate new markets, and create customer-centric offerings.

- Intellectual Property Management: AI can enhance the identification, protection, and monetization of intellectual assets in intellectual property management. Patent analysis, copyright protection, and intellectual property valuation can be aided by AI-powered tools, allowing businesses to capitalise on technological innovations.

3. Implications and Challenges

Exploration and exploitation of technological opportunities in the era of AI offer enormous potential, but there are significant ramifications and obstacles to consider.

- As AI becomes more incorporated into economic systems, ethical considerations regarding privacy, transparency, bias, and accountability arise. Organisations must navigate these obstacles and guarantee the responsible and ethical use of AI technologies for technological exploration and exploitation.

- Competencies and Workforce: The adoption of AI technologies necessitates a competent workforce capable of maximising these tools' potential. Organisations must invest in upskilling and reskilling their employees to navigate the ever-changing technological landscape and maximise the benefits of artificial intelligence (AI) in investigating and exploiting technological opportunities.

- Regulatory Frameworks: The dynamic character of technological advancements driven by AI necessitates adaptable and flexible regulatory frameworks. Governments and policymakers play a crucial role in fostering innovation and protecting consumer rights, data privacy, and equitable competition by fostering an enabling environment.

AI technologies have a significant impact on the exploration and exploitation of technological opportunities in economic systems. AI enables organisations to investigate uncharted territories, unearth insights, and leverage emerging technologies. Utilising these opportunities increases productivity, creativity, and competitiveness. To harness the full potential of AI in investigating and exploiting technological opportunities in the age of AI, however, organisations must navigate ethical considerations, cultivate necessary skills, and adapt to shifting regulatory landscapes.

Chapter 9: AI and Market Regulation

Artificial intelligence (AI) has ushered in a new period of technological advancements and transformative opportunities across multiple sectors of the global economy. AI technologies have the potential to transform market dynamics, disrupt traditional business models, and reshape market regulation. The chapter "AI and Market Regulation" examines the complex relationship between artificial intelligence (AI) and market regulation, with a concentration on understanding the challenges, implications, and potential solutions that arise in this evolving landscape.

Rapid AI advancements have introduced new dimensions to market behaviour, raising crucial issues regarding the role of regulation in an AI-driven economy. AI's potential to enable firms to circumvent market regulations and engage in practises that may contribute to market manipulation is a crucial factor. The ability of AI algorithms to process enormous quantities of data, recognise patterns, and make intelligent decisions presents both opportunities and risks. AI can increase market efficiency and innovation, but it can also lead to unjust advantages and market distortions. Consequently, it is essential to investigate the potential implications of AI for market manipulation and the necessary mechanisms to mitigate these risks.

Moreover, the emergence of AI technology necessitates adaptable regulatory frameworks capable of addressing the unique challenges and complexities of AI-driven market activities. Traditional regulatory approaches may struggle to keep up with the rapid advancements in AI, necessitating the consideration of new strategies and instruments by regulators. The chapter explores the need for comprehensive regulation that incorporates a variety of aspects, including data privacy, algorithmic transparency, accountability, and consumer protection. It emphasises the significance of forging a delicate balance between encouraging innovation and protecting the market's integrity, ensuring that AI technologies operate within ethical and legal parameters.

AI has the potential to improve market regulation, but it must be viewed as a complementary actor to the state, not as a replacement for effective regulation. The state continues to play an essential role in establishing market regulations, enforcing compliance, and ensuring accountability. This chapter examines the role of artificial intelligence in enhancing regulatory capabilities, such as automating surveillance, detecting anomalies, and evaluating risks. Nonetheless, it emphasises the need for human supervision and the participation of regulatory authorities in monitoring AI-driven market activities. In order to ensure that market regulation aligns with societal objectives and values, human judgement, ethics, and context-awareness continue to be crucial in decision-making processes.

In addition, the rise of large AI-based corporations has raised concerns regarding their market dominance, potential anti-competitive behaviour, and disproportionate value and wealth extraction. This chapter examines the effectiveness of existing antitrust norms, regulations, and laws in addressing the challenges posed by AI-driven markets. It examines the unique dynamics introduced by AI, such as the exploitation of network effects, the accumulation of enormous amounts of user data, and the establishment of entry barriers. The examination of existing antitrust frameworks seeks to identify gaps and potential modifications required to promote fair competition, innovation, and consumer welfare in the era of artificial intelligence.

This chapter provides a comprehensive analysis of the challenges, implications, and potential solutions associated with artificial intelligence and its effect on market regulation. It acknowledges the transformative potential of AI as a driver of innovation and economic development, but emphasises the need for comprehensive regulation to address the risks and obstacles that arise in an AI-driven economy. Understanding the potential for market manipulation, the role of AI in enhancing regulatory capabilities, and the efficacy of extant antitrust norms enables policymakers and stakeholders to effectively navigate the evolving landscape of AI and market regulation. In the age of AI, we can aspire to create a regulatory framework that fosters innovation, ensures fair competition, and protects the market's integrity through the use of thoughtful and flexible approaches.

The potential of AI to help firms circumvent market regulation and encourage market manipulation

Rapid advances in artificial intelligence (AI) technology in recent years have ushered in a new era of innovation and disruption across multiple industries. Particularly, the finance and trading industries have witnessed the transformative power of AI systems, which have become increasingly adept at analysing immense quantities of data and making complex decisions in real time. While it is widely acknowledged that AI has the potential to improve market efficacy and decision-making, there is growing concern that it could be abused to circumvent market regulations and facilitate market manipulation.

The integrity and stability of financial markets are gravely threatened by market manipulation, which intentionally distorts market prices or deceives market participants for personal benefit. It undermines equitable competition, erodes investor confidence, and can have far-reaching adverse effects on market participants and the economy as a whole. Historically, market manipulation has been conducted through a variety of methods, including the dissemination of false information, covert trading, and manipulation of order books. With the advent of AI, however, the landscape of market manipulation has changed, posing new challenges to regulators and market participants.

This chapter seeks to explore the potential for AI to assist businesses in evading market regulations and promoting market manipulation. It examines the fundamental mechanisms and techniques employed by AI systems for manipulative purposes, the risks and challenges associated with AI-driven manipulation, and the resulting regulatory implications. By examining these crucial facets, we can obtain a comprehensive understanding of the intersection between artificial intelligence and market manipulation, enabling regulators, policymakers, and market participants to effectively address and mitigate the associated risks.

1. Underlying Mechanisms and Techniques

AI technology advancements have introduced innovative techniques and strategies that can be utilised for market manipulation. One such mechanism is algorithmic trading, in which artificial intelligence (AI) algorithms analyse market data and implement trades with remarkable speed and accuracy. This can enable businesses to profit from price disparities or market imbalances. High-frequency trading (HFT), a subset of algorithmic trading, employs artificial intelligence (AI) algorithms to execute a large number of transactions in fractions of a second, thereby increasing the likelihood of market manipulation. In addition, AI-driven sentiment analysis and social media manipulation can be used to gauge public sentiment, generate artificial market sentiment, and disseminate fraudulent information in order to manipulate stock prices. Concerns about market transparency and fairness are raised by the capacity of AI systems to generate and disseminate false news and manipulate narratives.

Indeed, technological advancements in AI have created new opportunities for potential market manipulation, raising concerns about market transparency and equity. Due to its capacity to analyse vast amounts of data and execute trades with incredible speed and precision, AI-powered algorithmic trading has acquired popularity in financial markets. However, firms can utilise this technology to engage in manipulative practises.

Algorithmic trading enables businesses to identify and capitalise on price disparities or market imbalances, giving them an unwarranted advantage. By utilising AI algorithms, these firms are able to execute transactions at the speed of light, capitalising on fleeting opportunities and possibly distorting market prices. High-frequency trading (HFT), a subset of algorithmic trading, increases the volume and velocity of transactions, thereby increasing the likelihood of market manipulation.

Concerning is also the use of AI-driven sentiment analysis and manipulation of social media for market manipulation. AI systems can analyse social media data and data from other sources to determine market and public sentiment. This data can be utilised to generate artificial market sentiment, manipulate stock prices, and influence investor behaviour. In addition, AI can be used to generate and disseminate false news or manipulate narratives, which further complicates market dynamics and distorts investor perception.

The use of artificial intelligence for market manipulation presents significant regulatory challenges. These concerns should be addressed by establishing mechanisms for detecting and preventing manipulative activities. This may involve monitoring trading activities to identify suspicious patterns, instituting circuit breakers and other safeguards to prevent excessive market volatility, and conducting audits to ensure adherence to ethical and legal standards.

Additionally, regulations should emphasise enhancing market transparency and equity. This can be accomplished by mandating increased disclosure requirements, particularly regarding trading strategies and algorithms powered by artificial intelligence. By requiring firms to disclose comprehensive information about their AI systems and trading practises, regulators can improve market surveillance and detect potentially manipulative activities.

In addition, comprehensive regulation should encourage collaboration between regulators, industry participants, and AI experts in the development of effective supervision frameworks. This may include establishing regulatory sandboxes for testing and evaluating AI-driven trading strategies, undertaking regular risk assessments, and promoting market participant transparency and accountability. Comprehensive regulation should continuously adjust to the changing landscape of AI-driven market manipulation in order to preserve market integrity. This may necessitate close collaboration between regulators, technology experts, and industry stakeholders in order to anticipate emergent risks and create effective regulatory responses.

2. Risks and Challenges Associated with AI-Driven Manipulation

Utilising AI for market manipulation presents significant risks and obstacles that must be resolved. First, the complexity and opaqueness of AI algorithms make it difficult for regulators to effectively detect and prevent manipulative activities. The complexity of artificial intelligence (AI) systems, often referred to as "black boxes," can obscure the decision-making process and impede regulatory supervision and enforcement efforts. In addition, AI-driven market manipulation can result in the emergence of micromarkets with limited liquidity, potentially destabilising the market as a whole. The lightning-fast speed of AI-driven trading can outpace conventional risk management and surveillance mechanisms, making it difficult to maintain regulated markets and promptly detect manipulative behaviour. In addition, adversarial assaults against AI systems introduce vulnerabilities that can be exploited by manipulators, necessitating the development of effective defences against such attacks.

Indeed, the use of AI for market manipulation presents significant dangers and obstacles that must be effectively addressed to protect market integrity. To ensure equitable and transparent markets, comprehensive regulation should address these difficulties. The complexity and opaqueness of AI algorithms is one of the greatest obstacles, making it difficult for regulators to detect and prevent manipulative activities. Artificial intelligence (AI) algorithms frequently operate as "black boxes," making it difficult to comprehend the decision-making processes and identify potential manipulative strategies. Comprehensive regulation can address this issue by emphasising the need for AI algorithm and trading strategy transparency. This can include requiring companies to reveal the key features and mechanisms of their AI systems, thereby facilitating regulatory oversight and enabling the identification of potentially manipulative behaviours.

The application of AI-driven manipulation can also result in the emergence of micromarkets with limited liquidity. This fragmentation has the potential to disrupt the overall market dynamics, resulting in price distortions and diminished market efficiency. This risk should be mitigated by promoting measures to strengthen market resilience and discouraging manipulative practises that exploit market fragmentation. This may include imposing restrictions on order cancellations, regulating dark pools and other alternative trading venues, and instituting mechanisms to ensure the fair and orderly operation of markets.

A further challenge for regulatory supervision is posed by the rapid pace of AI-driven trading. The lightning-fast execution of transactions by AI algorithms can outpace conventional risk management and surveillance mechanisms, making it difficult for regulators to keep up with market developments and detect manipulative behaviour in a timely manner. Comprehensive regulation should encourage the development and deployment of advanced technological solutions, such as surveillance tools based on machine learning, to monitor and detect manipulative activities in real time. It is imperative that regulators have access to sophisticated tools capable of analysing vast quantities of data and identifying abnormal trading patterns associated with market manipulation.

Moreover, adversarial assaults against AI systems introduce vulnerabilities that manipulators can exploit. Adversarial assaults involve manipulating input data to deceive or mislead AI algorithms, resulting in unintended and potentially manipulative outcomes. Comprehensive regulation should promote the development and adoption of robust defences against adversarial attacks to mitigate this risk. This may involve employing techniques such as data cleansing, anomaly detection, and model validation to ensure the robustness and dependability of AI trading systems.

Therefore, the use of AI for market manipulation presents significant dangers and challenges that should be addressed by comprehensive regulation. Regulators can effectively mitigate the risks associated with AI-driven manipulation and foster fair and transparent markets by promoting transparency, enhancing market resilience, leveraging advanced surveillance tools, and developing defences against adversarial attacks.

3. Regulatory Implications

The proliferation of market manipulation facilitated by artificial intelligence necessitates a proactive regulatory response to safeguard market integrity and investor protection. Regulators are faced with the daunting task of keeping up with the rapid evolution of artificial intelligence (AI) technologies and devising suitable frameworks to mitigate the associated risks. To effectively identify patterns, anomalies, and suspicious activities indicative of market manipulation, it is essential to strengthen surveillance and detection capabilities. This involves employing sophisticated data analytics, machine learning, and AI to monitor market behaviour in real time. In addition, greater transparency and explicability of AI trading systems are essential for effective oversight. By requiring firms to disclose their algorithms, data sources, and trading strategies, regulators can better assess the potential for manipulation and take the necessary regulatory action.

Furthermore, it is essential to develop and enforce ethical guidelines and industry standards specific to AI-driven trading. These guidelines should address data privacy, algorithmic accountability, and the responsible use of content generated by artificial intelligence. It is essential that regulators, industry associations, and market participants work together to establish and assure the effective implementation of these standards. In addition, fostering international cooperation between regulatory bodies can assist in addressing the transnational character of AI-driven manipulation and establishing standardised regulatory frameworks. The proliferation of market manipulation facilitated by artificial intelligence necessitates a proactive regulatory response to safeguard market integrity and investor protection. Regulators are faced with the daunting task of keeping up with the rapid evolution of artificial intelligence (AI) technologies and devising suitable frameworks to mitigate the associated risks.

To combat AI-driven market manipulation effectively, regulators must strengthen their surveillance and detection capabilities. This requires using sophisticated data analytics, machine learning, and AI to monitor market behaviour in real time. Regulators can identify potential instances of market manipulation and take prompt regulatory action by analysing immense amounts of data and detecting patterns, anomalies, and suspicious activities. The use of AI-based surveillance tools can enhance the efficacy and effectiveness of monitoring efforts by augmenting conventional surveillance techniques. In addition to surveillance, it is essential for effective supervision to ensure greater transparency and explainability of AI systems used in trading. Regulators can require firms to disclose their algorithms, data sources, and trading strategies, allowing them to evaluate the potential for manipulation and identify anomalies. Transparent AI systems permit greater oversight, accountability, and comprehension of the involved decision-making processes. This transparency enables regulators to make informed decisions and take the necessary regulatory measures to curtail manipulative practises.

It is imperative to develop and enforce ethical guidelines and industry standards specific to AI-driven trading. These guidelines should address a variety of concerns, including data privacy, algorithmic accountability, and the responsible use of content generated by artificial intelligence. Regulators can work with industry associations, market participants, and other stakeholders to establish and assure the effective implementation of these standards. Regulators can mitigate the risks associated with AI-driven market manipulation and cultivate a more reliable and resilient market environment by establishing clear ethical boundaries and promoting responsible practises.

Moreover, given the global nature of financial markets, it is essential to cultivate international cooperation among regulatory bodies. Collaborative efforts can aid in addressing the international challenges posed by AI-driven manipulation, establishing harmonised regulatory frameworks, and facilitating the exchange of information and enforcement actions. Coordination at the international level is essential for ensuring uniform regulatory standards, promoting fair competition, and preventing regulatory arbitrage. The rise of AI-driven market manipulation necessitates a proactive and flexible regulatory approach. Enhancing surveillance capabilities, promoting transparency and explainability, developing ethical guidelines, and nurturing international cooperation are essential components of comprehensive regulation to protect market integrity and investors in the ever-changing landscape of AI-driven trading.

Rapid advances in AI technology have unleashed enormous potential for market effectiveness and decision-making. However, the same technology presents new challenges, including the potential for artificial intelligence to assist businesses in evading market regulations and promoting market manipulation. Understanding the underlying mechanisms, evaluating the associated risks, and implementing the appropriate regulatory measures are necessary to mitigate the negative effects of AI-driven manipulation. By employing a proactive and collaborative strategy, regulators and market participants can harness the benefits of artificial intelligence while protecting the integrity, fairness, and stability of financial markets.

The need for comprehensive regulation and the role of AI as a complementary actor to the state

In today's rapidly evolving technological landscape, the concept of the need for comprehensive regulation and the function of AI as a complementary actor to the state is an essential topic. As AI technology continues to advance and permeate various industries, including finance, healthcare, and transportation, the need for regulatory frameworks to ensure the responsible and ethical use of AI systems is increasingly acknowledged. In addition, the integration of AI as a complementary actor to the state can provide distinct opportunities for enhancing governance, decision-making processes, and the delivery of public services.

1. The Need for Comprehensive Regulation

The increasing autonomy and decision-making capabilities of AI systems raise ethical concerns such as accountability, impartiality, transparency, and confidentiality. Comprehensive regulation can provide guidelines and standards to ensure that artificial intelligence (AI) systems are designed and implemented in accordance with ethical principles. Ethical concerns regarding the increasing autonomy and decision-making capabilities of AI systems require comprehensive regulation. Accountability, impartiality, transparency, and privacy are essential ethical considerations that must be upheld in the design and deployment of artificial intelligence systems.

Accountability involves establishing distinct responsibility lines and defining the roles and responsibilities of various stakeholders involved in AI development and use. Regulatory frameworks should mandate that organisations have mechanisms in place to address the consequences of AI decisions, ensuring that individuals or entities can be held liable for any potentially detrimental or unethical outcomes. To prevent bias and discrimination in AI systems, fairness is crucial. Regulations should require organisations to actively mitigate biases that may result from the use of biassed training data or defective algorithms. Regular audits can be required to evaluate the fairness of AI systems, and organisations should be required to resolve any identified biases and take corrective action to ensure equitable outcomes. Transparency is essential for fostering confidence and comprehension in AI systems. Regulatory frameworks can mandate organizations to provide straightforward explanations of how AI systems make decisions, enabling users and stakeholders to comprehend the underlying processes. This can include documentation requirements, data source disclosure, algorithmic explanations, and information access to promote transparency and accountability.

Privacy protection is of the utmost significance for AI systems that handle personal information. Comprehensive regulations are required to ensure that AI systems adhere to extant data protection laws and principles, such as the General Data Protection Regulation (GDPR). Organisations should be required to implement privacy-by-design principles, such as secure data storage, data minimization, and informed consent collection. Societies can harness the benefits of AI while minimising risks and ensuring the responsible and ethical use of these technologies by instituting comprehensive regulations that address ethical concerns. Such regulations provide a framework for organisations to navigate the complex ethical landscape of AI, foster the development of AI systems that are transparent, fair, accountable, and respectful of privacy, and create public trust.

Reducing Bias and Discrimination: Inadvertently, AI algorithms can perpetuate biases present in training data, leading to discriminatory results. Comprehensive regulation can enforce AI system transparency, requiring organisations to monitor and address bias, as well as promote fairness and equity. Reducing bias and discrimination in AI systems is a crucial aspect requiring extensive regulation to ensure fairness and equity. When AI algorithms are trained on biassed or unrepresentative data, existing biases can be perpetuated and amplified, leading to discriminatory outcomes. In order to address this issue, regulations can enforce transparency and accountability in AI systems, compelling organisations to monitor and resolve bias throughout the lifecycle of AI.

Comprehensive regulations can require organisations to implement detection, evaluation, and mitigation mechanisms for bias. This requires frequent monitoring and auditing of AI systems in order to identify and correct any potential biases. Organisations can be required to conduct comprehensive analyses of training data to identify potential sources of bias, and to implement strategies to minimise or eradicate biases during data preprocessing and algorithm development. In addition, regulations can encourage the use of diverse and representative datasets, thereby promoting inclusivity and minimising the risk of perpetuating biases. Organisations may be required to demonstrate efforts in ensuring data diversity, such as actively pursuing diverse data sources and taking multiple demographic factors into account when creating more inclusive training datasets.

In addition to data-related measures, comprehensive regulation can encourage algorithmic transparency to promote fairness and equity. This entails mandating that organisations provide explanations for algorithmic decisions, allowing affected individuals or groups to comprehend how decisions were made and providing recourse in the event of unjust treatment. Transparency measures can include documenting the criteria, variables, and weighting factors used by AI decision-making algorithms, allowing for independent evaluation and auditing of the decision-making processes.

Comprehensive regulation can advocate for the participation of diverse stakeholders in the development and deployment of AI systems to further promote equity. This may include requiring organisations to establish diverse AI ethics boards or external advisory groups, assuring multiple perspectives and preventing undue power concentration or bias in AI decision-making. Comprehensive regulation can help mitigate bias and discrimination in AI systems by mandating transparency and requiring organisations to actively monitor and resolve bias, thereby promoting fairness, equity, and societal trust. These measures can ensure that artificial intelligence (AI) systems are designed and deployed with an emphasis on mitigating bias and delivering equitable outcomes for all individuals, regardless of their demographic characteristics.

AI relies heavily on data, and comprehensive regulation can protect the data privacy rights of individuals by assuring proper consent, secure storage, and appropriate use of personal information. In the context of AI systems, which significantly rely on data for training and decision-making, ensuring robust data protection is crucial. Comprehensive regulation can play a crucial role in protecting the data privacy rights of individuals and establishing clear guidelines for the proper management of personal information. Comprehensive regulation can enforce the requirement that organisations obtain consent from individuals prior to collecting and processing their personal information. This involves ensuring that individuals are aware of the purpose, scope, and duration of data acquisition, as well as any potential international data transfers or sharing with third parties. In addition, regulations can mandate that organisations provide individuals with easily accessible and intuitive withdrawal mechanisms.

Comprehensive regulation can also resolve the secure storage of personal data, which is a crucial factor. Organisations should be required to implement stringent data protection measures to prevent unauthorised access, loss, and mistreatment of personally identifiable information. This may include encryption, access controls, routine security audits, and adherence to industry-recognized security standards.

A comprehensive regulatory framework should also establish guidelines for the appropriate use of personal data within AI systems. This includes limitations on data retention periods, ensuring that personal data is only retained for as long as necessary and deleted securely when it is no longer required. In addition, regulations can mandate the use of anonymization and pseudonymization techniques to safeguard the privacy of individuals during data processing.

In addition, regulations can establish accountability frameworks for organisations, holding them accountable for the proper management of personal information. This can include requiring data protection impact assessments, internal data protection officers, and regular audits to ensure adherence to data protection principles. In the event of data breaches or unauthorised access, comprehensive regulation can mandate prompt notification of individuals and relevant authorities, as well as the implementation of appropriate corrective measures.

Individuals' privacy rights can be safeguarded in the context of AI systems through the implementation of extensive data protection regulations. This promotes responsible and ethical data practises and builds trust between individuals and institutions. In addition, it can assist in mitigating potential risks associated with data breaches, unauthorised access, and misuse of personal information, thereby enhancing data governance in the AI ecosystem. Establishing Liability and Accountability: Clear regulations can establish liability frameworks to assign blame when AI systems cause damage or engage in unethical behaviour. This helps guarantee accountability and gives individuals affected by AI-related issues recourse.

In the context of AI systems, establishing liability and accountability is a crucial aspect of comprehensive regulation. When AI systems cause injury or engage in unethical behaviour, clear regulations can play a critical role in assigning responsibility and ensuring accountability. These regulations provide a framework for addressing the ethical and legal implications of AI-related issues. Comprehensive regulation should define the liability frameworks applicable to the various stakeholders involved in the development, deployment, and use of artificial intelligence (AI) systems. This comprises AI system designers, manufacturers, operators, and users. By explicitly defining the responsibilities and obligations of each party, regulations allow for the assignment of liability in the event of harm or unethical behaviour.

Regulatory frameworks should define the criteria for determining liability in incidents involving artificial intelligence. This may involve negligence, malice, or noncompliance with regulatory standards. Regulations may also contemplate strict liability, in which liability is imposed regardless of fault if AI systems cause harm.

Individuals affected by AI-related issues should be able to seek redress and compensation through mechanisms established by a comprehensive regulatory regime. This can include provisions for legal remedies, dispute resolution procedures, and the establishment of specialised bodies or courts to handle disputes involving artificial intelligence. These mechanisms ensure that individuals have access to justice and can hold accountable those liable for the negative effects of AI systems. In addition, regulations should encourage organisations to implement risk management practises and ethical guidelines to prevent potential injury or unethical AI system behaviour. This may involve undertaking risk assessments, implementing protections, and adopting responsible AI development practises. Audits, inspections, and reporting requirements can be utilised to monitor and enforce compliance with such practises.

Comprehensive regulation offers a legal and ethical framework for addressing the potential risks and damages posed by AI systems by establishing liability frameworks and ensuring accountability. It allows affected individuals to seek redress, encourages responsible behaviour among stakeholders, and ultimately fosters confidence in the development and deployment of AI technologies.

2. AI as a Complementary Actor to the State

AI technologies can aid governments in analysing enormous quantities of data, recognising patterns, and making informed decisions. Algorithms based on artificial intelligence can efficiently process data and provide insights that can inform policymaking and governance processes.

AI technologies can play a crucial role in the improvement of governance and decision-making. Comprehensive regulation can leverage the potential of artificial intelligence to assist governments in analysing enormous amounts of data, identifying patterns, and making informed decisions. Governments can improve the efficiency and efficacy of policymaking and governance processes by employing AI algorithms.

AI technologies enable governments to process and analyse large volumes of data in real time, yielding valuable insights that can inform policymaking based on empirical evidence. These insights can vary from the identification of emerging trends and patterns to the prediction of future scenarios and their potential effects. Using AI, governments can improve their capacity to comprehend complex issues and make decisions based on a thorough analysis of available data.

In governance processes, regulatory frameworks can encourage the adoption of AI tools and technologies. This can include providing governments with incentives, guidance, and support to implement AI-powered analytics platforms, data management systems, and decision support tools. By doing so, governments can optimise their data-driven processes, improve their analytical capabilities, and expedite decision-making.

Governance can benefit from AI algorithms in a number of ways, including increased efficiency and precision in data analysis. They are able to rapidly process large volumes of data, identify patterns, detect anomalies, and generate insights that may not be readily attainable through manual processes. This enables governments to make better-informed decisions, optimise resource allocation, and effectively respond to emergent challenges and opportunities.

Nevertheless, comprehensive regulation should also address potential difficulties and dangers associated with the use of AI in governance and decision-making. This includes assuring the transparency and explainability of AI algorithms in order to facilitate accountability and prevent excessive power concentration. Regulations can stipulate that organisations must provide explanations for algorithmic decisions, allowing for independent examination.

In addition, regulatory frameworks should take into account the ethical implications of AI-driven decision making. This involves addressing issues such as AI algorithm impartiality, inclusivity, and potential bias. Regulations can mandate the use of diverse and representative datasets, regular audits to monitor algorithmic performance, and the establishment of ethical guidelines for the development and use of artificial intelligence in governance processes.

Comprehensive regulation can facilitate data-driven decision-making, enhance efficiency, and improve the overall quality and efficacy of public policy by harnessing the potential of AI in governance. However, it is essential to ensure the deployment of AI technologies in a responsible and ethical manner, with appropriate oversight and mechanisms to resolve potential challenges and risks. AI can be used to expedite and enhance the delivery of public services including healthcare, transportation, and public safety. For instance, AI-powered chatbots can provide 24/7 support, AI-driven traffic management systems can optimise traffic flow, and AI-powered predictive models can assist with disaster response and resource allocation. It is a significant benefit that comprehensive regulation can facilitate the improvement of public service delivery through the application of AI technologies. AI has the potential to expedite and enhance a variety of public services, such as healthcare, transportation, and public safety. By utilising AI-powered solutions, governments can optimise service delivery, boost efficiency, and improve citizen outcomes.

Healthcare is one area where AI can improve the provision of public services. AI-powered chatbots and virtual assistants can provide support 24 hours a day, seven days a week, with immediate and individualised responses to frequent healthcare questions. This can reduce the workload of healthcare professionals and increase access to healthcare information and services. By analysing medical data and images, AI algorithms can also assist in medical diagnostics, allowing for the early detection of diseases and providing valuable insights to healthcare professionals.

The transportation industry is another sector that can benefit from AI technologies. Traffic management systems powered by AI can optimise traffic flow, decrease congestion, and improve road safety. Various sources of real-time data, such as sensors and cameras, can be analysed by AI algorithms to provide intelligent traffic control and predictive modelling. This can enhance commuting, reduce travel times, and contribute to more sustainable transportation systems.

Disaster response and resource allocation can be substantially aided by AI-powered predictive models. By analysing data from multiple sources, including weather patterns, social media, and historical data, AI algorithms can help foretell and identify potential disaster events. This allows governments to proactively allocate resources, plan evacuations, and implement prompt response measures. By analysing real-time data and facilitating the efficient distribution of supplies and personnel, AI can also support resource optimisation during emergencies. By providing governments with guidelines, standards, and incentives to integrate AI technologies effectively, comprehensive regulation can promote the adoption of AI in the delivery of public services. Regulations can encourage governments to prioritise citizen-centric approaches, ensuring that AI solutions are created with the goal of enhancing public welfare and addressing societal demands.

However, comprehensive regulation is necessary to resolve potential challenges associated with the application of AI to the delivery of public services. This includes assuring the privacy and security of data, addressing biases in AI algorithms, and maintaining human oversight in crucial decision-making processes. Regulations can mandate compliance with data protection laws, require transparency in artificial intelligence algorithms, and establish mechanisms for auditing and accountability. By adopting AI technologies in public service delivery and instituting comprehensive regulation, governments can capitalise on AI's potential to improve the efficiency, accessibility, and responsiveness of serving the needs of citizens. This can result in improved outcomes, improved user experiences, and a more efficient allocation of resources in public services.

Adoption of AI technologies has the potential to increase government operations' efficacy and reduce expenses. Automating routine duties and optimising processes via AI can free up human resources and reduce administrative burdens, enabling governments to allocate resources more efficiently. Efficiency and cost reduction are significant benefits that can be unlocked through the incorporation of AI technologies in government operations with the aid of comprehensive regulation. By utilising artificial intelligence, governments can streamline processes, automate commonplace tasks, and optimise resource allocation, resulting in increased operational efficiency and cost savings.

Human-performed repetitive and time-consuming duties, such as data entry, document processing, and basic customer service inquiries, can be automated by AI technologies. By automating these duties, governments can free up personnel for more complex and value-added endeavours. This not only increases productivity but also decreases administrative burdens, allowing government employees to focus on higher-level tasks requiring critical thinking and creativity.

Comprehensive regulation can incentivize and direct the adoption of AI technologies by governments in order to optimise their operations. It can provide guidelines for identifying areas appropriate for automation and effectively implementing AI-driven solutions. By streamlining workflows, reducing operational bottlenecks, and eliminating redundant processes, governments can increase their efficacy and optimise their resources. Moreover, AI is able to analyse large volumes of data and generate valuable insights that assist in the making of informed decisions and the allocation of resources. Governments can identify patterns, trends, and correlations in data that may not be readily apparent through manual analysis by employing AI-driven analytics. This allows for more accurate forecasting, resource planning, and policy development, which ultimately results in a more effective and efficient allocation of resources.

Implementing AI technologies in government operations can result in substantial cost savings. Governments can reduce labour costs, reduce errors, and eliminate inefficiencies by automating duties and optimising processes. In addition, analytics powered by AI can facilitate proactive resource management, thereby optimising budgetary planning and allocation. By anticipatorily identifying potential hazards and bottlenecks, governments can more effectively allocate resources, thereby avoiding unnecessary expenditures and maximising cost-effectiveness. However, comprehensive regulation should also address potential challenges associated with the adoption of artificial intelligence in government operations. This includes ensuring data privacy and security, addressing concerns about algorithmic biases, and contemplating the ethical implications of AI-driven decisions. Regulations can provide guidelines for responsible data governance, security protocols, and algorithmic transparency in order to preserve public confidence and mitigate potential risks.

By leveraging the benefits of AI technologies and instituting comprehensive regulation, governments can increase operational efficiency, reduce costs, and enhance the delivery of services to citizens. Strategic adoption of AI in government operations has the potential to improve public administration, optimise resource allocation, and ultimately provide citizens with improved outcomes.

Ethical Considerations and Oversight: While AI can complement the state, comprehensive regulation should include mechanisms to ensure the ethical and responsible use of AI by both public and private entities. This includes establishing transparency, impartiality, and accountability guidelines for AI systems used by the government. When artificial intelligence complements the state, comprehensive regulation must address ethical considerations and oversight. While AI can provide numerous benefits, it is essential that both public and private entities use it responsibly and ethically. To accomplish this, regulations should include comprehensive mechanisms for oversight and establish guidelines for transparency, fairness, and accountability in AI systems used by the government.

Transparency is essential to assuring the responsible use of artificial intelligence. State and other entities can be required by regulation to disclose their use of artificial intelligence systems, including their purpose, data sources, algorithms employed, and potential consequences. Transparent AI systems permit public scrutiny, allowing individuals and organisations to comprehend and assess the fairness and biases incorporated in these systems. Additionally, fairness should be a primary consideration in the state's use of AI. Comprehensive regulation can require organisations to assess and mitigate biases in artificial intelligence (AI) algorithms, ensuring fair outcomes for all individuals regardless of their characteristics or circumstances. Regulations can encourage the use of diverse and representative datasets, promote fairness assessments, and require organisations to take corrective action if biases are identified.

Accountability mechanisms are necessary to ensure that the government and other entities utilising AI are held accountable for their actions. The regulations should establish distinct responsibility lines and define the obligations of various stakeholders. This includes holding individuals accountable for the design, development, and implementation of AI systems, as well as decisions made based on AI-generated insights. Individuals affected by AI decisions can seek redress and challenge potential injury or unethical behaviour through accountability frameworks.

A comprehensive regulation should also resolve privacy concerns related to government AI systems. It should mandate compliance with existing data protection laws and establish guidelines for the acquisition, storage, and use of personally identifiable information. Regulations can mandate the adoption of privacy-by-design principles, ensuring that privacy concerns are incorporated into the development and deployment of artificial intelligence systems. This includes instituting suitable security measures, obtaining informed consent, and giving individuals control over their personal data. Comprehensive regulation can establish autonomous bodies or agencies responsible for monitoring and evaluating the state's use of AI to ensure effective oversight. These organisations can conduct audits, evaluations, and impact assessments to determine the ethical implications of AI systems. In addition to providing guidance, enforcing compliance, and imposing penalties for noncompliance with ethical guidelines and regulations, they can also provide direction.

By incorporating ethical considerations and supervision mechanisms into comprehensive regulation, the state's ethical and responsible use of artificial intelligence can be ensured. This promotes public confidence, reduces the likelihood of discriminatory outcomes, and aligns AI technologies with societal values and expectations.

The efficacy of current antitrust norms, rules, and laws in preventing large AI-based firms from extracting value and wealth

The efficacy of current antitrust norms, rules, and laws in preventing large AI-based firms from extracting value and wealth is a pressing concern in the digital age. As AI continues to advance and play a significant role in various industries, including technology and e-commerce, there is a growing realization that traditional antitrust frameworks may need to be reevaluated and updated to address the unique challenges posed by AI-driven firms.

One key challenge is the potential for AI-based firms to gain and maintain dominant market positions, leading to concerns about anti-competitive behavior and the extraction of excessive value and wealth. AI technologies can enable these firms to amass vast amounts of data, develop sophisticated algorithms, and leverage network effects, granting them significant market power. This concentration of power can limit competition, stifle innovation, and result in unfavorable outcomes for consumers.

Comprehensive regulation should address these concerns by adapting antitrust laws to the digital era. This could involve reevaluating the criteria used to assess market dominance, taking into account factors such as data access, algorithmic advantage, and network effects. Additionally, regulations should consider the potential for AI-based firms to engage in discriminatory practices or engage in predatory pricing strategies that may harm competition.

To prevent the extraction of excessive value and wealth, regulations can address issues related to data ownership, interoperability, and data portability. These measures can promote competition and allow smaller players to access and utilize data on a more level playing field. By ensuring fair and equitable access to data, regulations can prevent AI-based firms from gaining an unfair advantage and facilitate greater market competition.

Furthermore, regulators should consider the potential for AI-based firms to engage in anti-competitive practices through mergers and acquisitions. Existing antitrust laws may need to be updated to include more rigorous scrutiny of AI-related transactions and to assess potential harm to competition and innovation. This can involve enhanced scrutiny of merger and acquisition activities, stricter enforcement of competition laws, and the introduction of measures to encourage divestiture or sharing of critical assets in cases where market concentration becomes a concern.

International cooperation is crucial in addressing the challenges posed by AI-based firms. Collaboration among regulatory bodies can foster the exchange of best practices, harmonize regulatory approaches, and prevent regulatory arbitrage. International coordination can also facilitate the sharing of insights and experiences in dealing with AI-driven antitrust issues, enabling regulators to stay ahead of emerging challenges.

The efficacy of current antitrust norms, rules, and laws in preventing large AI-based firms from extracting excessive value and wealth has become a critical concern in the digital age. As AI technologies continue to advance, they have become a key driver of economic growth and innovation. However, there are growing concerns about the market power and dominance of large AI-based firms, which can potentially lead to anti-competitive behavior and hinder market competition.

One of the challenges with applying traditional antitrust frameworks to AI-based firms is the unique nature of these companies. AI-based firms often rely on vast amounts of data, sophisticated algorithms, and network effects to gain a competitive advantage and maintain dominance. As a result, their market power may not be solely derived from traditional factors such as market share or pricing power. Thus, there is a need to reevaluate the criteria used to assess market dominance in the context of AI-based firms.

Comprehensive regulation should consider factors such as data access, algorithmic advantage, and network effects when assessing market dominance. Data has become a valuable resource, and AI-based firms often have access to large amounts of data, which can give them a significant advantage over their competitors. Therefore, regulations should address data ownership, data interoperability, and data portability to ensure fair and equitable access to data. This can help level the playing field and promote competition among AI-based firms.

Moreover, regulations should focus on potential discriminatory practices and predatory pricing strategies employed by AI-based firms. Discriminatory practices can involve leveraging AI algorithms to manipulate pricing or engage in personalized pricing strategies that unfairly target certain customer segments. Predatory pricing, on the other hand, involves temporarily lowering prices to drive competitors out of the market. Comprehensive regulation should monitor and prevent these practices to protect competition and ensure fair market conditions.

Mergers and acquisitions (M&A) involving AI-based firms also require scrutiny to prevent anti-competitive behavior. AI-based firms may engage in M&A activities to consolidate their market power and limit competition. It is important for regulators to evaluate the potential impact of these transactions on competition and innovation. This may involve conducting in-depth assessments of the potential harm to market competition and considering remedies such as divestitures or asset sharing to address any concerns.

To effectively address the challenges posed by AI-based firms, international cooperation among regulatory bodies is crucial. AI-driven antitrust issues are not limited to national boundaries, and collaboration can foster the exchange of best practices, harmonize regulatory approaches, and prevent regulatory arbitrage. International coordination can also enhance the sharing of insights and experiences in dealing with AI-driven antitrust challenges, enabling regulators to stay ahead of emerging issues.

The efficacy of current antitrust norms, rules, and laws in preventing large AI-based firms from extracting excessive value and wealth requires a comprehensive understanding of the unique challenges and dynamics presented by the digital economy. The rise of AI-based firms has brought about transformative changes in various industries, with these companies leveraging advanced algorithms and vast amounts of data to gain significant market power.

One challenge in applying traditional antitrust frameworks to AI-based firms is the need to reevaluate the criteria used to assess market dominance. Traditional measures, such as market share or pricing power, may not capture the true influence and competitive advantage held by AI-based firms. These companies often rely on factors such as data access, algorithmic sophistication, and network effects to establish and maintain their dominant positions.

Comprehensive regulation should recognize the value of data as a strategic asset in the digital economy. AI-based firms often have access to vast quantities of data, enabling them to train sophisticated AI algorithms and enhance their competitive advantage. To prevent the extraction of excessive value and wealth, regulations can address data ownership and access issues. This may involve promoting data interoperability and portability, ensuring that data can be shared among market participants to foster competition and innovation.

Additionally, comprehensive regulation should consider the potential for discriminatory practices and predatory pricing strategies employed by AI-based firms. Discrimination can occur when AI algorithms are used to personalize pricing or target specific customer segments unfairly. Regulations should address these practices by promoting transparency, non-discrimination, and fairness in pricing. Similarly, predatory pricing, which involves temporarily lowering prices to drive competitors out of the market, should be monitored and prevented to maintain a level playing field.

The evaluation of mergers and acquisitions involving AI-based firms is another crucial aspect of comprehensive regulation. Given the potential for AI-based firms to engage in M&A activities to consolidate their market power, regulators must carefully assess the impact on competition and innovation. This may involve conducting thorough assessments of the potential harm to market competition and considering remedies such as divestitures or asset sharing to address any anti-competitive concerns that arise.

To effectively address the challenges posed by AI-based firms, international cooperation among regulatory bodies is essential. The digital economy is inherently global, and AI-driven antitrust issues transcend national boundaries. Collaborative efforts can facilitate the exchange of best practices, harmonize regulatory approaches, and prevent regulatory arbitrage. By fostering international coordination, regulators can establish a unified and coherent regulatory framework that promotes competition, protects consumers, and ensures fairness in the AI-driven market.

In conclusion, the efficacy of current antitrust norms, rules, and laws in preventing large AI-based firms from extracting excessive value and wealth requires a comprehensive and nuanced approach. Adapting antitrust frameworks to account for factors such as data access, algorithmic advantage, and network effects is crucial. Addressing discriminatory practices, predatory pricing strategies, and carefully evaluating AI-based mergers and acquisitions are also essential elements of comprehensive regulation. Through international cooperation, regulators can develop a cohesive global regulatory framework that fosters competition, protects consumers, and ensures a level playing field in the AI-driven market.

Chapter 10: Ethics, Responsibility, and Governance in AI-Driven Economic Systems

In the swiftly changing environment of the 21st century, artificial intelligence (AI) has emerged as a transformative force with far-reaching implications for global economies. Its integration into diverse industries and economic systems promises unprecedented advancements, efficiency gains, and innovative answers to long-standing problems. Nonetheless, as AI becomes more pervasive, it raises significant ethical concerns and poses difficult questions about responsibility and governance. This chapter explores the complex relationship between artificial intelligence, economic systems, ethics, responsibility, and governance in an effort to cast light on the multifaceted nature of this paradigm shift.

The first section of this chapter discusses the ethical implications of artificial intelligence and their effect on economic systems. The exponential development of AI technologies raises ethical questions that require careful consideration. As AI algorithms permeate more and more aspects of economic systems, they exert unprecedented influence over decision-making. From automated trading platforms to personalised consumer recommendations, artificial intelligence algorithms impact market dynamics, resource allocation, and even individual preferences. As it becomes difficult to articulate the reasoning behind their decisions, the black-box nature of certain AI models presents challenges in terms of transparency, fairness, and accountability. This section investigates the ethical implications of AI's impact on economic systems, including algorithmic bias, privacy concerns, and the potential for economic inequality. In addition, it examines the ethical implications of job loss due to automation as well as the responsibility of both private businesses and governments to resolve these socioeconomic challenges.

The second section examines the role of corporations and governments in governing AI-driven economic systems. As artificial intelligence continues to revolutionise economic systems, stakeholder responsibility becomes paramount. As the primary creators and implementers of AI technologies, private companies are accountable for ensuring the ethical and responsible use of AI in their business operations. This involves incorporating ethical guidelines into their AI development process, actively mitigating bias in algorithms, protecting user data, and communicating the capabilities and limitations of AI-driven products and services in an open and transparent manner. Governments, on the other hand, play a crucial role in establishing a regulatory framework that encourages innovation while maintaining ethical standards. This section examines the various approaches taken by governments around the globe to regulate AI-driven economic systems, from light-touch policies to comprehensive regulations. It investigates the difficulties in striking the right balance between innovation and accountability and the potential for international cooperation to effectively address global AI governance issues.

The third section explores the potential for AI to contribute to societal objectives and advance economic prosperity. AI offers opportunities to resolve pressing societal issues and promote economic growth amidst its ethical complexities and governance challenges. This section examines how AI-driven economic systems can be utilised to advance societal objectives such as sustainable development, poverty reduction, and enhanced access to healthcare and education. The predictive capabilities of artificial intelligence can optimise resource allocation and decision-making across multiple domains, resulting in more efficient and equitable outcomes. In addition, the potential of AI to promote economic development is investigated, including how it can boost productivity, foster innovation, and create new avenues for economic expansion. From optimising pricing strategies to streamlining supply chains, AI offers innovative solutions that can revolutionise conventional economic paradigms.

The chapter emphasises that the incorporation of AI into economic systems represents a turning point in human history, presenting both opportunities and challenges that require a deliberate and balanced approach. This chapter examined the ethical implications of artificial intelligence, the responsibility of firms and governments in governing AI-driven economic systems, and the potential for AI to contribute to societal objectives and economic well-being. As the influence of artificial intelligence (AI) continues to expand, proactive and accountable governance will be required to leverage its potential for the greater good and to ensure that ethical considerations remain at the forefront of decision-making processes. By navigating this landscape with foresight and a commitment to ethical principles, societies can set the foundation for an AI-driven future that is prosperous, inclusive, and ethically sound.

The ethical implications of AI and their impact on economic systems

Integration of AI technologies into economic systems has unquestionably resulted in numerous benefits, including increased efficiency and productivity as well as enhanced decision-making processes. Nonetheless, this swift advancement in AI raises significant ethical concerns that necessitate careful consideration and proactive measures to address. Algorithmic bias and fairness, privacy and data protection, job displacement and labour market effects, autonomy and accountability, transparency and explainability, and social and economic inequality are among the most significant ethical implications of AI on economic systems. These significant ramifications are discussed in depth here.

1. Algorithmic Bias and Fairness

Algorithmic bias is one of the most pressing ethical concerns in AI-driven economic systems. AI algorithms, particularly machine learning models, are trained on enormous quantities of data, which may contain societal biases. AI systems can therefore perpetuate and amplify these biases, leading to unjust outcomes and discrimination. This bias can manifest in economic contexts such as employment decisions, loan approvals, and pricing algorithms, potentially reinforcing market inequalities. For instance, Obermeyer et al. (2019) found that a widely used healthcare algorithm exhibited racial bias, resulting in significant disparities in predicting medical requirements and allocating healthcare resources across racial groups.

In AI-driven economic systems, algorithmic bias has emerged as a complex and multifaceted ethical challenge. The source of bias is the training data used to construct AI models. Since machine learning algorithms learn patterns from historical data, the AI system learns and replicates any biases present in that data. These biases may be based on race, gender, ethnicity, socioeconomic status, or any other characteristic evident in the data.

In economic contexts, algorithmic bias can have significant repercussions. Due to historical hiring patterns and implicit biases in the data, AI-powered recruitment systems may inadvertently favour candidates from certain demographic groups during the recruiting process. This perpetuates existing workforce disparities and reinforces systemic inequality. Similarly, AI-based loan approval algorithms can unjustly disadvantage certain groups, resulting in diminished access to credit for marginalised communities. Frequently used in online marketplaces, pricing algorithms can inadvertently charge higher prices to users based on their location or other sensitive attributes, resulting in economic discrimination. In addition to having social effects, algorithmic bias can also have significant economic repercussions. When certain groups are systematically excluded or disadvantaged in economic transactions, it reduces their purchasing power and impedes their ability to completely contribute to the economy, resulting in a less inclusive and less prosperous economic system as a whole.

To combat algorithmic bias, a comprehensive and proactive approach is required. It begins with examining the data used to train AI models in order to identify and mitigate bias to the greatest extent feasible. The acquisition of data should be conducted ethically, with an emphasis on diversity and inclusivity, to ensure that datasets adequately represent all segments of society. In addition, it is crucial to include diverse teams in the development and testing of AI systems, as diverse perspectives can help identify and challenge biases that may not be immediately apparent. Moreover, the development of explainable AI (XAI) techniques is essential for comprehending how AI algorithms make decisions. By providing transparent explanations for AI predictions, XAI facilitates the identification of biases and the comprehension of their effect on outcomes. This transparency also encourages accountability and permits stakeholders to contest unjust decisions.

There should be regulatory frameworks in place to ensure that companies and organisations utilising artificial intelligence adhere to ethical standards and continuously monitor for bias. Before deploying AI applications, ethical review boards or committees can be formed to assess their prospective societal impact. In addition, ongoing research in the field of algorithmic fairness seeks to develop techniques that can mathematically quantify and mitigate AI model biases. This includes the development of fairness-aware algorithms that take into consideration various fairness definitions and constraints during model construction. Consequently, addressing algorithmic bias and promoting impartiality in AI-powered economic systems is an essential and ongoing endeavour. By understanding the potential hazards of AI bias, stakeholders can collaborate to develop systems that are more inclusive, equitable, and in line with societal values. To harness the full potential of AI in shaping a better economic future for all, it is necessary to strike the proper equilibrium between technological innovation and ethical considerations.

2. Privacy and Data Protection

Provide personalised services and recommendations, AI-powered economic systems rely significantly on data collection and analysis. This data-driven methodology raises concerns regarding user privacy and data security. Companies must ensure that user data is collected, stored, and used responsibly, with the necessary consent and safeguards in place to prevent unauthorised access to or misuse of sensitive information. The General Data Protection Regulation (GDPR) in Europe and comparable data protection laws in other regions are examples of regulatory efforts to address these ethical concerns by emphasising individual data rights and mandating stringent data handling requirements.

AI-driven economic systems that rely on data collection and analysis present a delicate balance between providing personalised services and safeguarding user privacy. The vast amounts of data generated and processed by AI algorithms enable businesses to offer customised experiences and recommendations, thereby increasing consumer engagement and satisfaction. Nonetheless, this data-driven strategy also raises significant ethical concerns regarding user privacy and data protection.

Data privacy is a fundamental human right, and the responsible management of user data is essential for maintaining confidence and trust in AI-driven economic systems. Companies must be transparent with users regarding the categories of data they collect, the purposes for which it is used, and the safeguarding mechanisms in place. This requires the explicit consent of users for data collecting and processing activities, ensuring that individuals have meaningful control over their personal data. In addition, businesses must implement stringent data security measures to prevent unauthorised access, data breaches, and misuse of sensitive data. Encryption, access controls, and routine security audits are crucial components of a successful data protection strategy.

Mishandling user data can have severe consequences, including damage to the company's reputation and injury to individuals through identity theft, fraud, and other privacy violations. Such incidents may also result in regulatory penalties and legal repercussions, highlighting the significance of data protection as a crucial ethical factor. In response to these ethical concerns, regulatory bodies around the globe have endeavoured to establish legal frameworks that protect the data rights of individuals. The European Union's General Data Protection Regulation (GDPR), which went into effect in 2018, is a prime example of a comprehensive data protection law. GDPR grants individuals greater control over their personal data, including the right to access, rectify, and delete their information. In addition, it mandates that organisations implement privacy-by-design principles and promptly notify authorities of data breaches. Other regions have enacted similar data protection legislation, such as the California Consumer Privacy Act (CCPA) in the United States and the Personal Data Protection Bill in India. The purpose of these laws is to standardise data protection and encourage businesses to adopt more ethical data practises.

Such regulations are essential steps in the right direction, but the dynamism of AI and data collection necessitates ongoing efforts to remain ahead of emerging privacy challenges. Companies must remain abreast of the most recent privacy regulations, invest in data protection technologies, and educate their employees on the best data management procedures on an ongoing basis. The ethical obligation to protect user data transcends legal requirements. Companies should consider implementing ethical principles, such as data minimization and purpose limitation, to ensure that data is only collected and used for legitimate and clearly defined purposes.

AI-driven economic systems have the potential to revolutionise industries and improve user experiences, as demonstrated. However, the ethical consideration of the responsible handling of user data must be at the vanguard of AI implementation. By prioritising data privacy, obtaining informed consent, and adhering to data protection regulations, businesses can cultivate a culture of trust and respect, thereby paving the way for AI-driven economic systems that are sustainable and ethically sound.

3. Job Displacement and Labor Market Effects

In certain industries, the automation capabilities of AI have the potential to disrupt the labour market and displace workers. Automation can increase productivity and reduce costs, but it can also lead to unemployment and income inequality, especially for workers in low-skilled or routine occupations. Ethical considerations arise in how companies and governments navigate this transition, ensuring that affected workers have access to retraining and reskilling opportunities to partake in the new AI-driven employment landscape.

Regarding its impact on the labour market, the advent of AI's automation capabilities in economic systems has generated both exhilaration and concern. While automation has the potential to increase business productivity, streamline processes, and reduce operational costs, it also raises ethical concerns regarding job displacement and its effects on workers.

Certain job roles could be rendered obsolete by AI-driven automation, particularly those involving repetitive or routine duties. This presents a significant challenge, as displaced workers may experience unemployment and transitional difficulties. Large-scale worker displacement can also contribute to income inequality and exacerbate socioeconomic disparities, with low-skilled or vulnerable workers suffering the most.

How companies and governments respond to this disruptive transformation of the employment landscape raises ethical concerns. Responsible corporate conduct requires proactive measures to mitigate the negative effects of automation on employees. Instead of focusing solely on profit maximisation, businesses should also prioritise the welfare of their employees and the greater community.

An essential ethical principle to adopt is that of "human-centered automation," in which the integration of artificial intelligence is designed with a focus on augmenting rather than replacing human capabilities. By recognising the unique strengths and qualities that humans contribute to the workplace, AI can be used to boost human productivity and creativity, resulting in more fulfilling and meaningful work experiences.

Companies and governments must also invest in reskilling and upskilling programmes for workers to be able to adapt to a shifting employment landscape. This involves providing training opportunities that equip employees with AI-relevant skills and competencies. Through policies, funding, and partnerships with educational institutions and enterprises, governments can play a crucial role in facilitating such programmes.

Moreover, ethical considerations extend to ensuring equitable distribution of the benefits of AI-driven economic growth. It is essential to address income inequality and advocate for equitable wages and social safety nets that support workers who may be displaced by automation or experience temporary disruptions. A balanced approach to automation entails engaging in open dialogues with workers and labour unions, soliciting their input and insights during the planning and implementation of AI-driven initiatives. By involving stakeholders in the decision-making process, businesses can obtain valuable perspectives and identify potential challenges before they become severe.

In conclusion, the potential displacement of jobs caused by AI's automation capabilities necessitates cautious ethical consideration and responsible governance. Companies must prioritise the well-being of their workforce and invest in reskilling and upskilling initiatives in order to equip employees to adapt to the shifting employment landscape. Adoption of ethical AI should prioritise human-centered automation, promoting an environment where AI augments rather than replaces human potential. Ultimately, by embracing ethical principles in the integration of AI into economic systems, societies will be able to navigate the transition to an inclusive and equitable AI-driven job market, which will benefit both employees and the economy.

4. Autonomy and Accountability

As AI systems become more autonomous, concerns of responsibility and accountability arise. In crucial industries such as healthcare, finance, and transportation, the decisions made by AI algorithms can have significant repercussions in the real world. It becomes imperative to establish clear lines of responsibility to ensure that humans can intervene, comprehend, and override decisions made by AI when necessary. The increasing autonomy of AI systems raises critical questions of responsibility and accountability from an ethical standpoint. In crucial industries such as healthcare, finance, and transportation, where AI algorithms make decisions that directly affect human lives and well-being, it becomes essential to strike a balance between autonomy and human oversight.

It is difficult to completely comprehend and predict AI algorithms due to their complexity and capacity to learn and adapt from data. As AI systems evolve and become more sophisticated, they may make decisions that are not fully explicable to humans, creating the so-called "black-box" problem. This lack of transparency can be a significant ethical concern in critical applications because it hinders our ability to comprehend the reasoning behind AI decisions.

To address this problem, the "explainable AI" (XAI) principle enters into play. XAI aims to develop methods and techniques that offer human users insight into how AI models reach their conclusions. By enabling AI systems to provide transparent justifications for their decisions, it becomes possible for humans to comprehend the underlying logic and verify the impartiality and ethical soundness of AI outcomes.

Establishing clear responsibility boundaries is another crucial aspect of ensuring the ethical use of artificial intelligence. Even as AI becomes increasingly autonomous, it should not absolve humans of responsibility for AI actions. The ultimate responsibility for the outcomes of decisions made using AI should rest with the organisations or individuals employing the technology. The decision-making process of AI-driven systems requires transparency. Companies and developers should be transparent regarding the level of autonomy granted to AI algorithms and the areas where human supervision is maintained. Transparent communication fosters trust and ensures that users, stakeholders, and regulators are aware of the capabilities and limitations of the system.

"human-in-the-loop" AI systems can be used to establish a balance between autonomy and human intervention in highly critical applications. These systems permit humans to actively participate in the decision-making process, with the ability to override AI decisions when required. This ensures that ethical considerations and human judgement and values are incorporated into the final product. In addition, the deployment of AI in scenarios with high consequences should involve rigorous testing, validation, and risk assessment procedures. Ethical review boards or committees can be established to assess the potential societal impacts of AI systems and ensure that they comply with ethical and legal requirements.

Ultimately, establishing exhaustive guidelines for AI accountability and governance requires a collaborative effort between AI developers, ethicists, policymakers, and industry stakeholders. This multidisciplinary approach permits a comprehensive examination of potential risks and ethical implications, leading to the establishment of frameworks that promote the responsible and accountable use of artificial intelligence.

The increasing autonomy of AI systems necessitates careful consideration of responsibility and accountability, as is evident here. Transparency and explainability are indispensable for ensuring that AI decisions are explicable and justifiable. Organisations must assume responsibility for AI outcomes and implement human oversight to ensure adherence to ethical considerations. Through transparent communication, human-in-the-loop approaches, and collaborative efforts, societies can leverage the power of artificial intelligence (AI) while maintaining a solid ethical foundation and protecting human welfare.

5. Transparency and Explainability

The opaque nature of some AI algorithms makes it difficult to comprehend how decisions are made, which can hinder accountability and confidence in AI systems. Ethical guidelines recommend that AI models provide transparent explanations for their results, particularly in high-stakes applications such as medical diagnosis and loan approvals. Explainable Artificial Intelligence (XAI) research aims to resolve this issue by developing techniques to make AI decision-making more interpretable to humans, allowing them to comprehend the reasoning behind AI predictions.

Transparency and explainability are fundamental components of ethical AI development, particularly as AI algorithms become more complex and sophisticated. The "black-box" nature of certain AI models refers to their opaqueness, i.e., they make decisions without providing obvious insight into how those decisions were made. This lack of transparency raises concerns regarding accountability and trust, as users and stakeholders may be reluctant to rely on AI systems if they are unable to comprehend their inner workings.

In high-stakes applications such as medical diagnoses and loan approvals, the consequences of AI decisions can have significant effects on individuals and society. Ethical guidelines emphasise the need for AI models to be explicable and transparent in such situations. When AI algorithms can provide clear explanations for their results, it not only increases accountability but also nurtures user and stakeholder trust. The objective of explainable AI (XAI) research is to enhance the interpretability of AI decision-making processes through the development of techniques. The objective is to close the gap between the extremely complex character of AI algorithms and human comprehension. XAI seeks to answer queries such as why a particular decision was made, what features or factors influenced the decision, and how confidently the AI's prediction can be trusted.

Various approaches to XAI, including model-specific methods and post hoc explanations, have been investigated. Model-specific methods seek to directly incorporate interpretability into the design of artificial intelligence models. These methods may involve substituting simpler, more transparent models for complex AI models or incorporating attention mechanisms to emphasise pertinent features in the input data. Post hoc explanations, on the other hand, concentrate on explaining AI decisions after they have been made. Techniques such as feature visualisation, attribution methods, and rule-based explanations aim to illuminate the inner workings and decision-making processes of AI models.

The application of XAI techniques is advantageous not only in high-stakes situations, but also in situations where impartiality and bias reduction are crucial. By comprehending how AI models reach their conclusions, it becomes possible to identify and eliminate biases, thereby ensuring that AI-driven economic systems adhere to ethical principles of fairness and equity. In addition to advancements in technology, ethical considerations in transparency and explainability necessitate making informed decisions regarding the deployment of AI systems. In certain circumstances, it may be preferable to use simpler, more interpretable models, even if they sacrifice some predictive performance, in order to maintain user trust and transparency.

In addition, organisations must explicitly convey to users and stakeholders the level of explainability provided by AI systems. This involves establishing expectations, elucidating the extent to which AI decisions can be comprehended, and emphasising the limitations of AI algorithms. Transparency and explainability are therefore fundamental pillars of ethical AI development. As AI algorithms become increasingly complex and autonomous, the need for XAI techniques to make AI decision-making understandable to humans grows. By pursuing transparency, organisations can improve their accountability, foster user trust, and ensure that AI-driven economic systems adhere to ethical principles. As XAI research advances, it will be possible to establish a balance between AI's capabilities and human comprehension, thereby advancing the deployment of AI technologies in a responsible and transparent manner.

6. Social and Economic Inequality

AI has the potential to exacerbate social and economic disparities that already exist. If AI-driven economic systems favour certain individuals or groups disproportionately, this could lead to a further concentration of wealth and power. Ethical considerations necessitate that AI be utilised to develop inclusive economic systems that benefit the entire society. The potential for artificial intelligence to exacerbate social and economic inequalities is a crucial ethical issue that must be addressed proactively. AI-powered economic systems can either exacerbate existing inequalities or promote greater inclusion and equitable distribution of opportunities and benefits.

If artificial intelligence algorithms are trained on biassed data or deployed in a manner that favours certain individuals or groups, it can result in disproportionate benefits for those who are already in advantageous positions. AI-powered recruiting systems that inadvertently learn from historical hiring patterns may perpetuate biases and limit opportunities for underrepresented groups, thereby reinforcing social inequalities in the job market.

Moreover, AI's influence on pricing and resource allocation can disproportionately affect vulnerable populations. If pricing algorithms result in dynamic pricing strategies that exploit consumers with limited options, the economic divide between the privileged and the disadvantaged can widen. This emphasises the obligation to ensure that AI-powered economic systems prioritise justice and social welfare.

To combat potential inequalities, it is imperative that AI is utilised to develop economic systems that are inclusive and beneficial to all members of society. In the development and deployment of AI technologies, ethical guidelines must prioritise fairness, equity, and social impact. Implementing measures that actively mitigate bias in AI algorithms is one approach.

This includes auditing AI models for fairness on a regular basis and adjusting them to guarantee equitable outcomes. By designating fairness as an essential performance metric for AI systems, businesses can align their technological advances with ethical considerations.

Diverse teams of developers, data scientists, and ethicists should be involved in inclusive AI design to ensure that AI systems are sensitive to the requirements and perspectives of various communities. Diverse representation in the development process prevents the perpetuation of biases and encourages the creation of AI-powered solutions that are more inclusive and considerate of diverse user populations.

As previously discussed, transparency and explainability also play a crucial role in addressing social and economic inequalities. By gaining a comprehension of how AI algorithms make decisions, it becomes easier to identify and combat biases. Transparent AI systems also enable stakeholders to hold corporations and governments accountable for the potential deleterious social and economic effects of AI.

Moreover, collaborations between the public and private sectors can result in AI-based social benefit initiatives. Governments can encourage the use of AI to resolve societal issues like healthcare accessibility, education, and poverty reduction. Partnerships between the public and private sectors can ensure that AI technologies are applied to initiatives that benefit the larger community and help bridge the digital divide.

As seen, AI has the capacity to either exacerbate or reduce social and economic disparities. Ethical considerations necessitate that AI-powered economic systems prioritise inclusiveness, equity, and societal welfare. We can harness the transformative potential of AI to create a more equitable and just society by proactively addressing bias, fostering diversity in AI development, ensuring transparency and accountability, and directing AI initiatives towards socially impactful projects. In order to shape an AI-driven future that benefits all members of society and fosters prosperity and well-being for all, responsible and ethical AI practises are essential.

The multifaceted nature of the ethical implications of AI in economic systems necessitates a holistic approach. By recognising and proactively addressing issues such as algorithmic bias, privacy concerns, job displacement, accountability, and inequality, we can design AI-driven economic systems that prioritise fairness, transparency, and social welfare. Effective regulations, industry best practises, and interdisciplinary collaboration between policymakers, technologists, and ethicists will play a crucial role in guiding AI to have a positive impact on economic systems while protecting ethical principles.

The responsibility of firms and governments in governing AI-driven economic systems

Artificial intelligence (AI) integration into economic systems has ushered in a period of unprecedented innovation, productivity gains, and transformative opportunities. As artificial intelligence (AI) technologies continue to advance, they are reshaping industries and generating significant changes in the global economy. Alongside these advancements, however, the rise of AI-driven economic systems has ushered in a plethora of ethical, social, and economic challenges that demand deliberate and accountable governance.

1. Ethical Considerations and Responsible AI Deployment

Ethical implications of AI-driven economic systems must be thoroughly grasped for the development and deployment of AI technologies in a responsible manner. As the primary creators and implementers of AI solutions, private companies have a significant obligation to ensure that their AI applications are designed and utilised in accordance with ethical principles. Adopting ethical AI frameworks that govern the entire lifecycle of AI initiatives, from data collection to model deployment, is required.

Concerning algorithmic bias, impartiality, accountability, and transparency, the ethical considerations centre on addressing these issues. To reduce algorithmic bias, businesses should implement diverse, inclusive, and demographically-representative data collection strategies. Regular audits and bias testing of AI models are necessary for identifying and mitigating any unjust biases that may emerge during training.

Companies must also prioritise the ethical aspects of AI algorithms and ensure that they are designed with openness in mind. Transparent AI models enable users and stakeholders to comprehend how the AI system makes decisions, thereby nurturing trust in its outcomes. In high-stakes applications such as healthcare diagnosis or financial decisions, where the ability to articulate the reasoning behind AI predictions is of utmost importance, transparent AI is of utmost importance.

2. Transparency and Explainability in AI Systems

Transparency and explainability are essential components of accountable AI governance, particularly as AI algorithms become more complex and opaque. Economic systems propelled by AI frequently operate as black-box algorithms, making decisions that are difficult for humans to comprehend or interpret. This absence of transparency can reduce accountability and trust in AI systems, thereby impeding their widespread adoption and acceptance.

In pursuance of transparency, businesses must invest in the research and development of explainable artificial intelligence (XAI) techniques. XAI aims to make AI decision-making processes more comprehensible to humans, allowing them to comprehend the logic behind AI predictions. Techniques such as feature visualisation, attribution methods, and rule-based explanations shed light on the inner workings and decision-making processes of AI models.

To further promote transparency and accountability, businesses should adopt human-in-the-loop AI system principles. By incorporating humans into the decision-making process, AI models can be subject to human judgement and values, allowing for responsible interventions and overrides as needed.

3. Data Privacy and Security

In order to provide personalised services and suggestions, AI-driven economic systems significantly rely on vast amounts of data. However, this reliance on data raises serious concerns regarding user privacy and data security. As stewards of sensitive user data, businesses must prioritise data privacy as a fundamental ethical obligation.

Businesses should implement stringent data security measures to prevent data breaches and unauthorised access. Encryption, access controls, and routine security audits are crucial components of a successful data protection strategy. In addition, businesses should obtain users' explicit consent for data acquisition and processing activities, ensuring that individuals have meaningful control over their personal data.

Ethical data handling requires companies to be transparent with users regarding the categories of data collected, the purposes for which it is used, and the safeguards in place to protect that data. This transparency fosters confidence and empowers users to make informed decisions regarding the data they share with AI-powered systems.

4. Mitigating Economic and Social Disparities

Automation propelled by AI has the potential to disrupt the labour market and lead to the displacement of workers, particularly those in low-skilled or routine positions. The responsibility for addressing economic and social disparities caused by AI-driven economic transformations is shared by governments and private businesses.

Employers are obligated to provide retraining and upskilling opportunities for affected employees, enabling them to transition to new positions in the AI-driven employment landscape. Collaborations between businesses and governments can result in the formulation of policies that ensure the equitable distribution of the benefits of AI-driven economic growth. This may involve incentivizing companies to invest in retraining programmes or establishing social safety nets to assist employees during transitions.

In addition, businesses can prioritise the ethical recruiting and advancement of diverse talent, ensuring that underrepresented groups have access to AI development and deployment opportunities. Diverse teams are more likely to consider the perspectives of various communities, thereby reducing the likelihood of perpetuating biases and inequities in AI-driven economic systems.

5. Regulating AI-driven Economic Systems

Governments play a prominent role in establishing a regulatory framework that governs economic systems driven by AI. Governments are responsible for establishing standards, enforcing ethical guidelines, and safeguarding consumers and citizens from potential harm caused by AI applications.

The creation of specialised bodies to oversee AI governance and establish ethical guidelines may be part of regulatory efforts. It is possible to establish transparent reporting and auditing mechanisms to monitor AI systems and assure adherence to ethical principles. In addition, governments should encourage collaborations with industry stakeholders, researchers, and ethicists in order to formulate informed and balanced regulations.

The responsibility of corporations and governments in governing AI-driven economic systems extends well beyond the adoption of AI technologies. It involves upholding ethical standards, prioritising transparency, protecting data privacy, and reducing economic disparities. By fostering a culture of responsible AI deployment, firms and governments can harness the transformative power of AI to advance societal objectives, promote economic prosperity, and create an inclusive and equitable AI-driven future. In order to shape an AI-driven future that benefits all members of society and fosters prosperity and well-being for all, responsible and ethical AI practises are essential.

The potential for AI to contribute to societal goals and promote economic welfare

Artificial intelligence (AI) is one of the few technological innovations that has so profoundly captivated the world's imagination and potential for revolutionary change. As we stand on the precipice of the AI revolution, the far-reaching ramifications of this revolutionary technology extend well beyond individual applications to incorporate broader societal aspirations and economic prospects. The unprecedented capabilities of artificial intelligence have sparked great optimism and anticipation for its potential to accelerate progress, enhance human lives, and propel economies to new heights.

The advent of AI-driven systems promises to solve some of humanity's most pressing problems and substantially contribute to the accomplishment of societal goals. This introduction explores the multifaceted potential of AI in nurturing social progress and economic prosperity, focusing on how this transformative technology can reshape industries, empower individuals, and pave the way for a more equitable and prosperous future.

1. Unleashing New Frontiers of Innovation

AI's ability to process massive quantities of data at unprecedented speeds and identify intricate patterns enables it to discover insights that were previously incomprehensible to humans. This capability establishes AI as an indispensable resource for scientific research, medicinal advancements, and environmental monitoring, where the potential for transformative effects is limitless.

AI-driven data analysis and modelling have accelerated the rate of discovery across multiple scientific disciplines. From particle physics to astronomy, artificial intelligence algorithms sift through enormous datasets to identify patterns, detect anomalies, and aid researchers in formulating hypotheses. AI's simulation and optimisation prowess enables scientists to explore complex systems and devise experiments with previously unattainable precision. As a result, AI-enabled research contributes to a deeper understanding of the universe and inspires innovations that influence the trajectory of human knowledge.

In the medical field, AI emerges as a revolutionary force in diagnostics, treatment, and drug development. By analysing complex data sets, AI enables medical professionals to make more precise predictions, diagnose diseases with greater precision, and create individualised treatment plans based on patient profiles. The remarkable accuracy of AI algorithms in detecting early signs of disease has led to more timely interventions and enhanced patient outcomes. In addition, AI's ability to analyse enormous amounts of genomic data expedites the discovery of targeted therapies and potential cures for genetic disorders and complex diseases.

Climate change and pandemics are two of the most critical global issues that AI has the potential to transform. Platforms for environmental monitoring employ AI algorithms to analyse satellite imagery, meteorological data, and sensor networks, thereby providing crucial insights into climate patterns, natural disasters, and ecosystem health. Predictive models powered by artificial intelligence aid policymakers in the development of proactive strategies for climate adaptation and mitigation, thereby contributing to the formulation of sustainable policies and practises.

In the agricultural sector, AI-driven precision agriculture offers a promising avenue for enhancing food security and environmental sustainability. By optimising resource utilisation, AI systems enable producers to make data-driven decisions regarding irrigation, fertilisation, and pest control, resulting in higher crop yields and less waste. The implementation of artificial intelligence in agriculture reduces environmental impact, conserves water resources, and reduces the use of toxic chemicals, thereby promoting more sustainable agricultural practises.

In the energy sector, artificial intelligence plays a transformative role in optimising energy generation, distribution, and consumption. Powered by artificial intelligence, demand forecasting models predict fluctuations in energy consumption patterns, enabling utilities to optimise energy distribution, balance supply and demand, and reduce waste. In addition, AI facilitates the efficient utilisation of solar, wind, and other sustainable energy technologies by improving their integration with conventional energy sources. AI contributes to the transition towards greener, more sustainable energy systems by maximising energy efficiency and promoting the adoption of renewable energy.

Autonomous vehicles powered by artificial intelligence have the potential to revolutionise transportation safety, accessibility, and efficacy in the transportation industry. Autonomous vehicles utilise AI algorithms to navigate complex environments, foresee potential dangers, and optimise traffic flow. The widespread adoption of autonomous vehicles has the potential to reduce traffic accidents, improve road safety, and establish more efficient transportation networks that optimise resource utilisation and minimise environmental impact.

The unprecedented capacity of artificial intelligence to process immense amounts of data and detect intricate patterns paves the way for new frontiers of innovation in scientific research, healthcare, environmental monitoring, and other economic sectors. By analysing complex data sets and enabling more precise predictions and diagnoses, artificial intelligence facilitates ground-breaking medical advancements and addresses global challenges such as climate change and pandemics. Precision farming, renewable energy integration, and autonomous vehicles have the potential to revolutionise industries, improve sustainability, and boost economic well-being thanks to the transformative effects of AI in agriculture, energy, and transportation. To maximise the benefits of this transformative technology for the betterment of society as a whole, it is essential to address ethical considerations, promote inclusivity, and ensure responsible governance as we leverage the potential of artificial intelligence.

2. Advancing Healthcare and Improving Quality of Life

The ability of AI to revolutionise healthcare is a pillar of its profound societal impact. By analysing vast medical databases and genomic data, AI-powered systems have the potential to substantially transform healthcare delivery, making it more precise, individualised, and accessible for all.

One of the most significant contributions of AI to healthcare is disease detection and diagnosis. AI algorithms excel at processing complex medical data, including medical images, patient records, and molecular information, in order to identify patterns and subtle indicators that may evade human perception. Thus, AI facilitates earlier disease detection, allowing medical professionals to intervene at earlier phases of illness, when treatments are frequently more effective and less invasive. In the context of cancer detection, for instance, AI-driven tools have demonstrated remarkable accuracy in detecting early indications of malignancies, thereby providing patients with a vital lifeline and increasing their chances of long-term survival.

Beyond diagnostics, AI's potential in healthcare extends to personalised treatment plans. By integrating patient data with medical knowledge from a vast array of sources, AI can identify optimal treatment options based on a patient's unique genetic composition, medical history, and lifestyle. This strategy, known as precision medicine, enables medical practitioners to provide targeted therapies, thereby minimising deleterious side effects and maximising treatment efficacy.

Artificial intelligence expedites the identification of prospective drug candidates in the field of drug discovery. Algorithms powered by artificial intelligence can analyse massive chemical libraries, simulate molecular interactions, and predict drug properties with unprecedented speed and precision. This capability accelerates the drug development process, reduces costs, and increases the likelihood of identifying novel therapeutics for a variety of diseases, including rare and neglected ones.

AI's transformative influence extends beyond traditional healthcare contexts to telemedicine, which bridges gaps in access to medical expertise, especially for underserved and remote communities. Remote consultations are facilitated by diagnostic tools propelled by artificial intelligence, allowing patients to receive timely medical advice and diagnoses from experts located at a distance. This has significant implications for the improvement of healthcare in rural areas and regions with a physician shortage.

In addition, AI plays a crucial role in improving the quality of life for people with disabilities. AI-powered assistive technologies offer innovative solutions to the difficulties confronted by individuals with visual or auditory impairments, motor disabilities, or cognitive limitations. Advanced image recognition and natural language processing capabilities enable artificial intelligence to assist individuals with visual impairments with tasks such as reading text, identifying objects, and navigating their environment. Similarly, speech recognition and text-to-speech technologies powered by artificial intelligence enable individuals with hearing impairments to communicate more effectively. In addition, AI-powered devices and robotics assist individuals with motor disabilities, allowing them to perform daily tasks with greater independence.

In mental health, AI-powered chatbots and virtual therapists provide scalable support, counselling, and early intervention. These AI-powered mental health platforms can provide immediate access to support and resources, thereby reducing the burden on overburdened mental health services and enhancing the overall accessibility of mental healthcare.

As demonstrated, AI's societal impact is driven by its immense potential to revolutionise healthcare. From earlier disease detection and personalised treatment plans to drug discovery and telemedicine, artificial intelligence empowers medical professionals and enhances patient outcomes. In addition, its transformative influence extends to enhancing the quality of life for people with disabilities and providing scalable mental health support. As AI evolves, it is essential to establish a balance between maximising its potential and addressing ethical concerns, ensuring that AI-driven healthcare innovations are deployed responsibly and equitably for the benefit of all members of society.

3. Augmenting Economic Growth and Driving Innovation

There is no denying the transformative potential of artificial intelligence (AI) to stimulate economic development and drive innovation. As AI technologies continue to advance, businesses in a variety of industries are adopting AI-driven solutions to streamline processes, optimise operations, and uncover new insights. The integration of AI across industries paves the way for unprecedented economic output, cost effectiveness, and market responsiveness.

The ability of AI to revolutionise conventional business practises is one of the main factors influencing its effect on economic growth. Technologies powered by artificial intelligence automate repetitive duties, allowing businesses to reallocate human resources to more strategic and creative endeavours. This not only improves overall operational efficiency, but also fosters a more agile and adaptable business environment in which companies can swiftly respond to shifting market demands and emergent opportunities.

The transformative potential of AI extends beyond mere automation because it enables data-driven decision-making. AI algorithms can analyse vast amounts of information in real-time by leveraging the power of big data and advanced analytics, enabling businesses to identify trends, predict consumer behaviour, and gain valuable market insights. With this wealth of information, businesses are able to tailor their strategies and offerings to meet the specific requirements of their customers, thereby increasing customer satisfaction and loyalty.

Moreover, the incorporation of AI into numerous industries fosters an innovation-driving positive feedback loop. As businesses adopt AI technologies to obtain a competitive edge, they unlock new revenue and expansion opportunities. For instance, AI-powered recommendation systems provide individualised product recommendations, thereby increasing cross-selling and upselling opportunities. The resultant increase in sales revenue permits businesses to invest more in AI research and development, thereby fueling the innovation cycle.

AI has a transformative effect on the development of novel business models. The incorporation of AI technologies enables businesses to reimagine their value propositions, resulting in the development of novel products and services that meet the evolving needs of consumers. By providing novel solutions and leveraging network effects to swiftly scale their businesses, AI-powered platforms disrupt conventional industries.

In addition, the rise of AI-driven economic systems increases the demand for AI-specific skills and knowledge. As businesses invest in AI research and development, opportunities arise for data scientists, AI engineers, machine learning specialists, and other AI-related professions. As individuals seek to acquire the skills necessary to participate in an AI-driven economy, this not only drives employment growth but also stimulates the education and training sectors. The symbiotic relationship between AI-driven innovations and economic growth fosters a cycle of innovation that reinforces itself. As businesses employ AI technologies, they gain a competitive advantage, resulting in higher profits and increased investment in AI research and development. This, in turn, promotes further technological advancements and economic growth.

As AI's impact on economic growth continues to develop, it is essential to address prospective challenges and ethical concerns. Concerns regarding data privacy, algorithmic bias, and the potential impact of AI on employment must be addressed to ensure the responsible deployment of AI. To create an AI-driven economic landscape that benefits society as a whole, it is crucial to strike a balance between leveraging AI's transformative potential and resolving these ethical concerns. AI is a transformative force across industries as a result of its undeniable potential to boost economic growth and promote innovation. As businesses adopt AI-driven technologies to streamline operations, obtain market insights, and improve customer experiences, they enter a positive innovation feedback loop, resulting in the creation of novel business models, new revenue streams, and new jobs. As we harness AI's potential to drive economic growth, it is essential that we do so responsibly, addressing ethical concerns and ensuring that the benefits of AI are distributed equitably for the benefit of society.

4. Fostering Inclusive Growth and Reducing Disparities

As the transformative potential of AI becomes increasingly apparent, there is a growing awareness of the need to ensure that its benefits are distributed equitably and promote inclusive growth. Despite the fact that AI-driven economic systems have the potential to drive progress and economic prosperity, there are concerns that, if unfettered, AI adoption could exacerbate existing social inequalities and exacerbate disparities. Despite this, it is crucial to recognise the unprecedented opportunity that AI presents to bridge these gaps and establish a more inclusive and just society.

Prioritising reskilling and upskilling programmes is one of the most effective ways to promote inclusive growth with AI. As AI technologies reshape the employment landscape and render certain skills obsolete, it is crucial to equip the workforce with the skills required to flourish in the changing job market. Investing in comprehensive reskilling and upskilling initiatives prepares individuals to leverage the potential of AI-driven technologies and gain access to new employment opportunities. By providing access to continuous learning and training, societies can equip individuals to transition into AI-relevant positions, thereby reducing unemployment and boosting economic mobility.

Moreover, addressing the digital divide is essential to ensure that all members of society have access to the benefits of AI. Digital infrastructure, internet access, and digital literacy are indispensable for AI-driven economic systems. To close the disparity between digitally connected and underserved communities, therefore, concerted efforts are required. Initiatives that promote digital literacy and facilitate access to affordable and dependable internet services can help balance the playing field, allowing all individuals to participate in an AI-driven economy.

An unwavering commitment to minimising biases and promoting impartiality in AI algorithms is also required for the responsible deployment of AI. Existing societal prejudices can be perpetuated and amplified by the inherent bias in training data, leading to discriminatory outcomes in AI-driven systems. Identifying and mitigating discriminatory patterns is facilitated by AI algorithms that are transparent and subject to rigorous testing for bias. In addition, comprehensive regulatory frameworks must be established to hold AI developers and deployers accountable for ensuring that their systems adhere to ethical guidelines and principles of fairness.

Ethical AI principles are crucial to shaping a more equitable future propelled by AI. These principles prioritise human values, transparency, and individual rights to ensure that artificial intelligence (AI) systems are developed and deployed with society's best interests in mind. Transparency in AI decision-making processes fosters confidence among users and stakeholders, enabling them to comprehend and, when necessary, challenge AI outcomes. In addition, ethical AI principles advocate for human-centered design, in which the development of AI technologies is driven by a profound comprehension of human requirements and societal context. This strategy ensures that AI solutions are tailored to address real-world issues and have a positive social impact.

As discussed, as the transformative potential of AI reshapes economic systems, inclusive development and the reduction of disparities become of paramount importance. By prioritising reskilling and upskilling programmes, bridging the digital divide, minimising biases, and adhering to ethical AI principles, societies can maximise the potential of AI to create a future that is more equitable and just. We can ensure that AI becomes a potent instrument for social progress, economic welfare, and the betterment of all members of society through concerted effort and responsible governance.

To conclude, artificial intelligence is at the vanguard of technological innovation, poised to transform industries, empower individuals, and contribute to the achievement of societal objectives. The transformative potential of AI to fuel advancements in healthcare, scientific research, energy, and transportation, among other fields, is undeniable, with enormous promise to improve human lives and promote economic prosperity. Responsible adoption of AI, governed by ethical principles, ensures that its benefits are shared equitably and sustainably as the world navigates this technological frontier. By leveraging AI to address global challenges, foster inclusive development, and drive innovation, societies can shape a future that maximises AI's potential for the greater good, thereby creating a world where economic prosperity and societal well-being go hand in hand.

Chapter 11: AI and Job Displacement

Artificial Intelligence (AI) has emerged as a transformative force that is reshaping industries, redefining the nature of work itself, and revolutionising business processes. As artificial intelligence (AI) technologies continue to advance at a rapid pace, the implications for employment and job displacement have become the subject of intense scrutiny and discussion. Despite the fact that AI promises unprecedented advances in efficiency, productivity, and innovation, there are legitimate concerns regarding its potential impact on the workforce, with fears of significant job displacement in a variety of industries.

This chapter examines the multifaceted landscape of AI and job displacement, including its effects on employment across various sectors, the role of institutions in managing the transition, and potential strategies for retraining and upskilling the workforce to adapt to the changing job market in the age of AI.

The first section of this chapter discusses the effects of artificial intelligence on employment and job displacement across industries. This section discusses how the incorporation of AI into industries is causing a radical shift in the labour market. Certain tasks and job positions may be disrupted and replaced by AI-powered automation, leading to potential job displacement in traditional sectors. Particularly susceptible to AI-driven automation are industries that rely heavily on repetitive duties, data processing, and manual labour. Among the occupations susceptible to displacement are those in manufacturing, administrative support, customer service, and transportation.

AI creates new job opportunities in emerging disciplines such as data science, machine learning engineering, and AI ethics and governance. As AI technologies become more pervasive, there is a developing need for professionals who can design, implement, and manage AI systems.

The second section discusses the role of institutions in overseeing the transition and assisting displaced employees. Governments, businesses, and educational institutions confront an urgent and complex challenge in managing the workforce transition in the face of AI-driven automation. Effective policies and programmes are required to provide employees displaced by AI-driven automation with support and reemployment opportunities.

Government institutions play a crucial role in formulating policies that strike a balance between technological advancement and social welfare. This requires the development of comprehensive labour market policies that facilitate the reintegration of displaced employees, such as unemployment benefits, job placement services, and financial assistance for retraining programmes. By providing incentives and subsidies, governments can also encourage businesses to invest in retraining and upskilling initiatives.

Businesses are responsible for anticipating and managing the effects of AI-driven workforce automation. This includes undertaking skill-gap analyses and developing retraining and redeployment strategies for workers impacted by automation. Companies that prioritise employee reskilling and upskilling foster a more motivated and adaptable workforce, resulting in increased productivity and creativity.

Educational institutions and training facilities play a crucial role in preparing the workforce for an AI-driven economy. This requires the development of flexible and adaptable training programmes for emerging AI-related employment roles. Collaborations between industry and academia can facilitate the alignment of educational curricula with the changing demands of the labour market, thereby ensuring that the workforce remains relevant and adaptable.

The third section explores potential strategies for retraining and upskilling the workforce in the era of artificial intelligence. To equip employees with the skills required in an AI-driven economy, the workforce transition requires a proactive approach to retraining and upskilling. This necessitates the identification of the most critical skill deficits and the development of targeted training programmes to address them. By emphasising digital literacy, critical thinking, problem-solving, and adaptability, it is possible to increase the workforce's resistance to automation.

Public-private partnerships are crucial to the successful implementation of retraining and upskilling initiatives. By leveraging the expertise and resources of both sectors, such collaborations are able to develop comprehensive and market-responsive training programmes. In the era of AI, lifelong learning initiatives are becoming increasingly important. Encouraging a culture of continuous learning enables employees to embrace opportunities for skill development throughout their careers, ensuring that they remain competitive and receptive to technological advances.

In conclusion, the rise of AI has the potential to have a significant impact on employment, with job displacement in certain industries being a major concern. Nevertheless, this transformative technology also generates new employment opportunities and boosts productivity and creativity. Governments, businesses, and educational institutions must work together to provide assistance, retraining, and upskilling opportunities for displaced workers in order to effectively manage the workforce transition. By investing in comprehensive labour market policies, fostering public-private partnerships, and promoting lifelong learning, societies can navigate the challenges posed by AI-driven automation and leverage its potential to create a workforce that thrives in the ever-changing AI era landscape. We can ensure that AI-driven advancements in the employment market are beneficial to individuals, industries, and the global economy by employing strategic planning and sound governance.

The effects of AI on employment and job displacement in various industries

The effects of artificial intelligence on employment and job displacement in various industries are extensive and multifaceted. As AI technologies continue to advance, the potential displacement of human employees by automated systems is becoming a growing concern. The ability of AI-powered automation to perform routine-based tasks, data analysis, and decision-making with increasing accuracy and efficiency is reshaping the employment market in a number of industries.

In industries that significantly rely on repetitive and predictable tasks, AI-driven automation is especially influential. As an example, manufacturing industries confront the possibility of increased robotization and AI-powered assembly lines, which can replace human workers in tasks like assembly, welding, and quality control. Self-checkout systems and AI-powered inventory management may reduce the need for cashiers and stock employees in the retail industry. Moreover, administrative support roles, such as data input and customer service, are vulnerable to AI-driven automation displacement. Natural language processing and chatbot technologies are becoming more adept at managing customer inquiries and providing support, potentially displacing a number of customer service positions.

While AI-driven automation can displace workers in certain industries, it is essential to note that AI also generates new employment opportunities. As more industries incorporate AI technologies, there is an increasing demand for professionals who can design, implement, and manage AI systems. AI has generated a variety of new occupations, including data scientists, AI engineers, machine learning specialists, and AI ethicists.

As with any technological revolution, the effects of AI on employment are complex and vary by industry and job function. Some jobs may be entirely replaced, while others may endure transformations necessitating the collaboration of humans and AI. It is imperative that societies prepare for this shift in the labour market by investing in education, training, and reskilling programmes to ensure that the workforce is adaptable and endowed with the necessary skills to thrive in an AI-driven economy.Effects of AI on Employment and Job Displacement in Various Industries:

1. Manufacturing Industry

The manufacturing sector is one of the industries most affected by AI-driven automation. As robotics and artificial intelligence (AI) technologies advance, manufacturers are increasingly employing automated systems to streamline production processes and increase efficiency. With their ability to perform repetitive tasks with precision and consistency, robots endowed with AI algorithms are ideally suited for assembly line work, welding, and quality control.

While this automation increases manufacturers' productivity and lowers their expenses, it also raises concerns about job displacement. Numerous manual labourers and assembly-line employees may be at risk of being replaced by machinery. This change necessitates workforce adaptation and the acquisition of new skills in order to remain pertinent in the evolving manufacturing landscape. Technicians and engineers specialising in robotics and artificial intelligence (AI) maintenance and programming are in high demand, as businesses seek professionals capable of supervising and optimising automated systems.

2. Retail Industry

The retail industry is undergoing a significant transformation as a result of AI-driven automation, especially in customer service. With the introduction of natural language processing and chatbot technologies, AI-powered customer service systems have become more adept at comprehending and responding to consumer inquiries. Self-service checkout is gaining prominence in retail stores, reducing the need for cashiers.

While AI-powered customer support systems can improve customer experiences and reduce operational costs for retailers, they may result in the loss of some retail employment. The roles of cashiers and customer service representatives may be redefined or eliminated by AI-powered systems. However, new opportunities are emerging for those who are able to design, implement, and maintain these AI systems. In addition, the value of retail analytics specialists who can interpret customer data and utilise AI-driven insights to enhance marketing strategies and customer targeting is rising.

3. Transportation Industry

Autonomous vehicles place the transportation industry at the vanguard of AI-driven disruptions. Transportation networks and logistics are being revolutionised by AI-powered technologies, which may result in changes to employment patterns. As self-driving vehicles become a reality, truck drivers, for example, may experience job loss.

Nevertheless, the rise of autonomous vehicles creates opportunities for a new generation of employees who specialise in autonomous vehicle design, testing, and regulation. Moreover, there is a growing demand for fleet managers and transportation analysts who can utilise AI-powered data analytics to optimise logistics and reduce operational costs. In addition, the transition towards electric and autonomous vehicles increases the demand for skilled labour in the renewable energy and electric vehicle maintenance industries.

4. Administrative and White-collar Jobs

Administrative and white-collar positions that involve data entry, data processing, and routine decision-making are also being impacted by AI-driven automation. Software powered by AI is capable of processing massive datasets and conducting complex analyses at incredible speeds, potentially displacing certain administrative duties.

Administrative assistants and data entry clerks may experience job displacement as administrative tasks become increasingly automated. Nonetheless, this creates opportunities for those with expertise in AI, data analytics, and programming. Data scientists and AI specialists are becoming indispensable to businesses as their ability to interpret and make decisions based on AI-generated insights drives business strategies and innovation.

5. Healthcare Industry

With the incorporation of AI technologies, the healthcare industry is undergoing a substantial transformation. Tools powered by AI can analyse vast amounts of medical data, aid in diagnosis, and accurately foretell patient outcomes. AI-powered medical imaging systems, for instance, can assist radiologists in detecting abnormalities in medical images, thereby reducing the need for manual image analysis.

While AI in healthcare has the potential to enhance diagnostic accuracy and patient outcomes, there are concerns that certain healthcare roles will be eliminated. As AI systems take on tasks such as medical imaging analysis and pattern recognition, the roles and responsibilities of radiologists and pathologists may alter.

Nevertheless, AI also creates new employment opportunities in the healthcare industry. AI specialists and data scientists are indispensable to the development and maintenance of AI-powered healthcare systems. In addition, healthcare professionals with knowledge of AI and data analytics are in high demand to interpret AI-generated insights and collaborate with AI systems to provide personalised patient care.

6. Financial Services Industry

Enhancing data analysis, risk assessment, and fraud detection, AI is transforming the financial services industry. AI algorithms can analyse financial data faster and on a larger scale than humans, resulting in enhanced decision-making and risk management.

In the financial services industry, AI-driven automation may affect jobs such as data entry, data analysis, and customer service. Routine duties such as transaction processing and customer inquiries can be automated, potentially resulting in job loss.

However, the development of AI also creates new opportunities in the financial services industry. Experts in data science and artificial intelligence are in high demand for developing complex algorithms for financial analysis, trading, and risk modelling. Moreover, AI-powered financial advisors and chatbots are emerging, necessitating the employment of professionals who can incorporate AI technologies into personalised financial planning.

7. Education Sector

The impact of AI on education is multifaceted. Adaptive learning platforms can personalise educational content and provide students with individualised learning experiences. Additionally, chatbots and virtual assistants powered by AI offer assistance and respond to student inquiries, reducing the need for human intervention in certain administrative and support roles.

Administrative positions, such as data entry and administrative support, may be displaced as a result of the incorporation of AI in education. However, new opportunities present themselves in the field of educational technology (EdTech) development, where AI experts and educational content developers collaborate to design innovative and personalised learning solutions.

8. Legal Industry

By automating document review, contract analysis, and legal research, AI is leaving its impact on the legal industry. Platforms powered by AI can analyse vast quantities of legal documents, resulting in increased productivity and decreased time spent on repetitive duties.

Due to AI-driven automation, the roles of paralegals and legal assistants who customarily handle document review and legal research may change in the legal profession. However, AI also presents new opportunities for legal professionals with expertise in AI and data analytics, as they can use AI-generated insights to provide clients with more informed legal advice and to develop strategies.

In conclusion, the effects of artificial intelligence on employment and job displacement vary across industries, with some sectors undergoing substantial changes due to AI-driven automation. AI creates new opportunities in emerging disciplines, such as data science, AI development, and EdTech, while displacing certain job roles. To manage the workforce transition in the era of artificial intelligence, it is essential to invest in reskilling and upskilling programmes to equip the workforce with the skills required by the changing job market. Governments, businesses, and educational institutions must collaborate to ensure that individuals are prepared to respond to the evolving employment landscape and capitalise on the opportunities AI technologies present. Moreover, responsible AI adoption and ethical considerations are essential for ensuring a future in which AI-driven advancements benefit both industries and the workforce, fostering a society in which AI is utilised to boost productivity, innovation, and economic welfare while minimising potential negative effects on employment.

The role of institutions in managing the transition and providing support for displaced workers

In navigating the workforce challenges posed by AI-driven automation, the role of institutions in managing the transition and providing assistance to displaced employees is crucial. Institutions such as governments, businesses, educational organisations, and labour unions play crucial roles in supporting workers through this transition and ensuring a smooth and equitable adaptation to the changing employment landscape as the job market evolves with the incorporation of AI technologies.

1. Government Institutions

Indeed, government institutions play a central role in defining responses to the challenges posed by AI-driven workforce automation. Governments are tasked with ensuring that the benefits of AI are balanced with the welfare of labourers and society as a whole as AI technologies continue to advance. Let's delve into the specifics and offer additional analysis:

The Comprehensive Labour Market Policies are one solution. Comprehensive labour market policies are required to assist employees who are at risk of losing their jobs due to AI-driven automation. In addition to unemployment benefits, job placement services, and financial assistance for retraining programmes, governments should prioritise the development of flexible and adaptable policies that cater to the particular requirements of displaced workers. This involves identifying the industries most impacted by the implementation of AI and customising assistance programmes to facilitate their reintegration into the labour market.

Moreover, investments in reskilling and upskilling initiatives should not be restricted to those directly impacted by job displacement. Governments should foster a culture of lifelong learning, promoting continuous education and upskilling opportunities for all employees to ensure their adaptability in an ever-changing employment environment.

Encouraging Business Investment in Retraining and Upskilling is another solution. Governments must actively encourage corporations to invest in rehabilitation and upskilling programmes. In addition to tax incentives and subsidies, governments may also offer grants or matching funds to businesses that engage in comprehensive employee training initiatives. It is possible to cultivate public-private partnerships in order to jointly design and implement retraining programmes that are aligned with industry needs and address emerging skill requirements resulting from AI adoption.

In addition, governments should actively engage with businesses to comprehend their AI adoption strategies and evaluate their workforce's potential effects. Governments can develop proactive policies and programmes that anticipate the changing job market and the skills required in an AI-driven economy by collaborating closely with industry leaders.

A third solution could be the Implementation of Responsible AI Regulation. To ensure that AI-driven job displacement is handled ethically and equitably, the implementation of AI must be subject to stringent oversight. Transparent and accountable AI algorithms are necessary for establishing public confidence in AI systems. Governments should mandate transparency in AI decision-making processes so that individuals can comprehend how AI algorithms arrive at particular conclusions. This transparency not only promotes accountability, but also permits individuals to challenge decisions when necessary.

Ethical principles that prioritise fairness, equality, and nondiscrimination are essential for guiding the development and deployment of AI technologies in a responsible manner. Governments can establish advisory committees composed of AI ethics, labour rights, and social impact experts to provide guidance on ethical AI practises.

The Addressing Socioeconomic Implications is a final option. The potential socioeconomic consequences of AI-driven employment displacement are substantial. Governments must anticipate and address the effects of artificial intelligence on income distribution, social equality, and opportunity access. This may necessitate a reevaluation of social safety nets, welfare programmes, and tax policies to accommodate the shifting nature of the workforce.

To support workers in an AI-driven economy, policymakers should consider innovative approaches, such as a universal basic income or portable benefits untethered to traditional employment arrangements. In addition, governments can foster partnerships with academic institutions to develop targeted educational programmes that equip workers with the skills necessary to flourish in the era of artificial intelligence.

Government institutions play a crucial role in regulating the effects of artificial intelligence on employment and job displacement, as is evident. Governments can cultivate a supportive environment for workers and businesses by designing comprehensive labour market policies, encouraging business investment in retraining and upskilling, and regulating AI implementation in a responsible manner. Proactive measures that prioritise ethical considerations and resolve socioeconomic implications can lead to a more inclusive and equitable transition in the age of AI, ensuring that all members of society reap the benefits of technological advancements.

2. Businesses

In the face of AI-driven automation, businesses play a crucial role in overseeing the workforce transition. As early adopters of AI technologies, businesses have the opportunity to create a positive and long-lasting impact on their employees and the larger workforce. Let's delve into the specifics and offer additional analysis:

The primary tactic is proactive workforce planning. Businesses that take a proactive approach to workforce planning are better able to adapt to the changes brought about by AI-driven automation. Businesses can identify skill gaps and emerging employment roles if they anticipate the impact of AI on their workforce. This foresight enables them to develop targeted training and upskilling programmes that are aligned with future employment demands, ensuring that employees have the skills necessary to thrive in an AI-driven economy. Effective workforce planning also involves fostering an organization-wide ethos of continuous learning and adaptability. Businesses that prioritise employee development and foster a growth mindset produce a workforce that is more adaptable and open to change.

Investing in Training and Upskilling Initiatives is another strategy. Investing in training and upskilling initiatives to prepare the workforce for AI adoption is a strategic move for businesses. Instead of focusing exclusively on recruiting new talent, businesses can invest in developing the potential of their current workforce. Businesses demonstrate their commitment to employee development and job security by providing opportunities for continuous learning and skill development.

Training programmes for employees should go beyond traditional skill development and take into account the interdisciplinarity of AI-driven technologies. For instance, fostering cross-functional collaboration between technical and non-technical teams can improve the incorporation of AI in numerous business aspects, resulting in more innovative solutions and business processes.

A third strategy could be the Implementation of Ethical and Responsible AI. Businesses are obligated to implement AI in an ethical and responsible manner in order to minimise negative effects on their employees. Instead of viewing AI as a job-replacement tool, businesses can use AI technologies to augment existing job positions and boost human productivity.

Business executives should prioritise the well-being of their employees and consider the human element in AI-driven processes. This includes transparent communication regarding AI's function in the organisation and its potential impact on job roles. Transparency in AI decision-making processes inspires confidence and promotes collaboration between AI systems and human employees. By responsibly integrating AI technologies into the workforce, businesses can create a more harmonious work environment in which employees and AI systems collaborate to accomplish common goals.

Therefore, businesses play a crucial role in shaping the transition of the workforce in the era of AI. Businesses can create an AI-ready workforce by employing proactive workforce planning, investing in training and upskilling initiatives, and implementing AI technologies in a responsible manner. Ethical considerations and a focus on human-centric AI implementation foster a collaborative and productive work environment in which employees and AI systems drive innovation and success in tandem.

3. Educational Institutions

Educational institutions play a crucial role in preparing the workforce for the opportunities and challenges presented by an AI-driven economy. To accomplish this, they must adapt their curricula to include AI-related fields such as machine learning, data science, and artificial intelligence, aligning their educational programmes with the needs of the real-world labour market. Collaboration with industry and businesses is essential for obtaining insights into emerging technologies and industry trends, thereby exposing students to cutting-edge AI applications and practises.

To equip individuals with the pertinent skills demanded by the AI-driven job market, it is necessary to enrol in training programmes that offer specialised AI-focused education. From introductory courses for novices to advanced training for seasoned professionals, these programmes are designed to accommodate a variety of skill levels and job functions.

It is essential to promote a culture of perpetual learning through initiatives in this area. This enables professionals to remain abreast of AI developments and embrace opportunities for skill enhancement throughout their careers. In addition to collaborating with businesses to offer customised training programmes that address specific business requirements related to AI adoption, educational institutions may also offer such programmes.

By remaining adaptable and receptive to changing trends, educational institutions can close the skills gap and ensure that graduates are well-equipped to flourish in the age of artificial intelligence. Through their efforts, educational institutions cultivate a workforce that is adaptable and resilient in the face of technological advancements, thereby moulding a future in which individuals can seize the opportunities and overcome the obstacles presented by AI-driven transformations.

4. Labor Unions

In the face of AI-driven automation, labour unions play a vital role in advocating for the rights and interests of workers. As AI technologies transform industries and alter job functions, labour unions play a crucial role in ensuring the well-being of employees during workforce transitions. These transitions frequently involve redundancies, reorganisations, and job displacement, creating uncertainty for employees and their families. Unions negotiate with employers to secure equitable treatment for displaced workers, ensuring that they receive adequate severance packages, benefits, and assistance with job transition.

In addition to addressing immediate issues, labour unions work to maintain equitable labour practises in the context of AI implementation. They advocate for ethical and transparent AI decision-making processes to prevent discriminatory algorithms and practises that could be detrimental to the interests of employees. By actively engaging with employers, labour unions contribute to the creation of an environment in which AI technologies are incorporated in a manner that prioritises the rights and welfare of workers.

Moreover, labour unions support retraining and reskilling programmes for displaced employees. They devise and implement effective initiatives that equip workers with the skills necessary to transition to new job roles and industries in collaboration with businesses. These retraining programmes are essential for empowering workers to adapt to a shifting employment landscape and maintain their competitiveness in an AI-driven economy.

A collaborative approach between labour unions and corporations goes beyond addressing the urgent obstacles of workforce transition. Cooperative efforts in AI-driven job design enable employees to actively shape their work environment despite technological advancements. By involving employees in the development and implementation of AI technologies, businesses can benefit from their insights and expertise while ensuring that the technology enhances rather than replaces existing job responsibilities.

This collaborative approach fosters a more inclusive and supportive workplace, where employees feel valued and empowered in the face of AI-driven change. It fosters a sense of shared responsibility and dedication to employees' interests. As businesses and labour unions collaborate to navigate the complexities of AI implementation, they pave the way for a more equitable and sustainable AI-driven future, where workers' rights are protected and the workforce is prepared to embrace the opportunities and challenges of the changing job market.

As seen, labour unions play an indispensable role in the context of AI-driven automation in advocating for employees' rights and interests. Their efforts to negotiate equitable treatment, support rehabilitation programmes, and promote a collaborative approach to technology adoption contribute to a more diverse and resilient workforce. In the era of AI-driven advancements, labour unions play a crucial role in shaping policies and practises that prioritise employees' welfare through collaboration with businesses and government institutions.

In conclusion, the era of artificial intelligence, institutions play crucial roles in managing the workforce transition and assisting displaced workers. Governments, businesses, educational institutions, and labour unions must collaborate to ensure that individuals are prepared to respond to the changing job market and capitalise on the opportunities AI technologies present. Effective policies, responsible incorporation of AI, and investment in education and training programmes are required to equip the workforce with the skills demanded by a dynamic labour market. By prioritising ethical considerations and a proactive approach to workforce planning, institutions can foster a future in which AI-driven advancements benefit industries and the workforce, resulting in a society that is more resilient, adaptable, and inclusive.

Potential strategies for retraining and upskilling the workforce in the age of AI

In the era of artificial intelligence, retraining and upskilling the workforce are crucial strategies for equipping individuals with the skills necessary to thrive in a swiftly changing job market. As artificial intelligence (AI) technologies continue to disrupt traditional employment roles, workers must adapt to the shifting demands of the digital economy. This requires a comprehensive approach that includes targeted training programmes, initiatives for lifelong learning, reskilling for changing industries, apprenticeship and on-the-job training, and industry-academia collaboration.

Targeted training programmes are designed to address specific skill gaps and emerging employment roles influenced by the adoption of artificial intelligence. By identifying the industries and sectors most impacted by AI-driven automation, policymakers and educational institutions can tailor training initiatives to meet the evolving demands of these labour markets. For instance, training programmes can emphasise AI-related disciplines, data science, coding, and other in-demand technical skills across industries. Simultaneously, non-technical skills such as critical thinking, problem resolution, and creativity should be emphasised in order to complement AI-driven technologies effectively.

It is essential to promote initiatives for continuous learning to ensure that the workforce remains adaptable to technological advances. Rather than viewing education as a one-time event, a culture of continuous learning should be cultivated to encourage individuals to take advantage of opportunities to advance their skills throughout their careers. Online courses, seminars, and webinars provide convenient and adaptable opportunities to acquire new skills and knowledge. Moreover, partnerships between educational institutions, businesses, and industry associations can facilitate the deliverance of pertinent and timely learning opportunities, allowing workers to remain competitive in an AI-driven employment landscape.

As the adoption of AI transforms industries, reskilling initiatives are crucial to assisting employees in their transition into new fields. For example, employees displaced from traditional manufacturing positions may benefit from retraining programmes that equip them with the skills required in emerging industries such as renewable energy or digital marketing. Government-funded reskilling programmes can provide financial assistance to employees undergoing career transitions, making it easier for them to pursue new opportunities.

Apprenticeship and on-the-job training programmes provide highly effective hands-on learning opportunities for developing practical skills. Individuals can acquire relevant experience while learning directly from seasoned professionals in their field through these programmes. Encouraging businesses to invest in apprenticeship and on-the-job training programmes can strengthen the talent pipeline and ensure that the workforce has the necessary AI-integration skills.

Collaboration between academia and industry is required for the development and delivery of current and relevant training programmes. Industry partners can provide insight into the most recent technological developments and skill requirements, allowing educational institutions to modify their curricula accordingly. In addition, industry-academic partnerships can result in internship and mentoring opportunities, allowing students and employees to gain practical experience in AI-driven environments. This exposure to the actual world bridges the gap between theoretical knowledge and practical applications.

Policymakers, educational institutions, businesses, and labour unions can ensure that workers are adequately prepared for the challenges and opportunities presented by an AI-driven economy by investing in these strategies. In doing so, they contribute to a more resilient and adaptable workforce, thereby shaping a future in which individuals can flourish in a world driven by AI that is swiftly changing. In addition to the strategies mentioned earlier, several emerging research and ideas can further enhance the effectiveness of retraining and upskilling the workforce in the age of AI:

Personalised Learning Paths: Tailoring training programmes to individual learning styles and skill levels can substantially increase the effectiveness of upskilling efforts. Adaptive learning platforms enabled by AI can analyse the progress and preferences of learners, allowing for the delivery of personalised content and pacing. This strategy increases worker engagement and ensures that they acquire the most pertinent skills for their specific career objectives.

Virtual Reality (VR) and Augmented Reality (AR) Training: By utilising VR and AR technologies, immersive training experiences that simulate real-world scenarios can be created. For example, industries such as healthcare, manufacturing, and engineering can benefit from VR/AR simulations that enable employees to practise complex procedures and problem-solving techniques. The hands-on experience acquired from these simulations can accelerate the development of skills and confidence.

While technical skills are crucial in an AI-driven economy, the importance of interpersonal skills should not be overlooked. In workplaces where human-AI collaboration is common, empathy, emotional intelligence, adaptability, and originality are becoming increasingly valuable. Integrating reskilling programmes that emphasise the development of these skills can facilitate more harmonious human-machine interactions and provide employees with a competitive advantage.

Mentorship and Reverse Mentoring: It is highly advantageous to establish mentorship programmes that combine experienced workers with those undergoing upskilling. The guidance and insights provided by mentors are invaluable for navigating career transitions and effectively utilising new skills. In addition, the concept of reverse mentoring, in which junior employees mentor senior colleagues on tech-savvy practises and digital trends, can establish a two-way learning environment and encourage intergenerational collaboration.

Utilising social learning networks and communities of practise can facilitate knowledge sharing and collaboration among employees. Online platforms that foster interaction between students and subject matter experts permit real-time feedback, problem-solving, and the exchange of ideas. These networks can play a crucial role in fostering a culture of continuous development within organisations by fostering a learning ecosystem.

To ensure the optimal alignment of reskilled workers with job openings, AI can be used to match newly acquired skills with in-demand roles. By analysing job postings and employee skill profiles, AI algorithms can identify potential connections, providing job seekers and employers with valuable insights. This approach to skill matching streamlines the job search process for reskilled workers, resulting to a more seamless integration into the labour market.

Accessible retraining and upskilling opportunities must be made available to all segments of the population in order to foster inclusive growth. Governments and educational institutions are obligated to prioritise initiatives that address digital literacy disparities and provide assistance to underserved communities. Societies can mitigate inequalities exacerbated by AI-driven economic transformations by providing equal access to education and resources.

In conclusion, the continuous development of AI technologies necessitates robust and creative approaches to workforce retraining and skill enhancement. Personalised learning paths, VR/AR training, and a focus on soft skills are just a few ways that these strategies can be improved. In addition, mentorship programmes, social learning networks, AI-driven skill matching, and inclusive learning access contribute to a comprehensive and future-ready workforce. Policymakers, educational institutions, businesses, and labour unions can proactively shape a resilient and adaptable workforce capable of prospering in an AI-driven world by embracing this new research and ideas.

Chapter 12: AI and Income Inequality

Few phenomena have captivated the collective imagination and intrigue as profoundly as artificial intelligence (AI) in the history of technological advancement. With its promise of unprecedented efficiency, innovation, and transformative potential, AI has rapidly established a foothold in numerous sectors of the global economy. AI has ushered in a new era of possibilities, reviving industries spanning from healthcare and finance to transportation and manufacturing.

Nonetheless, as the trajectory of AI continues to ascend, a complex and multifaceted challenge emerges, one that compels us to consider the potential repercussions of its proliferation. The pervasive issue of income inequality, which has simmered beneath the surface of societal consciousness for decades, now intersects with the momentum of AI in profound and nuanced ways. This chapter undertakes an exploratory journey into the intricate relationship between AI adoption and income inequality, dissecting the mechanisms through which AI exerts its influence, the role of institutions in shaping outcomes, and the policy interventions that may pave the way for a more equitable future.

The Relationship between AI Adoption and Income Inequality

As societies incorporate AI into their economic infrastructure, the distribution of income undergoes a remarkable transformation. The initial appeal of artificial intelligence stems from its potential to increase productivity, streamline operations, and generate novel avenues for economic development. However, the implementation's broader implications are not uniform. While it is undeniable that AI has the potential to create new employment and industries, it also has the potential to exacerbate existing disparities between labour and capital, skillsets, and geographic regions. This section explores the complex relationship between AI's disruptive potential and the intricate fabric of income inequality, casting light on the mechanisms underlying its impact.

The Role of Institutions in Mitigating Negative Impacts

The importance of institutions in shaping the outcomes of AI adoption cannot be overstated in a world increasingly characterised by the combination of human ingenuity and machine intelligence. Governments, regulatory bodies, educational institutions, and labour organisations play a crucial role in mitigating the adverse effects of AI-induced income inequality. Institutions have the ability to channel the momentum of AI towards a more inclusive and equitable future through the formulation of thoughtful policies, the implementation of forward-thinking regulations, and the promotion of continuous learning. This section describes the main actors and mechanisms that can influence the trajectory of income distribution in the age of artificial intelligence.

Potential Policy Interventions to Address the Widening Income Gap

A multifaceted strategy is required to combat the widening income disparity, one that draws inspiration from potential policy interventions aimed at recalibrating the scales of economic equity. From the implementation of universal basic income to the promotion of reskilling and upskilling initiatives, policy interventions hold the potential to steer AI's effect on income distribution in a way that is beneficial to society as a whole. By fostering an environment that encourages innovation, social mobility, and equal access to opportunities, policymakers can leverage AI's potential while mitigating its unintended effects. This section examines a spectrum of policy pathways that can pave the way for a future in which AI is a driver of equitable development.

As AI advances inexorably, an intricate dance between technological innovation and socioeconomic dynamics transpires on a global scale. The sections that follow explore each facet of this story, illuminating the intricate threads that connect AI and income inequality. In exploring the profound interplay between these forces, we undertake a mission not only to comprehend their complex dynamics, but also to harness AI's potential as a catalyst for transformative change — an agent that, when guided by thoughtful institutions and enlightened policies, can help forge a more just and inclusive future.

12.1. The relationship between AI adoption and income inequality

The incorporation of Artificial Intelligence (AI) into a variety of economic sectors has resulted in significant advancements and transformative changes. Nonetheless, this rapid technological advancement has complex socioeconomic ramifications, especially in the realms of income distribution and inequality. The relationship between AI adoption and income inequality is multifaceted and influenced by a complex web of interconnected factors. In this in-depth analysis, we explore the mechanisms, drivers, and consequences that define the evolving dynamics between AI and income inequality.

Mechanisms Underpinning the Relationship

1. **Labor Market Disruption**

Automation and robotics powered by artificial intelligence have surfaced as transformative forces reshaping the modern labour market. The potential for these technologies to displace jobs, especially those involving routine and repetitive activities, has significant implications for income distribution and socioeconomic dynamics. A closer look at this phenomenon exposes a complex environment characterised by intricate interactions, varying effects, and potential mitigation strategies.

At its foundation, AI-powered automation has the potential to streamline processes and increase industry-wide efficiency. Previously laborious and time-consuming tasks can now be performed quickly and precisely by machines with cognitive capabilities. This innovation offers indisputable advantages in terms of increased productivity, decreased costs, and accelerated production cycles. However, the flip side of this development is the displacement of human employees, particularly those who perform repetitive tasks and follow standard procedures.

This displacement has far-reaching consequences, particularly for low- and middle-skilled employees who frequently perform routine tasks amenable to automation. These workers confront a double whammy: job losses and stagnant wages. As AI technologies assume routine responsibilities, positions formerly held by humans are progressively eliminated, resulting in unemployment and economic insecurity. Concurrently, the increased availability of automated solutions can reduce the demand for human labour in these fields, exerting downward pressure on wages and limiting income development for those who are able to maintain their jobs.

This phenomenon, known as skill-biased technological change, exacerbates wage disparities between employees with varying levels of skill. High-skilled employees who are able to design, implement, and supervise AI systems are better positioned to adapt to the shifting environment and reap the benefits of technological advances. Their ability to interact with and utilise the potential of AI technologies enables them to remain competitive and relevant in a job market that is constantly evolving. On the opposite end of the spectrum, low- and middle-skilled employees are at a disadvantage because they frequently lack the necessary skills to navigate this new terrain. As a result, the wage disparity between these distinct groups widens, which contributes to the worsening of income inequality.

To address these obstacles and mitigate the negative effects of AI-driven labour market disruption, multifaceted strategies are essential. Individuals can maintain their competitiveness and adaptability by investing in education and training programmes that equip employees with the skills required by an AI-enhanced economy. To ensure that the workforce remains resilient in the face of technological disruption, it is crucial to foster a culture of continuous learning and skill development. In addition, policies designed to promote job transitions, social safety nets, and support mechanisms can provide a buffer for workers negatively impacted by automation, mitigating the impact on their livelihoods and income stability.

Consequently, the disruption brought about by AI-powered automation presents a complex interplay of challenges and opportunities in the labour market. Education, training, and well-considered policy interventions can pave the way for a more equitable and inclusive future, despite the high likelihood of job displacement and wage stagnation. By leveraging the transformative potential of AI while protecting the interests of all segments of society, the path to mitigating income inequality in an era of technological advancement becomes more feasible.

2. Skill Polarization

The incorporation of Artificial Intelligence (AI) into the fabric of the labour market has led to a dynamic shift in the demand for skills, resulting in a phenomenon known as skill polarisation. This intricate process reveals a multifaceted landscape in which the fortunes of high-skilled and low-skilled workers diverge, resulting in complex repercussions for income distribution, economic mobility, and social cohesion.

Adoption of artificial intelligence heralds in an era in which technical expertise and specialised knowledge are increasingly valued commodities. Those with the expertise to design, implement, and manage AI technologies are in an advantageous position. They are at the vanguard of the technological revolution due to their ability to navigate complex AI systems, decipher complex algorithms, and utilise data-driven insights. As industries and organisations adopt AI-driven efficiencies, these experienced professionals become innovation catalysts, driving productivity gains and influencing strategic decision-making processes.

The dynamics of the labour market are cognizant of this increase in demand for highly competent workers. In actuality, it manifests as wage increases and robust income growth. High-skilled individuals, armed with the competencies to leverage the potential of AI, enjoy compensation and career advancement. As the demand for their specialised skills exceeds the supply, competitive forces increase their earnings, resulting in a concentration of economic gains in this segment of the labour force.

In contrast, the narrative for low-skilled employees reveals a path characterised by diminishing opportunities and wage stagnation. As AI technologies assume centre stage, positions that once comprised a substantial portion of the labour market are susceptible to displacement or reorganisation. These roles, which are frequently characterised by routine and repetitive duties, bear the brunt of the changes brought about by automation. Low-skilled employees are confronted with fewer employment opportunities and a shrinking job market, where positions requiring minimal technical expertise are becoming increasingly scarce.

In tandem with diminished employment opportunities, a lack of engagement with AI systems can result in wage stagnation for low-skilled employees. The transition in labour market demand towards AI-relevant skills can cause a mismatch between the capabilities of the labour force and the requirements of a technology-driven economy. As a result, the earning potential of low-skilled employees may stagnate or decline, perpetuating income disparities and limiting their access to economic advancement.

To navigate the landscape of AI-driven skill polarisation, a comprehensive approach encompassing education, training, and policy interventions is required. By providing low-skilled employees with opportunities for upskilling and reskilling, it is possible to equip them with the skills necessary to interact with AI technologies and open up new employment opportunities. In addition, fostering a culture of continuous learning can enable individuals to adapt to changing labour market demands, ensuring that they remain relevant and competitive in an AI-enhanced economy.

The trajectory of skill polarisation in the context of AI adoption illustrates the complex relationship between technological advancement and income distribution. While high-skilled employees ride the demand and growth wave, their low-skilled counterparts must adapt and survive in an ever-changing environment. Societies can aspire for a balance that bridges skill gaps and cultivates a more inclusive and equitable economic future by making strategic investments in education, training, and policies that promote equitable access to AI-driven opportunities.

3. **Concentration of Economic Gains**

The widespread adoption of Artificial Intelligence (AI) heralds in a paradigm shift in the distribution of economic gains, aptly referred to as the concentration of economic gains. This intricate aspect of the AI revolution shines a light on the distribution of wealth within specific industries, revealing the intricate interweaving of opportunity, wealth, and income inequality.

At its core, AI adoption amplifies growth and profitability in industries that enthusiastically implement AI technologies. Industries that leverage the power of AI to drive efficiencies, optimise operations, and extract insights from enormous data repositories experience a productivity and innovation increase. As vehicles of economic development, these AI-driven industries become centres of accelerated growth, allowing them to outpace their counterparts in the conventional economy.

Nonetheless, this meteoric rise in certain industries ushers in a harsh reality: the concentration of economic advantages. The benefits of this development, which is enabled by AI-driven efficiencies, are not distributed uniformly throughout society. Rather, they accrue to a limited group of individuals who are uniquely positioned to take advantage of the opportunities presented by AI technologies. This unequal distribution of economic prosperity exacerbates existing income disparities, creating a chasm between those who have access to AI-driven avenues of advancement and those who are marginalised.

This concentration has far-reaching and multifaceted repercussions. For those with access to AI-driven opportunities, the ascent is marked by increased earning potential, broader career prospects, and greater wealth accumulation. As they navigate industries enabled by AI technologies, these individuals experience an improvement in their standard of living and socioeconomic standing as a result of the economic windfall.

Individuals and communities that lack access to AI-driven industries confront a formidable obstacle. The limited availability of AI-enhanced opportunities confines them to industries that may remain unaffected by the AI revolution or have delayed adoption rates. This divergence in economic trajectories can exacerbate income disparities, with those outside the AI-driven growth sphere experiencing stagnant wages, restricted career mobility, and diminished opportunities for financial advancement.

To address the concentration of economic advantages generated by AI, a concerted effort to democratise AI-related opportunities is required. Individuals can be empowered to transition into sectors that utilise AI technologies if policies promote equitable access to education and training in AI-related skills. Moreover, promoting an environment of innovation and entrepreneurship across diverse communities can facilitate the diffusion of AI-driven growth, resulting in a more equitable distribution of economic prosperity.

The landscape of income distribution and inequality is shaped by the intricate interaction between AI adoption and economic gain concentration. As AI technologies reshape economic trajectories, the challenge is to create a future in which growth dividends are accessible to all sectors of society. By eliminating entry barriers, fostering inclusive innovation, and implementing policies that reconcile disparities, societies can work towards an equitable distribution of the opportunities and benefits provided by the AI revolution.

4. Digital Divide

The arrival of the AI era brings with it transformative opportunities, but also reveals a digital divide that may exacerbate existing socioeconomic disparities. The digital divide, a complex consequence of Artificial Intelligence (AI) integration, arises as a multifaceted challenge that interweaves issues of technological infrastructure, digital literacy, and access to economic opportunities. Understanding the complexities of this divide is necessary for navigating the complex relationship between AI adoption and income inequality.

Integrating AI is fundamentally dependent on a robust technological infrastructure and a foundation of digital literacy. The ability to engage with AI technologies, utilise data-driven insights, and employ the power of automation is contingent upon having access to the required tools and skills. However, the stark reality is that not all individuals and communities have equal access to and proficiency with technology.

Socioeconomic disparities, which are frequently entrenched in factors such as income, education, and location, play a crucial role in perpetuating the digital divide. In a landscape dominated by AI, individuals and communities without access to sophisticated technological infrastructure are at a disadvantage. They are unable to take advantage of the opportunities presented by AI technologies without the necessary hardware, software, and high-speed internet connection.

In addition, digital literacy emerges as a critical factor in bridging or widening the divide. The ability to comprehend, navigate, and utilise AI-related tools and platforms effectively is a defining characteristic of the digital age. Those lacking exposure to digital literacy training or educational resources are ill-equipped to interact with the AI ecosystem. This skill gap widens the disparity between those who can leverage AI technologies for economic advancement and those who are left behind.

The digital divide has far-reaching effects on income distribution and inequality. Those with the necessary technological access and digital literacy can leverage AI-driven efficiencies to boost productivity, launch new entrepreneurial ventures, and gain access to online education and employment opportunities. This expands opportunities for income growth and socioeconomic mobility.

In contrast, those on the disadvantaged side of the digital divide encounter a number of obstacles. Their limited access to AI-related tools and resources hinders their ability to capitalise on AI's economic benefits. This perpetuates income disparities because they lose out on the potential benefits of AI-driven innovation, limiting their economic growth and social mobility opportunities. Reducing the digital divide necessitates a multifaceted strategy. To ensure that marginalised communities have access to reliable and high-speed internet connectivity, policymakers must prioritise investments in technological infrastructure. In addition, educational institutions and organisations can play a crucial role by providing digital literacy programmes that equip individuals with the skills necessary to effectively interact with AI technologies.

As can be seen, the digital divide caused by the incorporation of AI highlights the complex relationship between technology, education, and income distribution. Unlocking the transformative potential of AI for all members of society requires bridging this divide. By removing access barriers, promoting digital literacy, and fostering an inclusive AI ecosystem, societies can make significant advances towards reducing income disparities and ensuring that the benefits of the AI revolution are available to all.

Drivers of AI-Induced Income Inequality

1.Technological Advancement

The rapid rate of AI development and adoption heralds a new era of technological progress, one that introduces a profound shift in the landscape of skills required by the labour market. This disparity in skill sets is a crucial component of the complex relationship between AI adoption and income inequality, revealing a narrative of opportunities seized, opportunities ignored, and the repercussions for socioeconomic equilibrium.

At its root, the rising tide of AI-driven innovation reshapes the very structure of industries and occupations. Emerging AI-driven industries require a unique combination of skills, including data analysis, algorithm development, machine learning, and AI programming. As technology becomes the foundation of economic development, those with the necessary technical competencies will be at the forefront of this transformational wave.

However, this surge in demand for AI-related skills casts a shadow over traditional industries that do not involve AI. As certain industries transition to AI-driven models, individuals with skill sets aligned with these emerging paradigms are better positioned to obtain high-paying positions that leverage AI. This dichotomy creates a two-tiered job market, where opportunities in AI-driven sectors promise lucrative careers while individuals in traditional sectors may have limited opportunities for professional advancement.

This technological divergence has significant and multifaceted repercussions. Those who engage on a journey to acquire AI-relevant skills are equipped to navigate the ever-changing landscape of emerging industries. Their ability to interact with AI technologies and contribute meaningfully to AI-driven projects opens the door to high-paying positions, career advancement, and the opportunity to influence the trajectory of AI innovation.

In contrast, those who lack access to AI-centric education and training confront an uphill battle. As they navigate the terrain of traditional sectors that are less influenced by AI, their earning potential and career advancement opportunities may stagnate. This divide between AI-enabled sectors and traditional domains can contribute to the perpetuation of income inequality, as those utilising cutting-edge technology enjoy the benefits of the AI revolution while others experience relative economic stagnation.

To mitigate the effects of this skill divergence, a multifaceted strategy is required. Education and training programmes must equip individuals with the skills required by both AI-driven and conventional industries. Fostering a culture of continuous learning and adaptability can empower the workforce with the skills necessary to navigate the changing job market. Moreover, policymakers and industry leaders must collaborate to ensure that AI-driven development is not confined to a select number of industries, but rather permeates a broad spectrum of industries and offers a variety of opportunities.

AI-driven technological progress brings to the forefront a crucial challenge: the disparity between the skills required by emergent AI-driven sectors and traditional industries. This terrain necessitates a commitment to equitable access to education, training, and opportunities, ensuring that the benefits of the AI revolution are available to people of all backgrounds. Societies can aspire for a more equitable distribution of economic opportunities and advancement by fostering a balanced ecosystem that values both AI expertise and traditional skills.

2. Globalization and Market Concentration

The integration of AI technologies introduces a new dimension to the global economic landscape, one that is characterised by the possibility of globalisation and market concentration. As AI transcends geographic borders, it enables multinational corporations to exert unprecedented influence, thereby reshaping market dynamics and income distribution. This complex interaction between AI adoption and economic concentration reveals a tale of power asymmetry, profit accumulation, and the difficulties of ensuring equitable economic participation.

At its foundation, AI's ability to transcend borders and operate seamlessly across diverse markets increases corporations' global reach. Armed with AI-driven capabilities, multinational corporations can centralise their operations, optimise their supply chains, and capture efficiencies that bolster their competitive advantage. This consolidation of power and resources enables these corporations to establish dominance in their respective industries, thereby exerting a substantial impact on market dynamics and economic outcomes.

The effects of this phenomenon reverberate through local economies and income distribution. On the one hand, multinational corporations that utilise AI technologies enjoy substantial profit margins, utilising AI-driven insights to target consumer preferences and boost operational efficiency. This profit concentration can result in substantial economic gains for a select group of individuals and stakeholders, thereby exacerbating income inequality.

In contrast, local economies and lesser businesses may face obstacles posed by AI-driven market concentration. The dominance of multinational corporations can reduce market competition, thereby limiting the opportunities for local businesses to prosper and grow. As these smaller actors struggle to compete with AI-enabled behemoths, their ability to generate profits and sustain economic growth may be diminished.

There are far-reaching implications for income distribution. The concentration of profits within a small group of multinational corporations can result in an unequal distribution of income, with a disproportionate share of economic advances accruing to a subset of society. This dynamic can exacerbate income disparities within and across nations, as multinational corporations profit from AI-driven efficiencies while local economies struggle to keep up. In the era of artificial intelligence, mitigating the potential effects of globalisation and market concentration necessitates a multifaceted strategy. Promoting global economic integration and protecting local economies requires policymakers to establish a delicate balance. By implementing regulations that promote healthy market competition while fostering innovation, it is possible to create a setting in which AI technologies can benefit society as a whole. Moreover, fostering a culture of innovation and entrepreneurship at the local level can enable small businesses to effectively leverage AI technologies and compete on the global market. By providing assistance, resources, and access to AI-related tools, policymakers can ensure that the benefits of AI-driven development are distributed more equitably across a broad spectrum of economic actors.

Therefore, the interaction between AI adoption and globalisation results in a paradigm shift in the market concentration and income distribution dynamics. It is essential to strike a balance between global economic integration and local economic resilience to ensure that the benefits of AI-driven growth are accessible to all segments of society. Societies can navigate the challenges posed by AI-induced market concentration and promote a more inclusive and equitable economic future by nurturing an environment that values diversity, innovation, and fair competition.

3. Education Disparities

The profound impact of Artificial Intelligence (AI) on the contemporary economy highlights the importance of education as a catalyst for individual empowerment and a pillar of equitable socioeconomic progress. The complex relationship between AI adoption and education disparities constitutes a crucial juncture where economic opportunity, skill acquisition, and income distribution converge.

At its core, access to quality education is a crucial determinant of an individual's capacity to interact with AI technologies and exploit their potential. The skills, competencies, and adaptability required to navigate the complexities of the AI era are built upon the foundation of education. It empowers individuals with the cognitive tools necessary to decipher complex algorithms, create AI-driven innovations, and make informed decisions in a world increasingly dominated by data.

Nonetheless, socioeconomic disparities continue to cast a long shadow over educational access and achievement. Individuals from disadvantaged circumstances frequently face obstacles that restrict their access to quality education. A cycle of limited access to the knowledge and skills necessary to flourish in an AI-driven economy can be perpetuated by factors such as income inequality, geographical location, and systemic biases.

These education disparities have ripple effects on income distribution and socioeconomic mobility. As AI technologies become ingrained in a variety of industries, those with fewer educational opportunities are disadvantaged. They may lack the necessary foundational knowledge to comprehend AI principles, the computational skills to work with AI tools, or the critical thinking skills to apply AI-driven insights to real-world problems.

Individuals who lack access to a quality education are excluded from the AI revolution's economic benefits as a result of this educational deficiency, resulting in a significant income disparity. As sectors driven by AI experience growth and innovation, those without the required educational background are relegated to low-skilled, low-paying jobs or left to contend with economic stagnation.

In the era of AI, mitigating the effects of education disparities requires a multifaceted strategy. The implementation of initiatives that bridge educational disparities and provide resources to underserved communities must be a top priority for policymakers. Investing in digital literacy programmes, STEM education, and the development of AI-related curricula can empower individuals to utilise AI technologies and realise their full potential.

In addition, collaboration between educational institutions, industry stakeholders, and community organisations can cultivate a learning ecosystem that transcends socioeconomic boundaries. Scholarships, mentorship programmes, and vocational training initiatives can help individuals from all walks of life acquire the necessary skills to flourish in an AI-driven economy.

As observed, the intersection of AI adoption and education disparities reveals a crucial intersection where the keys to economic empowerment are unequally distributed. To shape a future in which the benefits of the AI revolution are accessible to all segments of society, it is crucial to close educational disparities and ensure equitable access to AI-related knowledge. By removing barriers to education, fostering a culture of lifelong learning, and cultivating an inclusive AI ecosystem, societies can endeavour to bridge the gap between AI technologies and income distribution, thereby fostering a more just and equitable economic environment.

4. Policy and Regulation

The unprecedented wave of innovation ushered in by Artificial Intelligence (AI) brings to the fore a crucial necessity: the formulation of robust policies and regulations that guide its integration in a manner that ensures equitable benefits and safeguards against the escalation of income inequality. The complex interplay between AI adoption and policy dynamics reveals a landscape in which proactive governance plays a crucial role in defining the contours of economic opportunity, societal well-being, and income distribution.

In the ecosystem of artificial intelligence, policy and regulation are the guardians of equity, equality, and accountability. In the absence of adequate safeguards against bias in AI algorithms, systemic inequities can be perpetuated, resulting in discriminatory outcomes that disproportionately affect certain groups. Inadequate worker protections in the face of automation may exacerbate job loss and wage stagnation, thereby exacerbating income disparities. In the absence of substantial investments in education and retraining programmes, workforce adaptability can be hindered, leaving individuals ill-equipped to navigate the changing demands of an AI-driven economy.

Inadequate policies and regulations have profound effects on income distribution and socioeconomic stability. Unchecked, AI technologies can exacerbate existing disparities by reinforcing biases, marginalising vulnerable employees, and restricting access to opportunities. The potential for economic stratification and social unrest overshadows the promise of AI-driven growth, emphasising the necessity of responsible governance.

To mitigate the potential risks, policymakers must adopt a multifaceted strategy that includes proactive measures, anticipatory regulations, and comprehensive interventions. Robust frameworks for auditing AI algorithms, identifying and correcting biases, and ensuring transparency can assist in mitigating the risk of discriminatory outcomes and levelling the playing field for all members of society. These measures can foster an AI landscape that is more inclusive and cognizant of broader socioeconomic implications.

In addition, worker protections must adapt to the challenges posed by automation and AI-driven disruptions. This may entail redefining labour standards, fostering collective bargaining mechanisms, and designing social safety nets that serve as a buffer against technologically-induced economic shocks. Providing employees with the tools to transition into new roles and industries through comprehensive education and retraining programmes is crucial to ensuring that the benefits of artificial intelligence are accessible to all, as opposed to a select few.

The relationship between AI adoption and policy and regulation has a significant impact on the progression of income inequality. A more equitable distribution of AI-related benefits can be achieved through proactive governance that addresses biases, protects worker interests, and fosters an environment of continuous learning. By harnessing the transformative potential of AI through ethical, forward-looking policies, societies can steer the AI revolution towards a future where technological advancement is in harmony with socioeconomic well-being, allowing all individuals to flourish in an inclusive and just economic landscape.

Consequences of AI-Induced Income Inequality

1. Social Mobility

In the tapestry of societal development, social mobility represents the promise of upward economic advancement and the realisation of individual aspirations. The complex relationship between AI adoption and social mobility reveals a narrative in which widening income inequality casts a shadow over the prospects of those striving to transcend their circumstances, reiterating the need for proactive measures that illuminate pathways to opportunity for all.

The rapid adoption of AI has a twofold effect on social mobility. On the one hand, AI technologies have the potential to unlock new avenues of economic development by fostering innovation and generating new employment opportunities. As industries adopt AI-driven efficiencies, a variety of roles emerge that require data analysis, machine learning, and AI implementation skills. AI becomes an enabler of professional development for those with the necessary skills, paving the way for upward economic mobility and the prospect of a better future.

Nonetheless, the flip side of this narrative exposes a sobering truth: escalating income inequality can erect formidable barriers to social mobility. As AI adoption intensifies, it becomes increasingly difficult for individuals from disadvantaged backgrounds to access the opportunities necessary for upward mobility. Lack of access to quality education, training, and resources can leave them ill-equipped to meet the demands of an AI-driven job market, perpetuating a cycle of diminished economic prospects.

This vicious cycle is exacerbated by the incorporation of AI technologies into numerous industries. Individuals lacking the necessary skills and resources may find themselves marginalised, relegated to low-paying jobs, or unemployed for extended periods. As a result of the rapid tempo of AI development and adoption, individuals who lack the resources to keep up with evolving technological demands risk falling behind.

Social mobility impairment has far-reaching consequences. Inequality in income impacts not only individuals' access to economic opportunities, but also educational attainment, healthcare access, and well-being as a whole. This can perpetuate a cycle of disadvantage in which people from disadvantaged backgrounds struggle to escape the constraints imposed by limited resources and unequal access to AI-related opportunities.

The intersection between AI adoption and social mobility necessitates a comprehensive strategy encompassing education, workforce development, and policy reform. Equitable access to high-quality education, particularly in AI-related disciplines, is essential for equipping individuals from all backgrounds with the skills necessary to participate in emerging industries. Investing in vocational training, apprenticeship programmes, and reskilling initiatives enables individuals to adapt to the changing demands of the labour market and opens doors to economic advancement.

The trajectory of social mobility in the context of AI adoption has far-reaching implications for future opportunities and income distribution. By proactively removing barriers, nurturing a culture of lifelong learning, and designing policies that prioritise inclusive growth, societies can overcome the obstacles posed by rising income inequality. By doing so, they can ensure that the promise of social mobility remains accessible to all individuals, regardless of socioeconomic background, and foster a future in which the transformative potential of AI is in harmony with the principles of upward economic mobility and societal well-being.

2. Labor Market Polarization

The advent of Artificial Intelligence (AI) heralds in a profound transformation of the labour market, revealing a narrative of labour market polarisation with far-reaching consequences for social dynamics, economic stability, and shared prosperity. The intricate interplay between AI adoption and labour market shifts reveals a landscape in which the distribution of opportunities, income, and societal well-being endures a radical reconfiguration.

Integration of AI into the labour market heralds in polarisation, characterised by the emergence of distinct strata within the workforce. Once the bastion of economic stability, the middle class is now flanked by two contrasting factions. On the one hand, a growing population of low-wage, low-skilled employees is confronted with the spectre of diminished opportunities and constrained earning potential. On the other hand, a select group of high-skilled, high-paying professionals flourish in the context of AI-driven innovation's transformative potential.

This polarisation has profound repercussions for the social fabric as a whole. The growth of the low-wage, low-skill sector highlights the difficulties encountered by workers relegated to jobs susceptible to automation or outsourcing. The deterioration of job security, restricted opportunities for career advancement, and wage stagnation can result, perpetuating cycles of economic vulnerability and diminished upward mobility. In contrast, the growth of high-skilled, high-paying professionals increases the concentration of economic benefits among a small number of individuals. Those with the technical expertise to navigate the complexities of AI technologies stand to benefit from a swiftly evolving employment landscape. Their access to well-paying positions, augmented by AI-driven efficiencies, consolidates their socioeconomic status, thereby driving income inequality and contributing to the polarisation of societal fortunes.

The repercussions extend beyond economic disparities, affecting broader aspects of social stability and cohesion. Polarisation on the labour market can burden the social fabric, eroding trust and communal cohesion. A severe economic divide can contribute to feelings of alienation, disenfranchisement, and social unrest. This erosion of social cohesion threatens the basis of harmonious coexistence, highlighting the critical significance of addressing the effects of labour market polarisation.

To mitigate the effects of AI-induced labour market polarisation, a multifaceted strategy encompassing education, workforce development, and policy interventions is required. To foster a resilient and adaptable workforce, it is crucial to equip individuals with the skills required to interact with AI technologies. Investing in education and training programmes that close skill gaps enables employees to transition into roles that align with the changing demands of an AI-driven economy.

In order to mitigate the polarising effects of AI adoption, policy measures that promote equitable access to opportunities, fair remuneration, and social safety nets can be utilised. By prioritising worker protections, promoting job quality, and fostering an inclusive growth environment, policymakers can aspire to create a labour market that promotes both economic growth and social harmony. Therefore, the trajectory of income distribution, societal stability, and shared well-being is determined by the intricate tango between AI adoption and labour market polarisation. By adopting proactive strategies that prioritise education, equity, and social cohesion, societies can navigate the challenges of labour market polarisation and unlock the potential for a more inclusive, equitable, and harmonious future in which the benefits of AI-driven innovation are shared by all members of society.

3. Innovation Disparities

Within the tapestry of technological progress, the advent of Artificial Intelligence (AI) unfurls a complex story that interweaves the dynamics of innovation, income distribution, and the evolution of ground-breaking ideas. The interplay between AI adoption and innovation disparities sheds light on a landscape where access to resources, opportunities, and diverse perspectives shapes the trajectory of progress, fostering an environment either conducive to ground-breaking technologies or hindered by income-based restrictions.

Innovation is, at its root, the vital force that propels societies forward, transforms industries, and enriches lives. However, innovation diffusion is not uniform, and AI adoption can both exacerbate and mitigate this inequality. Significant portions of the population may be hampered in their capacity to contribute to the creative process by the income disparity resulting from the widespread adoption of AI.

The correlation between income inequality and innovation disparities is evident. A lack of equitable access to education, training, and resources can limit the talent pool capable of utilising AI technologies and influencing the future of innovation. It is possible for individuals from disadvantaged backgrounds to be excluded from pursuing careers in AI-related disciplines, thereby limiting the diversity of perspectives and ideas that fuels transformative progress.

This disparity in access to resources and opportunities can hinder the creation of innovative technologies and solutions. The absence of diverse voices can result in a myopic approach, impeding the investigation of novel concepts that could address complex societal challenges. As innovation stagnates in segments of the population hampered by income inequality, advancements with the potential to revolutionise industries or resolve pressing global issues may remain unrealized.

Beyond technology and entrepreneurship, the implications permeate disciplines such as healthcare, environmental sustainability, and social justice. As certain populations are excluded from the creative process, the necessary collective ingenuity to develop solutions to complex problems fragments. This fragmentation impedes progress and limits the capacity to leverage AI's transformative potential for the greater good of society.

In order to address innovation disparities in the context of AI adoption, education, research, and policy must collaborate. By prioritising access to quality education and training in AI-related disciplines, policymakers can ensure that individuals from all backgrounds have the opportunity to contribute to the innovation ecosystem. Access to the tools that drive innovation can be democratised through scholarships, mentorship programmes, and other initiatives that facilitate hands-on experience with AI technologies. In addition, promoting an environment that values diverse perspectives and inter-disciplinary collaboration can increase the impact of innovation. Research institutions, corporations, and governments must actively promote diversity and inclusion to foster a fertile environment for creative problem-solving that transcends income, background, and culture.

The intersection of AI adoption and innovation gaps provides a compelling narrative of unrealized potential and lost opportunities. By removing obstacles to education, fostering diversity, and implementing policies that promote equitable access to resources, societies can establish an ecosystem in which innovation flourishes without restriction. In doing so, they pave the way for a future in which the benefits of AI-driven innovation are utilised for the collective advancement of humanity, regardless of socioeconomic status, nurturing a society that is enriched by the diverse tapestry of human creativity.

In essence, the relationship between AI adoption and income inequality is complex, dynamic, and has far-reaching consequences. Factors such as labour market disruption, skill polarisation, economic concentration, and the digital divide influence the underlying mechanisms of this relationship. Technological progress, globalisation, disparities in education, and policy considerations all contribute to AI-induced income inequality. This inequality has ramifications for social mobility, labour market polarisation, and innovation gaps. A comprehensive approach is required to address the difficulties posed by AI-induced income inequality. Policymakers, institutions, and industry leaders must collaborate to develop and implement strategies that ensure equitable access to AI-related benefits, promote inclusive education and training, and establish safeguards against economic power concentration. As AI continues to reshape our societies, the pursuit of a fair and equitable distribution of its benefits will continue to be crucial.

12.2. The role of institutions in mitigating the negative impacts of AI on income distribution

In the complex and swiftly changing landscape of AI adoption, the role of institutions emerges as a determining factor in determining the trajectory of income distribution and societal well-being. Institutions, including governments, regulatory bodies, educational institutions, and labour organisations, have a significant obligation to mitigate the potential adverse effects of AI on income distribution. Institutions have the ability to ensure that the benefits of AI-driven innovation are distributed equitably to all segments of society by implementing thoughtful policies, fostering inclusivity, and cultivating a supportive ecosystem.

1. Policy Formulation and Regulation: Guiding the Path of Ethical AI Adoption

As policy and regulation architects, institutions have a unique opportunity to influence the ethical contours of AI adoption. To prevent the perpetuation of existing social inequalities, it is crucial that policies address the potential biases embedded in AI algorithms. Institutions can require AI systems to be transparent, ensuring that decision-making processes are transparent and accountable. This not only protects against discriminatory outcomes, but also fosters public confidence, which is essential for pervasive AI acceptance.

Moreover, regulations can guide the responsible deployment of AI to prevent undue power and economic concentration. Institutions can prevent monopolistic tendencies and ensure that the benefits of AI are distributed to a diverse range of economic actors by implementing policies that promote competition and equitable market practises. In order to strike a balance between innovation and equity, institutions must anticipate artificial intelligence's effect on income distribution and respond proactively with adaptive regulations.

2. Lifelong Learning and Reskilling: Nurturing Human Capital in the AI Era

As AI transforms the essence of work, educational and training paradigms must be rethought. Supported by educational institutions and policymakers, lifelong learning initiatives enable individuals to perpetually update their skills, thereby ensuring their continued relevance in an ever-changing labour market. Reskilling programmes tailored to the needs of AI-driven industries can help displaced employees transition into new roles, bridging the gap between economic change and personal development.

Additionally, institutions play a crucial role in promoting collaboration between academia and industry. By aligning educational curricula with the skill sets demanded by AI technologies, institutions can enhance workforce readiness, ensuring that graduates possess the skills necessary to excel in AI-driven industries. This collaboration extends to the development of flexible learning pathways, micro-credentialing, and upskilling initiatives that cater to the diverse requirements of individuals seeking to thrive in the era of artificial intelligence.

3. Labor Protection and Social Safety Nets: Upholding Workers' Rights Amidst Change

The disruption brought on by AI adoption highlights the significance of institutions in protecting labour rights. Labour unions can advocate for equitable wages, safe working conditions, and protection against unfair relocation. Collective bargaining mechanisms can ensure that workers have a voice in negotiating AI-related changes, allowing them to secure improved terms in the midst of technological disruption.

Government- and institution-supported social safety nets serve as a crucial safety valve against income disruptions caused by AI-induced job displacement. Robust unemployment benefits, wage subsidies, and remedial assistance provide a safety net that strengthens economic security and reduces the likelihood of income inequality. Institutions are able to design these safety nets to be adaptable and responsive in order to meet the unique challenges posed by the rapidly changing nature of labour.

4. Inclusive Innovation Ecosystem: Fostering Diversity for Comprehensive Progress

Institutions play a crucial role in fostering an innovation ecosystem that values diverse perspectives and abilities. Institutions of higher education can take proactive steps to encourage underrepresented groups to utilise AI technologies. By offering scholarships, mentorship programmes, and initiatives that reduce entry barriers, institutions increase the number of people who contribute to AI-driven innovation.

In addition, institutions can facilitate the development of incubators, accelerators, and research centres that foster interdisciplinarity. By fostering an environment in which professionals from diverse backgrounds collaborate to address complex problems, institutions increase the potential for holistic solutions to multifaceted problems. This diversity of thought not only fosters innovation, but also ensures that AI technologies are created with an acute awareness of their societal impact.

5. Collaboration and Partnerships: Collective Action for Equitable AI

The multifaceted character of AI-induced income inequality requires institutions, industries, and civil society to collaborate. Institutions can serve as catalysts for dialogue and cooperation, facilitating the formation of partnerships that leverage collective expertise. Collaboration across sectors permits the co-development of initiatives that promote equitable access, skill development, and economic opportunities.

Government institutions and businesses can collaborate on the design and funding of education and training programmes to close AI-related skill gaps. Industry associations and labour organisations can collaborate to develop ethical guidelines for the adoption of artificial intelligence that prioritise worker rights and social equity. By merging resources, knowledge, and perspectives, institutions can create a more inclusive and equitable economic landscape by forming a united front against the negative effects of AI on income distribution.

In conclusion, the multifaceted function of institutions in mitigating the negative effects of artificial intelligence on income distribution transcends policy formulation. Institutions wield a transformative influence on the AI landscape through judicious regulation, support for lifelong learning, labour protection, nurturing inclusivity, and fostering collaboration. By promoting ethical practises, cultivating human potential, and fostering an inclusive environment, institutions can navigate the challenges posed by AI-induced income inequality and pave the way for a future in which AI-driven progress benefits society as a whole.

12.3. Potential policy interventions to address the widening income gap caused by AI

As the advent of Artificial Intelligence (AI) transforms economic landscapes, addressing widening income disparities assumes centre stage. To ensure that the benefits of AI-driven progress are distributed equitably throughout society, it becomes crucial to develop effective policy interventions. Policymakers can navigate the challenges posed by AI-induced income inequality and pave the way for a more equitable and inclusive future by deploying a comprehensive array of strategies spanning education, workforce development, taxation, and social support.

1. **Universal Basic Income (UBI)**

Universal Basic Income (UBI) is a transformative policy intervention designed to counteract the widening income disparity resulting from the widespread adoption of artificial intelligence. Under this programme, the government provides a regular, unconditional financial payment to all citizens and residents. UBI serves as a safety net, providing a reliable source of income that assures individuals can meet their basic needs regardless of job loss or AI-driven economic shifts.

Implementing UBI necessitates careful consideration of funding mechanisms, distribution quantities, and potential economic consequences. By providing a consistent income floor, UBI strengthens economic security, allowing individuals to withstand job transitions and navigate the uncertainties posed by AI-driven disruptions. UBI also encourages entrepreneurship and innovation by providing individuals with the financial freedom to investigate new ventures without fear of poverty.

2. **Progressive Taxation and Wealth Redistribution**

Progressive taxation policies are a potent instrument for addressing income inequality in the age of artificial intelligence. Such policies impose higher tax rates on individuals and corporations with higher incomes, resulting in a more equitable distribution of tax burdens. Social programmes, education, and workforce development initiatives that empower individuals to engage with AI technologies and exploit new opportunities can be funded with progressive tax revenue.

Mechanisms for wealth redistribution, such as inheritance or wealth taxes, can further reduce income disparities by preventing the accumulation of enormous fortunes by a select group of society members. These policies encourage a more equitable distribution of resources, fostering a socioeconomic environment in which the benefits of AI-driven progress are more evenly distributed.

3. Education and Reskilling Initiatives

Comprehensive education and reskilling initiatives are required to combat AI-induced income inequality. Policymakers can allot funds for the development of AI-centric curricula, the establishment of vocational training centres, and the provision of financial aid to individuals seeking to acquire AI-related skills. Education and reskilling programmes can bridge skill gaps, improve employability, and enable individuals to pursue higher-paying positions by equipping employees with the knowledge and skills required to interact with AI technologies.

In addition, partnerships between educational institutions and businesses can ensure that curricula are aligned with the needs of AI-driven industries. Initiatives such as apprenticeships, internships, and online learning platforms can facilitate continuous upskilling, allowing individuals to remain pertinent in an AI-driven, rapidly transforming job market.

4. Sectoral Development and Innovation Incentives

Policies that foster the expansion of sectors propelled by artificial intelligence can stimulate economic growth and provide avenues for reducing income inequality. Governments can offer businesses incentives to invest in R&D, employment creation, and technological innovation within AI-intensive industries such as healthcare, renewable energy, and advanced manufacturing.

Grants, tax exemptions, and access to capital for startups and small businesses in these industries can foster entrepreneurship and promote economic diversification. By fostering an environment conducive to AI-driven innovation, policymakers can generate employment opportunities, boost competitiveness, and facilitate upward mobility for workers in these burgeoning fields.

5. Job Guarantee Programs

Job guarantee programmes can serve as a mechanism to maintain economic stability and reduce income inequality in the face of AI-induced job displacement. These programmes provide meaningful roles in public service projects, infrastructure development, and community initiatives, assuring employment opportunities for all individuals who wish to work.

By providing stable employment and remuneration, job guarantee programmes mitigate the negative effects of AI-driven job losses. In addition to reducing income disparities, these initiatives contribute to societal cohesion and collective well-being. Job guarantee programmes uphold the principle of economic inclusivity by redefining the nature of work and ensuring that everyone has access to employment.

6. Data Ownership and Privacy Regulations

Data ownership and privacy regulations play a crucial role in ensuring the equitable distribution of the benefits of AI-driven progress. Policies that grant individuals ownership of their personal data and regulate its use by businesses protect against the concentration of data-driven profits among a small number of entities.

Institutions can establish frameworks that give individuals control over the collection, processing, and monetization of their data. This strategy ensures that individuals are equitably compensated for the value generated by their data and reduces the likelihood of AI-driven economic disparities resulting from unequal access to data resources.

7. **Support for Entrepreneurship and Small Businesses**

Policies that encourage entrepreneurship and assist small businesses can stimulate economic vitality and contribute to a more equitable distribution of income. Governments can provide financial incentives, access to capital, and resources for business development to enable entrepreneurs to leverage AI technologies and create new economic opportunities.

Policymakers can democratise access to economic development by fostering a culture of innovation and facilitating the success of small businesses in AI-driven industries. Supporting entrepreneurs from disparate backgrounds fosters an environment in which a broader range of individuals can contribute to AI-driven innovation, thereby reducing income inequality by increasing the number of economic beneficiaries.

In conclusion, a nuanced combination of these policy interventions has the potential to effectively address the widening income disparity caused by the widespread adoption of artificial intelligence. Policymakers can navigate the complex challenges posed by AI-induced income inequality by adopting strategies such as Universal Basic Income, progressive taxation, education and reskilling initiatives, sectoral development, job guarantee programmes, data ownership regulations, and support for entrepreneurship. Together, these interventions create a more equitable and inclusive economic landscape in which the transformative power of AI-driven progress is harnessed for the advantage of all members of society.

Chapter 13: AI and Intellectual Property Rights

The emergence of artificial intelligence (AI) threatens established paradigms of intellectual property (IP) rights in the annals of human brilliance and invention. The dynamics of invention, ownership, and protection undergo a significant transformation as humanity rushes headlong into an AI-driven economy. As it explores the delicate relationship between AI and intellectual property, Chapter 13 reveals the tangled web of problems, fixes, and reforms that characterises this period of extraordinary technological development.

The chapter's scope is broad, covering the many difficulties that come with protecting and enforcing intellectual property in a world where AI-generated material predominates. The story takes place in a world where artificial intelligence (AI) has the power to produce works of art, music, literature, and even scientific breakthroughs, blurring the distinction between human authorship and algorithmic production. Fundamental problems regarding the nature of ownership, the function of institutions, and the requirement for flexible IP laws arise as innovation assumes new dimensions and creators now include machines.

The first stroke explores the difficulties associated with preserving intellectual property in the face of the unrelenting advance of automation brought on by AI. In a world where algorithms help produce a variety of works, the chapter examines how the basic definition of creativity and originality is altered. It struggles to develop a paradigm that supports the complex dance between human creativity and machine augmentation as well as the complexities of determining authorship, attributing ownership, and these other issues. This investigation's central thesis is that institutions are essential to establishing just and functional IP rights in the era of AI. Governments, judicial systems, and regulatory agencies are revealed as the guardians of a precarious equilibrium, tasked with stimulating innovation while making sure that creators are fairly acknowledged and compensated for their efforts. The processes by which institutions adjust to the new aspects of AI-driven creativity are explored in this part, ensuring that intellectual property rights continue to serve as a pillar of support for creators and a catalyst for societal advancement.

The chapter's conclusion sketches out possible changes to IP regulations that would take into account their special properties as they relate to AI-generated content. The story examines the necessity for legal frameworks that successfully balance encouraging innovation, rewarding creators, and protecting against the dangers of overreach or misuse. It imagines the possibilities of a world in which AI and human creators coexist, establishing a culture that fosters interaction, promotes experimentation, and fosters a sense of collective authorship. The chapter in this symphony of ideas captures the creative symphony between humans and machines that characterises the AI era. In order to take readers on a thought-provoking trip into the core of AI's impact on intellectual property rights, it dissects the intricate melodies of creativity, ownership, and legal adaptation. This chapter aims to not only analyse the problems at hand but also to shed light on the way forward—a way that embraces both human ingenuity and the transformative potential of AI in determining the future of intellectual property in the digital age. As the lines between authorship blur and the canvas of invention expands.

13.1 The challenges of protecting intellectual property in an AI-driven economy

The protection of intellectual property (IP) is undergoing a complex evolution in the transformative wake of Artificial Intelligence (AI) spread. The difficulties of protecting intellectual property in an AI-driven economy become a compelling narrative of complexity as AI technologies help to produce a wide variety of innovative works. This calls for an in-depth exploration of brand-new issues that intersect the legal, ethical, and practical realms. AI-generated material blurs the distinctions between traditional authorship and ownership in one of two ways. It is vital to determine if the AI system itself, the human programmer, or a cooperative relationship between the two should be given credit. When AI algorithms change and adapt information over time, creating doubts about the temporal aspect of authorship, this difficulty becomes especially pressing. Creating a fair and consistent structure for authorshipattribution becomes a crucial task.

- Rapid Generation and Monitoring: The monitoring and enforcement of IP rights are significantly hampered by AI's capacity to quickly generate a vast amount of content. Artificial intelligence can create works at a rate that is faster than the capacity of traditional enforcement methods. The decentralised nature of the internet makes it more difficult to track the distribution and use of AI-generated material across different online platforms, which further exacerbates this problem.

- Originality and Infringement: The astonishing accuracy with which AI can imitate existing styles, genres, and artistic expressions raises questions regarding originality and accidental infringement. The distinction between inspiration and infringement is made more difficult by the AI's ability to accidentally duplicate copyrighted works and perhaps recreate them in a transformative way. Redefining what original material is entails evaluating the delicate line between AI-generated content that honours preexisting works and stuff that illegally copies them in order to address this difficulty.

- Jurisdictional Difficulties: The fact that the digital world has no borders makes it more difficult to safeguard intellectual property (IP) created by AI. AI-generated material can instantly cross international borders, pushing the bounds of national IP laws and enforcement procedures. Harmonising international attempts to protect authors' rights in the context of AI-generated content is hampered by the disparate legislative frameworks across various jurisdictions.

- Fair Use and Transformative Works are Being Redefined: AI-generated content challenges accepted notions of fair use and transformative works. The distinction between creative transformation and replication is muddled by AI's capacity to produce derivative works that use preexisting resources. In the context of AI, courts and legal systems struggle to define fair use's parameters, necessitating new legal interpretations to strike a balance between encouraging creativity and protecting intellectual property.

- Algorithmic Discrimination and Ethical Issues: The difficulties of preserving IP transcend beyond the realm of the law and include moral worries about algorithmic prejudice and potential violations of cultural, artistic, or human rights. The datasets that AI systems draw inspiration from can unintentionally reinforce biases or produce content that is offensive to certain cultural sensibilities. This calls for a reconsideration of the relationship between IP protection and the moral implications of AI-generated material.

As seen, there are numerous and extensive difficulties with intellectual property protection in an AI-driven economy. To overcome these obstacles, current IP frameworks must be completely revised to incorporate AI's special characteristics. It need interdisciplinary cooperation between legal experts, ethicists, engineers, and legislators to strike a balance between promoting innovation, rewarding creators, and guarding against the unintended effects of AI-generated material. In the end, ensuring that innovation thrives while creators' rights and social values are protected in the face of this revolutionary technological tide will depend on a cogent and flexible approach to IP protection in the AI era.

13.2 The role of institutions in ensuring fair and effective IP rights in the age of AI

The protection and fair enforcement of intellectual property (IP) rights take centre stage in the dynamic environment of innovation fostered by artificial intelligence (AI). To successfully navigate the potential and challenges presented by this revolutionary technological era, institutions must ensure fair and effective IP rights. Institutions are crucial in determining the laws, rules, and procedures that promote innovation, safeguard the rights of creators, and uphold ethical standards as AI-generated content blurs the lines between authorship and creation, challenges conventional notions of creativity, and pushes the bounds of legal frameworks.

1. **Framing New Definitions and Guidelines**

Institutions have the authority to create fresh definitions and rules that take into account the specifics of AI-generated content as it relates to intellectual property. When AI is used to create content, specific criteria are required to handle issues with authorship, ownership, and originality. Institutions lay the groundwork for a cogent and just IP framework that is in line with the dynamics of the AI era by creating thorough definitions that cover human-AI collaboration and properly assigning credit. Institutions have a significant need to reconfigure intellectual property (IP) regimes in the AI era in order to solve the complex problems presented by AI-generated content. This transformative function involves creating new definitions and rules that take into account the changing dynamics of human-AI collaboration, going beyond simple adaptation.

Redefining the basic nature of authorship and ownership is one of the biggest difficulties institutions face. Authorship has typically been attributed to specific human creators, but the development of AI has eroded these distinctions. Institutions struggle to come up with a definition of authorship that encompasses both the work of human programmers and the autonomous AI systems. As equitable acknowledgment of all contributors' contributions becomes increasingly important, institutions must adopt rules to prevent excessive underrepresentation of human innovation.

Institutions have to handle an additional layer of complexity brought on by the collaborative nature of AI-generated material. The distinction between human and AI influence must be carefully drawn to account for both situations in which AI systems serve as creative tools under human direction and those in which AI takes the initiative in content creation. The degree of IP protection and acknowledgment given to the joint output depends on this distinction.

The idea of authorship is further complicated by AI's iterative and temporal character. Institutions must consider how authorship changes as a result of the ongoing iteration and revision of content by AI algorithms. Guidelines must take into account the possibility of early human contributions being gradually modified by AI systems in order to adequately represent the fluidity of authorship in the context of content produced by AI systems.

Another challenging issue is how to balance the independence of AI systems with the impact of human designers. Institutions must carefully adjust policies to reflect the degree of independence that AI has in the generation of content while simultaneously acknowledging that it is dependent on human-designed algorithms. By striking this equilibrium, it will be possible to produce an IP framework that truly captures the interaction between AI and humans.

The importance of these definitions and rules' enforceability and clarity cannot be overstated. Institutions are responsible with developing language that is not only sound legally but also clear to both artists and consumers as well as legal experts. Ambiguities in ownership, attribution, or collaborative authorship may result in disagreements that inhibit innovation and creativity. In order to ensure that the framework they design provides a strong foundation for the peaceful coexistence of human and AI-driven creativity, institutions play a crucial role.

Therefore, it is a difficult and delicate task for institutions to define new definitions and norms for AI-generated material within the context of intellectual property. Institutions pave the way for a future where IP rights and AI-driven creativity intersect smoothly, providing a climate that encourages innovation, respects creators, and welcomes the dynamism of the AI era by forging a path that honours both human ingenuity and AI's revolutionary potential.

2. Evolving Legal Frameworks

The rules governing IP rights must change to take into account the distinctive qualities of content produced by AI. Institutions can take the initiative in revising the definitions of transformative works, fair use rules, and current copyright laws. Updating laws to protect creators, whether they are led by humans or artificial intelligence, while promoting an environment that supports innovation is a proactive approach. In the era of AI-generated content, institutions' duty for transforming the legal systems controlling intellectual property (IP) rights assumes greater significance. Rethinking current copyright laws, fair use rules, and transformative work interpretations is necessary given the innovative and dynamic nature of AI's creative contributions.

Institutions are at the forefront of reviewing copyright rules as AI-generated content challenges conventional ideas of authorship and creativity. It is no longer possible to cover the collaborative efforts between human creators and autonomous AI systems using the old paradigm of human-authored products. In order to protect the rights of all contributors, whether they are human or AI-driven, institutions must redefine copyright limitations. In the age of AI, fair use doctrines—which define the extent of legal consumption of protected content—need to be thoroughly reevaluated. When AI algorithms are used to create material, institutions must take the lead in defining the parameters of fair use. In order to ensure that the transformative nature of AI-generated material is consistent with the principles of fair use, they must strike a balance between encouraging innovation and defending the rights of content creators.

A new viewpoint is necessary in the field of artificial intelligence (AI) given how transformative work interpretations affect the distinction between original works and derivative works. The obligation to define what constitutes transformative AI-generated material rests with institutions. This includes balancing the AI system's independence from preexisting materials in order to shape how derivative works are viewed and safeguarded.

An climate that fosters innovation while defending creators' rights requires a proactive approach to legislative revisions. Institutions must take the lead in implementing legislative changes that take into account the distinctive characteristics of information produced by AI. In order to achieve this, a legal framework must be established that not only acknowledges the achievements of AI systems but also develops mechanisms to guarantee creators—human or AI—are appropriately compensated and safeguarded.

Institutions are important in achieving the delicate balance between fostering innovation and safeguarding the rights of artists. They must watch out that new laws do not impose too onerous constraints that hinder AI's innovative potential. Institutions create an environment where creators are motivated to explore the endless potential of AI-driven innovation by creating laws that offers a clear and flexible framework. In the era of AI-generated material, the development of legal frameworks controlling intellectual property rights is a complex and diverse task. Institutions have a proactive and transformative role in updating fair use guidelines, revising copyright laws, and defining how transformative works are interpreted. By doing this, institutions help to create a legal environment that encourages innovation, defends the rights of artists, and accommodates the complex interaction between human and AI-driven creation.

3. Collaborative Ownership Models

Institutions can support the creation of cooperative ownership models that recognise the contributions of both human creators and AI systems as AI becomes a more significant element of the creative process. These models can assist in allocating incentives, kudos, and duties in a way that respects the individual contributors' unique roles. Institutions can reduce potential conflicts and provide equitable recompense for all stakeholders by prioritising collaboration over conflict.

Institutions take on a new role in the world of AI-driven creativity as the designers of cooperative ownership models that go beyond conventional paradigms and embrace the delicate interaction between human creators and AI systems. This transformative function involves creating a framework that promotes equitable allocation of incentives, recognition, and responsibilities, establishing an environment where innovation thrives while reducing conflicts. It goes beyond simply acknowledging contributions. Institutions take on the responsibility of developing collaborative ownership models that capture the multifaceted nature of AI-generated material as AI integrates itself more deeply into the creative process. These approaches fundamentally acknowledge the unique roles that autonomous AI systems and human creators play. Institutions build a foundation that values the particular skills and contributions of each stakeholder by doing this.

These cooperative ownership forms' main goal is to make it easier to distribute rewards fairly. Institutions are aware that individual authorship is no longer the only form of creativity. They strive to make sure that both human and AI creators receive just compensation for their contributions. This calls for a sophisticated strategy that weighs the level of AI creativity and its influence on the result. Another crucial aspect incorporated into joint ownership models is recognition. The atmosphere in which the innovative contributions of both human and AI contributors are adequately appreciated is greatly influenced by institutions. This recognition goes beyond naming the author; it also takes into account the contribution of AI to the final artistic expression. These models carefully distribute duties so that each contributor's contribution is valued and recognised. Institutions design procedures that specify the responsibilities of both human and artificial intelligence (AI) participants, encouraging a sense of shared accountability. By doing this, organisations foster a collaborative mindset that goes beyond conventional ideas of competitiveness and equips content producers to successfully negotiate the intricacies of AI-generated content.

One fundamental principle of these ownership arrangements is the importance of collaboration over conflict. Institutions serve as arbitrators, making sure that ownership and attribution-related conflicts are settled through cooperative means. Institutions foster an environment where creators collaborate to address issues and reach decisions that uphold the integrity of the creative process by fostering open debate and communication. The function that institutions play in these arrangements includes mitigating potential disagreements. They form the foundation for contracts that specify the conditions of ownership, the division of benefits, and initial acknowledgement of collaboration. Creators are free to concentrate on invention rather than legal problems thanks to this proactive strategy, which not only avoids conflicts but also develops an atmosphere of trust and transparency.

As can be observed, collaborative ownership models developed by institutions represent a paradigm shift that recognises the complex dance between the contributions of humans and artificial intelligence in creative endeavours. Institutions foster an ecosystem where creativity thrives, conflicts are reduced, and the synergistic potential of human-AI collaboration is realised through building frameworks that distribute rewards, recognition, and responsibilities in an equitable manner.

4. IP Monitoring and Enforcement

In the AI context, institutions are essential for improving IP monitoring and enforcement methods. Institutions can create cutting-edge AI-driven technologies that can spot unauthorised use and potential violations by working with technology specialists. These systems may track material across several digital platforms, look for patterns, and notify content producers of potential infractions. In a rapidly changing digital world, effective enforcement systems support artists' rights and discourage infringement. Institutions—both public and private—have emerged as key actors in supporting the monitoring and enforcement of intellectual property (IP) in the dynamic field of artificial intelligence (AI). Due to the growing significance of AI in numerous industries and the possible hazards of IP theft and infringement, this progression has become crucial.

In this endeavour, cooperation between institutions and technology professionals has become crucial. Together, they create cutting-edge AI-driven solutions that can spot unauthorised use and potential intellectual property violations. These cutting-edge tools use deep learning and machine learning algorithms to examine a large amount of digital content spread across numerous platforms, including websites, social media, and digital repositories. To find similarities and irregularities, they compare this content to already-existing databases of works protected by copyright, patents, and trademarks. The capacity of AI-driven IP monitoring solutions to inform content producers, patent owners, and trademark owners in almost real-time is a huge advantage. Automated notifications are delivered when potential infractions are found, enabling quick action to safeguard intellectual property rights. In a rapidly changing digital economy where infringements can spread easily, reaction is essential.

Institutions are also attempting to develop centralised databases of IP-related data that will be accessible to all parties, including corporations, law enforcement, and content providers. These databases offer a thorough picture of all IP assets currently in existence, making it simpler for rights holders to establish their claims and for law enforcement to find and punish IP violators. In addition to defending the rights of artists, effective IP enforcement measures are essential in discouraging potential infringers. Knowing that AI-powered surveillance technologies are actively looking for IP infringement in digital spaces acts as a powerful deterrent, discouraging people and organisations from engaging in illegal activities that can result in legal repercussions.

Therefore, the importance of institutions in creating, implementing, and continually upgrading IP monitoring and enforcement methods cannot be emphasised as AI continues to alter the future of technology and innovation. These institutions help to create an environment where innovation is protected, creators are recognised for their work, and the digital landscape continues to be a fair and equitable place for all stakeholders by utilising the power of AI.

5. Ethical and Cultural Considerations

Institutions can address issues with algorithmic bias, cultural sensitivity, and social effect by including ethical and cultural factors into IP protection initiatives. Institutions may guarantee that AI algorithms respect human values and diversity by establishing ethical standards for AI-generated material. Institutions can support the creation of AI models that respect moral principles and cultural norms while avoiding content that might reinforce biases or violate cultural norms.

Institutions take on a crucial role in increasing intellectual property (IP) monitoring and enforcement systems as guardians of creative integrity in the dynamic world of AI-generated content. Institutions work with technological specialists to develop sophisticated AI-driven tools that preserve authors' rights while preserving the ideals of IP protection. The complexity and size of AI-driven content creation necessitate creative solutions. The creation of cutting-edge AI-driven technologies that transform IP monitoring is at the heart of this position. Institutions use engineers' knowledge to develop algorithms that can quickly spot unauthorised use and potential violations. These technologies analyse huge amounts of digital content across platforms using machine learning algorithms, comparing patterns, and spotting instances of possible IP infringement.

These tools' capacity to spot content patterns and similarity even in the vastness of the digital sphere is a crucial feature. In order to develop algorithms that can identify situations where AI-generated content resembles already-existing copyrighted material, institutions work with AI experts. These technologies act as early warning systems by spotting probable infringements, allowing creators to take preventative steps to safeguard their works.

To ensure prompt intervention, alert systems are essential. When suspected IP infringement are found, institutions develop AI-driven alert systems that swiftly notify the producers. The ability to assess the issue, communicate with the appropriate people, and take appropriate action to remedy infringements before they worsen is provided by this real-time notification. These initiatives' spirit of cooperation goes beyond technological advancement. Institutions provide as a conduit for communication and conflict resolution between creators, platforms, and users. They enable interactions that promote adherence to IP rights, allowing parties to resolve disagreements through dialogue and cooperation as opposed to pursuing drawn-out legal fights. At the core of this effort are efficient enforcement tools. Institutions make an effort to make enforcement actions fair and prompt so that there is no doubt about the repercussions of IP violation. They discourage potential offenders and uphold the value of creators' rights in the digital sphere by doing this.

Institutions have a dynamic role in policing and enforcing intellectual property rights. It requires ongoing evolution and adaptation to keep up with the shifting strategies used by infringers. Institutions work together with engineers to improve and tweak AI algorithms so that the tools continue to be reliable and accurate at spotting fresh IP infringement. Institutions are leading the creation and implementation of cutting-edge AI-driven systems that monitor and uphold intellectual property rights in the AI era, serving as examples of creative integrity. Institutions build a digital ecosystem where authors' rights are honoured, AI-generated content is protected, and the equilibrium between innovation and IP protection is rigorously maintained through collaboration, innovation, and proactive measures.

6. International Collaboration

Institutions must promote international cooperation and the harmonisation of intellectual property norms due to the global nature of the digital landscape. Institutions can promote cross-border agreements to ensure that authors' rights are protected globally as AI-generated content crosses borders. Nations can address jurisdictional complications and create cogent global rules for IP rights protection through cooperative efforts.

In order to protect AI-generated content, institutions are essential in promoting international collaboration and harmonising intellectual property (IP) rules. Institutions have a transformative influence as they traverse the globalised digital age. Institutions become the builders of cross-border agreements that transcend geographical boundaries as a result of their recognition of the international nature of artificial intelligence's creative outputs. This creates a unified front to defend creators' rights on a worldwide scale.

International cooperation facilitated by institutions is fundamentally a reaction to the ubiquity and fluidity of AI-generated material. Institutions serve as catalysts for cooperative efforts across nations as innovations swiftly cross international borders. To resolve jurisdictional difficulties, collaborative frameworks are formed, guaranteeing that authors' IP rights are widely acknowledged and protected. The creation of international agreements demonstrates institutions' commitment to developing world standards that regulate AI-generated content. These agreements bridge cultural and legal divides and foster a common awareness of the value of artists' rights and the necessity of their protection in a world connected to the internet. Institutions support communication and bargaining to harmonise IP norms, creating a stable and predictable environment for both authors and users.

Recognising the jurisdictional issues that develop in the digital sphere is a crucial part of international collaboration. Institutions serve as brokers, bringing nations together to address problems including cross-border enforcement, content distribution, and infringement detection. Institutions pave the path for standardised solutions that go beyond the constraints of different legal systems by encouraging communication and cooperation. Institutions play a crucial role in promoting awareness-raising and instructional campaigns in addition to enforcing legal agreements. Institutions work together to spread information regarding AI-generated content and its repercussions for global governments, users, and producers. Institutions enable governments to take informed decisions and actively engage in the international debate on IP protection by promoting best practises and increasing knowledge of the issue.

Importantly, institutions that allow international cooperation encourage an atmosphere of respect and cooperation between states. Collaboration efforts transcend political differences and emphasise the shared objective of fostering innovation while preserving creators' rights by recognising the importance of each nation's creative contributions and the need to protect them. Therefore, international cooperation facilitated by institutions emphasises the interconnectivity of the digital age and the necessity of setting up unified systems for safeguarding intellectual property produced by AI. Institutions become the architects of a worldwide framework that promotes creativity, stimulates innovation, and ensures that artists' rights are protected regardless of geographical boundaries through cross-border agreements, standardisation efforts, and awareness-raising campaigns.

7. Education and Awareness

Institutions are essential in educating the public about AI-generated content and its effects on IP rights, as well as artists, customers, and the broader public. Institutions enable stakeholders to make wise decisions by increasing awareness of the risks, rewards, and ethical implications of AI-driven innovation. A culture of respect for IP is cultivated by educating creators about their rights and obligations, which supports compliance and moral content production.

Institutions emerge as defenders of a new intellectual property (IP) frontier in the era of artificial intelligence (AI), championing knowledge and awareness to negotiate the complicated terrain of AI-generated material. They play a multidimensional function that involves a diverse range of duties that come together to help design a future in which AI innovation coexists peacefully with respect for IP rights.

Institutions' core purpose is to empower people by educating them on the subtleties of AI-generated content for producers, consumers, and the general public. Creators build a deeper knowledge of the dynamic dance between human creativity and AI algorithms via workshops, lectures, and interactive projects. Institutions enable consumers to make ethical decisions about the information they engage with and the ethical considerations inside it by bridging the gap between technical wonders and those choices through education. In order to give stakeholders the discernment needed to negotiate AI's ethical footprint, institutions have supported a global discourse on the ethical challenges of AI, including algorithmic bias, cultural sensitivity, and social effects.

Traditional ideas of authorship and ownership are becoming more ambiguous in the context of AI-generated content, which has forced institutions to revise their definitions and policies. Prioritising concerns of credit distribution between human programmers and AI systems, clear frameworks for authorshipattribution become crucial. By ensuring that creators are aware of their rights and obligations, institutions help to foster a culture of respectful IP practises. The chance of inadvertent infringements is decreased when legal knowledge and ethical considerations are combined to give authors the power to negotiate the complexities of copyright laws, fair use rules, and attribution standards.

Institutions also venture into the area of international partnerships, going beyond the national boundaries of AI-generated IP. In order to recognise the efforts of both human and AI producers and to ensure that rewards, recognition, and obligations are shared fairly, collaborative ownership models have been developed. Institutions reduce disputes and provide just recompense for all parties by encouraging cooperation over conflict.

Monitoring and enforcing IP rights provide significant issues in the digital age, calling for creative solutions. Institutions use the power of AI technology to create sophisticated systems that track material across digital platforms, identify similarities, and notify creators of suspected infringements. This ongoing watchfulness, supported by institutions, defends artists' rights and promotes a respect for intellectual property (IP) culture.

Institutions also have an impact on international partnerships, which promotes the harmonisation of IP standards in a globalised digital environment. To safeguard artists' rights globally, agreements are created that cut across jurisdictional boundaries and harmonise regulatory frameworks. Institutions act as champions for universal standards that traverse difficult jurisdictional issues and guarantee that the creative works of creators are appreciated internationally.

Institutions also provide a knowledge ecosystem that links policymakers, technologists, and experts from industry and academia. The ethical frameworks and best practises that govern the production and consumption of AI-generated material are shaped by this collaborative approach, which fosters a comprehensive awareness of AI's promise and drawbacks. Institutions act as guiding lights, enabling a climate where AI innovation thrives while preserving moral and legal principles.

Essentially, education and awareness become the pillars of institutions' efforts, providing a context where the revolutionary potential of AI converges with a strong respect for IP rights. Institutions enable a wide range of stakeholders—creators, consumers, and the general public—

to navigate the complex landscape of AI-generated content by taking a comprehensive approach to education. Institutions offer a way that fosters ethical content practises, empowers responsible decision-making, and maintains the sanctity of intellectual property in the digital age at this era of tremendous technological evolution.

8. Adaptive Governance and Policy Formation

To keep up with the rapidly changing AI landscape, institutions must maintain an adaptive approach to governance and policy formulation. Because of how quickly technology is developing, institutions must constantly review and adapt their IP frameworks to handle new problems. The protection of creators' rights and the promotion of innovation are made possible by this proactive approach to policymaking.

Institutions emerge as architects of adaptive governance and policy formulation in the midst of an era marked by transformative Artificial Intelligence (AI) advancement, holding a crucial mandate to navigate the constantly changing AI landscape. Institutions take on the role of foresight, continually recalibrating intellectual property (IP) frameworks to handle emerging difficulties as technology's unrelenting march sweeps us into unfamiliar territory. The ability of regulations to protect creators' rights and foster creativity in the age of AI is ensured by their continual reinvention.

Institutions adopt an adaptable stance, responding quickly to the ongoing technological evolution since they are highly aware of the speed of AI. A continual cycle of assessment, reevaluation, and improvement is a requirement of adaptive governance. Institutions are conducting a dynamic symphony in which each note indicates a measured response to the changing AI landscape. Institutions foresee possible disruptions by carefully examining the constantly evolving features of AI-generated material, ensuring that IP frameworks are durable and adaptive. Because of how quickly technology is developing, institutions must be on guard and proactive in revising their IP policies to keep up with the story of AI as it develops. Swift solutions to new issues, such as the authorship of AI-generated work or the effects of algorithmic bias, demonstrate institutions' ability to adapt to the future without sacrificing the principles underlying IP protection. This flexible approach creates an ecosystem where the rights of artists are maintained, moral issues are at the forefront, and innovation is fostered within a sustainable framework.

Institutions find themselves not only in a reactive mode but also in an anticipating one in the complex dance of adaptive governance. The trajectory of AI can be projected, which enables institutions to create policies that anticipate potential problems. This foresight guarantees that authors' rights are strengthened, consumer trust is maintained, and society as a whole is still in a position to profit from AI's creative fabric. Institutions weave new paradigms into the vast tapestry of adaptive governance, in addition to enhancing current regulations. Traditional definitions must be rethought in light of AI, whether they pertain to fair use, ownership, or authorship. Institutions set out on this complex path as the architects of policy, creating frameworks that are inherently indicative of AI's revolutionary character. This in turn helps to create a climate in which both producers and customers behave morally and legally. However, adaptive governance and policy development go beyond the bounds of legal frameworks. They accept the expanded ethical implications that AI brings. The challenge of institutions is to strike a balance between AI-driven innovation and the upholding of societal values. Institutions must strike a delicate balance between encouraging creativity and making sure that it is cultivated within a framework that respects human rights and societal well-being as AI-generated material becomes a cultural force.

As seen, institutions raise their flag for adaptive governance and policy development, navigating the complex space where AI innovation converges with IP protection and societal ethics. Institutions are the definition of agility, ensuring that IP frameworks keep up with the rate of technological development through an uncompromising commitment to change. Their role encompasses the complexities of ethics, cultural integrity, and creativity in addition to the legal system. Institutions act as the curators of balance in the AI age's mosaic, constantly readjusting the scales to maintain creators' rights and protect society's moral compass.

In conclusion, institutions play a critical role in maintaining just and effective IP rights in the era of AI, which will ultimately determine the direction of innovation and creativity. Institutions act as the designers of a vibrant and inclusive IP environment as AI-driven content challenges established paradigms. Institutions lay a foundation that upholds creators' rights while fostering an environment favourable to AI-driven innovation by defining new terms, modifying legal frameworks, encouraging collaboration, enhancing enforcement mechanisms, addressing ethical issues, promoting international cooperation, and raising awareness. Institutions play a revolutionary role in defining an AI and IP coexistence future through these concerted efforts, ensuring that innovation thrives while ethical standards and artists' rights are respected.

13.3 Potential reforms to adapt IP laws to the unique characteristics of AI-generated content

Artificial intelligence (AI) is rapidly advancing, ushering humanity into an era where machine innovation and intellectual property (IP) rights collide, creating a compelling need for prospective reforms. In order to assure fair protection, innovation, and ethical considerations in this rapidly changing environment, the emerging field of AI-generated material challenges the entire foundation of conventional IP regulations.

1. **Redefining Authorship and Ownership**

Potential improvements must start by rethinking the fundamental ideas of authorship and ownership. The special interaction between human programmers and AI algorithms makes conventional attributions more difficult. As AI systems produce content on their own, the issue of authorship gets more complex. A new category of collaborative authorship that acknowledges both human contribution and AI's creative influence could be established as part of reforms. This revision ensures that creators are fairly recognised and compensated in addition to recognising the achievements of AI.

The issue of redefining authorship and ownership stands as a key difficulty in the quickly changing universe of AI-generated material, necessitating a sophisticated and thorough approach. Traditional ideas of creative contributions have been radically changed by the complicated dance between human programmers and AI algorithms, prompting future adjustments that align with the intricate symbiosis between human inventiveness and machine-generated material.

Complexities are introduced by the interaction of human programmers with AI algorithms that are difficult for traditional attributions to handle. AI-generated content blurs the distinction between main authorship and technology facilitation, in contrast to traditional works where a single human author's vision is clearly identifiable. A new conception of authorship is necessary to encompass this hybrid collaboration since the question of who has creative agency transforms into a complex riddle.

The issue of just pay and acknowledgement is at its core. Traditional intellectual property regulations frequently fail to take into consideration the creative influence of AI, potentially undermining the crucial contributions of human programmers. Reforms that uphold the idea of shared authorship are a workable approach. This redefinition more closely reflects the collaborative nature of content creation by recognising AI's function as a co-creator alongside human programmers. By ensuring that both human and machine creative energies are appropriately acknowledged and rewarded, these measures support a healthy environment where innovation is encouraged and intellectual property rights are safeguarded.

In addition to reflecting the complicated reality of AI-generated work, this reimagined concept of collaborative authorship also acts as a mechanism to sustain the moral and ethical commitments connected with creative endeavours. A legal framework that can adequately capture the nuances of this innovative kind of collaboration, which results from the convergence of human brilliance with AI's computational power, is needed. Creators are protected from potential marginalisation and given a platform to discuss just compensation and attribution through collaborative authorship.

This reform also opens up a wider discussion about what creativity actually is. The notion of what it means to be a creator is challenged by AI algorithms' capacity to produce original and innovative content as they get more sophisticated. A paradigm change in cultural attitudes is brought about by the redefinition of authorship, which challenges us to reconsider the nature of creativity and the influence of technology on artistic expression.

Therefore, a crucial first step in creating a fair and harmonious framework for the digital age is to redefine authorship and ownership in the context of AI-generated content. The complex interplay between human and AI contributions calls for reforms that not only take legal complexities into account but also connect with the ethical, cultural, and financial aspects of innovation. By recognising collaborative authorship, we uphold the values of fairness, creativity, and appreciation for creators' contributions in this constantly changing environment, while simultaneously embracing the transformational potential of AI.

2. **Time-Dependent Attribution**

The temporal aspect of intellectual property rights is challenged by AI's capacity to change and adapt content over time. A dynamic attribution approach that changes with AI-generated content may be suggested as a reform. An authorship and ownership approach like this would recognise the dynamic nature of AI-generated works while accurately representing collaborative contributions based on AI's role at each step of content creation. A fundamental reworking of intellectual property (IP) rights is embodied by the idea of time-dependent attribution in the context of AI-generated material, which captures the dynamic interaction between AI systems and creative progress. The requirement for a flexible and adaptive structure that reflects the fluidity of content creation and the progressive nature of AI's engagement is highlighted by this proposed revision.

Traditional IP regulations are ill-equipped to handle the temporal complexity that arises from AI's unique capacity to evolve and improve content over time. AI-generated material, in contrast to traditional works with static attributes, morphs, adapts, and improves itself as it interacts with data and gains new knowledge. As a result, the conventional model of fixed authorship and ownership faces a significant obstacle that calls for a paradigm shift in favour of a more subtle and flexible strategy. A dynamic attribution model appears as a potential remedy in light of this. This methodology calls for ongoing evaluation of AI's contribution throughout the process of content generation. The role of AI is assessed and assigned in accordance with each key turning point or stage of development. A similar strategy ensures that authorship and ownership are not just established at the outset but develop alongside the content itself, reflecting the iterative nature of AI's creative process.

This change embraces the idea of a symbiotic relationship between humans and AI, where writing is a joint effort that develops through time. This concept recognises the incremental contributions of both creators by allocating authorship and ownership based on AI's cumulative involvement. While AI improves and polishes the work, it respects the dynamic nature of content production by promoting an atmosphere where creators are adequately compensated for their continued contributions. Additionally, the idea of time-dependent attribution is consistent with the larger IP protection philosophy, which promotes innovation while defending the rights of artists. This methodology creates a fair distribution of praise and payment by bridging the temporal gap between the original input and continued contributions from AI. It circumvents the difficulties of locating significant turning points in the development of the text, permitting an accurate representation of joint efforts.

A time-dependent attribution model's implementation does, however, provide some practical difficulties. Careful thought must be given to selecting the precise stages at which AI's contributions are evaluated, developing precise evaluation standards, and resolving any potential conflicts. It is a challenging endeavour that necessitates cooperation between legal professionals, technologists, and producers to strike a balance between the growing nature of AI-generated material and the demand for legal clarity. Time-dependent attribution is essentially a possibility The essence of AI's disruptive impact on creativity and the changing landscape of content development is captured by IP reform. This reform honours the iterative character of invention while also addressing the temporal difficulties faced by AI-generated works by embracing a flexible and dynamic framework. It highlights the complex interplay between human creativity and AI's dynamic influence, creating a future where intellectual property rights are protected, innovation flourishes, and artists are fairly acknowledged throughout the growing process of content production.

3. **Enhanced Fair Use and Transformative Work Guidelines**

The areas of fair use and transformative works should also be subject to reform. Fair use principles must be updated in light of AI's capacity to replicate existing work and create transformative versions. To distinguish between transformational AI-generated material that adds value and simple reproduction, strict rules should be created. This difference guards against unexpected violations while encouraging innovation and artistic expression within moral bounds.

An important turning point in the development of intellectual property (IP) laws is the recalibration of fair use and transformative work rules to account for the special dynamics of AI-generated content. In order to find a balance between fostering innovation and defending artists' rights, we must reassess and strengthen these doctrines in light of AI's revolutionary potential as well as its propensity for replication. The cornerstone of copyright law, fair use, allows for the limited use of works protected by copyright without obtaining consent from the original author. However, the strength of AI adds problems that test the conventional limits of fair usage. The line between disruptive innovation and simple reproduction becomes more hazy as AI systems imitate and reinterpret previous information. Fair use reforms must include a thorough analysis of the revolutionary potential of AI-generated material.

The key to reform is the creation of strict rules that can distinguish between two different types of AI-generated content. On the one hand, innovative AI-generated works that offer significant value through insightful criticism, parody, or creative reinterpretation ought to be protected under fair use laws. However, a simple copying or slight adjustment without a significant contribution does not qualify as transformation and should not be considered fair use. This difference protects against unintentional violations and supports the rights of creators.

Reforms enable content producers, AI programmers, and content consumers by defining this border. Creators profit from a reinforced intellectual property system that safeguards their original works while encouraging a creative environment. Clearer standards are provided to AI programmers, encouraging responsible development that supports the creation of ethical content. Customers then have access to AI-generated content that upholds creators' intellectual property and fosters a respect for creators' rights. But putting into practise the improved fair use and transformative work principles comes with its own set of difficulties. Careful thought must go into developing the standards that accurately distinguish AI-generated material from replicative content. To ensure that the reform accomplishes its intended goals without limiting innovation, it is essential to define these criteria through cooperation between legal experts, AI developers, and content producers.

Furthermore, these reforms' ethical components deserve critical consideration. The potential for AI to copy current content prompts moral questions about the integrity of original thought and innovation. As regulations are developed, it becomes increasingly important to find a balance between promoting AI-driven innovation and upholding the moral propriety of content production. This balance supports the overarching goals of IP protection, which are to foster innovation while upholding society values and creators' contributions.

As can be observed, efforts to improve fair use and transformative work rules represent an important step in bringing AI-generated content under the purview of intellectual property laws. These reforms demonstrate the adaptability of legal frameworks in the face of technological advancement by fostering an atmosphere that is favourable for innovation, creativity, and the creation of ethical content. These rules guarantee that the core of fair usage persists while preserving authors' rights and social norms as AI continues to redefine the limits of creativity.

4. Establishing AI as a Legal Entity

Potential amendments could include recognising AI systems as legal entities that are capable of possessing intellectual property rights in order to facilitate legal clarity. A clear foundation for assigning ownership can be developed by giving AI legal personality. This opens the door for direct legal recognition of content produced by AI, making it possible for AI to be more easily incorporated into current IP systems. A paradigm-shifting reform that promises to simplify the complex landscape of intellectual property (IP) rights in the era of AI-generated material is the idea of giving AI systems legal entity status. This change, which is based on the idea that AI is a legal entity, presents a novel framework that is compatible with AI's potential for transformation while resolving the difficulties associated with assigning ownership and authorship.

Fundamentally, the legalisation of AI represents a break from accepted legal norms. It recognises the growing autonomy and inventiveness of AI systems and their participation as active contributors to content creation. This acknowledgement, which is comparable to bestowing legal personhood, raises AI systems above the status of simple tools and puts them as independent legal persons.

One of the major problems with AI-generated material, the attribution of ownership, is addressed by this reform. By giving AI systems legal personhood, a clear and standardised framework for assigning ownership to works produced by AI is created. By removing doubts and potential conflicts about authorship, this method makes it easier to incorporate AI-generated content into the current IP structure.

Direct legal recognition of AI-generated content is also made possible by the idea of AI as a legal entity. AI entities may be able to hold intellectual property rights in the same way as legal companies may. This acknowledgement speeds up the procedure for granting patents, copyrights, and other intellectual property (IP) protections to works produced by AI, guaranteeing that all creators—human or machine—are accorded equal legal status.

This reform is not without its complications and factors, though. When AI systems are given legal entity status, concerns regarding responsibility, accountability, and decision-making arise. The assessment of responsibility in situations involving infringement or ethical transgressions becomes complex as AI systems grow more independent. The creation of a framework that spells out the obligations and restrictions of AI entities while guarding against unforeseen effects calls for a careful balancing act between legal know-how and technological acumen.

Furthermore, careful consideration is required regarding the ethical implications of acknowledging AI as legal entities. Giving AI systems legal personality implies some level of agency and responsibility, obfuscating the distinction between humans and machines. To ensure that the change supports the larger values of justice, transparency, and social wellbeing, it is crucial to strike a balance between this acknowledgment and the ethical consequences of AI's actions and conclusions. A progressive reform that tackles the complexity of AI-generated content in the area of intellectual property is the legalisation of AI. This reform bridges the gap between technology and law by giving AI systems legal personality, providing a smooth transition for AI into the current IP framework. This reform is a cornerstone in sustaining the concepts of attribution, acknowledgment, and equitable protection for creators, both human and machine, in the dynamic and growing world of AI-generated material as AI's creative capacities continue to grow.

5. **Proactive Algorithmic Transparency**

Reforms may impose proactive algorithmic transparency requirements, requiring content producers to disclose the use of AI in their work. By fostering consumer trust through openness, customers are more equipped to choose the information they interact with. Reforms encourage openness while negotiating the issues of credit for AI-generated material by requiring unambiguous labelling or metadata standards.

In the world of intellectual property (IP) rights, the idea of proactive algorithmic transparency is emerging as a paradigm-shifting reform, providing a way to negotiate the complex interaction between AI-generated material and the informed consumer decisions. In order to provide transparency and foster trust in the digital age, this reform introduces a framework that requires content producers to disclose clear and understandable information regarding the role of AI in the content creation process.

Proactive algorithmic transparency, at its core, aims to address a significant issue: the secrecy surrounding AI's contribution to artistic production. The line between human and machine-driven creativity is becoming more hazy as AI systems get more complex and their influence on content creation frequently goes unnoticed. Reforms in this area are intended to clarify this issue by enabling users to distinguish between information written entirely by humans and that written jointly with AI.

Transparency is integrated into the fabric of content distribution by requiring creators to declare the use of AI. Users are given the crucial knowledge they need to comprehend the sources and nature of the content they engage with through clear labelling or standardised metadata. By enabling customers to choose the material they consume with knowledge, this transparency promotes trust and accountability in the digital environment. Effective attribution of AI-generated contributions is made possible by proactive algorithmic openness, which also helps to increase consumer confidence. Creators, whether they be people or businesses, can preserve their dedication to integrity by publicly admitting the use of AI in the production of material. A culture of responsible content creation that is in line with shifting society values is established thanks to this open disclosure, which also protects the reputations of content creators.

However, proactive algorithmic transparency implementation calls for serious evaluation of both technical difficulties and moral ramifications. The development of uniform labelling systems that accurately express the degree of AI engagement necessitates cooperation between creators, technologists, and regulatory organisations. Transparency measures must strike the correct balance between conveying pertinent information and preventing information overload. Otherwise, they risk becoming impractical and difficult for users to understand. Furthermore, it is necessary to consider ethical issues connected to algorithmic transparency. The amount of human involvement and control may vary as AI systems create content on their own. It highlights ethical concerns about the boundaries of disclosure and the ramifications of AI's impact on artistic expression in order to ensure that the reform appropriately represents the true nature of AI's contribution while also protecting authors' intellectual property.

A ground-breaking reform that connects creators, consumers, and the evolving world of AI-generated content is proactive algorithmic transparency. This reform enhances the digital experience by requiring standardised, explicit disclosures, empowering users to make informed decisions, and inspiring producers to value the collaborative synergy between humans and machines. Proactive algorithmic transparency changes the way intellectual property is used by promoting trust, creating responsibility, and advancing the responsible content production culture in the age of AI.

6. Flexible Duration and Termination of AI-Generated Rights

The quick growth of AI-generated content demands adaptable IP durations and termination procedures. In order to ensure that rights are upheld for as long as AI is actively contributing, reforms may push for dynamic IP lengths that take this creative contribution into account. In addition, termination clauses might be added to prevent perpetual ownership by dormant AI systems and provide creators the chance to take back control after AI stops contributing.

A revolutionary reform, the idea of flexible length and termination of AI-generated rights reconciles the temporal aspect of intellectual property (IP) with the dynamic character of AI-generated content. This reform highlights the need for a framework that secures both innovation and just ownership while attempting to overcome the inherent difficulties brought on by AI's quick evolution. Traditional fixed IP durations frequently fall short in the context of AI-generated content when it comes to conveying the spirit of creativity that develops over time. The idea of an unchanging IP lifespan becomes untenable as AI systems continue to learn, adapt, and contribute to content production. A paradigm shift towards dynamic IP lengths that reflect the ongoing contributions of AI is proposed by reforms in this field. This means an IP system in which authors are allowed to profit from their contributions for as long as AI is an active collaborator because the length of rights is inextricably linked to AI's active participation.

Additionally, the addition of termination provisions is a crucial component of this change. Termination clauses give artists the ability to restore control after AI's contributions stop, acknowledging that the creative partnership between humans and AI may be fleeting. By preventing perpetual ownership by inactive AI systems, this precaution promotes a system in which authors are still able to exercise their rights and modify their creations in response to shifting conditions.

To strike a balance between innovation, ownership, and ethical considerations, the adoption of adjustable duration and termination mechanisms, however, necessitates careful calibration. Collaboration between legal professionals, technologists, and creators is required to identify termination triggers, define the process of IP transition, and determine the requirements for active AI contribution. By striking this balance, the change is guaranteed to foster creativity while avoiding unforeseen outcomes, such as maintaining ownership of AI-generated works long after their collaborative creative process has ended. Additionally, ethical issues are raised, particularly with regard to the moral standing of works produced by AI after AI contributions have ceased. A comprehensive strategy that upholds the larger principles of cultural heritage and the public domain while respecting authors' rights is necessary to address issues relating to preservation, credit, and access to AI-generated work.

As a result, the reform relating to the flexible length and termination of AI-generated rights is an example of a progressive strategy that harmonises the fundamentals of intellectual property with the evolving field of AI. This reform recognises the collaborative nature of AI-generated material and equips artists to navigate the developing AI landscape with agency and accountability by adopting the idea of dynamic IP durations and implementing termination clauses. This reform demonstrates the adaptability of IP laws in stimulating innovation, defending creators' rights, and advancing a harmonic balance between technical advancement and artistic expression as the creative cooperation between humans and AI continues to develop.

7. Ethical and Cultural Considerations

To ensure that AI-generated material respects societal values and conventions, reforms should take ethical and cultural factors into account. It is imperative to establish rules to stop AI from creating information that upholds biases, offends cultural sensibilities, or violates human rights. Reforms open the door for ethical AI-generated content production by incorporating moral concepts into IP legislation.

A turning point in the development of AI-generated material is when ethical and cultural concerns are incorporated into the core of intellectual property (IP) regulations. By recognising the tremendous influence AI has had on our values, beliefs, and cultural heritage, this reform goes beyond the bounds of the law. This strategy serves as a cornerstone in ensuring that AI-generated content adheres to society standards, promotes inclusion, and upholds human rights by fusing ethical concepts with IP rules. This change primarily addresses the danger that AI-generated content could reinforce prejudices, stereotypes, or cultural sensitivities. The possibility of unintentionally incorporating current cultural prejudices into content creation looms big as AI systems learn from massive datasets. A safeguarding framework is created to reduce these dangers by incorporating ethical principles into IP changes. This approach requires the creation and use of algorithms that place a high value on fairness, diversity, and consideration of cultural differences.

The establishment of protections against content that violates human rights or cultural sensitivity is part of reforms that address ethical and cultural issues. To avoid AI-generated content from supporting hate speech, false information, or stuff that offends moral, religious, or cultural sensibilities, specific guidelines have been established. This makes sure that AI-driven creativity stays within the parameters of morally and responsibly producing material. The implementation of this change, however, is fraught with numerous difficulties. Understanding cultural nuances, moral principles, and changing societal norms in depth is necessary to determine the ethical standards that AI-generated material must conform to. Guidelines that strike the correct balance between stimulating innovation and protecting ethical integrity must be developed together by ethicists, sociologists, content creators, and legal specialists. Furthermore, issues with responsibility and decision-making arise from the complexity of AI's learning process. Who is accountable when AI-generated content unintentionally transgresses moral or cultural standards? In order to make sure that artists, programmers, and regulatory agencies all share responsibility for preventing ethical violations, it is essential to strike a balance between AI's autonomy and human oversight.

The importance of the ethical and cultural transformation goes beyond mere compliance; it fosters a climate in which AI-generated content benefits society. Reforms encourage a culture of responsible AI-driven innovation by requiring ethical considerations in IP legislation. Creators have the power to make their work consistent with social norms, and AI technologists are driven to create algorithms that contribute to rather than subtract from the cultural fabric.

A paradigm change in the field of AI-generated material can be seen in the inclusion of ethical and cultural issues in IP legislation. This reform supports an inclusive, responsible, and futuristic approach to AI-generated innovation by promoting a connection between ethical values, cultural understanding, and IP protection. The ability of IP laws to encompass not only legal principles but also the ethical imperatives that influence the trajectory of AI-generated material for the benefit of society as a whole is demonstrated by this revision as the digital world changes.

Interdisciplinary cooperation between legal experts, AI technologists, ethicists, legislators, and stakeholders is essential for navigating the path towards reforms. These reforms resonate with the very core of technical innovation and societal values, transcending the purview of the law. These reforms serve as the compass pointing humanity towards a future where innovation flourishes, creators are fairly compensated, and the integrity of IP rights is protected in the face of an AI-driven paradigm shift as the tapestry of AI-generated material continues to grow.

Chapter 14: AI and Cybersecurity

In the ever-changing landscape of technological development, the intersection of AI and cybersecurity appears as a symphony of opportunities and vulnerabilities. In this chapter, we'll begin our investigation into the interplay between different disciplines, peeling back the layers to show how difficult it can be to balance creativity with safety.

This narrative revolves around the central paradox of artificial intelligence. While AI has the potential to revolutionize industries and boost human abilities, it also offers weaknesses that could be used for malicious purposes. As AI spreads throughout vital sectors like healthcare, finance, transportation, and communication, it opens up a broader target for cyberattacks. Cyberattacks of unprecedented scale and sophistication can be planned with the help of artificial intelligence (AI) thanks to the capabilities of this technology, such as autonomous decision-making, flexibility, and data processing competence.

One of the most compelling examples of AI's vulnerability is adversarial attacks. Subtle changes to the input data can fool the AI model into producing inaccurate predictions. Consider the potentially lethal consequences of programming autonomous vehicles to misinterpret traffic signals or ignore barriers. Because of this, it's more important than ever to have robust defenses in place to protect the honesty of AI's judgment calls and keep out unwanted outsiders.

In this intricate tango between innovation and safety, institutions play the role of resilience designers. The cybersecurity landscape for AI is developed by cooperation between governments, regulatory agencies, research institutions, and corporate stakeholders. A significant obstacle that organizations must overcome is the design of safe AI systems that ensure the privacy, reliability, and availability of data and algorithms. When artificial intelligence (AI) systems are built from several datasets, it is imperative that strict data protection measures be taken, including best practices in data anonymization, encryption, and secure storage to reduce the risk of breaches. However, securing AI from cyber threats requires more than technological solutions alone; it also calls for coordinated efforts across borders and the establishment of new legal precedents. The initiative is being spearheaded by institutions, who are formulating policies to ensure the safety and dependability of AI systems. As a practical measure for gauging the security of AI applications, mandatory security audits are proposed. These third-party audits offer in-depth analyses and recommendations for enhancing safety protocols. Liability frameworks enhance accountability and promote responsible AI development by making AI developers liable for security breaches.

The worldwide nature of cyber dangers, however, emphasizes the need for consistent guidelines. Because cyberattacks know no geographical bounds, increasing the global resilience of AI systems requires cooperative efforts that combine information, share best practices, and establish norms. Working together on a global scale increases the likelihood of success in the group's mission to secure digital ecosystems.

Finally, the union of AI with cybersecurity is a treasure trove of creative problem solving and attentiveness. This chapter helps us navigate the shifting landscape by untangling the web of responsibilities, risks, and controls that exist across many institutions. Protecting the transformative potential of AI and securing our digital future calls for the proactive incorporation of robust cybersecurity safeguards. Our goal in analyzing this interplay is to arrive at a time when innovation and resilience are working together to ensure the security and integrity of our digital ecosystem in the face of ever-evolving threats. Through an in-depth and analytical examination of these aspects, this chapter aims to give readers a comprehensive understanding of the intricate relationship between AI and cybersecurity. Using the information in this chapter, we can navigate the uncharted seas of a technologically growing globe with confidence, knowing that the digital infrastructure that supports our interconnected world is secure.

The vulnerabilities and risks associated with AI systems in terms of cybersecurity

In the rapidly evolving world of technology, the combination of artificial intelligence (AI) with cybersecurity presents a unique paradox. While AI has the potential to revolutionize a wide range of sectors, such as healthcare, banking, transportation, and communication, it also introduces a variety of risks that could undermine the safety of online systems. This section delves into the myriad challenges brought on by the dynamic convergence of AI systems with cybersecurity threats and vulnerabilities.

1. Adversarial Attacks and Exploitation

At its foundation, AI's flaws are the unpleasant truth of adversarial attacks. These flaws are able to manipulate AI systems by quietly changing the data they use to make decisions. For instance, artificial intelligence (AI)-powered image identification systems can be fooled by making small adjustments to photographs, leading to misclassification. Attacks of this nature might have devastating effects on vital systems like autonomous vehicles, medical diagnostics, and defense systems.

Attacks from hostile actors are becoming increasingly sophisticated, which poses a serious threat. Using these vulnerabilities, bad actors can bypass security measures, jeopardize data integrity, and get access to private information. The very trust that AI systems are meant to create is undermined when they are entrusted with making crucial decisions, increasing the likelihood of manipulated outcomes.

Adversarial attacks, like technological progress, have become more subtle and varied. A variety of modern learning methods, including transfer learning, generative adversarial networks (GANs), and reinforcement learning, are being used by attackers to create more sophisticated and sneaky adversarial examples. These developments give adversaries more opportunities to exploit AI systems in a wider variety of contexts, making AI security an ever-increasing concern. Furthermore, the repercussions of successful adversarial attacks can reach far beyond the modification of data. It only takes a small change to the input data for autonomous vehicles to cause catastrophic failure. Misdiagnoses, postponed treatments, or erroneous prescriptions are among ways in which medical diagnostics can go wrong and put patients' lives in danger in the healthcare system. Adversarial assaults on defense systems pose a threat to national security because they can impede essential operations or cause the improper deployment of resources.

Researchers and companies working on AI technology now prioritize protecting their systems from being compromised by malicious actors. To lessen the blow of adversarial attacks, there has been a rise in the importance of robustness testing and the creation of resilient AI models. To further ensure that AI systems are thoroughly tested and secured against these dangers, regulatory agencies and standards organizations are increasingly focused on AI security requirements.

While artificial intelligence (AI) technology has tremendous potential, realizing that potential in a secure and safe manner is complicated by the fact that it is vulnerable to attacks by adversaries. As AI systems become more pervasive in everyday life, protecting them from malicious assaults is essential to ensuring that people can continue to trust AI-driven solutions.

2. Data Poisoning and Model Manipulation

Artificial intelligence (AI) systems rely heavily on large datasets for training and learning. However, data poisoning, in which attackers insert bad data to affect AI's learning process, can contaminate these datasets. If this issue is not addressed, it could cause AI algorithms to make biased predictions or evaluations. When AI systems incorporate user-generated content or public data for training, the potential for harm increases. Manipulated data can be used to train artificial intelligence (AI) models to disseminate misleading information, biased information, hate speech, and malicious content. This might have far-reaching effects in fields like social media, where AI algorithms influence information distribution, public discourse, and users' perspectives.

The scope and significance of these problems is an important consideration. The power of AI systems to mold data and sway judgment will increase as they become more pervasive in daily life. Recommendation systems powered by artificial intelligence, for instance, might reinforce biases and create filter bubbles in internet advertising, so limiting the audience's exposure to a variety of viewpoints. It can cause division in the public discourse and prevent well-informed choices. The ever-evolving methods used by cybercriminals further contribute to the difficulty of tackling data poisoning. It is becoming increasingly difficult to detect and successfully mitigate threats from adversaries who are constantly adapting and finding new ways to enter destructive data into AI training sets.

More secure methods of data cleaning and validation are being developed by academics and businesses as a defense against these threats. More and more people are calling for AI systems to be open and accountable so that flaws can be found and fixed as soon as possible. Ethical AI initiatives, together with legislation and guidelines, aim to make the AI ecosystem more secure and accountable.

Overall, the vulnerabilities of AI systems to data poisoning and the possibility of manipulated data shaping AI models constitute significant obstacles to the ethical development and deployment of AI technology. To maintain the values of justice, transparency, and dependability in AI systems as AI develops, it is critical that these problems be solved.

3. Model Inversion and Privacy Breaches

Concerns over privacy and security are warranted since model inversion attacks against AI systems, especially those employing deep learning techniques, can inadvertently divulge private information. Such attacks allow attackers to extract information about the training data and reverse-engineer parts of the AI model's architecture. This procedure may expose private information about individuals and hence endanger their safety.

Particularly worrisome are the repercussions of model inversion attacks on sensitive data-heavy systems like medical diagnosis, financial transactions, and user behavior monitoring. For instance, in the medical field, where AI systems aid in diagnosis, a model inversion attack could compromise patient privacy by disclosing their medical history, treatment plans, or even their identity. A similar risk of financial loss and identity theft exists in the financial sector should customer transaction history or account details become public.

In the face of model inversion attacks, the importance of robust privacy-preserving techniques cannot be overstated. Federated learning, secure multi-party computing, and differential privacy are just a few examples of AI solutions that protect users' privacy and are rising in popularity as viable defenses. By using these methods, AI models can acquire knowledge without having direct access to sensitive information. The issue of privacy in AI research and development is also being emphasized by regulators and industry standards. When designing and deploying AI systems, it is important to keep privacy in mind. Legislation like Europe's General Data Protection Regulation (GDPR) and ethical principles can help with this.

Not only is it a matter of compliance, but also of developing confidence and supporting the wider adoption of AI-powered solutions, to address the privacy threats connected with model inversion assaults. To fully embrace the benefits of AI technology while limiting the threats to privacy, users and businesses need to have confidence that their data will be treated with the highest care and security.

4. Resource Exhaustion and Infrastructure Attacks

The resource-intensive nature of AI computations makes AI systems vulnerable to resource exhaustion assaults. Disruptive and destructive effects on different essential AI applications may result from these assaults, which involve flooding AI infrastructure with a deluge of requests or malicious inputs. When AI models are stored and used in the cloud, resource exhaustion attacks can impede or even halt the execution of AI jobs. Because of this, organizations and individuals who rely on these services for tasks as varied as data analysis and natural language processing may experience interruptions in service. Also vulnerable to performance loss when under attack from resource exhaustion are edge computing deployments, which use AI for instantaneous decision making in remote places. This has potentially far-reaching consequences in areas like driverless vehicles, where making quick decisions in the interest of safety is essential.

In addition, AI systems can be weaponized to launch cyberattacks. Technology backed by artificial intelligence can be exploited by bad actors to send out massive amounts of spam, carry out phishing attacks, or spread malware. As AI spreads into other areas, this raises questions about the reliability of our digital infrastructure as a whole. Security measures of the highest order are required to protect against resource exhaustion attacks. Methods like rate limitation, access controls, and intrusion detection systems can help spot and counteract malicious request patterns. By spreading out computing demands, distributed AI models and redundancy in mission-critical AI systems might help mitigate the effects of resource fatigue assaults.

The use of artificial intelligence (AI) for malevolent purposes is a concern that must also be monitored closely. Monitoring AI systems for indicators of compromise and developing strategies to detect and counter AI-driven cyberattacks is a top priority for organizations and security specialists. It is imperative that ethical considerations and responsible AI development methods be implemented to prevent the misuse of AI technology for malicious ends and instead have it used for the welfare of society.

5. Zero-Day Exploits and Adaptive Threats

The vulnerability of AI systems to zero-day attacks is a growing cause for alarm in today's ever-changing cyber threat landscape. These attacks take advantage of flaws that haven't been discovered by programmers or the security community, making them difficult to patch. There is a risk that AI-driven systems, especially those that use open-source components or pre-trained models, would unwittingly introduce security flaws. These holes let attackers to gain unauthorized access to systems and compromise their functionality, frequently going undetected until serious harm has been done.

There are advantages and disadvantages to using AI in cyber security. Artificial intelligence (AI) has the potential to increase our ability to detect and respond to threats by rapidly sifting through massive amounts of data in search of anomalies. However, adversaries can also leverage AI to develop novel forms of assault. It is extremely difficult to protect against these threats using conventional static security solutions due to their capacity to develop and change their tactics in real-time in reaction to discovered countermeasures. New and flexible defenses are needed to counter these increasing dangers. Artificial intelligence (AI) and machine learning are being used in this area, allowing for better defenses against evolving threats. Anomaly detection, behavior analysis, and machine learning algorithms are all examples of how modern security solutions are helping businesses get ahead of adaptive threats.

To further lessen the likelihood of falling prey to zero-day vulnerabilities, businesses should make frequent vulnerability assessments and patch management top priorities. Sharing information about newly identified vulnerabilities and attack strategies within the cybersecurity community is also vital. So, cybercriminals' strategies change as rapidly as AI does. To protect the confidentiality, availability, and integrity of AI-driven apps and infrastructure, cutting-edge security mechanisms that can adjust to the ever-changing nature of cyber threats must be built into these systems. A dynamic and diverse environment, where innovation and security dance inextricably together, is revealed by the cybersecurity risks and vulnerabilities associated with AI systems. As AI develops its capabilities, more opportunities arise for malicious use. The ever-changing relationship between AI and cybersecurity highlights the importance of preventative, multi-pronged defense systems that can anticipate, recognize, and counteract emerging threats.

To solve these problems, the AI research community, the cybersecurity sector, lawmakers, and industry stakeholders must work together. A comprehensive plan that includes technical innovation, strong standards, ethical concerns, and international cooperation is vital for navigating the ever-evolving world of AI-driven cybersecurity. As society opens itself up to the transformative potential of AI, it must make a concerted effort to decrease vulnerabilities and manage risks to ensure that the promise of a technologically sophisticated future is safe and reliable.

The role of institutions in developing robust cybersecurity measures for AI applications

The convergence of AI and cybersecurity has reached a tipping point that will have far-reaching consequences for the future of our rapidly evolving digital civilization. As AI becomes increasingly prevalent across sectors including healthcare, banking, transportation, and communications, there is an increased demand for robust cybersecurity solutions. The cybersecurity safeguards required to protect AI applications are created and implemented by a wide range of institutions. Institutions can be anything from government agencies and regulatory groups to academic centers and business alliances. In this analysis, we delve into the nuanced and intricate function that institutions play in the creation of solid cybersecurity frameworks for AI applications.

1. Setting Standards and Best Practices

Beyond their consultative function, institutions have a crucial role in establishing the cybersecurity landscape for AI applications. These organizations bring together specialists from many fields (such as academia, business, and government) to share their expertise and develop all-encompassing standards and regulations. These rules are a road map for protecting the privacy and reliability of AI software.

The creation of AI-specific encryption algorithms is an important part of these institutional efforts. Since AI systems deal with enormous volumes of data, some of which may be highly confidential, safeguarding this data from prying eyes is of the utmost importance. Encryption standards and approaches that can reliably protect AI-generated insights and user data are now being defined by several institutions. These rules also include the topic of access control, which is crucial. Institutions understand the importance of regulating who has access to AI systems and at what levels of access. There must be clear guidelines for who can do what, how they can do it, and what happens if they don't.

Due to the complicated nature of AI algorithms and models, secure coding methods are essential during development. Common vulnerabilities and threats, such as injection attacks and buffer overflows, can be avoided by following the advice provided by institutions on how to write AI code that is secure. This improves the stability of the software ecosystem as a whole, and it also increases the safety of AI applications. In addition, AI-specific authentication solutions are designed to strengthen trust in the reliability of AI models and services for authenticating users and other systems. These safeguards are in place to ensure that AI algorithms are not misused or altered in any way.

Institutional initiatives to establish cybersecurity guidelines for AI will have far-reaching consequences. These efforts lay the groundwork for standardized procedures that will increase the compatibility of AI systems across industries. In today's ecosystem-integrated world, where AI is used in everything from healthcare and finance to transportation and manufacturing, this is more important than ever. These uniform procedures directly contribute to increased safety against threats. Vulnerabilities and exploits are less likely to spread when AI systems in different fields use the same security practices. Inconsistencies or lapses in security protocols are less likely to be exploited by cyberthreats.

Institutions help strengthen AI-powered applications by mitigating these threats. Organizations can reduce the potential impact of cyber threats by proactively addressing vulnerabilities and responding efficiently to security incidents. In addition, following organizational norms helps ensure conformity with applicable laws and regulations, which is especially important for businesses operating in sectors governed by privacy and security laws.

To sum up, institutions play a crucial role in establishing the AI cybersecurity landscape by providing the direction and standards required to safeguard AI systems, user data, and the broader digital ecosystem. Their combined efforts clear the path for widespread use of AI technologies that are safe, compatible, and reliable.

2. Regulatory Frameworks and Compliance

The regulatory frameworks that govern the security of AI applications are largely established by institutions. These frameworks are an important line of defense against new forms of cybercrime in the field of AI. They're more than just suggestions; they spell out roles, responsibilities, and penalties for individuals who fail to practice safe cyber hygiene. Institutions aggressively push businesses to invest in cybersecurity and provide adequate protection for AI systems.

The establishment and maintenance of AI applications in line with stringent security criteria is a key goal of these regulatory frameworks. Risks from security breakdowns or breaches can be greatly reduced by adopting practices that are in line with industry standards. Fortifying AI systems' cybersecurity posture, these frameworks often prescribe data encryption, access controls, threat monitoring, and incident response preparation.

In addition, regulatory compliance is about more than just following the rules; it's also about creating a culture of safe and responsible AI deployment. These policies assist lessen the likelihood of AI systems being vulnerable to assaults by pushing enterprises to integrate their AI operations with cybersecurity regulations. As the security landscape changes, they also stress the need for constant monitoring, evaluation, and adjustment of existing safeguards.

Practically speaking, regulatory frameworks lay the groundwork for making sure AI applications are not only cutting-edge technologically but also resistant to ever-evolving cyber dangers. These regulations emphasize the importance of keeping AI systems safe from intrusion by sending the message that cybersecurity is an essential aspect of developing and operating AI. In the end, they help make AI-powered solutions in all kinds of fields more credible and trustworthy.

3. Research and Development

Modern cybersecurity solutions optimized for AI applications are being developed primarily by academic institutions and research groups. Their combined efforts are crucial to improving the safety and robustness of AI programs. These groups do innovative studies to find new approaches to AI security issues, such as improved encryption techniques, anomaly detection algorithms, and intrusion detection systems.

Protecting the massive volumes of data handled by AI systems is a major part of their work, thus they are always pushing the limits of encryption solutions. The goal of this study is to advance data encryption methods that are both effective at preventing unauthorized access and lightweight enough to not slow down AI programs. Researchers in universities and think tanks also study AI's behavior in depth to develop complex algorithms that can spot outliers and potential dangers. This is crucial for identifying anomalous behavior within AI-driven systems that may indicate a hack or security compromise.

Another important area of study is intrusion detection systems. These programs are made to keep an eye out for any suspicious activity or intrusion into an AI environment. Researchers hope that by adapting these algorithms to AI's specific characteristics, they can develop more precise and efficient threat detection mechanisms. The advancement of AI cybersecurity relies heavily on cooperation between educational institutions and research firms. Researchers can pool their knowledge and resources to create ground-breaking answers to the ever-evolving problems in the field of AI-driven technologies by working together on collaborative projects. Institutions provide a safe space for scientists to do their work, contributing to an atmosphere that values new ideas and welcomes experimentation. An innovative mindset is crucial for the creation of cyber defenses that can keep up with the evolving dangers in the field of artificial intelligence.

In conclusion, the joint efforts and ground-breaking research conducted by academic institutions and research groups play a crucial role in enhancing AI cybersecurity. To protect AI systems and guarantee their dependability and trustworthiness across a wide range of applications and sectors, their work helps to the creation of rigorous security measures.

4. Training and Education

To effectively negotiate the complex convergence of cybersecurity and AI, institutions play a crucial role in providing workers with the necessary knowledge and abilities. In doing so, they assume the duty of training a workforce that is not only knowledgeable about AI technology but also capable of creating and maintaining trustworthy AI programs. This is accomplished through various workshops, seminars, and academic programs designed to meet the ever-changing needs of the cybersecurity industry.

Institutional support has been crucial in developing a competent cybersecurity workforce. These experts understand the nuances of AI and know how to easily incorporate strong security measures into AI infrastructure. As part of this process, it's important to learn about and prepare for AI-specific threats such adversarial assaults and model inversion. More than that, organizations actively contribute to fortifying the barrier against cyber threats and breaches that may affect AI programs. Institutions can guarantee the safety of AI systems since their developers and maintainers will have received the proper education and training. This then leads to the development of AI apps that can withstand attacks from the internet.

Organizational activities have far-reaching consequences. The security of entire AI ecosystems is included, not just that of certain individuals. Artificial intelligence (AI) solutions that are both technically advanced and inherently secure benefit from a staff that has received adequate training. As AI spreads into more areas of life, it's important that technology and security evolve in tandem to ensure everyone's safety.

So, institutions play a critical role in bridging the divide between cybersecurity and AI by offering the knowledge and training that professionals need to succeed in this dynamic field.

Together, they strengthen the safety and dependability of AI ecosystems across industries by developing cutting-edge, robust AI applications.

5. Collaboration and Information Sharing

When it comes to cybersecurity, it's crucial that institutions promote an atmosphere that values sharing knowledge and working together. Institutions understand the significance of fostering open lines of communication and collaboration among cybersecurity's many stakeholders because of the field's inherently collaborative nature. Cyber dangers, especially those related to AI, are complex and constantly growing, thus a collaborative strategy is necessary to combat them. Such cooperation is frequently sparked by government agencies, industry consortia, and international organizations. They facilitate forums and programs where interested parties can meet, discuss security issues, and pool resources to find solutions. These sites act as meeting places for professionals from many fields and areas to share their knowledge and thoughts.

The improved awareness of cyber threats connected with AI is a major gain from this cooperation. Cybercriminals' methods are evolving alongside the development of AI systems. Institutions keep the cybersecurity community apprised of new AI-related dangers and vulnerabilities by disseminating information and research findings. This pooled information is priceless for thwarting hackers and staying ahead of their schemes. Together, we can get the word out about effective countermeasures and defenses much more quickly. Collaboration amongst cybersecurity experts from different fields is essential for finding and creating solutions that operate in a wide variety of settings. Adapting to the ever-changing nature of threats calls for this kind of sharing of knowledge and methods.

Cybersecurity initiatives are less likely to be disjointed and more likely to present a cohesive front in the face of cyber threats if institutions are able to facilitate communication and coordination among enterprises. By expanding the scope of cybersecurity to include lessons from other domains and industries, we can better protect critical infrastructure.

As seen, organizations understand that cybersecurity is a team effort and deliberately foster an atmosphere where stakeholders can freely exchange data, conduct joint studies, and build resilient defenses. When it comes to protecting digital ecosystems around the world and addressing the special problems posed by cyber threats related to artificial intelligence, a joint approach is necessary.

6. International Cooperation:

In our interconnected world, cyber threats associated with AI are constantly growing, and international cooperation to combat them is crucial. Their contributions are more than crucial; they will shape the future of cybersecurity in a world driven by AI.

Harmonization of cybersecurity norms, policies, and procedures around the world is not simply a worthy objective; it is essential. Artificial intelligence (AI) technologies are not restricted by geographical location. Institutions are aware of this, which is why they are exerting so much effort into harmonizing cybersecurity measures to make them both effective and consistent across countries. An equal playing field in the fight against cyber risks related to AI necessitates this level of harmonization.

Institutions act as gatekeepers for a cyber border, stopping potential threats at the door. They foster a global spirit of cooperation, which unites people from all walks of life regardless of physical proximity. As cyberthreats related to AI continue to evolve, several groups are working together to develop better security measures. Collaborative efforts like this help institutions establish a global dedication to securing AI applications.

Institutions take on an increasingly important role in ensuring a secure and stable cyberspace as the societal impact of AI expands. Their work is becoming increasingly important as it contributes to maintaining the reliability and safety of AI programs. By doing so, organizations clear the way for a future in which AI-driven technologies can develop without fear in the face of a constantly shifting cyber threat scenario.

Potential regulations and standards to safeguard AI systems against cyber threats

As the technological landscape continues to evolve at an unprecedented rate, the absorption of AI systems into various aspects of society has become both a transformative force and a source of new vulnerabilities. Due to the intricate connection between AI and cybersecurity, a comprehensive regulatory framework and set of standards are required to adequately secure AI systems from the expanding number of cyberthreats. Here we investigate its numerous elements and examine in depth the likely regulations and standards required to secure AI systems against cyber threats.

1. Holistic Risk Assessment and Classification

In fact, an effective regulatory framework must first begin with a thorough risk analysis that takes into account the particularities of AI systems. Deeper exploration of this topic requires familiarity with the many uses of AI and the ever-changing nature of cybersecurity threats.

From creation and release to retirement and disposal, the AI application lifespan is a long and winding road. There are new vulnerabilities and new ways to be attacked with each new stage. An effective regulatory framework will acknowledge the importance of taking a comprehensive approach to AI applications as a whole. This method guarantees that security measures aren't just strong when an AI system is being deployed, but that they are also effective when an AI system is being developed or retired.

In addition, a thorough risk analysis takes into account the fact that AI systems are used for a wide variety of tasks in many fields, each of which presents its own set of challenges. Protecting user data may be a top priority for consumer-facing AI applications, but protecting

AI systems embedded in vital infrastructure from sophisticated assaults with catastrophic implications requires a different level of security. Regulators can respond to this variety by using a tiered risk classification scheme. This framework assigns varying levels of importance and risk to various AI applications. Cybersecurity measures are proportional to the potential consequences by being aligned with the tiered classification of risks, as required by authorities.

For instance, the most strict cybersecurity measures are required for top-tier AI applications that have an effect on essential infrastructure like power grids or healthcare systems. While consumer-focused AI chatbots and other lower-tier applications may not need as many layers of security, they should nonetheless provide the same level of privacy protections as their enterprise counterparts.

A dynamic nature of AI systems, distinct hazards in diverse application domains, and a sophisticated approach to risk assessment are fundamental to effective regulation of AI cybersecurity. This method guarantees that AI technology will be able to develop and help society even as cyber dangers change and advance. It also gives authorities a road map for adjusting their approach as the AI ecosystem evolves.

2. Mandatory Security by Design Principles

It would be a huge step forward for cybersecurity if security by design principles were mandated as part of the legislative process governing the creation of AI. To develop this idea further, it is important to acknowledge how this strategy might radically alter the way AI systems are developed and protected against cyber attacks.

Historically, security precautions have been tacked on at the end of the production cycle, leaving AI systems vulnerable. In contrast, requiring security by design principles ensures that cyber safety is built into an AI project from the ground up. This change places an emphasis on preventative security, making safe coding, thorough testing, and frequent system updates standard operating procedure.

By following best practices for secure coding, you may reduce the likelihood of typical vulnerabilities like code injection and data breaches in your AI. Comprehensive testing procedures guarantee that AI systems are thoroughly examined for vulnerabilities and weaknesses, lowering the possibility of exploitable faults going undetected. Developers of AI systems can stay one step ahead of evolving threats by quickly patching any newly revealed vulnerabilities in light of regular upgrades.

Artificial intelligence systems are intrinsically protected against cyber threats thanks to the regulatory mandate of security by design. By taking this route, the attack surface is minimized, making it harder for cybercriminals to sneak in and exploit vulnerabilities. It's a paradigm shift from the traditional approach to cybersecurity, which focuses on patching holes after they've been discovered. Moreover, implementing security by design principles is in line with the overarching objective of creating AI systems that are not just cutting-edge technologically but also resistant to the ever-changing threat landscape. Trust in AI applications is boosted by this method, which is appreciated by both end users and industry insiders.

Therefore, a proactive and transformational approach to cybersecurity is to mandate security by design principles in AI development through legal regulations. Building AI systems with security as a primary issue from the outset replaces the previous focus on addressing vulnerabilities after deployment. This not only strengthens AI systems' resistance to cyberattacks, but also promotes a mindset of cybersecurity as fundamental to AI research and development.

3. Transparent Accountability and Liability

Responsibility and culpability must be clearly delineated in any AI cybersecurity regulations. This includes outlining the responsibilities of end users, operators, and developers when it comes to the safety of AI applications.

For instance, it is the responsibility of operators to implement critical security measures and fix any vulnerabilities that may occur while AI systems are in use. Meanwhile, it is the obligation of developers to keep their systems secure by updating and patching them on a regular basis to counteract new vulnerabilities.

Consequences for violating regulations must be made clear in writing. These rules not only ensure that people are held to account, but they also encourage all relevant parties to make cybersecurity a top priority. Cybersecurity is not a luxury when it comes to AI development and operation, and this is made abundantly evident by transparent liability frameworks that lay out the potential legal repercussions.

In addition, these frameworks allow consumers and institutions to demand accountability from software creators and network administrators when security flaws occur. The availability of legal redress in the case of a breach encourages stakeholders to insist on rigorous security standards and practices from AI developers and operators. This fosters an ethos of accountability and due diligence within the AI community.

Strong cybersecurity procedures in the AI business can be greatly aided by the development of clear lines of accountability and liability through regulations. This furthers the argument that security measures must be built into every stage of the AI life cycle, not treated as an afterthought. This method aids in creating an AI environment where security is prioritized by all participants.

4. Continuous Monitoring and Incident Reporting

The ever-changing nature of cybersecurity necessitates constant supervision of AI systems via legal frameworks. As such, it protects AI systems in advance of any potential vulnerabilities or attacks.

Strong AI cybersecurity necessitates constant, real-time monitoring. It requires cutting-edge technology to spot outliers, single out risks, and launch prompt countermeasures.

Cybercriminals are always innovating new attack vectors and strategies, thus having access to these tools is essential. In addition, intrusion protection techniques are generally mandated by rules that demand for real-time monitoring. These safeguards serve as digital roadblocks, blocking intruders and foiling cyberattacks before they ever begin. Because they handle sensitive data and perform crucial tasks, AI systems require robust intrusion prevention techniques.

Regulations that require incident reporting standards are put in place to ensure openness and responsibility in the case of a data breach. According to these norms, it is mandatory to notify the proper authorities and impacted parties of any security incident or breach immediately. Effective incident response, threat containment, and damage mitigation all depend on timely reporting.

As can be seen, rules that require constant monitoring and event reporting play a crucial role in improving the security of AI systems. These safeguards prevent data breaches, secure sensitive information, and help keep the public confident in AI's usefulness. These legal protections are becoming increasingly important to guarantee the robustness and security of AI systems as their use spreads across more and more industries.

5. International Cooperation and Information Sharing

Regulations that encourage international cooperation and information sharing are crucial in the field of AI cybersecurity. Such precautions are necessary in today's globally interconnected society, where cyber threats know no borders. These rules ought to be international in scope, with the goal of fostering international cooperation.

Mechanisms for the seamless exchange of threat intelligence, sharing of best practices, and disseminating lessons learned should be established within regulatory frameworks. By working together, governments, businesses, and cybersecurity specialists may pool their resources and expertise. As a result, the international community will be better equipped to deal with the ever-changing cyber threats aimed at artificial intelligence (AI) systems. There are numerous wins to be had by encouraging global collaboration and exchange of data on AI security. The primary benefit is that it improves AI's built-in safeguards against attacks. It improves the ability to detect and respond to complex and nuanced threats that cross state lines by pooling the resources and skills of multiple stakeholders.

Together, the international community can respond swiftly and effectively to new cyber threats. The ability to quickly adapt is essential in a world where the threat landscape is changing at an unprecedented rate. Cooperation-promoting regulatory measures improve the resilience of AI systems and vital infrastructure against these kinds of attacks. Also, initiatives like this help spread a mindset of collective cybersecurity duty. They stress the importance of working together across national boundaries and special interests to protect AI systems. Regulations that foster this spirit of cooperation can contribute to a more secure digital ecosystem in which AI applications can flourish.

Finally, rules that encourage international cooperation and sharing of information are crucial in fighting back against transnational cyber threats to AI systems. They're the backbone of an international security system that allows us to better adapt to new dangers. This cooperative method not only improves AI systems' cybersecurity but also fosters a sense of collective duty to protect the internet.

6. Regular Compliance Audits and Penalties

Compliance audits should be built into regulatory frameworks in the field of AI cybersecurity to evaluate the efficacy of security measures put in place by AI developers and operators. Compliance with security policies, risk assessment methods, incident response plans, and other regulations can be strengthened with the help of audits.

Maintaining and improving the safety of AI systems relies heavily on impartial compliance audits. They offer a neutral assessment of current cybersecurity procedures, pointing out where tweaks or enhancements may be necessary. Audits strengthen the AI ecosystem's cybersecurity by evaluating the compliance of AI stakeholders. The deterrence impact is a major perk of routine compliance audits. Stakeholders are strongly encouraged to proactively engage in successful cybersecurity solutions by the threat of audits and the potential execution of penalties for non-compliance. As a result, the AI industry as a whole develops a sense of responsibility and accountability.

In addition, the security of AI systems is improved by methods that are both open and strict in their compliance requirements. They inspire a sense of urgency and commitment to cybersecurity because of the severe penalties of not complying. Protecting AI systems from potential incursions and hacks requires taking this preventative measure.

So, preserving the security of AI systems relies heavily on rules that call for regular compliance assessments. These audits give the AI sector a neutral evaluation of their cybersecurity processes, discourage noncompliance with punishments, and encourage everyone to take cybersecurity seriously. In the end, they help keep AI applications safe and reliable despite an ever-changing threat landscape.

Thorough regulations and standards must be established to safeguard AI systems from cyber threats. The intricacy and interdependencies of AI and cybersecurity need for a comprehensive, dynamic, and flexible regulatory framework. In this part, we examine a sample plan and emphasize its key features, including a risk assessment, security by design, accountability, continuous monitoring, international cooperation, and compliance audits. By harnessing the potential of effective regulation, society can create an environment where AI-driven innovations flourish while protecting the integrity of critical systems and maintaining the trust of users and stakeholders.

Chapter 15: AI and Environmental Sustainability

In a period of remarkable technological growth and mounting environmental concerns, the combination of AI with environmental sustainability emerges as a beacon of hope and creativity. As our globe struggles with pressing concerns like climate change, resource depletion, and ecological degradation, the incorporation of AI-driven solutions holds the possibility of transforming our relationship with nature. This chapter examines how artificial intelligence (AI) may usher in a new era of environmental sustainability and the critical role that institutions play in establishing this revolutionary course.

Environmental Sustainability with Artificial Intelligence: At the intersection of scientific progress and technological innovation lies the astounding potential of artificial intelligence to revolutionize the pursuit for environmental sustainability. Artificial intelligence's strengths in data processing, pattern recognition, and decision making allow us to tackle challenging ecological issues with unparalleled precision and efficacy. There is a wide variety of ways that artificial intelligence may help the environment, from improving ecosystem management to predicting natural disasters and optimizing renewable energy systems.

Given AI's inherent power to analyze massive datasets and its ability to simulate and predict complicated environmental interactions, next-generation green solutions hold great promise. AI's contributions to sustainability are essential to finding a way for people to live in harmony with the natural environment, as evidenced by developments in precision agriculture, the optimization of energy consumption, and the monitoring of animal populations.

Institutions, such as governments, international organizations, universities, and corporations, play a critical role in making the environmental benefits of AI a reality. They act as futurist architects, guiding the development, deployment, and distribution of AI-driven solutions to the world's most pressing environmental problems. In these groups, scientists, engineers, policy experts, and environmentalists can collaborate across traditional disciplinary boundaries. When environmental protection and AI advancement come together, resources can be better allocated toward the creation of game-changing technologies and rules. As the world recognizes the potential of artificial intelligence, a serious discussion about the challenges and trade-offs of this innovative approach to environmental sustainability is emerging. Institutions need to be careful and forward-thinking as they balance the conflicting goals of protecting the environment and growing the economy.

Artificial intelligence (AI) has the ability to provide both desirable efficiency and undesirable side effects. Insightful discussions on the ethical ramifications of AI in environmental applications, the potential for labor displacement in some industries, and the necessity for vulnerable populations to have fair access to AI-generated solutions are all explored in this chapter. The meeting point of AI and ecological sustainability is an important crossroads that transcends traditional academic, economic, and cultural boundaries. In this first installment, we embark on a trip into a future where AI becomes a beacon of hope in our pursuit of a sustainable future, guided by the stewardship of institutions.

Bringing together the potential of AI, the strategic vision of institutions, and the conscientious consideration of challenges, this chapter presents a panoramic view of a landscape where cutting-edge technologies and responsible policies converge to create a harmonious coexistence between humanity and the natural world. We embrace the transformative potential of AI-driven environmental solutions as we set sail for a greener, more sustainable future and reevaluate our connection with the planet.

The potential of AI to contribute to environmental sustainability and green technologies

In the intricate dance between scientific progress and ecological responsibility, the symphony of artificial intelligence (AI) emerges as a melodic harmony with the potential to alter Earth's future destiny. At a time when climate change, resource depletion, and ecological imbalance cast long shadows, the intersection of AI and environmental sustainability shines a bright light on the path toward a greener, more resilient planet. In this chapter, we delve deeply into the huge potential of AI to encourage the development of green technologies and contribute to environmental sustainability.

Unveiling the Virtuosity of AI: A Multifaceted Palette of Applications

The revolutionary promise of AI is founded on its amazing data processing, analysis, and inference capabilities. Thanks to its proven track record of success, AI is now widely recognized as a crucial component of innovative approaches to addressing environmental challenges. From careful monitoring of natural ecosystems to the optimization of resource management systems, AI offers an unparalleled toolkit that promises to change the parameters of sustainability.

Artificial intelligence (AI) is making waves in the renewable energy sector, where its predictive modeling capabilities are being utilized to increase the efficiency of solar and wind power generation. Modifications can be made in real time based on analysis of complicated weather patterns and energy usage data, leading to increased efficiency and less waste. Smart grids driven by AI can also automatically balance energy distribution, which can cut down on transmission losses and improve the efficiency of power networks.

Precision agriculture is another symphony of AI's contribution to environmental sustainability. Data-driven insights from AI systems allow for precise predictions of agricultural output, optimal fertiliser application, and fine-tuned irrigation plans. This integration of technology and nature increases food security while decreasing agricultural resource waste and its negative environmental impact.

Conservation efforts can also benefit from AI's music. Algorithms powered by artificial intelligence allow scientists and conservationists to track wildlife populations, pinpoint high-risk locations, and find illegal poaching by sifting through mountains of data. These real-time insights help conservationists craft targeted conservation plans that better protect the world's diverse ecosystems.

Green Technologies in the AI Age: A Flourishing Ecosystem of Innovation

The use of AI serves as a catalyst, pushing the development of green technology into uncharted territory. The harmony of AI-driven sustainability solutions resounds in eco-friendly urban design, where algorithms enhance city layouts, traffic flows, and waste management systems. By reducing traffic, energy consumption, and pollution levels, AI transforms cities into eco-friendly role models.

Under AI's watchful eye, waste management has also seen a noticeable transformation. Intelligent sorting systems powered by machine learning enable efficient garbage sorting and recycling. The environmental impact of trash disposal and landfill expansion can be mitigated with the help of sensors powered by artificial intelligence (AI), which monitor landfill capacity and alert workers to the most efficient waste collection routes.

The promise of AI is most evident in the disciplines of disaster prediction and climate modeling. Artificial intelligence systems analyze large datasets, climate models, and past weather patterns to learn more about the causes and effects of climate change. As a result, disaster managers and policymakers can take preventative measures to protect sensitive communities from natural disasters.

Beyond the Horizon: AI's Limitless Canvas of Sustainability

There is no upper bound on the creative, resilient, and coexisting world that artificial intelligence has the potential to paint for environmental sustainability. As humanity moves through the Anthropocene, AI lights the way toward ecologically benign practices and sustainable technology that respect the planet's intricate cycles. This section delves into the nitty-gritty of AI's contribution to sustainability, weaving a tale that considers institutional collaboration, the nuances of challenges, and the symphony of progress and responsibility. As a group, we're embarking on a journey through the revolutionary journey of AI, a place where responsible leadership and technological advancement meet, illuminating the promise of a brighter, greener future.

The role of institutions in promoting AI-driven solutions for climate change mitigation and resource management

Climate change and resource depletion are among the most pressing global issues and have the potential to have far-reaching consequences. The immense difficulty that humanity has in trying to preserve the delicate balance of the planet's ecosystems highlights the critical role that artificial intelligence (AI) may play as a powerful partner in this endeavour. To fully realize the potential of AI, institutions must play the role of visionary catalysts, driving the development and implementation of AI-driven solutions for climate change mitigation and sustainable management of finite resources. This chapter kicks off an in-depth exploration of the various ways in which institutions might help bring about the paradigm shift needed to create a sustainable and environmentally friendly future.

Institutions as Architects of Vision and Collaboration

When it comes to tackling the multiple problems of resource management and climate change mitigation, institutions play a crucial role. In order to achieve their lofty goals, these forward-thinking groups pool their knowledge and resources from several fields, including ecology, economics, technology, and policy. Together, experts from many fields can create a solid plan for fixing the world's most urgent environmental problems.

Regulations and policies established by government bodies are major motivators of sustainability initiatives. They create a regulatory climate that is amenable to good change by allocating money and offering incentives to enterprises who implement environmentally friendly practices. By sharing best practices, coordinating activities across borders, and encouraging data exchange, international organizations like the United Nations and the World Bank encourage global cooperation to enhance climate models and resource management techniques.

Science's grasp of environmental issues can be greatly advanced by the work done in research facilities. They do this through conducting ground-breaking studies that shed light on the complex dynamics of ecosystems and lead to the creation of novel technology that can aid in the monitoring and combating of climate change. To accelerate the creation of AI-driven solutions for sustainable resource management, they form partnerships with industry consortiums to translate academic knowledge into practical implementations.

Consisting of environmentally conscious firms, industry consortia collaborate with academic institutions to integrate AI-driven technologies into their daily operations. In addition to enhancing resource use efficiency, these partnerships help the business sector lower its carbon footprint and adopt more sustainable practices. They influence other industries to join the trend by adding to the ecosystem of innovation.

There is an urgent need for sustainable answers to global concerns, and these institutions have come together to create a symphony of environmental stewardship and AI innovation. They set the framework for collaborative projects that tap into the ingenuity of researchers, engineers, decision-makers, and technologists by funding research, cultivating industrial partnerships, and encouraging information sharing. When taken as a whole, they pave the way for a future where climate change and resource depletion are met head-on with AI-driven solutions that are sustainable, resilient, and effective.

Enabling Data-Driven Insights and Decision-Making

Data is a crucial asset in the fields of resource management and climate change, and institutions have the unique potential to make this resource more widely available to the public. They act as the hub where information from many sources comes together; this includes government agencies, environmental groups, academic institutions, and even citizen-scientists. When institutions work together in this way, they generate a thriving data ecology from which AI algorithms can draw profound insights and patterns.

Artificial intelligence algorithms are given the ability to conduct complex analyses through the combination of disparate data sources, which aids in the making of decisions based on evidence in the fields of resource management and climate change mitigation. By compiling data on climate, ecosystems, weather patterns, and more, institutions provide a more complete picture of environmental dynamics, empowering stakeholders to make educated decisions that affect Earth's future.

The use of AI is crucial to this data-driven procedure. Using it, businesses may keep tabs on environmental indicators on a global and regional scale in real time. The predictive skills of AI improve the accuracy of weather forecasting models, which is essential for catastrophe preparedness and response. Additionally, AI helps with sustainable resource management by optimizing the distribution of water and energy to reduce wastage and maximize productivity.

Artificial intelligence (AI) is being used by institutions to monitor air and water quality at a finer resolution than ever before, resulting in real-time data on pollution levels and the identification of potential health dangers. Additionally, AI-driven climate models may mimic the long-term implications of various policy actions, allowing institutions to develop plans with the greatest impact on climate resilience and preservation. Institutions can assess the results of actions like reducing emissions, planting trees, and switching to renewable energy by running simulations.

Evidence-based policies and tactical actions that promote resource preservation and strengthen climate resilience can be developed with the help of insights obtained from data processed by AI. By encouraging governments, corporations, and communities to embrace sustainable practices that safeguard our planet for future generations, institutions play a pivotal role in effecting positive change. Now more than ever, thanks to advances in artificial intelligence and widespread access to data, institutions are leading the charge in the fight against climate change and paving the way toward a brighter, more secure future.

Fostering Innovation and Technological Adoption

Institutions have a heavy burden not just in ensuring data availability, but also in creating a culture that encourages experimentation with new technologies and their widespread implementation. They spur innovation by fostering a community where businesses, universities, and government agencies work together to create ground-breaking products and services.

Institutions offer a great environment for the trial and error necessary to build and perfect AI-driven technology. As part of this proactive role, you'll be providing support for budding tech-driven enterprises by way of mentorship, advice, and access to resources. Synergies between these new businesses and more established ones contribute to the development of cutting-edge AI-driven tools and systems, and institutions play a key role in facilitating these partnerships.

An important function of institutions is to serve as intermediaries between the academic and professional worlds. They help move innovations from the laboratory into practical use. This guarantees that the exciting discoveries made in the field of artificial intelligence are not left in the abstract but rather are put into action in meaningful ways. Therefore, the findings of cutting-edge research are being applied in fields like energy efficiency and climate change adaptation.

Additionally, universities provide crucial infrastructure for AI-driven solution prototyping, testing, verification, and scaling. They provide the resources and knowledge to improve AI algorithms and technologies, making them more resilient, efficient, and adaptable to the difficult problems of resource management and climate change. With this system in place, environmental protection and climate change projects can more quickly incorporate AI-based solutions.

As was observed, institutions play a variety of roles that all contribute to the development and implementation of AI-driven solutions in the vital areas of resource conservation and climate change mitigation. Their work creates conditions favorable to new ideas, increasing the likelihood that the world's most serious problems will be solved with the help of artificial intelligence.

Policy Formulation and Regulatory Frameworks

The legislative frameworks that encourage the creation and implementation of AI-driven sustainability solutions are mostly the product of institutional decision-making. By passing laws and implementing new policies, they pave the way for a greener tomorrow by encouraging the use of renewable energy and cutting down on carbon emissions.

Institutions should primarily legislate to endorse and encourage the use of ecologically friendly technologies. Sustainable practices, investment in renewable energy, and carbon footprint reduction may be required by legislation. Institutions give businesses the incentive and the obligation to connect their operations with sustainability goals by establishing a legislative environment that promotes green innovation.

The role of institutions in encouraging funding for AI-powered solutions to climate issues is equally critical. They achieve this through enacting regulatory frameworks that provide incentives for spending money on environmentally friendly activities. Businesses are prompted to invest in artificial intelligence (AI) technology that minimize their emissions and carbon tax obligation by carbon pricing methods like these. Investment in AI solutions to tackle climate change is further encouraged by tax incentives targeted specifically at green technologies. In addition, institutions set quantifiable goals for reducing emissions and improving sustainability, providing a road map for businesses to follow. Institutions portray AI as a driver of long-term economic progress by establishing such lofty goals. In order to meet these goals, businesses are incentivized to use AI-driven innovations that improve efficiency, cut down on waste, and lessen their negative influence on the environment.

The adoption of artificial intelligence–driven sustainability solutions is boosted by institutional efforts to shape regulatory frameworks. They advocate for organizations and industries to adopt AI as a potent tool for achieving environmental sustainability and economic development through legislative measures, financial incentives, and goal-setting frameworks. This preventative approach makes institutions powerful agents in the movement toward a more resilient and sustainable future.

Capacity Building and Knowledge Dissemination

When it comes to AI-driven solutions for resource management and climate change, institutions play a vital role, with education and capacity building taking center stage. They facilitate the spread of information, providing access to the materials, workshops, and training courses that can help individuals and businesses make the most of AI's potential.

Institutions greatly aid the spread of AI-driven solutions by providing access to these educational materials. They are crucial in developing experts in the field of applying artificial intelligence to environmental problems. Institutions enable a wide variety of professionals, including legislators, scientists, and practitioners, to effectively integrate AI into their work through training programs and workshops. Institutions equip policymakers with the information they need to make educated decisions about how to use AI in resource management and climate change mitigation. Policymakers can boost sustainability initiatives, advance environmentally friendly technology, and incentivise socially and environmentally conscious behavior if they have a firm grasp on AI's capabilities and possibilities.

Institutions help scientists because they provide them with access to artificial intelligence-driven technologies and procedures. With these resources, scientists can examine massive data sets, simulate intricate ecological networks, and produce more reliable climate forecasts. With the help of AI, researchers can learn more quickly about the causes of climate change and how to better manage scarce resources.

Institutions help professionals in industries like agriculture, forestry, and energy by teaching them to use AI-driven solutions to maximize efficiency, lessen waste, and lessen their influence on the environment. They learn to use AI-powered technology to improve the environmental friendliness of their operations, which in turn leads to better resource management.

As a result, institutions are pivotal in facilitating widespread access to AI-based resource management and climate change adaptation expertise. Through training and education, they equip people and businesses to use AI to its fullest potential, accelerating the search for a more sustainable and resilient future.

Championing Equitable Access and Global Collaboration

Institutions play a crucial role in making AI-driven solutions accessible to people of all backgrounds and locations. They are in favor of equal access to resources like the internet, especially for marginalized communities who will feel the effects of climate change more acutely.

Joint ventures between institutions are one way in which international cooperation is fostered in order to tackle global environmental issues. Institutions strengthen the global effort to tackle climate change and resource depletion by creating a worldwide collective intelligence through information exchange, technological transfer, and cooperative research. Institutions play a leading role in the complex symphony of actions needed to prevent climate change and manage limited resources by coordinating effective responses, encouraging creativity, and guiding policy changes. As the chapter progresses, it delves deeper into issues including the nuances of AI-driven solutions, impending challenges, and the balance between responsibility and progress.

Institutions amplify the potential of AI to create a future that prioritizes climate resilience, resource abundance, and environmental harmony. Institutions, in their role as sustainability guardians, point the way to a brighter future, reshaping our connection to the natural world and setting off a symphony of change propelled by artificial intelligence that will reverberate well beyond the confines of our own era.

Potential challenges and trade-offs in balancing economic growth with environmental concerns in the AI era

In the ever-evolving narrative of human development, the junction of environmental sustainability and economic growth offers a dynamic crossroads replete with complexity and depth. With the advent of AI, the tension between these two priorities has never been greater, and it has sparked a fruitful dialogue about the challenges and trade-offs that may develop as we try to strike a middle ground between the two. This section kicks off a comprehensive exploration of the myriad elements that must be considered to strike a balance between rising economic ambitions and the need to conserve the planet's delicate ecosystems.

The Pinnacle of Prosperity and Planetary Pressures

Finding a happy medium between environmental protection and economic development is at the heart of the matter, and it's a tall order. Humanity's increasing need for natural resources, the breadth of industrial activity, and the relentless exploitation of ecosystems for commercial gain all put significant stress on the environment and contribute to this complex predicament. All of these things cast a pall over our efforts to protect the future of the earth from the likes of climate change, biodiversity loss, and resource depletion.

The rise of AI adds both new challenges and potential answers to this dynamic ecosystem. Technologies powered by AI have the potential to increase productivity, open up new markets, and stimulate economic growth. These innovations do have certain benefits, such as the opportunity to increase economic growth and productivity. However, they incur a high price in terms of environmental impact.

Artificial intelligence (AI) systems, data centers, and the accompanying expansion of supporting infrastructure all have a high power footprint. This increased energy use, mostly driven by traditional fossil fuels, can increase carbon emissions and put more stress on our planet's already stressed ecosystems. If not addressed, the environmental impact of AI technology has the potential to sabotage current environmental protection efforts and undo any progress achieved toward sustainability.

Therefore, it is essential to carefully evaluate the environmental ramifications of AI in order to effectively integrate it into our society and economies. In order to reap the benefits of AI while minimizing its negative effects on the environment, it is crucial to adopt environmentally responsible procedures during the design, construction, and use of AI systems. To make sure that AI-driven advancement is in line with the necessity of maintaining our natural world, we need to do things like adopt energy-efficient AI solutions, invest in renewable energy sources, and enact stringent environmental restrictions. Finding a happy medium between economic development and environmental protection in the AI era calls for creative approaches and unwavering dedication to a sustainable future.

Trade-offs in Technological Triumphs

Smart cities and driverless vehicles are two examples of how AI-driven inventions may soon enter the market and completely transform our economy. These developments have the potential to improve the quality of city life, transportation, and people's everyday experiences. However, it's crucial to keep in mind that the widespread use of AI-powered technology will have serious effects on the natural world.

For example, the complex network of devices, sensors, and data processing centers that underpins the functionality of smart cities requires significant energy and raw materials to power and maintain. Electronic waste is a rising problem, and its production and disposal add extra stress to our already overburdened ecosystem. Similarly, autonomous vehicles have the potential to raise energy consumption and emissions if they are not carefully regulated; this is because they still require energy for production, maintenance, and operation, despite the fact that they promise greater fuel efficiency and reduced traffic congestion.

However, this AI-driven revolution may not be all bad news. As AI develops further, it will be able to better manage available materials and streamline manufacturing procedures. Cities may better manage energy usage, decrease waste, and lessen their environmental effect with the help of smart systems. When connected to an intelligent transportation network, autonomous vehicles can improve traffic flow, cut down on pollution, and conserve valuable resources.

However, a level head is required when considering these developments. The depletion of natural resources and the destruction of crucial ecosystems could result from accelerating economic growth at the expense of sustainable practices. This calls for a far-sighted strategy that puts equal emphasis on sustainable development and economic growth. To maximize the potential of AI-driven economic growth without jeopardizing the health and stability of our planet, we must adopt eco-friendly technologies, embrace renewable energy sources, and enact tough environmental legislation. The successful introduction of AI into our economies will ultimately depend on how well we manage to balance development with ecological preservation.

Human Capital and Technological Displacement

An in-depth analysis of the social costs and benefits of AI-driven economic expansion is warranted. While AI has the potential to greatly increase productivity, encourage creativity, and create new job opportunities, it also presents a challenging challenge: the conundrum of technological displacement. Automation in routine industries and tasks creates a contradiction because it threatens to eliminate jobs, especially in fields where routine tasks predominate.

AI's ability to automate processes has the potential to reduce employment in several sectors. When a company implements AI-driven solutions to optimize operations and decrease expenses, it may reduce the size of its workforce if it relies largely on manual or regular labor. People and communities who have relied on these occupations in the past may feel economic insecurity as a result of their loss. Furthermore, the shift toward AI-driven economies requires human resources trained in the proper administration and development of AI tools. A chasm can open up inside societies without preventative actions to reskill and upskill workers, worsening income disparity. Those who have the skills to prosper in AI-driven environments may reap significant financial benefits, while those who do not may be left on the sidelines and at a disadvantage.

Governments, schools, and corporations must cooperate together on workforce development programs to lessen the likelihood of unintended repercussions from AI-driven economic expansion. To help people adjust to the new realities of the labor market, it's important to make training opportunities available and cheap. To mitigate the possibility of economic inequality and guarantee that the advantages of technological advancement are shared by a wider range of people, initiatives that promote continual learning and skill enhancement might equip workers to remain competitive in an AI-driven economy. To achieve a more inclusive and fair future, nations must leverage the revolutionary power of AI while also addressing the difficulties it creates.

Ethics, Governance, and Regulatory Balancing Act

Finding the appropriate regulatory balance is difficult but essential if we want to make sure that AI development serves long-term goals. Well-intentioned as it may be, excessive regulation can suffocate economic vitality and hamper innovation, impeding the development of AI-enabled sectors. The lack of regulation, on the other side, can cause ethical and environmental problems, along with questions of responsibility and openness, as well as the risk of unforeseen effects. Institutions must be equipped to deal with the moral complexities presented by AI-enabled businesses. They need to tread cautiously between the competing goals of economic expansion and the need for moral protections. Fostering a culture of responsible innovation that serves economic goals and environmental imperatives requires striking this balance.

Regulation that works well will foster innovation while also setting safeguards against any potentially damaging or immoral behavior. For instance, it should encourage openness in AI systems, making it such that algorithmic conclusions can be understood and defended. Mechanisms for holding AI-driven companies accountable for the effects of their technologies should also be established. In addition, legislation should take into account the environmental consequences of AI technology, such as energy usage, and promote the creation of AI solutions that are less taxing on the environment.

To make sure that rules are well-informed and address the concerns of all parties, institutions should actively interact with stakeholders such as AI businesses, environmental organizations, and the general public. By working together, we can build a regulatory framework that protects against unintended consequences and promotes ethical advancements in AI.

Finding the proper regulatory equilibrium in the age of AI-driven innovation is a complex task. Institutions must successfully negotiate the interplay between economic development, moral concerns, and environmental concerns. Institutions can aid in AI development by encouraging responsible innovation through carefully written rules, increasing the likelihood that AI will be developed in accordance with sustainable aims and ethical standards.

Mitigation Strategies and Pathways Forward

This part reveals a wide variety of strategies for coping with the problems and trade-offs, as well as exciting new avenues for development. These methods provide a road map for maximizing AI's usefulness while handling the challenges of environmental responsibility.

Propagating the idea of a "circular economy," which centers on the reduction of waste through the development of products and systems that give top priority to recycling and reuse, is an important tactic. Businesses can lessen their negative effects on the environment and save money on resources by adopting this strategy.

Another important strategy is investing in renewable energy sources to power AI infrastructure. In addition to reducing the carbon footprint of AI systems, shifting to clean and renewable energy is in line with broader environmental aims. The environmental impact of AI-driven technologies may be mitigated by this transition to green energy. In addition, robust legal frameworks play an essential role in fostering eco-friendly behaviors. Incentives for sustainable company practices, reduced emissions, and corporate social responsibility can be achieved by well-crafted rules. These legislative actions foster an atmosphere where economic expansion and environmental protection are mutually supportive.

Leveraging AI's skills as a tool for resource optimization, climate modeling, and environmental monitoring is one effective strategy. Solutions powered by AI have the potential to improve resource management, leading to less waste and more sustainable practices across industries. Better predictions and well-considered policy choices can be made in light of climate change thanks to climate models powered by artificial intelligence. Enhanced by AI, environmental monitoring systems reveal the state of an ecosystem in real time, allowing for more preventative conservation measures to be taken.

The future of environmental protection and economic progress can be shaped via strategic investments in eco-innovation, green technologies, and sustainable supply chains. Institutions, organizations, and governments may set an example for a more sustainable and prosperous world by investing in these efforts. It's clear that we can achieve economic growth and environmental protection at the same time by making these investments in artificial intelligence and sustainability.

The chapter concludes with a summary of the lengthy investigation, synthesizing the various threads of issues, trade-offs, and potential solutions. This article highlights the importance of institutions, decision-makers, corporations, and society at large in charting the course toward a future in which environmental preservation and economic growth are compatible goals. Brushstrokes of innovation, governance, and judgments that go beyond monetary metrics are painting a picture of the AI era. To help humanity achieve a prosperous, equitable, and sustainable future, the AI era presents an opportunity to forge a new nexus where human creativity harmonizes with ecological knowledge. It's a fine art to strike a balance between economic development and environmental protection.

Chapter 16: AI and Consumer Behavior

An intriguing tale that develops at the intersection of human psychology and technological progress, the inseparable union of AI and consumer behavior in the contemporary business and consumer landscape. Artificial intelligence (AI) has had revolutionary implications on the intricate web of consumer decision-making processes, preferences, and the nuanced dance between individual choice and state-of-the-art algorithms, which this chapter begins to explore.

The influence of AI on consumer behavior is intriguing and deserves careful attention as the technology becomes increasingly pervasive in our daily lives, from online entertainment and shopping to individualized suggestions and digital assistants. In this chapter, we'll look at the myriad ways in which AI is changing the mechanics of the marketplace and how individuals interact with it. It's founded on AI's extraordinary capacity to sift through mountains of data in search of trends and make educated guesses about what people want.

The Impact of AI on Consumer Decision-Making: Decoding Preferences in the Digital Age

Artificial intelligence's fascinating and far-reaching impact on consumer choice is fascinating in and of itself. This is a pivotal point in the development of this complex field, as it allows AI to unearth previously hidden insights and preferences that influence consumers' decisions to buy a product by combining algorithms with consumer psychology. AI ushers in a new era of consumer decision-making, one in which personalized product recommendations based on past habits and AI-driven trend predictions are commonplace.

Here, we explore deeper into how AI improves the consumer journey by serving as a digital compass and expertly leading individuals through the maze of options accessible in today's online marketplace. We will explore how AI works behind the scenes to shape the complicated dance between human aspirations, desires, and the countless opportunities made possible by AI-driven technologies. AI's ability to provide customized experiences is one of the most noticeable ways in which it influences purchasing decisions. Artificial intelligence (AI) can make highly accurate product suggestions by evaluating massive datasets that include consumer behaviors, interests, and demographics. By tailoring options to each user's specific tastes and requirements, customization not only reduces cognitive load but also boosts user happiness.

Further, AI's ability to foresee future trends and consumer wants is invaluable. Businesses can benefit greatly from AI-powered systems that analyze data in order to predict future trends and create products and services that meet the needs of a diverse customer base. Companies may adapt their plans to meet the demands of the market with the help of this proactive approach to trend forecasting.

Therefore, the incorporation of AI into consumer decision-making processes represents a fundamental change in the way people interact with the digital world. It allows businesses to better understand and serve their target demographic while also providing customers with a more tailored and time-saving experience. As AI develops further, it will play an ever-increasing role in molding consumer tastes and easing the process of making well-informed decisions, demonstrating the revolutionary potential of this technology in the dynamic realm of consumption.

Guardians of Consumer Rights and Privacy: The Institutional Stewardship

Institutions take on a central role in the digital era as the key protectors of consumer rights and privacy in an AI-driven landscape. Institutions are at the forefront of a delicate balancing act as artificial intelligence (AI) technologies continue to proliferate, bringing unprecedented levels of convenience and innovation to consumers while simultaneously posing threats to the rights and privacy they are meant to protect.

In this pivotal position, institutions employ a multipronged strategy to negotiate the complex landscape of AI-powered markets. They are responsible for analyzing legal structures, creating data governance regulations, and resolving the ethical questions that lie at the heart of the AI revolution. This chapter delves into the methods used by these organizations to ensure customer confidence, lessen the likelihood of negative outcomes, and foster an environment where AI and consumer rights can live without conflict. Their primary duty is to create and uphold regulatory frameworks that are appropriate for the dynamic state of AI today. These frameworks are the backbone of consumer safeguards, outlining how AI should be created, used, and deployed. Institutions carefully create these regulations to achieve a balance between encouraging innovation and protecting customers' rights and interests, thereby restricting the scope of legal gray areas in which AI systems can operate.

Institutional oversight is not complete without data governance policies. Institutions are committed to implementing sound data governance procedures in light of the fact that AI depends critically on massive amounts of data. Data collection, storage, dissemination, and utilization are all covered by these rules. By taking such precautions, businesses hope to ensure that customer information is treated with the utmost confidentiality, protecting individuals' right to oversight of their data. The potential for AI algorithms to amplify prejudice, bigotry, and inequality is also not lost on institutions. To combat this, they perform regular audits and checks on AI systems to check for and fix any biases that may be present. By pushing for openness in AI research and development, organizations provide consumers more agency over AI-driven decisions by giving them insight into the decision-making process.

As was demonstrated, the onus of protecting consumers' rights and privacy in an AI-driven environment falls squarely on the shoulders of institutions. Their concerted efforts across legal frameworks, data governance laws, and ethical concerns are crucial to creating a setting in which AI's benefits can be realized without jeopardizing basic ideals of consumer protection.

Institutions remain dedicated to protecting these rights while AI continues its rapid progress, which will help maintain trust and ethical innovation in the digital era.

AI-Driven Advertising and Consumer Welfare: Pioneering New Paradigms

Together, personalized marketing and AI-driven advertising are ushering in a new era of dialogue that is changing our concept of consumer welfare in the era of digital change. This study digs into the complex relationship between AI-driven advertisements and the happiness of consumers, illuminating the enormous impact that AI has had on the dynamics of contemporary advertising.

In this engrossing story, we explore in detail how AI is radically altering the field of advertising. The days of generic, one-size-fits-all marketing are numbered in favor of hyper-targeted campaigns that are tailored specifically to each consumer's tastes and habits. With the use of AI, marketers can develop cutting-edge tactics that infuse all digital interactions with smart algorithms, allowing them to cater content to each individual user's preferences. However, our investigation goes farther than simply looking into the practical implications of AI-driven advertising for consumers. Concerns about manipulation in this data-rich ecosystem are naturally prompted. We strike a balance between the privacy concerns that can arise when AI algorithms gain access to sensitive personal information and the benefits of offering tailored recommendations that improve the customer experience.

Because of the wide-ranging nature of the effects, we will be looking at both the advantages and disadvantages of AI-powered advertising. On the one hand, artificial intelligence allows marketers to create compelling stories that hit home with customers on an emotional level and increase loyalty. On the other side, as AI algorithms constantly learn and adapt to customer behavior, there are worries about privacy, data security, and unintended effects.

In the end, our investigation sheds light on the groundbreaking new paradigms appearing at the crossroads of AI-driven advertising and consumer welfare. It sheds light on how the marketing landscape is shifting in this brave new AI-driven world, particularly at the intersection of technology and ethics and how the choices taken by firms and authorities will affect the future of digital advertising and the safety of consumers.

The Harmonious Symphony of Choice and Technology

As we delve deeper into the intertwined worlds of artificial intelligence and consumer behavior, we hope to weave together a tapestry of insightful analysis and meaningful musings. We seek equilibrium between the revolutionary impact of AI on consumer choice, the watchful and ever-evolving role of institutions in protecting consumer rights, and the ever-shifting terrain of AI-driven marketing. All of these factors come together to form the complex landscape that characterizes the modern consumer's journey.

As we set out on this adventure through the rapidly changing digital age, where AI is constantly honing its grasp of human tastes and habits, we are moved to ponder the broader ramifications of this technological revolution. Recognizing that AI, while a potent instrument for increasing the consumer experience, also offers problems and ethical implications, we ponder the delicate balance that must be achieved between innovation and consumer well-being.

Society must address issues of privacy, security, and justice in this era of unprecedented connectivity and data-driven decision making. In order to ensure that consumers' rights are safeguarded and their data is used ethically, institutions play a crucial role in developing legislative frameworks governing ethical AI use. As the reach and influence of AI continue to grow, their watchful eye and flexibility are more important than ever.

In addition, the growing influence and personalization of AI-driven advertising prompts serious concerns about the balance of power between corporations and consumers. There is a delicate balance to be struck between really helpful recommendations and overbearing manipulation of customers when using personalization. We are guided by ethical considerations as we navigate this space, which highlight the significance of openness, informed consent, and consumer agency.

In conclusion, we approach this ever-changing terrain of artificial intelligence and consumer behavior with a healthy dose of self-awareness and introspection. The promise of AI and consumer preferences working together is a future where people may use technology to make decisions that are true to their beliefs and goals. Navigating this landscape with a common goal of protecting consumers' and society's best interests in the digital age requires a dedication to ethics, education, and teamwork.

The impact of AI on consumer decision-making processes and preferences

The ubiquitous presence of artificial intelligence (AI) in today's connected world has sparked a revolutionary shift in the nuanced world of consumer choice. The fascinating phenomena of how AI-powered technologies are changing the dynamics of modern consumption is becoming increasingly apparent as they invade more and more areas of our lives, from online shopping to entertainment. In this section, we begin our investigation into how AI affects consumers' decision-making processes by deconstructing the various mechanisms by which AI modifies and tests people's tastes.

Personalization and Precision: Redefining Consumer Preferences

Artificial intelligence's ability to tailor user experiences to each individual is a major factor in how it affects purchasing decisions. Artificial intelligence (AI) algorithms, fed by massive amounts of data, examine patterns, habits, and preferences to curate individualized offerings. With the help of AI, businesses can now produce hyper-targeted content that speaks to the preferences and goals of each individual customer, putting an end to the era of generic marketing.

Beyond only suggesting products, this method is highly tailored to each individual customer. Insights powered by AI probe deeply into daily routines, anticipating future wants and affecting purchases. The more AI interacts with its users, the more it learns about them and their tastes, leading to a mutually beneficial relationship in which both parties benefit. As a result, shoppers enjoy greater ease and contentment as they confidently make purchases in a market that has been carefully arranged to meet their specific requirements.

The introduction of AI-driven personalisation has caused a paradigm shift in the way consumers make choices. AI's unique capacity to re-calibrate consumer preferences is at the heart of this shift, giving rise to an unprecedented level of personalisation and precision throughout the whole shopping experience. AI's strength comes from its ability to process large amounts of data, which includes everything from a user's online activities and transactions to their social relationships and online habits. Using these data sets, AI systems may shape experiences for individuals in ways that were previously impossible. The constraints of traditional demographic categorizations are overcome as AI sorts through these complex patterns, uncovering the minute intricacies that determine individual preferences.

Casting a wide net in an effort to catch even a small number of interested consumers with mass ads is so last century. With the arrival of AI, every connection will be a chance to provide hyper-targeted material that perfectly matches the recipient's preferences and aspirations. This accuracy goes far beyond simple product suggestions and permeates the entire customer experience. Insights enabled by AI probe deeply into the complex web of consumer behaviours, revealing not only current tendencies but also anticipating dormant needs that have yet to be openly defined. Because of AI's predictive nature, businesses and consumers can get a taste of what they want before they even know they want it. The process is similar to a dance in which AI partners with humans to learn from their actions and grow in understanding over time.

As a result, the marketplace has been fundamentally reimagined, and shoppers now face challenges unique to their preferences. Products, services, and content are carefully selected so that they speak to a person's individual tastes and interests. With this much customization available, shopping becomes more than just an exchange of goods and services; it becomes an opportunity for the customer to explore their own identity. Despite the seeming perfection of this individualized paradise, several issues arise. Because of the massive amounts of data needed to power AI's personalisation engine, ethical and legal concerns have been raised. Convenience comes at the cost of consumers giving up some degree of control over their personal data. Concerns regarding the societal effects of hyper-personalization arise from the possibility of AI creating filter bubbles, which reinforce current preferences while limiting exposure to diverse ideas.

The impact of AI on consumer choice goes far beyond efficiency gains; it encompasses a radical reinvention of the modern customer's complete journey. Data, algorithms, and human desires have come together to usher in an era when each interaction is a unique path that ultimately leads to decisions that have profound significance for the individual. There will be a dynamic interplay between technology and human agency as AI-driven personalisation continues to develop, forcing us to strike a balance between individual agency and protection of ethical considerations.

Unveiling Latent Desires: AI as a Trend Forecaster

Artificial intelligence (AI) is being used more and more in consumer decision-making, and this is revealing previously hidden needs and trends. Analytics driven by AI can sift through large datasets to reveal hidden trends, track changing tastes, and forecast the future. This allows companies to provide cutting-edge goods and services that speak to the current mood of consumers before those needs become widely known.

What this means for customers is a future where their needs are not merely anticipated, but anticipated before they even ask for them. New goods that suit their changing tastes can be found with the help of AI. Consumer decision-making is enhanced by anticipation and discovery as AI-generated insights highlight what is beyond the horizon of conventional choices.

The advent of a new era of trend forecasting that goes beyond the limits of human intuition is heralded by the introduction of AI into the sphere of consumer decision-making. Artificial intelligence (AI) is playing an increasingly pivotal role in business, one that goes well beyond the obvious. By probing the underlying currents of consumer behavior, AI is able to reveal latent wants and emerging patterns that would otherwise remain hidden in the complex tapestry of data. The power of AI stems from its unrivaled capacity to navigate enormous datasets with dexterity and precision. This massive computing capacity acts as a lighthouse, pointing the way for organizations as they navigate the murky waters of new patterns, changing tastes, and prospective trends. As a result, there has been a dramatic change in the way that companies and consumers view and engage with the market.

The repercussions for businesses are significant. Artificial intelligence (AI) has the analytical power to sift through the digital footprints of innumerable consumers, interpreting the subtlest shifts in their behaviors and preferences. With the help of this dynamic analysis, organizations may not only respond to existing trends but also anticipate the emergence of brand new ones. To predict future trends, AI can act as a sentinel, monitoring the present and listening for hints about the future. With this insight, companies can create cutting-edge goods and services that perfectly capture the spirit of the times and give them an edge in the marketplace. Delivering on consumer expectations and fostering a sense of resonance and connection can be achieved through the timely launch of offerings that capture the pulse of rising trends. Consumers are no longer passive observers; instead, they actively shape new directions in the marketplace and foster a two-way dialogue with companies beyond the transactional level.

Consumers may look forward to a world of increased anticipation and discovery thanks to the use of AI as a trend forecaster. The process of choosing becomes a fascinating adventure, with each new purchase promising to reveal the latest and greatest in fashion. As AI-generated insights reveal what lies beyond the conventional, consumers navigate an unfamiliar terrain of options, each tinged with the excitement of discovery. There is a complicated interplay of ethical problems, however, that lurks underlying the attractiveness of this predictive utopia. There's a fine line between appealing to consumers' subconscious urges and altering their tastes. Businesses and institutions need a moral compass to help them harness AI's predictive capabilities in a way that doesn't end up exploiting people.

Artificial intelligence's ability to predict future trends has far-reaching implications for business and the arts. Data analytics, AI algorithms, and human desires all working in harmony to usher in a golden age of conscious spending. Future developments in AI-driven trend forecasting will force us to negotiate the intersection of creativity, responsibility, and free will, resulting in a state of equilibrium between foresight and surprise.

Enhancing Decision-Making Efficiency: The Rise of AI Assistants

The introduction of AI-driven virtual assistants will have an even greater effect on customer choice. These digital assistants are easy to incorporate into daily life, and they provide timely guidance and support for a variety of decisions. AI assistants deliver instantaneous information, reviews, and recommendations for a variety of tasks, including dining out, traveling, and shopping.

Effectiveness in selecting choices is consequently improved. Using AI's extensive database of information and analytical prowess, customers may instantly sort through available alternatives. This effect of streamlining not only saves time, but also reduces the mental strain associated with making decisions, giving people more assurance in their final selections. Artificial intelligence (AI) powered virtual assistants emerge as guiding beacons, lighting the way to educated and efficient decision-making in the complex tapestry of modern life, where every instant is saturated with choices. These AI-powered digital assistants are already a part of people's daily lives, lending a hand with everything from the most menial tasks to the most life-altering decisions.

These virtual assistants are the first step toward a cooperative relationship between artificial intelligence and the process of making choices. People can bring AI assistants into their lives with a simple invocation, giving them access to a wealth of information and advice. Whether it's helping you decide where to eat tonight, organizing an exotic vacation, or finding your way through the maze of shopping possibilities, AI assistants are at the ready to deliver personalized, up-to-the-moment information and guidance. The resulting increase in productive deliberation is nothing short of revolutionary. With such a wealth of data at their disposal, consumers can confidently wade through seemingly endless options with the help of AI-powered assistants. Once a demanding task, sorting through possibilities, weighing consequences, and making predictions is now reduced to a conversation with a computer program.

The impact on one's mental environment when making decisions goes much beyond the undeniable ease of use. Decision fatigue is a serious problem that can get in the way of good judgment in a world full with options. Artificial intelligence (AI) assistants, with their speedy information synthesis and personalized recommendations, become allies in reducing this mental strain. Because they don't have to agonize over every possible outcome, people are able to make decisions with greater certainty and clarity.

However, the proliferation of AI helpers raises a wide range of concerns, just as any new technology does. Despite their convenience, these digital aids have been linked to a decline in critical thinking. In order for AI to enhance decision making without inhibiting the development of human judgment and discernment, a fine balance must be maintained in the symbiotic interaction between humans and AI. As AI assistants get more involved in people's daily lives, they learn more about them and their habits, leading to privacy and security concerns. Institutions and governments have a critical problem when trying to find a middle ground between providing individualized support and protecting sensitive data.

The advent of AI helpers ushers in a new era of consumer decision-making marked by increased productivity, ease of use, and agency for the buyer. A future where judgments are guided by insights that go beyond individual capacities is hinted at by the coming together of human agency and artificial intelligence. However, moving forward necessitates careful thought of what this transformation means. The ethical compass must lead us to a peaceful coexistence where digital companions enhance human potential rather than destroy it as society navigates the uncharted waters of AI-powered decision-making.

Challenges and Considerations: The Duality of AI Influence

However, there are some challenges associated with incorporating AI into the decision-making processes of consumers. There are growing privacy and security risks associated with the increasingly tailored recommendations generated by AI. Concerns have been raised concerning the morality of collecting, using, and storing the massive amounts of user data needed to power AI algorithms. The dangers of AI creating "filter bubbles" or reinforcing preexisting biases also merit investigation. However, because AI bases its suggestions on users' past actions, it may unintentionally prevent them from being exposed to novel ideas and perspectives.

A seductive dichotomy, combining the wonders of customisation with the nuanced threads of ethical considerations, develops in the hypnotic dance between artificial intelligence and consumer decision-making. While the revolutionary surge of personalisation and convenience brought about by AI's incorporation into the very fabric of decision-making processes is undeniably appealing, underlying this fascinating surface lurks a tapestry of problems and complexities that require our undivided attention.

Artificial intelligence's prowess in tailoring results to each individual is founded on the mountains of data it consumes, processes, and analyzes. An increasingly pertinent question arises as AI-driven recommendations go from merely suggestive to eerily attuned to human preferences: what is at the intersection of customization, privacy, and data security? Concerns about the ethical gathering, use, and storage of personal data are at the heart of the symbiotic dance between artificial intelligence and the customer.

This moral conundrum has repercussions in many areas of society, not just the technological ones. Institutions and stakeholders must consider how to strike a balance between using AI's ability to decipher consumer preferences and protecting the sacred sphere of privacy. To keep the light of data misuse and illegal access from dimming the synergy between AI and personalisation, we need a strong framework that provides openness, informed consent, and data protection.

To paint a vivid picture of a world enriched by personalized insights and recommendations, AI's palette goes far beyond simple personalization in the broad tapestry of consumer decision-making. The ability to understand and predict human behaviour, which is what gives AI its power, also raises a delicate concern. Inadvertently reinforcing existing prejudices and restricting exposure to alternative perspectives, known as "filter bubbles," throw a pall over the available options.

There is a real danger that the horizon of options may be narrowed as AI systems filter ideas based on past behaviour. Artificial intelligence (AI) led journeys that perpetuate pre-existing views may eclipse the organic exploration of new territory in decision-making, the chance contact with novel notions, and the mosaic of contrasting opinions. Once a vivacious orchestra of songs, the symphony of consumer choice now risks becoming an orchestrated monotony.

Institutions and technologists must work together to strike a balance between individualization and variety. The onus is on us to cultivate AI systems that not only understand preferences but also embrace the art of serendipity, presenting customers with viewpoints they might not have encountered otherwise. Institutions may foster a culture in which AI serves as not just a decision-making confidant but also a motivator for discovery by weaving together the essence of personalisation with the richness of variety. The beautiful symphony of customization highlights the tremendous possibilities of the space where artificial intelligence and consumer decision-making interact with one another. The halls of confidentiality, data ethics, and the search for multiple viewpoints all reverberate to the tune of this beautiful song. To successfully navigate this dichotomy, we need a balanced strategy that protects personal freedoms while tapping on AI's revolutionary potential. Institutions must use their batons of leadership wisely as the AI and personalization symphony evolves, ensuring that the music strikes a balance between creativity and accountability.

In conclusion, the influence of AI on consumer choices is complex, involving issues of accessibility, individualization, and morality. How people make their way through the modern economy is rethought in light of AI's enhanced ability to refine preferences, foresee trends, and improve decision-making efficiency. A fine balance must be struck between maximizing the benefits of AI and protecting privacy, diversity, and consumer agency as this technology continues to change preferences. The AI-driven consumer decision-making landscape promises a future where options are more personalized and perceptive, allowing people to make educated choices that are in line with their ever-changing wants and needs.

The role of institutions in protecting consumer rights and privacy in AI-powered markets

Institutions play a pivotal role in the delicate tango between artificial intelligence (AI) and consumer involvement, using their clout to safeguard individuals' rights and privacy in AI-enabled markets. The revolutionary potential of AI reshapes the dynamics of business and engagement, necessitating the construction of rigorous frameworks to assure ethical standards, informed consent, and accountability.

Ensuring Ethical Practices

When it comes to ethics in markets driven by artificial intelligence, it is institutions that function as the vanguards. New ethical problems arise with the introduction of AI into interactions with consumers, such as the need to be open about how data is being used, to avoid bias, and to prevent discrimination. Institutions ensure that AI-powered systems run in a way that doesn't violate basic rights, puts justice first, and prevents the unintentional reinforcement of biases through the use of regulations and norms.

Coming to talk about shaping the ever-changing landscape of AI-powered markets, institutions are the unwavering vanguards of ethical conduct. A new era of unimaginable possibilities begins with the seamless integration of artificial intelligence (AI) into consumer interactions, but with this new era comes a plethora of ethical problems that require careful analysis and action.

Artificial intelligence (AI) changes the fundamentals of customer interaction by adding layers of complexity to the process that were not previously present. Among them, the need for clear explanations of how data is being used stands out as a top need. Institutions are beginning to acknowledge the importance of being transparent and clear with consumers about how their data is being gathered, processed, and used by AI-powered systems. In order to provide customers more agency over their personal data, institutions have enacted tough regulations to ensure that companies are held accountable for reporting the breadth and purpose of data utilization. In addition, a firm dedication to fighting bias and preventing discrimination is essential as businesses increasingly use AI in their dealings with customers. Organizations are aware that the underlying algorithms and AI systems powering these exchanges can inherit biases from their training data. As a result, they established exhaustive rules that force businesses to do thorough audits and assessments of their AI models in an effort to eradicate discriminatory outcomes and correct underlying biases that may seep into decision-making processes.

Institutions' roles in the ever-changing world of AI-powered markets go far beyond basic regulatory monitoring; they have significant sway in shaping an environment that protects fundamental rights and principles of fairness. Institutions' overarching goals lay the groundwork for AI systems to serve as agents of empowerment and accessibility rather than the upkeep of inequality. The goal is to forge an atmosphere where technological innovation flourishes hand in hand with ethical considerations, giving customers the comfort that their rights will be protected as they interact with AI-powered services. For a future where AI-powered markets are bastions of fairness, transparency, and inclusivity, enhancing consumer experiences while protecting the underlying values that characterize our society, institutions must chart the way for ethical AI practices.

Fostering Informed Consent

The concept of "informed consent" takes on new significance in the context of markets driven by artificial intelligence. Consumers need to be well-informed about the use of their data, the scope of AI-driven personalization, and the potential ramifications of their decisions, and institutions play a crucial role in this regard. Consumers are given agency in an AI-driven world when organizations are required to provide transparent information about how their customers' data is used.

In the ever-changing universe of AI-powered marketplaces, informed consent is more important than ever as the bedrock of moral consumer interaction. In this new context, institutions play an important role as watchdogs over consumers' rights and agency, defining the parameters of openness and agency that regulate people's interactions with AI-driven technologies. The importance of consumers knowing how their data is used and how much artificial intelligence-driven personalisation affects their experiences has been acknowledged by institutions. This understanding drives the creation of stringent guidelines that call for transparent communication that is brief, to-the-point, and easy to understand. Institutions enforce these standards to ensure that businesses provide clear and understandable information to customers about the data utilization and AI-powered decision-making processes that affect their lives.

Institutions' responsibilities go beyond simply enforcing rules; they also represent a dedication to creating a setting in which people can exercise choice and control over their interactions with AI. Institutions may better equip consumers to deal with the complexities of AI-powered markets if they advocate for informed consent and help people make choices that are in line with their beliefs and goals.

There is a growing culture of trust and responsibility in AI as organizations define the boundaries of informed consent. Consumers' interactions with AI-driven systems thrive on this foundation of trust, turning what was once cause for concern into a world of agency and possibility. When institutions work together, AI-enabled markets emerge as spaces where consumers make educated decisions, where data is used as a tool of empowerment, and where the principles of informed consent strengthen the bond between technology and humanity.

Upholding Data Privacy

Against the backdrop of AI-powered markets, institutions have taken on the role of data guardians in this era defined by data proliferation. Strong data protection standards, such as the General Data Protection Regulation (GDPR), allow organizations to specify clear boundaries for the gathering, storing, and sharing of personal information. Institutions can rest easy knowing that AI-driven systems are secure from intrusion by upholding stringent data privacy requirements.

As AI-driven businesses continue to proliferate, information on consumers' habits and preferences will become increasingly valuable. Institutions play a pivotal role as gatekeepers in today's data-rich environment, exercising their responsibility to safeguard individuals' right to privacy. In the complex ecosystem of artificial intelligence systems and consumer interactions, institutions perform the role of sentinels, developing and enforcing rules to protect individuals' privacy.

Strong data protection standards, such as the General Data Protection Regulation (GDPR), are at the forefront of this safeguarding effort. These regulations were established with the firm belief that customers should have control over their personal information and that such information should be protected, and they give organizations the ability to define the parameters within which such information may be acquired, maintained, and shared. In order to protect against the subtle infiltration of unauthorized access and the dangers of data exploitation, institutions provide strategic direction that establishes a comprehensive and severe set of rules that AI-driven systems must comply to.

Because of their steadfast commitment to the well-being of their customers, institutions take data privacy seriously enough to make it the foundational concept around which AI-powered markets are built. Institutions guide the balance between technological progress and the protection of individual rights by establishing the ground rules for interaction. As data continues to weave the complex tapestry of consumer interactions in the age of artificial intelligence, it is the vigilance of institutions that bolsters the walls of defense, creating an atmosphere where trust and confidence flourish and consumer data is protected from unauthorized access.

By protecting individuals' right to privacy, organizations are sending a clear statement that the game-changing potential of AI must be exploited in accordance with the ethical principles of responsible data handling. By doing so, institutions not only foster a digital landscape where individuals can engage without apprehension, fully aware that their data is shielded by the watchful guardianship of institutions, but also contribute to the long-term growth of AI-powered markets.

Navigating Algorithmic Transparency

The complicated algorithms supporting AI-powered markets add a new level of opaqueness. To help customers make sense of AI processes and conclusions, institutional advocates for "algorithmic transparency" are crucial. In order to build confidence in AI-powered interactions and make sure consumers understand how decisions are made, institutions enforce policies that make it necessary for businesses to reveal the inner workings of their AI-driven systems.

When it comes to making sense of the complex decision-making processes at play in today's AI-driven markets, institutions shine as beacons of light and clarity. The basic foundation of these markets rests on intricate algorithms that exert outsized influence over customer actions. Unfortunately, this level of complexity frequently results in a cloud of obscurity, leaving consumers to puzzle over the mysterious workings of algorithms. Institutions provide a guiding light in this complex environment by promoting algorithmic openness as essential to consumer agency and confidence.

Transparency in algorithms is a paradigm shift toward making the inner workings of AI systems more accessible to the general public. Awareness of the disparity in power between technology and consumers has led to calls for rules requiring companies to reveal the inner workings of their AI so that customers may make more informed decisions. Consumers benefit from this advocacy because it helps them understand the reasoning behind suggestions, forecasts, and individualized services. As algorithms manage more and more of the options available to consumers, increased openness about how they work will help humans better understand artificial intelligence. By pushing this imperative, institutions encourage companies to be transparent about the algorithms they use, giving customers more information with which to make informed decisions in the digital sphere. Institutional advocates for algorithmic transparency embody ethical stewardship that goes beyond simple disclosure. Organizations are obligated to make sure their AI systems are in line with ethical norms and customer interests if institutions push for easily understandable algorithms. This open approach guarantees that the benefits of AI are used not just for profit, but for the general good of consumers as a whole.

With their regulatory muscle, institutions cause a seismic shift that reshapes the foundations of AI-driven markets. Openness about algorithms helps develop a mutually beneficial relationship between businesses and their customers. Institutional leaders in the movement for more openness are like beacons, illuminating the road toward a future in which consumers are empowered, informed, and confident in their interactions with the algorithms that define the options available to them in AI-powered markets.

Redefining Accountability

Institutions are rethinking what it means to be accountable in AI-powered marketplaces as AI systems become more embedded in consumer interactions. They promote a culture of responsibility that goes beyond human actions by establishing frameworks that make organizations liable for the outcomes of AI-driven decisions. That corporations are nonetheless responsible for their actions in the face of AI-powered interactions is reinforced by the fact that institutions provide customers with avenues for redress in the event of AI-related errors, prejudices, or malfunctions.

The traditional contours of accountability undergo a fundamental revision in the ever-changing universe of AI-powered marketplaces, where computers traverse the intricate terrain of customer interactions. Institutions will be at the forefront of changing accountability paradigms in the new era ushering in with the advent of AI systems as active actors in decision-making. This revolutionary effort is more than just a change in terminology; it is a fundamental rethinking of accountability in a society where machines play an ever-greater role.

Institutions play a crucial role in this fast-paced field by designing frameworks that go beyond the traditional notion of responsibility. As institutions promote a culture of accountability that goes beyond human activities, it naturally expands into the realm of AI systems and the consequences of those actions. Accountability is therefore redesigned to include not only human behavior but also the biases and results produced by AI entities. Institutions may ensure that businesses take responsibility for AI-driven actions by exercising their regulatory authorities. Although these decisions are made by algorithms, their effects on user experiences and decisions are far-reaching. Therefore, institutions provide the groundwork for a systematic approach that requires businesses to claim responsibility for AI-generated results. By promoting a culture in which responsibility is not compartmentalized but rather accepted on a whole, this framework protects consumers' interests.

Additionally, institutions play the role as recourse architects, strengthening consumer rights in the face of AI-related faults or prejudices. Institutions' ethical duty emphasizes the concept that organizations are not immune from resolving unexpected repercussions of AI-powered interactions. In order to protect consumer rights in the face of the revolutionary tide that is AI, a new paradigm is required in which institutions provide channels for redress, restitution, and correction.

The institutional watchful eye has reshaped the accountability framework to go beyond the traditional confines of duty. It exemplifies the evolution of AI-driven markets into an ecosystem in which businesses, spurred on by institutional requirements, accept their responsibility as gatekeepers of AI-driven interactions. To successfully navigate the dynamic interplay between human agency and machine influence, this new paradigm is crucial, as it creates a coherent narrative in which businesses are held responsible not only for their actions but also for the intricate orchestration of AI-powered decisions that shape the consumer landscape.

Nurturing Innovation within Ethical Bounds

Institutions do a fine balancing act between creativity and morality in markets driven by AI. They simultaneously create a climate that promotes AI-driven innovation and defines the ethical limits within which that innovation can occur. By finding this middle ground, organizations can promote AI-powered solutions that give consumers more agency without sacrificing on ethical standards. This unlocks AI's full potential to improve consumers' lives without infringing on their rights.

In the world of AI-powered markets, where the climax of innovation is in tune with the ethical undercurrents, institutions stand out as the conductors of a nuanced symphony. Orchestration is more than just putting things next to one other; it's a sophisticated activity that encompasses things like encouraging a crescendo of innovation while keeping it in tune with the ethical limits that serve to protect consumers. There is a precise ballet taking place between innovation and ethics, and institutions are the ones at the helm.

The awareness that new ideas are the fuel that keep AI-driven marketplaces humming is the driving force behind this concerted effort. Institutions use their sway as gatekeepers of development to prod businesses toward innovative uses of AI. They create a climate where the infinite potential of AI may be used to open up new avenues of consumer connection, redefine experiences, and accelerate revolutionary transformations through legislation, grants, and incentives. However, ethical sensibilities underlying society norms and consumer expectations must act as a brake on the rising tide of innovation. Understanding the precarious nature of this balance, institutions lay forth the parameters of ethical constraints that direct AI-powered innovation. Even as innovation reaches new heights, they provide a moral compass that protects the protection of consumer rights, data privacy, and societal well-being.

Institutions play a delicate role, striking a balance between stifling innovation and compromising ethics. They are responsible for developing frameworks that encourage the creation of AI-powered solutions that are in tune with the symphony of progress while also being sensitive to the ethical harmonies. These guidelines outline the limits of what constitutes good innovation, so that progress isn't made at the expense of customers' rights and freedoms.

It is clear from the institutional mediation of innovation and ethics that the development of AI-powered markets is not a zero-sum game. Instead, it's a group effort to bring together the creative potential of businesses with the ethical requirements of larger institutions. This concordant coming together gives rise to a milieu where AI-powered inventions flourish, infused with a feeling of duty and dedication to the common good.

Markets driven by AI are becoming concert halls where the music of development can be heard echoing through the halls of consumer experiences as institutions cultivate an atmosphere that embraces the union of innovation and ethics. It's a symphony that builds to a crescendo of a future where innovation, constrained by ethical considerations, boosts consumer well-being and reimagines the very fabric of involvement in AI-powered markets.

Enabling Consumer Empowerment

In the end, institutions give people the tools they need to confidently and actively engage with an AI-powered world. Consumers are empowered through regulation, education, and activism to make smart choices, take charge of their data, and stand up for their rights. Consumers go from observers to decision-makers as a result of this empowerment, altering the dynamics of AI-driven markets to better serve their needs. Institutions play a critical role as the orchestrators of consumer agency in the emerging world of AI-powered markets, where computers choreograph interactions and data flows like a symphony. Their job description goes well beyond monitoring, since it also includes giving customers the tools they need to successfully negotiate this complex ecosystem. Consumers go from being onlookers to being the architects of their own AI-driven futures thanks to the dynamic interaction of rules, education, and advocacy provided by institutions.

Regulations that protect consumer rights and data privacy are the background onto which institutions paint this transition. Regulations, like brushstrokes on a painting, mold the form of markets driven by AI so that they are consistent with principles of fairness, transparency, and accountability. Consumers gain confidence in their interactions inside AI-powered ecosystems because of these regulatory frameworks' adherence to principles that put their needs first.

Another pillar of consumer empowerment, education serves as the paintbrush that brings the picture to life. Institutions play the role of teacher, distributing information on how AI systems function, the risks associated with data sharing, and the processes by which individualization is achieved. This effort to educate customers makes them active decision-makers who can distinguish between the algorithms that influence their preferences and the moral principles on which such algorithms are based.

Advocacy serves as a rousing climax to the consumer empowerment symphony, raising consumers' voices to a higher pitch in the AI-driven arena. Institutions protect consumers' rights, making sure AI systems are morally sound in addition to cutting-edge in terms of technology. Consumers' voices are heard and addressed by institutions, which in turn creates a culture where consent, fairness, and autonomy permeate all interactions and data sharing. This institutional symphony embodies a reimagined concept of interaction in the AI-powered economy, going well beyond the simple act of buying and selling. Knowledgeable customers become more than passive beneficiaries of AI-driven products and services; they shape their own digital experiences through advocacy and regulation.

The empowering journey fueled by institutions exemplifies the essence of democracy in AI-powered markets: a world in which every action is infused with free will, every choice is grounded in insight, and every piece of information is a reflection of personal agency. Institutions set the groundwork for an AI-powered market that respects and amplifies consumer sovereignty through legislation, education, and lobbying, ensuring that the symphony of progress is in harmony with the individual notes of empowerment.

In conclusion, institutions play a nuanced and significant role in safeguarding consumer rights and privacy in AI-powered marketplaces. Institutions have an important role to play as AI continues to alter business-to-consumer interactions by protecting values like openness, responsibility, and data privacy. Institutions can protect consumers' interests and create an environment where artificial intelligence's transformational potential can be realized without compromising the ideals that support a just and equitable society by establishing an ecosystem that harmonizes innovation with ethics.

Potential implications for advertising, personalized marketing, and consumer welfare in the AI era

Advertising, tailored marketing, and consumer welfare are just few of the fields that are feeling the effects of the AI era's transformational wave. The prospective effects of evolving AI technology in these areas are so far-reaching that they require careful examination. This essay explores the nuances of these consequences and provides a thorough analysis of the future landscape.

Revolutionizing Advertising and Marketing

Like an earthquake that upends the landscape, AI will shake up the marketing and advertising industry. As a result of AI's pattern recognition and data analysis capabilities, companies can more effectively communicate with their ideal customers. Advertisements are transformed into one-on-one discussions as personalization takes center stage and allows marketers to target consumers with pinpoint accuracy. Since customers are more likely to connect with material that reflects their interests, behaviors, and aspirations, this shift increases the possibility for engagement.

With the use of AI-powered predictive analytics, businesses can better position their wares in response to consumer demand. This foresight optimizes resource allocation and makes contacts with consumers relevant rather than obtrusive, reducing the reliance on the hit-or-miss strategy of conventional marketing. As a result, customers experience less noise in the advertising world and are more likely to come across messages that are relevant to them. Artificial intelligence (AI) is at the center of a seismic shift occurring in the advertising and marketing industry. Artificial intelligence (AI) is shaking up the landscape of how businesses and customers interact in significant ways. Because of AI's dynamic powers, traditional marketing techniques have been propelled into a new era of exceptional personalization and engagement. These skills stem from AI's unique capacity to scan enormous datasets and discover nuanced patterns.

The concept of customization, which AI has taken to new heights, is at the center of this transformation. Using AI, companies can now have meaningful, one-on-one discussions with customers, rather than just broadcasting standardized messages to a wide demographic. As a result of this shift in thinking, commercials are no more one-way broadcasts but dynamic conversations that speak directly to the tastes, habits, and goals of their target audiences. With such granular targeting, participation might increase dramatically. Once subjected to an onslaught of generic commercials, consumers are now more likely to come across content that is tailored specifically to them. By catering to individual tastes, this method goes beyond the typical one-size-fits-all method and fosters a sense of resonance and connection. Therefore, consumers are more inclined to interact with information that they find relevant and intriguing, which in turn increases the likelihood of ad clicks, ad views, and brand loyalty.

In addition to its impact on personalisation, AI has also revolutionized predictive analytics, which is used by marketers to foresee and prepare for customer behavior. With this skill, companies can understand the complex web of customer wants and desires and position goods and services in ways that strike a chord with customers. Precision-driven methods, in which resources are used optimally and contacts with consumers are meaningful rather than intrusive, are replacing shotgun approaches to marketing. For companies and customers alike, this shift has far-reaching repercussions. Contrast this with the current advertising landscape, where content that isn't relevant to the viewer's interests competes for their attention. This not only improves the quality of life for consumers but also increases the efficiency of advertising. The possibility for even more nuanced and accurate targeting becomes more evident as AI continues to improve and enhance its predictive abilities, creating a virtuous cycle of refinement that benefits both sides.

Artificial intelligence's revolutionary effects on advertising and marketing are revising best practices for connecting with consumers. Brands can now connect with their customers on a more meaningful level because to AI's analytical prowess, which has facilitated the shift from mass communication to individualized discourse. As a result of this revolutionary change, customers will have a more fulfilling and interesting experience, which is exactly what they want. Consumers should expect a new era of extraordinary personalisation, relevance, and engagement as businesses continue to use AI-driven information to hone their marketing efforts.

The Ethical Tightrope of Personalized Marketing

While tailored marketing has a lot of potential, it also has some ethical issues to work out. There's a narrow line between customization and prying eyes, so tread carefully. Privacy protections should be balanced with the accuracy of artificial intelligence-driven personalization. Institutional support for strong data protection policies and rules protecting personal information is essential for achieving this delicate balancing act, which will result in the ethical and transparent use of consumer data.

Moreover, there are concerns regarding the variety of ideas due to the possibility of AI creating "filter bubbles," in which individuals are exposed only to material that corresponds with their previous beliefs. Institutions face a difficult problem in preventing biased marketing practices from stifling creativity and innovation. To find your way through this minefield of moral quandaries, you'll need to strike a careful balance between catering to individual preferences and encouraging a balanced and inclusive data ecosystem.

While AI-enabled tailored marketing ushers in a new era of consumer-business interactions, it also introduces new ethical challenges. Businesses must walk a fine line between satisfying customers and protecting their personal information as AI enables them to provide content that is perfectly tailored to each individual. This paradox highlights the importance of organizations addressing the moral challenges of targeted advertising in the age of AI. Personalized marketing is, at its essence, a balancing act between being useful and annoying. While it's important to give customers individualized services that cater to their tastes, it's also crucial to protect their privacy in the process. The fine-grained accuracy made possible by AI requires stringent adherence to privacy and security laws. It is the responsibility of institutions to create and enforce strict rules for the gathering, storing, and use of individual data. The best way for businesses to secure their customers' private information against theft, misuse, and data breaches is to advocate for and implement strong data protection regulations.

Another ethical consideration that organizations need to take into account is the potential for "filter bubbles" to form. Inadvertently reinforcing existing prejudices and limiting exposure to other perspectives are both possible outcomes of AI's ability to personalize content based on past behaviors and preferences. In order to overcome this obstacle, institutions must push for policies that promote a balanced and varied information ecosystem. One way to accomplish this goal is to publicize algorithms that sprinkle a bit of randomness or serendipity into consumers' individualized recommendations.

The foundation of morally sound tailored marketing is openness. Institutions play a critical role in promoting transparent and understandable disclosure methods that educate customers on the scope of data collection, the motivations behind personalization, and the risks to their personal data and privacy. Consumers need to have control over their data and the ability to make decisions based on accurate information. Additionally, the ethical discussion includes the role of institutions in closing the digital divide. Institutions have the potential to shape regulations that guarantee everyone has equal access to AI-powered personalized experiences, halting the widening of existing class divides. Making sure the advantages of targeted advertising reach everyone requires supporting programs that increase digital literacy and level playing fields.

Thus, the many factors that institutions must weigh are highlighted by the ethical precipice presented by personalized marketing in the age of AI. Institutions may build a framework that takes use of the revolutionary potential of individualized marketing while protecting consumers' privacy, diversity, and the right to equal access. Creating a tailored marketing landscape that gives consumers agency while protecting their privacy requires a fine balancing act between innovation and personal privacy.

Augmenting Consumer Welfare

The welfare of consumers becomes increasingly important as well as a major beneficiary of the AI-driven marketing revolution. Ads that are specifically tailored to a user's interests improve the user experience by decreasing the amount of noise they have to wade through and encouraging them to focus on the most relevant information. When shopping, customers are more likely to come across goods and services that are tailored specifically to their need. In addition to improving advertising, AI could also improve overall customer satisfaction. By analyzing consumer spending patterns with AI, businesses may create items and services that are more suited to individual tastes. Increased efficiency and economic growth are two outcomes of this better matching of supply and demand.

As AI-driven marketing radically alters the landscape of consumer behavior, a complicated story of worry and agency emerges, leading to a substantial improvement in consumers' well-being. The AI's multifarious implications for consumer well-being are highlighted by this impact's dualistic nature, which is characterized by the pinpoint accuracy of targeting and the greater breadth of market innovation.

In the age of AI, precision and relevance are central to the idea of customer welfare. Ads are redirected from a sea of generic information and into a world of hyper-personalized relevance, thanks to AI's capacity to analyze massive databases and recognize complex patterns. As a result, the flood of useless adverts is much diminished, relieving consumers of the need to wade through meaningless information. This simplification results in a more productive use of time, allowing customers to zero in on material that truly speaks to them.

Transforming the shopping experience is fundamental to AI's positive effect on consumers. Artificial intelligence and consumer data are coming together to usher in a new era of razor-sharp judgment. Businesses can better meet the needs of their target markets by analyzing their customers' prior actions and preferences. This mutually beneficial interaction between AI-driven insights and consumer expectations not only improves the retail experience, but also helps bring supply and demand into better harmony. Beyond the area of advertising, the improvement of customer well-being has far-reaching effects. The predictive analytics of artificial intelligence have the ability to completely alter the market landscape by adapting goods and services to consumers' ever-changing tastes. This in-depth familiarity with customer wants and needs is the bedrock of innovation, allowing for the development of fresh approaches to old problems. Markets respond positively to this innovation, which boosts growth and efficiency across the board.

However, difficulties also arise throughout this period of change. Careful navigation is required due to the presence of ethical problems relating to data privacy, the possibility of algorithmic biases, and the risk of reinforcing filter bubbles. Institutions play a critical role in determining how to best utilize AI-driven marketing strategies while minimizing risks. Transparency, justice, and accountability in the application of AI are crucial to the pursuit of consumer welfare. As can be seen, the marketing revolution fueled by AI is a potent tool for social change. Central to this shift are improvements in targeted accuracy, consumer experience, and innovation generation. Institutions and enterprises must walk a fine line between advancing technology and being ethically responsible as they traverse the complex network of AI-powered customer interactions. Institutions can magnify the positive influence of AI on consumer welfare by advocating for consumer rights, data privacy, and different perspectives. This will usher in a new era of consumer empowerment, efficiency, and contentment.

In conclusion, artificial intelligence (AI) has far-reaching and ever-evolving ramifications for commercials, targeted promotions, and the general well-being of consumers. Customized interactions that boost participation and minimize waste are the hallmark of the age of artificial intelligence. However, privacy, diversity, and consumer agency must all be protected by this shift in focus to ethics. Institutions may use the advantages of AI-powered personalisation to improve customer experiences and well-being while minimizing risks in a dynamic environment. How businesses interact with their audiences and how customers navigate the market will be profoundly impacted by the future of marketing as the industry strives to strike a balance between precision, ethics, and consumer interests.

Chapter 17: AI and Healthcare Economics

In a period marked by swift technological progress, there are limited fields that possess the potential to significantly transform human welfare and societal structures to the same extent as artificial intelligence (AI) within the domain of healthcare economics. The ongoing development of advanced AI technologies and their integration with the complex dynamics of the healthcare sector has revealed a growing promise for transforming healthcare delivery and improving economic efficiencies. This chapter initiates a thorough examination of the intricate connection between artificial intelligence (AI) and the field of healthcare economics. It delves into the potential for transformation that AI brings, emphasises the importance of ensuring equal access to its benefits, and acknowledges the ethical complications that arise in this transformational process.

The Potential of AI to Revolutionize Healthcare Delivery and Reduce Costs

The current discussion surrounding artificial intelligence (AI) and healthcare economics mostly revolves around the significant transformation occurring in the delivery and management of medical services. The incorporation of artificial intelligence (AI)-enabled systems and algorithms has introduced a novel framework in the field of healthcare, which presents significant potential in terms of accurately and swiftly detecting, treating, and preventing diseases. The utilisation of machine learning algorithms, natural language processing, and computer vision technologies is significantly transforming the field of medical research, diagnostic processes, and patient care protocols.

Artificial intelligence (AI) is facilitating a paradigm shift in healthcare by enabling early disease identification using data-driven predictive models and optimising treatment regimens using real-time patient data, thus paving the way for personalised and targeted healthcare. The redefinition of healthcare systems' cost structure is being driven by the ability to decrease inefficiencies, eradicate diagnostic errors, and optimise resource allocation. Through the automation of administrative duties, the optimisation of resource utilisation, and the enhancement of clinical decision-making, artificial intelligence (AI) not only holds the potential to ease budgetary pressures but also gives the opportunity to reallocate resources to areas that are of utmost importance.

The Role of Institutions in Ensuring Equitable Access to AI-based Healthcare Technologies

The revolutionary potential of AI-driven healthcare advances is indisputable; yet, ensuring equal distribution and accessibility of these advancements is of utmost importance. The integration of AI technology into healthcare systems necessitates the consideration of potential amplification of pre-existing gaps in healthcare access. In the realm of artificial intelligence (AI), the involvement of institutions and policymakers is of utmost importance as they have a significant influence on the direction of AI implementation. Their role is crucial in ensuring that the progress made in AI is utilised to bridge existing gaps in society, rather than exacerbating them.

The task encompasses not only the implementation of technology but also the resolution of obstacles such as safeguarding data privacy, overcoming infrastructural constraints, and accommodating differing degrees of digital literacy. This chapter will explore the collaborative endeavours necessary for the establishment of inclusive frameworks that facilitate the utilisation of AI-driven healthcare by underserved communities. The event will emphasise efforts to promote equal access, encourage collaborations between public and private sectors, and cultivate a healthcare environment that empowers marginalised people.

Ethical Considerations and Privacy Concerns in the Use of AI in Healthcare Economics

The increasing integration of artificial intelligence (AI) into the healthcare sector brings forward prominent ethical considerations and privacy concerns. The need to strike a balance between the potential benefits of data-driven insights and the obligation to protect patient privacy requires the establishment of a comprehensive ethical framework. This chapter aims to examine the ethical quandaries that arise in the context of artificial intelligence (AI) implementations within the healthcare sector. These problems encompass various aspects, such as the use of confidential patient information, the likelihood of algorithmic biases, and the consequences associated with autonomous decision-making.

Through the analysis of case studies and the examination of regulatory methods, this chapter aims to shed light on the dynamic and changing ethical considerations within the realm of AI-powered healthcare. Furthermore, it will emphasise the significance of interdisciplinary cooperation among healthcare practitioners, technologists, policymakers, and ethicists in order to effectively navigate the intricate landscape of artificial intelligence (AI) integration while upholding the fundamental principles of patient autonomy, consent, and confidentiality.

In summary, this chapter will establish the foundation for a thorough investigation into the mutually beneficial connection between artificial intelligence and the field of healthcare economics. This study aims to examine the revolutionary potentials, equity imperatives, and ethical nuances associated with the use of artificial intelligence (AI) in healthcare. By conducting a comprehensive analysis, this research will offer a strategic framework for leveraging AI's capabilities to restructure the delivery of healthcare services, promote equal access to healthcare, and uphold the ethical principles that underpin contemporary healthcare economics.

The potential of AI to revolutionize healthcare delivery and reduce costs

The use of artificial intelligence (AI) inside the healthcare industry has substantial potential for transforming healthcare provision and generating substantial cost reductions. Artificial intelligence (AI) technologies, which include machine learning, natural language processing, computer vision, and predictive analytics, have the potential to revolutionise various aspects of the healthcare industry. These advancements can significantly impact areas such as diagnoses, treatment, administrative procedures, and patient involvement. This section examines the various ways in which artificial intelligence (AI) is positioned to transform healthcare delivery, enhance patient outcomes, and help to cost control.

1. Precision Diagnostics and Personalized Treatment

The capacity of artificial intelligence (AI) to effectively handle and evaluate extensive quantities of medical information, encompassing electronic health records (EHRs), medical imaging, and genomic sequences, has resulted in a fundamental transformation in the field of diagnosis. Machine learning algorithms possess the capability to swiftly discern intricate patterns and correlations within these datasets, hence facilitating expedited and more precise disease identification. One example is the utilisation of artificial intelligence (AI)-powered algorithms to assist radiologists in the identification of initial indications of cancer within medical imaging. This application has demonstrated potential in enhancing patient prognosis and increasing survival rates.

In addition, artificial intelligence enables the tailoring of treatment strategies according to specific patient attributes. Through the analysis of patient data, artificial intelligence (AI) systems have the capability to forecast treatment responses and anticipated bad effects. This empowers physicians to customise medicines according to the individualised requirements of each patient. The implementation of a personalised strategy not only serves to improve patient outcomes, but also serves to mitigate the reliance on trial-and-error methods in treatment, resulting in a reduction of healthcare expenses associated with ineffective interventions.

2. Predictive Analytics and Preventive Care

The predictive analytics capabilities of artificial intelligence (AI) have considerable potential for transforming the healthcare sector's emphasis from a reactive approach to a proactive one. Through the examination of past patient data, artificial intelligence (AI) has the capability to discern individuals who are at a heightened risk and forecast the emergence of specific ailments. This empowers healthcare providers to take proactive measures and intervene prior to the exacerbation of these problems. The implementation of this proactive strategy not only enhances the overall health and wellness of patients, but also mitigates the economic strain associated with the management of severe diseases.

Furthermore, wearable gadgets and mobile applications that utilise artificial intelligence have the capability to consistently monitor the vital signs of patients, thereby offering immediate and up-to-date information for the timely identification of abnormalities. The implementation of this early warning system has the potential to provide prompt interventions, hence mitigating the occurrence of hospital readmissions and emergency room visits, both of which significantly contribute to healthcare expenditures.

3. Streamlined Administrative Processes

The complexity and expenses associated with administrative tasks in the healthcare sector, such as billing, coding, and claims processing, are widely recognised. The implementation of AI-driven automation has the potential to mitigate this burden through the optimisation of administrative operations. The field of natural language processing encompasses the ability to analyse medical documents, extract pertinent details, and effectively assign appropriate codes for diagnoses and procedures, hence facilitating proper billing operations. Not only does this practise decrease the occurrence of errors, but it also expedites the process of payment, hence enhancing the revenue streams for healthcare providers.

Additionally, artificial intelligence (AI)-powered chatbots and virtual assistants have the capability to manage routine enquiries from patients, facilitate appointment scheduling, and offer information. Consequently, this relieves administrative personnel of these responsibilities, enabling them to concentrate on more intricate assignments. This not only improves patient involvement but also adds to cost reduction through increased operational effectiveness.

4. Drug Discovery and Clinical Trials

The pharmaceutical sector is being transformed by artificial intelligence (AI), which is accelerating the processes of drug research and development. Machine learning algorithms provide the capability to analyse extensive datasets encompassing molecular structures, pharmacological profiles, and clinical trial outcomes, hence facilitating the identification of prospective drug candidates. The expedited medication discovery process diminishes the duration and resources needed for introducing novel therapies to the market, hence reducing the expenses linked to research and development.

In addition, artificial intelligence (AI) has the potential to enhance the optimisation of clinical trial design through its ability to identify appropriate patient populations, forecast patient responses, and provide real-time monitoring of trial progress. The implementation of this streamlined strategy improves the efficiency of trials and decreases the period of clinical development, leading to cost reductions for pharmaceutical corporations and healthcare systems alike.

5. Remote Monitoring and Telemedicine

The significance of remote healthcare delivery was underscored by the COVID-19 pandemic. AI-enabled telemedicine solutions offers the potential to administer medical consultations, oversee patient well-being, and conduct subsequent care from a distance. This not only enhances patient accessibility to healthcare, particularly in areas with little resources, but also alleviates the burden on healthcare institutions and diminishes the necessity for in-person appointments. The utilisation of AI-driven remote monitoring systems has the capability to identify even the most minor alterations in the health condition of patients, thereby notifying healthcare professionals of potential concerns at an early stage, thereby preventing their escalation. The implementation of timely interventions informed by real-time data has the potential to mitigate hospitalisations and complications, hence resulting in cost savings through the reduction of high-cost healthcare service utilisation.

The clear potential of artificial intelligence (AI) to bring about a transformative impact on the delivery of healthcare and cost reduction is observed across a wide range of applications, encompassing diagnosis, treatment, administrative procedures, and patient involvement. By using the capabilities of artificial intelligence (AI) in precision diagnostics, predictive analytics, improved administrative processes, medication discovery, and remote monitoring, healthcare systems have the potential to improve patient outcomes while maximising the efficient use of resources. The ongoing advancement of AI technology presents the potential to revolutionise the healthcare industry by enhancing its efficiency, prioritising patient needs, and optimising cost-effectiveness.

The role of institutions in ensuring equitable access to AI-based healthcare technologies

The integration of artificial intelligence (AI) inside the dynamic and ever-changing healthcare sector holds the promise of transforming medical practises and enhancing patient outcomes. However, in order to fully realise the advantages of healthcare technologies based on artificial intelligence, it is imperative to make a collective endeavour to guarantee fair and equal access for all sectors of the population. Inclusive access to AI-driven healthcare solutions is facilitated by several institutions, including governments, regulatory agencies, healthcare providers, and industry stakeholders. These entities assume a crucial role in advocating for and executing strategies that effectively tackle inequities in healthcare and promote equitable access. This extensive discourse examines the various aspects of the role that institutions must fulfil in order to provide fair and equal access to healthcare technology based on artificial intelligence.

1. Policy and Regulation

The establishment of institutional frameworks and laws has a pivotal role in influencing the implementation and availability of healthcare technology driven by artificial intelligence. It is the duty of governments and regulatory agencies to formulate and implement policies aimed at mitigating the occurrence of health inequities resulting from technological advancements. This entails the establishment of criteria for safeguarding data privacy, ensuring security measures, promoting interoperability, and formulating ethical principles for the application of artificial intelligence in the healthcare sector. It is imperative for regulations to include provisions that enforce openness in artificial intelligence (AI) algorithms and decision-making processes. This measure is necessary to address biases and guarantee equitable treatment for various patient populations.

In addition, it is imperative for institutions to engage in collaborative efforts with experts, researchers, and industry stakeholders in order to establish a regulatory framework that both encourages innovation and ensures the protection of patient rights, as well as the promotion of fair and equal access. In order to mitigate the unequal distribution of AI benefits across different demographics or socioeconomic groups, institutions can ensure the establishment of a fair and equitable environment.

2. Education and Awareness

In the realm of AI-based healthcare technology, institutions play a crucial role in cultivating public awareness and comprehension. Education initiatives ought to be strategically crafted with the objective of elucidating AI principles, debunking prevalent myths, and accentuating the prospective advantages for both individuals and communities. It is imperative that healthcare personnel undergo comprehensive training in order to proficiently utilise artificial intelligence (AI) tools and seamlessly incorporate them into clinical practise. This will guarantee that patients from diverse backgrounds may fully reap the advantages of AI-driven diagnoses, treatment, and care.

Targeted interventions are crucial in tackling differences in digital literacy, so guaranteeing that marginalised people are not disproportionately disadvantaged as a result of limited access or comprehension. Institutions may effectively enable citizens to interact with AI-based healthcare solutions by proactively educating both healthcare professionals and the general public.

3. Infrastructure Development

The utilisation of AI-based healthcare solutions necessitates a strong and dependable digital infrastructure. It is imperative for institutions to allocate resources towards the enhancement and enlargement of healthcare information systems, high-speed internet connectivity, and telehealth platforms, with a specific focus on underprivileged and geographically isolated regions. The convergence of public and private sectors through collaborative initiatives has the potential to address the digital gap and facilitate the provision of essential infrastructure for marginalised groups, enabling them to access healthcare services driven by artificial intelligence.

In addition, it is imperative for institutions to actively support the incorporation of artificial intelligence (AI) technology into current healthcare systems, with a focus on guaranteeing compatibility, interoperability, and seamless data interchange. This promotes the efficient provision of healthcare services across various contexts and facilitates equal opportunities for utilising AI-powered advancements.

4. Inclusive Research and Development

It is incumbent upon institutions to actively foster research and development endeavours that place emphasis on inclusivity and effectively tackle the distinctive healthcare requirements of various populations. It is imperative to build and evaluate AI technologies using inclusive datasets that adequately reflect diverse demographic groups. This approach guarantees that the resultant solutions are both useful and accurate when applied to a wide range of patient profiles.

Institutions may contribute to the mitigation of biases and the equitable distribution of benefits from AI-based healthcare technologies by allocating funds towards research that specifically addresses diseases that exhibit a disproportionate impact on marginalised communities. Additionally, increasing diversity in clinical trials is crucial in order to ensure that these technologies are effective and beneficial for individuals from all backgrounds and circumstances.

5. Affordability and Reimbursement

It is imperative for institutions to actively promote policies that guarantee the accessibility and cost-effectiveness of healthcare technology based on artificial intelligence (AI). This entails engaging in negotiations to establish equitable pricing with technology suppliers, fostering a competitive environment, and providing incentives to promote the creation of cost-efficient solutions. Furthermore, it is imperative to build compensation procedures that might provide financial support to healthcare practitioners that are willing to embrace artificial intelligence (AI) technologies, particularly in contexts where resources are limited.

In order to mitigate inequities in access to AI-based healthcare technologies due to economic constraints, it is imperative for institutions to prioritise the accessibility and financial feasibility of these technologies for both healthcare practitioners and patients. The diverse and far-reaching nature of institutions in guaranteeing fair access to AI-based healthcare technology is evident. By implementing comprehensive regulatory frameworks, educational activities, infrastructure development, inclusive research, and affordability measures, institutions have the power to establish an inclusive environment that ensures the accessibility of AI-driven healthcare benefits to all sectors of society. Institutions have a crucial role in promoting equity, thereby fostering a future in which AI technologies enhance healthcare outcomes and mitigate gaps, irrespective of socioeconomic, geographic, or demographic variables.

Ethical considerations and privacy concerns in the use of AI in healthcare economics

The convergence of artificial intelligence (AI) and healthcare economics gives rise to a multitude of ethical and privacy concerns that necessitate thoughtful examination and proactive interventions. The integration of AI technologies into healthcare systems and economic frameworks necessitates the examination of complex ethical challenges and privacy concerns that arise. This thorough discourse explores the intricate realm of ethical considerations and privacy concerns linked to the utilisation of artificial intelligence (AI) in the field of healthcare economics. It scrutinises the intricate environment that institutions, politicians, and stakeholders must traverse.

1. Patient Privacy and Data Security

The utilisation of artificial intelligence (AI) within the realm of healthcare economics is contingent upon the comprehensive examination of extensive quantities of patient data, encompassing electronic health records, medical imagery, and genomic data. Nevertheless, the dependence on sensitive data gives rise to substantial privacy apprehensions. It is imperative for institutions and stakeholders to implement comprehensive data security measures in order to effectively protect patient information from unauthorised access, breaches, and cyber threats. The implementation of encryption, anonymization techniques, and stringent access controls plays a crucial role in upholding patient privacy when leveraging the potential of artificial intelligence for economic analysis.

In addition, it is imperative that the sharing and transfer of patient data for economic research driven by artificial intelligence (AI) comply with rigorous privacy standards, such as the Health Insurance Portability and Accountability Act (HIPAA) in the United States. This is necessary to guarantee the preservation of patients' rights and confidentiality.

2. Algorithmic Transparency and Bias Mitigation

The ethical dilemmas in healthcare economics arise from the lack of transparency in AI systems. The utilisation of artificial intelligence (AI) in economic decision-making processes holds significant consequences for the allocation of resources, pricing mechanisms, and the creation of policies. Ensuring transparency, interpretability, and accountability of these algorithms is of utmost importance. It is imperative for institutions to actively promote the advancement of explainable artificial intelligence (AI) models, which enable stakeholders to comprehend the underlying reasoning behind algorithmic judgements and identify any potential biases.

The reduction of bias holds similar importance. Artificial intelligence (AI) algorithms have the potential to unintentionally sustain and reinforce pre-existing biases that are inherent in the data they are trained on, hence resulting in inequitable economic consequences. It is imperative for institutions to actively advocate for the thorough examination and evaluation of AI algorithms in order to identify and rectify any instances of unfairness and prejudice. This process should aim to mitigate inequities and guarantee that economic decisions are characterised by equity and impartiality.

3. Informed Consent and Patient Autonomy

The incorporation of artificial intelligence (AI) into the realm of healthcare economics entails the use of patient data for economic evaluations, frequently without obtaining explicit patient agreement for such objectives. The aforementioned situation gives rise to ethical concerns pertaining to the principles of informed consent and patient autonomy. It is imperative for institutions to actively promote and prioritise the establishment of unambiguous and open channels of communication pertaining to the utilisation of patient data for economic research. This approach empowers patients by equipping them with the necessary information to make well-informed choices regarding their involvement in such studies.

Furthermore, it is imperative to uphold patients' autonomy in deciding whether their data should be used for economic studies, thereby guaranteeing individuals the authority to determine the use of their health information. Within this particular framework, institutions assume a pivotal function in formulating rules that effectively reconcile the advantages of economically-driven insights derived from artificial intelligence with the autonomy and privacy desires of patients.

4. Accountability and Liability

The integration of AI technologies into healthcare economics presents a multifaceted ethical dilemma about the assignment of blame and culpability. It is imperative for institutions and governments to construct comprehensive frameworks that effectively outline the specific roles of various parties, such as AI developers, healthcare providers, and economic analysts. The establishment of unambiguous lines of accountability is necessary in situations where economic decisions, which are impacted by artificial intelligence, result in unexpected repercussions or poor outcomes.

Furthermore, it is imperative for institutions to actively encourage the advancement of insurance and liability frameworks in order to effectively mitigate the potential negative consequences that may arise from economic assessments powered by artificial intelligence. This measure guarantees the sufficient protection of patients and stakeholders in instances where errors or bad effects arise as a consequence of economic advice derived by artificial intelligence.

5. Human Oversight and Decision-Making Autonomy

Although artificial intelligence (AI) has the potential to offer significant contributions to economic decision-making, it is crucial to acknowledge the ethical considerations associated with relinquishing excessive decision-making authority to algorithms. It is imperative for institutions to actively promote a harmonious coexistence between AI-generated recommendations and human supervision. It is imperative that human specialists possess the capacity to engage in critical evaluation of economic insights obtained from artificial intelligence (AI), so guaranteeing that judgements made based on these insights are in accordance with ethical standards and societal norms.

It is recommended that institutions develop explicit standards to delineate the extent of decision-making authority granted to artificial intelligence (AI) systems. These guidelines should underscore the significance of human judgement and involvement, particularly in situations where economic decisions carry substantial societal and ethical implications. The utilisation of artificial intelligence (AI) in healthcare economics raises intricate and dynamic ethical and privacy issues, necessitating meticulous examination, the establishment of regulatory structures, and collaborative endeavours including institutions, legislators, and stakeholders. In order to uphold ethical standards and protect patient rights, institutions should effectively traverse the complex landscape of AI-driven healthcare economics by placing a high priority on patient privacy, ensuring algorithmic transparency, obtaining informed permission, establishing accountability mechanisms, and maintaining human oversight. By engaging in such actions, individuals make a valuable contribution towards a future in which artificial intelligence (AI) technologies play a pivotal role in enhancing economic analyses. Simultaneously, these actions ensure the preservation of the integrity, privacy, and autonomy of persons within the healthcare ecosystem.

Chapter 18: AI and Financial Markets

Within the dynamic realm of global finance, the incorporation of artificial intelligence (AI) has emerged as a formidable influence, altering the dynamics of financial markets and rethinking the conceptualization and implementation of trading and investment strategies. This chapter undertakes a thorough examination of the complex association between artificial intelligence (AI) and financial markets. It elucidates the effects of AI on market efficiency, emphasises the crucial role of institutions in regulating this domain, and highlights the intricate network of risks and challenges that arise from the widespread adoption of AI-driven strategies.

The Implications of AI for Financial Market Efficiency and Stability

The core of the AI-driven revolution in financial markets is centred around the potential for increased efficiency, transparency, and resilience. The utilisation of machine learning algorithms, natural language processing, and predictive analytics has brought about a significant transformation in the field of data analysis. This advancement has empowered market participants to efficiently handle large quantities of data and derive practical and valuable insights from it. The emergence of enhanced agility in trading has resulted in a significant shift in the prevailing paradigm, thereby elevating algorithmic and high-frequency trading to a prominent position.

The utilisation of artificial intelligence (AI) has facilitated the identification of nuanced patterns and correlations within historical market data, hence enabling enhanced precision in price forecasting, risk evaluation, and identification of market trends. Consequently, the enhancement of financial market efficiency has provided investors with increased capabilities to make well-informed judgements and optimise their portfolio management techniques. This chapter explores the impact of AI-enhanced trading algorithms on market liquidity, bid-ask spreads, and price discovery, leading to increased market stability.

The Role of Institutions in Regulating AI Algorithms in Trading and Investment

The undeniable transformative influence of artificial intelligence (AI) on financial markets is accompanied by various hurdles that hinder its widespread implementation. Various institutions, including as regulatory organisations, central banks, and participants in financial markets, are currently faced with the challenge of creating a regulatory framework that effectively manages the tension between promoting innovation and mitigating risks. The emergence of artificial intelligence (AI)-powered algorithms has prompted inquiries regarding the integrity of markets, the concept of fairness, and the possibility of exacerbating systemic hazards.

This chapter elucidates the complex role that institutions play in formulating and implementing policies that govern trading and investment techniques powered by artificial intelligence. This paper explores the imperative of creating clear principles pertaining to algorithmic openness, risk assessment, and accountability. The significance of the cooperative endeavours between institutions and industry players cannot be overstated in the context of preventing market manipulation, mitigating algorithmic biases, and guaranteeing the responsible utilisation of AI's transformational capabilities.

Potential Risks and Challenges Associated with AI-Driven Financial Markets

The growing dependence of financial markets on artificial intelligence (AI) gives rise to a novel set of risks and concerns. Although AI algorithms provide unparalleled levels of speed and precision, they are nonetheless susceptible to unforeseen errors and the subsequent propagation of consequences. The chapter explores the possibility of algorithmic malfunctions, flash crashes, and unanticipated market volatility that may arise from the interaction of intricate AI systems. Moreover, the widespread use of AI-driven methodologies gives rise to apprehensions over the consolidation of authority and the likelihood of collective decision-making patterns among algorithmic traders. This chapter delves at the potential hazards of excessive dependence on historical data, the opaque nature of AI algorithms, and the ethical quandaries linked to decision-making facilitated by AI.

This chapter establishes the foundation for a thorough examination of the complex interplay between artificial intelligence and financial markets. This statement highlights the significant impact that AI can have on improving market efficiency and stability. It also recognises the crucial role that institutions play in developing regulatory frameworks to enable responsible usage of AI. Furthermore, this phenomenon brings attention to the diverse array of risks and issues that emerge following the advent of artificial intelligence in the financial markets. The chapter endeavours to comprehensively examine these elements in order to establish a comprehensive comprehension of the impact of artificial intelligence on the financial realm. It seeks to provide valuable insights into the potential benefits and risks associated with this technology.

The implications of AI for financial market efficiency and stability

The convergence of artificial intelligence (AI) and financial markets has initiated a paradigm shift marked by unparalleled velocity, precision, and intricacy. The advent of AI technology, such as machine learning algorithms and predictive analytics, has significantly transformed the trading and investment domain, leading to significant ramifications for the efficiency and stability of financial markets. This section provides an in-depth analysis of the various ways in which artificial intelligence (AI) has significantly transformed the dynamics of financial markets.

It explores the effects of AI on market efficiency, liquidity, price discovery, and systemic stability.

1. Enhanced Market Efficiency

The integration of artificial intelligence (AI) into financial markets has resulted in a significant enhancement of market efficiency, leading to notable consequences for investors, traders, and the overall economic environment. The utilisation of artificial intelligence (AI) has significantly advanced the capabilities of financial markets, enabling them to engage in extensive data analysis, recognise patterns, and make quick decisions. This has resulted in a wide range of advantages that beyond the limitations of conventional trading methods.

Machine learning algorithms possess the ability to efficiently analyse vast amounts of historical and real-time market data, enabling them to identify complex patterns that may be difficult for human analysts to detect. This ability greatly enhances the speed at which information is absorbed and enables investors to make highly informed judgements with exceptional accuracy, frequently in an instant. The democratisation of real-time insights signifies a significant shift in paradigms, as it eliminates the previous limitations on decision-making caused by temporal constraints, resulting in financial markets becoming more dynamic and flexible.

Moreover, the rise of AI-powered trading tactics, as demonstrated by algorithmic and high-frequency trading, has introduced a period characterised by unprecedented levels of swiftness and precision. These methods leverage the analytical powers of artificial intelligence (AI) to rapidly execute trades, guided by complex algorithms that respond instantaneously to market occurrences. This speed not only decreases the temporal gaps between information distribution and action but also helps to a more equitable allocation of resources. AI-enhanced markets effectively address informational inefficiencies by swiftly incorporating new knowledge into asset prices. As a result, these markets facilitate the development of a pricing environment that accurately reflects the underlying fundamentals and minimises speculative distortions.

The implications of this heightened market efficiency have wide-ranging consequences. In addition to the advantages experienced by individual investors, such as enhanced decision-making capabilities and more efficient trading techniques, the wider financial ecosystem also derives benefits. An enhanced market infrastructure that is more responsive and efficient plays a crucial role in reinforcing market integrity, fostering investor confidence, and facilitating strong economic growth. The increasing presence of artificial intelligence (AI) in financial markets has prompted a persistent pursuit of enhanced efficiency and stability. This pursuit highlights the continual evolution of conventional economic models into advanced frameworks empowered by AI technology.

2. Expanded Market Liquidity

The influence of artificial intelligence (AI) on market liquidity, a crucial determinant of the ease with which assets can be bought and sold, has been substantial. The utilisation of artificial intelligence algorithms in high-frequency trading has resulted in a significant enhancement of market liquidity through the reduction of bid-ask spreads, which represent the disparity between the maximum price a buyer is ready to pay and the minimum price a seller is willing to take. The reduction in spreads results in decreased transaction costs for participants in the market, hence enhancing the cost-efficiency and accessibility of trading. Furthermore, liquidity providers powered by artificial intelligence possess the ability to promptly detect and capitalise on arbitrage possibilities, hence mitigating market disparities across various trading platforms. The execution of trades by liquidity providers at extremely fast speeds results in improved liquidity for market players across different assets and trading platforms, hence promoting a more integrated and efficient financial ecosystem.

The extensive influence of artificial intelligence (AI) on financial markets surpasses mere operational effectiveness and encompasses the complex notion of market liquidity. This crucial factor plays a pivotal role in determining the ease with which assets may be bought and sold, and forms the foundation for the interplay between supply and demand dynamics. The catalytic impact of artificial intelligence (AI) on liquidity has brought about a significant change characterised by increased ease of access, decreased costs associated with transactions, and an interconnection that redefines the boundaries of contemporary trading environments.

High-frequency trading (HFT), driven by artificial intelligence (AI) algorithms, serves as a fundamental aspect of this transformation in market liquidity. The proficiency of algorithms in efficiently handling data and carrying out trades has had a noticeable impact on the dynamics of market liquidity. Significantly, the utilisation of artificial intelligence (AI) in high-frequency trading (HFT) has emerged as a powerful factor in reducing bid-ask spreads. These spreads represent a fundamental measure that quantifies the difference between the prices at which assets are bought and sold. The process of narrowing, which is made possible by the efficient and precise nature of AI-powered trading, gives rise to a ripple effect that permeates the entire market. Decreased bid-ask spreads result in diminished transaction costs for market players, hence enhancing the cost-efficiency and accessibility of asset trading for a wider range of investors.

Moreover, the capabilities of artificial intelligence (AI) extend to promoting a more unified and balanced trading environment by using the services of liquidity providers. The utilisation of AI-powered entities, which possess the ability to rapidly detect and exploit arbitrage opportunities, assumes a crucial function in mitigating discrepancies among various trading platforms. The efficient execution of trades, facilitated by algorithmic precision, serves to connect disparate elements and reduce disparities, so establishing a smooth interface across various assets and platforms. Consequently, this process enhances the availability of liquid assets and facilitates trading in many markets, creating an environment in which market participants can profit from improved convenience in purchasing and selling, regardless of geographical or technological limitations.

The consequences of this increased market liquidity have a profound impact on the financial environment. The integration of artificial intelligence (AI) with liquidity results in the democratisation of market participation, facilitating investors to interact with enhanced agility and efficiency. Furthermore, the decrease in transaction costs, which is a significant characteristic of AI-powered liquidity, is evident in various financial transactions, hence enhancing the accessibility of financial markets and strengthening investor trust. The ongoing advancements in artificial intelligence (AI) contribute to the enhancement and expansion of liquidity mechanisms in financial markets. This progress pushes the boundaries of what can be accomplished in these markets, leading to a new era characterised by increased accessibility, improved efficiency, and more interconnection.

3. Improved Price Discovery

The capacity of artificial intelligence (AI) to effectively handle and evaluate extensive datasets in real-time has significantly enhanced the efficiency of processes for determining prices. Price discovery is the mechanism via which market players jointly reach a consensus over the equitable valuation of a particular asset. AI-driven algorithms integrate many data sources, such as news sentiment, social media trends, and macroeconomic indicators, in order to evaluate market sentiment and analyse the dynamics of supply and demand.

AI-driven models offer a more thorough understanding of market patterns and possible asset prices by integrating a wide range of inputs from various sources. The process of increased price discovery offers valuable assistance to investors in making well-informed trading decisions. Additionally, it plays a significant role in promoting the accuracy and stability of asset pricing, hence mitigating the occurrence of speculative bubbles or abrupt market distortions.

The use of artificial intelligence (AI) in financial markets has brought about a significant change in the traditional practise of price discovery. This revolution holds ramifications that reach beyond the mere mechanics of trading, resonating with profound effects. The ability of artificial intelligence (AI) to efficiently handle and analyse large datasets in real-time has played a crucial role in enhancing the accuracy and effectiveness of price discovery mechanisms. This has contributed to a more sophisticated comprehension of the dynamics involved in asset valuation.

Price discovery is a fundamental aspect of market functioning, representing the complex process by which market participants collectively determine the appropriate value of an object. Artificial intelligence (AI), with its ability to rapidly acquire and integrate diverse streams of information, revolutionises this procedure by combining a wide range of data sources. These sources go beyond conventional market indicators and include a diverse range of inputs such as news mood, social media trends, macroeconomic statistics, and other dynamic factors. This novel methodology for determining prices surpasses the limitations of traditional data, encompassing a broad range of information that effectively captures the frequently elusive market sentiment. The integration of these heterogeneous data serves as evidence of the analytical capabilities of artificial intelligence. The AI-driven models that are generated offer stakeholders a wide-ranging perspective, providing in-depth understanding of market trends, the complexities of supply and demand dynamics, and the various factors that influence asset prices. This broadened perspective provides investors with a more knowledgeable framework to analyse market conditions and assess the prospective value of assets.

In addition to its immediate benefits, this improved process of determining prices has significant ramifications for the wider financial ecosystem. The utilisation of artificial intelligence in price discovery serves to limit the occurrence of speculative bubbles and minimise the effects of significant market distortions, so fostering a more equitable and steady market atmosphere. The incorporation of artificial intelligence (AI) into financial markets brings about a state of balance, guaranteeing that asset prices more precisely align with their underlying fundamentals. Consequently, this integration serves to reduce the level of volatility typically associated with financial markets.

During this transformative era of price discovery facilitated by artificial intelligence, investors are not only able to gain valuable insights but also navigate a market environment characterised by more rational valuations and less systemic risks. The ongoing development and adaptation of AI-driven models have led to a persistent pursuit of improved accuracy and knowledge in assessing asset prices. This pursuit has become a defining characteristic of financial markets, as it establishes a future where the interaction between technology and financial dynamics becomes increasingly interdependent.

4. Systemic Stability and Risk Management

The introduction of artificial intelligence (AI) in financial markets has brought about a multitude of advantages. However, the intricate nature and interdependencies of AI systems also give rise to apprehensions over the stability of the whole financial system. If not subjected to adequate regulation and monitoring, the practise of rapid algorithmic trading has the potential to exacerbate market volatility and give rise to sudden and rapid declines in prices, commonly referred to as flash crashes, which are then followed by swift recoveries. The interdependence of AI-driven tactics might potentially lead to a series of cascading consequences, wherein the malfunction or breakdown of a single algorithm initiates a chain reaction that impacts the entire market. In order to address these risks, institutions and regulatory authorities are responsible for formulating oversight procedures and implementing circuit breakers that have the ability to suspend trading activities in the event of very volatile market conditions. Furthermore, artificial intelligence (AI) is being utilised in the field of risk management and stress testing, allowing financial institutions to simulate different situations and evaluate potential weaknesses in their portfolios.

Within the complex framework of financial markets, intricately intertwined with the sophisticated elements of artificial intelligence, the quest for unparalleled effectiveness and ingenuity is pitted with the essential need for systemic stability and the mitigation of risks. The advent of artificial intelligence (AI) brings forth numerous advantages, although it also introduces a novel phase characterised by intricate interconnections. Consequently, this highlights a multifaceted landscape that is abundant with both opportunities and possible challenges. One of the primary considerations that artificial intelligence (AI) introduces into the structure of financial markets is the possibility of increased volatility and sudden disruptions to systemic stability. The rapid advancement of algorithmic trading, driven by the exceptional processing speed of artificial intelligence, presents the possibility of swift market fluctuations that surpass conventional patterns. The phrase "flash crash" has become a prominent part of financial terminology, describing situations in which prices undergo sudden and significant declines, only to swiftly recover. If these brief periods of disturbance are not addressed, they might potentially diminish the trust of investors and weaken the overall integrity of the market.

These risks are further exacerbated by the complex interplay between strategies powered by artificial intelligence. The utilisation of comparable algorithms across diverse trading platforms fosters a level of interconnectivity that has the potential to result in cascading consequences. The occurrence of a solitary algorithmic failure can act as a catalyst, initiating a chain reaction of events that propagate across the market and can result in extensive disruptions. The mitigation of these inherent hazards requires a unified and cooperative endeavour by various institutions and regulatory entities. In order to ensure the stability of the system, efforts are being made to establish extensive systems for oversight and the use of circuit breakers. The fail-safe procedures, which are specifically designed to suspend trading in times of significant market turbulence, serve as a protective measure against the uncontrolled escalation of volatility.

Furthermore, the potential of artificial intelligence (AI) as a tool for risk management and stress testing is being increasingly recognised as a significant asset. Financial organisations possess the capability to employ AI-driven models in order to simulate a wide range of scenarios, including economic downturns as well as geopolitical upheavals. These simulations offer a comprehensive perspective on possible vulnerabilities, allowing institutions to proactively customise risk management strategies and strengthen portfolios in response to a constantly changing landscape of uncertainty.

The role of institutions and regulatory bodies is of utmost importance in effectively managing the complex interplay between AI-driven innovation and systemic stability. The collective endeavours of individuals working together play a crucial role in shaping an atmosphere that effectively harnesses the transformative capabilities of artificial intelligence, while simultaneously reducing the probability of disruptive disturbances. The increasing integration of AI inside financial markets presents an ongoing challenge to strike a balance between innovation and stability. This pursuit unfolds as a continuous narrative, outlining a trajectory towards a future in which technological advancements seamlessly align with the fundamental principles of a robust and secure financial ecosystem.

In conclusion, the incorporation of artificial intelligence (AI) into financial markets has introduced a period characterised by exceptional levels of efficiency, liquidity, and price discovery. The utilisation of artificial intelligence (AI) has facilitated enhanced agility, interconnectivity, and responsiveness to information within financial markets through its capabilities in data analysis, real-time processing, and algorithmic execution. Nevertheless, as the effect of artificial intelligence (AI) becomes more profound, it is crucial for institutions and regulators to establish a harmonious equilibrium between leveraging its advantages and ensuring the preservation of systemic stability. To achieve a technologically advanced and efficient financial ecosystem, it is imperative to adopt a comprehensive approach that acknowledges both the potential benefits and drawbacks of artificial intelligence (AI).

The role of institutions in regulating AI algorithms in trading and investment

The widespread adoption of artificial intelligence (AI) algorithms in the domains of trade and investment has introduced a novel phase of opportunities and obstacles, hence demanding the proactive involvement of institutions to guarantee the responsible and ethical implementation of such technologies. The complex interaction of technological advancements, market forces, and regulatory supervision constitutes the central focus of the discussion on the role of institutions in governing artificial intelligence algorithms. The present research explores the complex range of responsibilities and factors that institutions must address in order to achieve a careful balance between promoting innovation and ensuring the integrity of the market.

1. Algorithmic Transparency and Fairness

The notion of algorithmic transparency is a key component of the regulatory framework that governs AI algorithms in the domain of trading and investment. With the advancement of AI algorithms, there is a growing capability for them to exceed human understanding, leading to the emergence of a phenomena known as the "black box." In this scenario, the rationale behind decision-making becomes opaque and difficult to comprehend. In the realm of AI-driven algorithms, institutions assume a crucial role in promoting transparency by imposing the obligation on market participants to divulge the fundamental workings of such algorithms.

Transparency plays a crucial role in enabling investors to acquire a comprehensive understanding of the risks connected with algorithmic trading. Additionally, it serves as a protective measure against potential biases that may be inherent in AI models. The issue of algorithmic bias, in which artificial intelligence (AI) systems unintentionally perpetuate discriminatory results, highlights the importance for institutions to require thorough evaluations that guarantee fairness and inclusivity. Regulatory entities possess the authority to establish rules aimed at scrutinising algorithms for potential biases, so ensuring that trading decisions are devoid of any partiality and uphold principles of fairness.

The legislative framework governing the integration of AI algorithms in trading and investment is centred around the principle of algorithmic transparency. This principle emphasises the need to strike a careful equilibrium between technological advancement and ethical responsibility. As the capabilities of artificial intelligence (AI) algorithms continue to advance, the intricacy of their decision-making processes might beyond human understanding, resulting in a lack of transparency that obscures the underlying mechanisms. This phenomena is widely known as the "black box."

In light of the potential consequences associated with this lack of clarity, institutions assume a crucial position as proponents of transparency. By cultivating a setting that prioritises transparency, institutions compel market participants to disclose the complex framework of their algorithms driven by artificial intelligence. The act of exposing in question is not solely a matter of revealing information, but rather a demonstration of responsibility, wherein the individuals accountable for these algorithms take an active approach in clarifying the internal mechanisms of their digital counterparts.

Transparency holds immense importance within the financial ecosystem, yielding wide-ranging ramifications. Primarily, it provides investors with an enhanced comprehension of the risks associated with algorithmic trading, enabling them to make more informed decisions and exercise cautious portfolio management. The revelation of algorithmic mechanisms elucidates the riddle surrounding market behaviours, empowering investors to evaluate the prospective ramifications of AI-driven tactics on their financial stakes. However, the concept of transparency goes beyond simply sharing information and also encompasses ethical integrity. In the era of artificial intelligence, the issue of algorithmic bias arises as a significant worry. The unintentional continuation of biassed results, even in the absence of clear human intention, highlights the pressing need to implement mechanisms that guarantee fairness and inclusion in algorithmic decision-making. In the present setting, it is the institutions that assume the task of ensuring algorithmic accountability. Regulatory entities possess the capacity to exercise their authoritative power in order to establish standards that thoroughly examine algorithms for any potential biases that may be present. The examination being conducted serves as evidence of the dedication to fairness, a protective measure aimed at mitigating the possibility of unfair outcomes stemming from the automated domain of artificial intelligence.

The role of institutions in the realm of algorithmic transparency and fairness extends beyond mere inspection. It represents a compelling imperative, emphasising the need for a cohesive integration of technology progress and ethical awareness. Institutions actively strengthen a regulatory framework that promotes the values of transparency, responsibility, and fairness, so guaranteeing that AI algorithms facilitate not only financial innovation but also a more balanced and comprehensive financial environment.

2. Risk Management and Model Validation

It is incumbent upon institutions to assume the burden of developing comprehensive risk management frameworks that take into consideration the distinct problems presented by artificial intelligence algorithms. The utilisation of artificial intelligence (AI) brings forth new and distinct types of risks, encompassing weaknesses in operational processes, inaccuracies in data, and instability inside systems. It is imperative for regulatory agencies to enforce the requirement for financial institutions to subject their artificial intelligence (AI) models to rigorous stress tests and scenario studies in order to detect and address any vulnerabilities. Moreover, institutions have the responsibility of regulating the validation processes of models, ensuring that artificial intelligence algorithms are appropriately tuned to efficiently respond to varying market situations. By conducting regular audits and compliance checks, institutions have the capacity to validate the precision and dependability of AI models, therefore reducing the probability of severe failures that may potentially disturb market stability.

In a dynamic environment characterised by the interplay between financial innovation and systemic stability, institutions assume the role of designers of resilient risk management frameworks that serve as safeguards against the always increasing challenges presented by AI algorithms. The integration of artificial intelligence (AI), with its exceptional capabilities, introduces a novel landscape of hazards that surpass the confines of conventional paradigms and require a fundamental shift in the practise of risk governance. The integration of artificial intelligence (AI) into financial systems gives rise to a variety of new dangers that require careful consideration and deliberate measures to address. The presence of operational vulnerabilities, which may not be immediately apparent due to the appearance of smooth automation, necessitates the implementation of customised protections that proactively mitigate any risks. The presence of data inaccuracies, which arise from the use of extensive datasets, has a potential for distorted outcomes. This highlights the critical importance of implementing data governance and ensuring data quality assurance.

Furthermore, the potential for systemic instability is a significant concern, particularly due to the speed and interconnectivity that characterises algorithmic trading. Institutions play a crucial role in effectively navigating the complex landscape of risks by developing risk management frameworks that are responsive to the evolving technology landscape. In order to achieve this objective, regulatory organisations play a pivotal role in defining the parameters of risk management through the implementation of rigorous requirements. The requirement for financial institutions to subject their artificial intelligence (AI) models to thorough stress tests and scenario analysis is identified as a fundamental aspect of this undertaking. Stress tests, which are specifically designed to exert significant pressure on AI systems, reveal flaws that may remain dormant under normal market conditions. By conducting simulations of unfavourable scenarios, institutions acquire valuable knowledge about anticipated challenges, hence enhancing the robustness of AI-driven policies in the face of future uncertainties.

Simultaneously, the task of model validation takes significant importance. It is the role of institutions to oversee thorough validation processes, ensuring that artificial intelligence algorithms are appropriately tuned to traverse the unpredictable fluctuations of market dynamics. Periodic audits and compliance checks are essential for assessing the precision and dependability of AI models. The purpose of these audits is to serve as a vigilant safeguard, preventing the occurrence of devastating failures that could spread throughout the industry, resulting in significant disruptions. By assuming these obligations, institutions surpass the function of mere protectors; they transform into stewards of market integrity and stability. As the advancements in AI algorithms progress, the dedication of institutions to proactive risk management and rigorous model validation plays a fundamental role in establishing a strong foundation for financial resiliency.

In conclusion, the domain of risk management and model validation represents a crucial frontier where institutions adeptly navigate the delicate equilibrium between the advancements of AI-driven innovation and the necessities of stability. By doing so, individuals express a narrative that combines technological expertise with caution, so supporting the flourishing of the financial ecosystem in the face of the dynamic interplay between innovation and protection.

3. Market Surveillance and Manipulation Prevention

The emergence of artificial intelligence algorithms requires a transformation in market surveillance methods. It is imperative for institutions to modify their surveillance capabilities in order to successfully monitor trading methods driven by artificial intelligence. The expeditious rate at which algorithmic trading occurs has the capacity to magnify market volatility and engender the possibility of market manipulation. It is imperative for regulatory entities to establish and enforce comprehensive monitoring systems capable of identifying irregularities, questionable trends, and potential violations of market ethics. Furthermore, it is imperative to acknowledge the significant contribution of institutions in mitigating market manipulation through the implementation of regulatory measures aimed at restraining the proliferation of algorithmic trading practises that may be deemed excessive. To mitigate the effects of algorithmic-driven operations during moments of significant market volatility, it is possible to implement measures such as circuit breakers and position limitations.

With the emergence of AI algorithms, there is a growing need for enhanced market surveillance and manipulation prevention in contemporary financial markets. The swift progression of technical advancements necessitates that institutions adjust their surveillance capabilities in order to effectively monitor algorithmic trading activities. The process of recalibration, which involves a balanced combination of innovative approaches and effective control, serves as the central point around which market integrity revolves.

The integration of artificial intelligence (AI) and trade gives rise to a complex situation that requires the development of advanced surveillance techniques. In light of this fundamental change in perspective, it is imperative for institutions to effectively utilise the inherent capabilities of artificial intelligence in order to oversee and analyse trading methods that are driven by AI. The inherent swiftness and cognitive capabilities of AI algorithms prove to be invaluable assets in detecting patterns, anomalies, and deviations that may otherwise defy human perception. By implementing artificial intelligence (AI) for the purpose of monitoring AI, institutions enhance their capacity to effectively adapt to the swiftly evolving market environment. Within the intricate fabric of surveillance, the ominous presence of market manipulation assumes significant proportions. The rapid responsiveness of algorithmic trading has the potential to increase market volatility, leading to the emergence of manipulative practises that break the equilibrium between supply and demand. In order to fulfil their responsibility as guardians of market integrity, institutions are required to develop and implement strong surveillance systems that function as virtual sentinels, actively monitoring and preventing any breaches.

The scope of these surveillance systems encompasses a wide range of functions. Detection methods must possess a high level of sensitivity in order to accurately identify patterns that deviate from established standards, hence prompting the need for greater investigation. Anomalies, aberrations, and atypical trading behaviours, which may suggest potential manipulation, should undergo thorough study to determine their underlying intent and impact. In addition, institutions have a diverse and complex role in the prevention of market manipulation. The implementation of regulations aimed at limiting excessive algorithmic trading practises serves as evidence of a dedication to ensuring fair competition. Safety valves, such as circuit breakers, are used to moderate the influence of algorithmic-driven operations in times of significant market volatility. These measures effectively reduce the potential for quick trading to trigger a chain reaction of adverse consequences.

In conclusion, the domain of market surveillance and prevention of manipulation is a rapidly evolving field where institutions utilise the capabilities of artificial intelligence to promote the integrity of the market. The dedication to preserving the integrity of financial markets in the face of the dynamic terrain of algorithmic trading is exemplified by this proactive approach, which combines technological expertise with regulatory oversight. When it comes to navigating these waters, institutions have a dual role, serving not only as custodians of stability but also as creators of a financial ecosystem that is resilient against the risks of manipulation and volatility.

4. Education and Expertise

A comprehensive comprehension of both technological subtleties and market dynamics is crucial in navigating the regulatory framework pertaining to AI algorithms. Institutions play a crucial role in cultivating education and competence within their respective communities. It is imperative for regulatory organisations to engage in collaborative efforts with specialists from academia, technology, and finance in order to establish a group of professionals capable of proficiently assessing the potential dangers and advantages associated with artificial intelligence (AI) algorithms.

Furthermore, it is possible for institutions to facilitate the promotion of ongoing learning and certification initiatives that ensure market players remain well-informed about the most recent innovations and regulatory obligations within the AI-driven trading domain. In the realm of incorporating AI algorithms into trading and investment, the significance of education and knowledge becomes apparent as fundamental pillars for effectively managing the convergence of advanced technology and the intricate complexities of financial markets. The complex and multidimensional nature of regulations need a group of skilled individuals that possess a deep comprehension of both the complexities of AI algorithms and the dynamics of the market in which they function.

Institutions have a crucial role in creating an atmosphere that promotes ongoing learning and the improvement of skills, as they are situated at the intersection of this convergence. The development of expertise involves a comprehensive approach that incorporates various aspects, including technology, market behaviours, risk governance, and ethical issues.

Collaboration serves as a crucial element in this endeavour. Regulatory organisations, with the jurisdiction to influence market practises, should establish collaborations with professionals from academia, technology, and finance. This multidisciplinary collaboration combines theoretical and practical ideas, creating a comprehensive body of knowledge that surpasses traditional disciplinary boundaries. Central to this undertaking is the cultivation of a group of experts who possess the knowledge and skills necessary to comprehensively assess the potential advantages and disadvantages presented by artificial intelligence algorithms. The function necessitates the implementation of comprehensive risk assessments, which possess the ability to identify potential vulnerabilities and predict the consequences they may have on the market. These individuals function as the forefront representatives, adeptly identifying the complex connections that intertwine technology advancement with market forces.

However, the process of acquiring knowledge and developing skills goes beyond a mere starting point—it transforms into a continuous voyage of intellectual growth. In light of the dynamic advancements in technology and market paradigms, it is imperative for institutions to take the lead in promoting and fostering a culture of ongoing learning initiatives. Certification programmes are designed with great care to encompass the most recent breakthroughs and regulatory requirements. These programmes provide a means for market players to remain informed about the constantly evolving field of AI-driven trading. So, the field of education and expertise serves as evidence of institutions' dedication to bridging the gap between AI algorithms and market dynamics. The commitment described is marked by the principles of teamwork, ongoing learning, and the improvement of skills. This commitment acts as a safeguard against the risks associated with making misinformed decisions and falling behind in terms of technical advancements. In light of this perspective, institutions play a crucial role in shaping a prospective future wherein artificial intelligence algorithms seamlessly integrate with financial markets. This integration is facilitated by a group of experts who adeptly navigate the intricate dynamics between innovation and accountability.

In summary, it can be argued that institutions play a crucial role in facilitating the responsible integration of AI algorithms in trading and investment. Their work encompasses activities such as lobbying for openness and fairness in algorithms, as well as ensuring strong risk management practises and surveillance methods. As artificial intelligence (AI) algorithms persistently reshape market dynamics, it is imperative for institutions to maintain a diligent approach in changing regulatory frameworks. These frameworks should effectively strike a delicate equilibrium between promoting innovation and safeguarding market integrity. By engaging in joint endeavours, institutions have the potential to cultivate a milieu in which breakthroughs propelled by artificial intelligence augment market efficiency and stability, all the while ensuring the ethical and responsible use of state-of-the-art technologies.

Potential risks and challenges associated with AI-driven financial markets

The incorporation of artificial intelligence (AI) into financial markets has ushered in a novel epoch characterised by exceptional efficacy, ingenuity, and the capacity for profound change. Nevertheless, the potential for transformation is not devoid of its associated dangers and obstacles. The increasing integration of AI algorithms inside financial environments necessitates a thorough comprehension and effective mitigation of associated risks. This discourse explores the various dangers and challenges that emerge as a result of artificial intelligence (AI) in financial markets, providing a comprehensive understanding of their consequences for the stability of the market, confidence among investors, and regulatory structures.

1. Algorithmic Complexity and Opacity

The inherent qualities of AI algorithms, namely their sophistication and complexity, give rise to many issues. The complex characteristics of these algorithms can surpass human comprehension, hence giving rise to the phenomena known as the "black box." Understanding the decision-making processes of algorithms becomes a formidable challenge as they rapidly make decisions in reaction to market occurrences. The lack of transparency and accountability associated with this opacity gives rise to concerns, particularly regarding potential unintended consequences.

Furthermore, the complex interaction of different algorithms inside the market ecosystem can give rise to systemic concerns. The expeditious dissemination of algorithmic techniques across trading platforms has the potential to generate linked vulnerabilities, hence exacerbating the spread of market disruptions. In order to maintain the vibrancy that algorithms contribute to financial markets, institutions and regulatory authorities are faced with the task of effectively managing systemic risks.

The domain of AI-driven financial markets is characterised by a strong attraction towards sophistication and complexity, which serves as evidence of the transformational potential that algorithms possess. However, as this enticing phenomenon entices individuals, it presents a series of difficulties, frequently concealed by the mysterious nature of its complexity. The complicated inner workings of AI algorithms give rise to the phenomena sometimes referred to as the "black box." Within this area, the decision-making processes of these algorithms remain mysterious and beyond human understanding, leading to a host of intricate problems. The crux of this difficulty resides in the inscrutability of algorithmic decision-making. The rapid operational capabilities of AI algorithms render the task of comprehending the underlying logic driving their behaviours comparable to unravelling a complex cryptographic system. The lack of transparency around these algorithms presents significant challenges in terms of comprehending the underlying reasoning behind critical trading choices, impeding both market players and regulatory entities.

The opacity of this phenomenon has far-reaching consequences within the financial domain, creating a sense of uncertainty regarding responsibility and openness, which are fundamental pillars for maintaining the integrity of the market. The absence of clear delineation of algorithmic decision-making gives rise to apprehensions over the attribution of accountability for the consequences of strategies driven by artificial intelligence. The occurrence of the "black box" phenomenon hinders the capacity to identify the root cause of atypical behaviours or undesired outcomes, creating a state of ambiguity that permeates the market. However, the difficulties arising from the lack of transparency in algorithms go beyond the scope of particular algorithms. The complex interaction among many algorithms operating inside the market ecosystem gives rise to the potential presence of systemic risks. The expeditious proliferation of algorithmic techniques across trading platforms gives rise to a complex network of interrelated risks. The dissemination of market disruptions, initiated by the errors of a solitary algorithm, has the ability to resonate across the ecosystem, intensifying the consequences and expanding the magnitude of possible crises. Within the intricate interplay of innovation and responsibility, various institutions and regulatory agencies encounter a critical juncture. The primary difficulty lies in effectively managing the equilibrium between maintaining the dynamic and efficient nature of algorithms in financial markets, while also addressing the potential unintended propagation of systemic hazards.

In summary, the domain of algorithmic complexity and opacity exhibits a duality marked by potential benefits and risks. As artificial intelligence (AI) algorithms increasingly permeate financial markets, it becomes crucial for stakeholders to confront the necessity of elucidating the enigmatic nature of the "black box" and implementing procedures that foster openness, accountability, and resilience. In the pursuit of navigating unfamiliar territory, the adoption of a collaborative approach becomes crucial in guiding the financial ecosystem towards a future that effectively harnesses the transformational capabilities of artificial intelligence (AI), while simultaneously addressing the issue of opacity through responsible innovation.

2. Systemic Stability and Flash Crashes

The utilisation of AI-driven algorithms, due to their exceptional computational efficiency, has the potential to unwittingly amplify market volatility. Flash crashes, colloquially referred to as sudden and dramatic market fluctuations, can be initiated by the rapid execution of deals and the swift transmission of information, hence causing cascading consequences. If left unaddressed, these instances of fast price changes have the potential to undermine investor trust and destabilise the stability of the market. To tackle this difficulty, it is necessary to implement procedures that mitigate the influence of algorithmic-driven operations in times of significant volatility.

Within the domain of AI-driven financial markets, the combination of algorithmic velocity and market stability presents itself as a dual-edged instrument, embodying both prospects and risks. The rapid speed at which algorithms controlled by artificial intelligence execute deals and send information can unintentionally disrupt the stability of market equilibrium. The outcome of this velocity gives rise to a phenomena that instills apprehension within the financial ecosystem—flash crashes, which are characterised by sudden and significant price swings. These events can provide challenges for both investors and regulators as they grapple with the potential consequences. The crux of this challenge lies in the fundamental nature of algorithmic decision-making. Given the rapid processing capabilities of AI algorithms, they are able to analyse market information at a rate that exceeds human capabilities. Consequently, their responses to market occurrences are conducted with a level of precision that approaches instantaneous. The rapidity of this phenomenon has the capacity to improve the effectiveness and fluidity of the market, but it also brings about a susceptibility, particularly in periods of increased market strain.

Flash crashes are distinguished by their abrupt and significant fluctuations in the market, which can rapidly unravel in a stunning manner. The cascading ramifications of these fluctuations arise from the intricate interaction of algorithmic algorithms, each responding collectively to perceived market signals. The convergence of these reactions has the potential to magnify the extent of price fluctuations, leading to a cascading impact that resonates across the market environment.

The ramifications of unregulated flash crashes are diverse in nature. The destabilisation of market stability can occur due to unpredictable and irregular price fluctuations, leading to a decline in investor confidence, which is a crucial factor. The market players face a substantial risk due to their failure to effectively foresee and respond to extreme market situations, which can result in financial losses. Moreover, the systemic ramifications of flash crashes, characterised by the contagious spread of market disturbances, emphasise the imperative for diligent protective measures. In order to tackle this complex dilemma, it is imperative to strengthen market mechanisms that can reduce the effects of algorithmic-driven activity in times of significant volatility. One strategy that can be employed is the utilisation of circuit breakers, which are deliberate interruptions in trading activities that aim to mitigate the rapid escalation of price fluctuations. Circuit breakers provide market players with a brief pause to reassess and recalibrate by briefly halting trade during such instances.

In summary, the convergence of rapid algorithms and stable market conditions in AI-powered financial markets necessitates the implementation of proactive strategies to minimise the potential impact of sudden market downturns. In the realm of market integrity, institutions and regulatory agencies bear the responsibility of maintaining a careful equilibrium. This entails harnessing the advantages of algorithmic trading in terms of efficiency, while also taking measures to prevent the unforeseen repercussions of excessive volatility. By implementing effective circuit breakers and employing various protective strategies, stakeholders may collaboratively negotiate the intricate landscape of market fluctuations caused by algorithms. This concerted effort aims to create a future where the balance between speed and stability is achieved, hence promoting a financially resilient and safe ecosystem.

3. Data Bias and Discriminatory Outcomes

The successful implementation of artificial intelligence (AI) algorithms in financial markets is contingent upon the availability and utilisation of extensive datasets. Nevertheless, it is important to acknowledge that these datasets may contain inherent biases, which can unintentionally result in discriminatory consequences. Algorithmic bias is a consequence of biassed training data, which can lead to decisions that create unfair advantages or disadvantages for specific groups. The utilisation of biassed algorithms by institutions not only gives rise to ethical considerations, but also exposes them to both reputational and legal risks. It is imperative for institutions to proactively adopt strategies aimed at identifying and addressing algorithmic bias, thereby guaranteeing that judgements made by AI systems are fair and encompassing.

Within the complex relationship between artificial intelligence (AI) algorithms and financial markets, data plays a fundamental role as the foundation upon which algorithms base their decision-making processes. The utilisation of extensive datasets, meanwhile, reveals a contradiction that stems from the capacity of data to reflect the prejudices ingrained in society, inadvertently compromising the principles of equity and fairness that financial markets essentially aim to maintain.

The coalescence of partial data and AI algorithms can result in the emergence of algorithmic bias, which refers to the situation where the decisions made by AI algorithms are influenced by the biases inherent in the training data. The presence of this subtle yet substantial prejudice can give rise to discriminatory consequences, wherein certain groups are unjustly favoured or disadvantaged by the judgements made. These consequences, which are in opposition to the ideals of equity, possess the capability to weaken the credibility of financial markets and diminish public confidence. The difficulties associated with mitigating algorithmic bias transcend the ethical domain. Institutions that implement biassed algorithms subject themselves to a range of potential hazards, including those related to reputation, legality, and finance. The financial sector has the potential to inadvertently perpetuate societal biases, which can lead to inequitable outcomes. This phenomenon not only damages the reputation of financial organisations but also exposes them to potential legal consequences.

Within the context of these challenges, there exists a pressing need for institutions to proactively identify and address algorithmic bias. This mandate adopts a comprehensive strategy that extends beyond the confines of technology in isolation. To address the inherent bias and prejudice encoded inside AI algorithms, institutions must employ a comprehensive approach that encompasses technical solutions, rigorous assessments, and human monitoring. One method of mitigating bias involves the utilisation of data preprocessing, a procedure in which biassed components are detected and rectified. Through a methodical examination of the training data and the subsequent rectification of any discrepancies, institutions have the ability to mitigate the transmission of bias from the data to the algorithm. Moreover, the implementation of varied and inclusive training datasets presents a potential solution to mitigate prejudice, allowing algorithms to acquire knowledge from a wider range of experiences and viewpoints. The necessity for continuous monitoring and evaluation is further emphasised by ethical issues. It is imperative for institutions to have procedures that consistently evaluate algorithmic judgements in order to identify and address any potential biases and discriminatory practises. The integration of diverse teams, consisting of individuals with expertise in several fields such as technology, ethics, sociology, and domain-specific knowledge, facilitates a comprehensive approach that thoroughly examines algorithms from many perspectives.

In summary, the complexities surrounding data bias and its capacity to produce discriminatory results highlight a critical juncture for institutions and regulatory entities. By effectively managing this critical point in time by a dedicated adherence to attentiveness, openness, and inclusivity, individuals and organisations involved can cultivate a financial environment where artificial intelligence algorithms play a role in promoting fairness rather than intensifying disparities. By implementing proactive strategies, establishing strong regulatory supervision, and maintaining a steadfast commitment to fairness, the incorporation of AI algorithms into financial markets has the potential to serve as a catalyst for beneficial change. This integration can uphold the values of equality and fairness, while also paving the way for a more inclusive future.

4. Cybersecurity and Technological Vulnerabilities

The need of AI-driven financial markets on resilient technology infrastructure is inherent. Nevertheless, this heavy dependence exposes the financial sector to many cyber risks and vulnerabilities. Adversarial entities possess the capability to exploit vulnerabilities within artificial intelligence algorithms, data pipelines, or trading platforms in order to engage in market manipulation, unauthorised acquisition of sensitive information, or the initiation of extensive disturbances. The primary difficulty resides in enhancing the security of artificial intelligence (AI) powered systems while still preserving the agility and rapidity facilitated by algorithms.

Within the complex framework of AI-powered financial markets, technology serves as the fundamental infrastructure that enables the dynamic and efficient functioning of algorithms. The significant advancements in technology have played a crucial role in transforming market dynamics. However, these advancements have also presented a complex issue, particularly in the domain of cybersecurity and the associated vulnerabilities. The dependence on resilient technological infrastructure presents opportunities for potential cyber threats, and in this context, the conflict between strengthening security measures and maintaining flexibility becomes a prominent concern. The convergence of artificial intelligence and financial markets presents a plethora of potential opportunities for malevolent entities. Artificial intelligence (AI) algorithms, due to their complex decision-making mechanisms, data pipelines, and interconnected trading platforms, are susceptible to being targeted for abuse. Cyber risks encompass a wide range of manifestations, spanning from intricate hacking endeavours to organised endeavours that seek to manipulate market behaviours.

One significant concern that arises is the possibility of market manipulation. The potential exists for malicious entities to enter artificial intelligence algorithms with the intention of manipulating market movements to their advantage, exploiting the rapid execution capabilities enabled by those algorithms. Through the development of algorithmic tactics that imitate authentic market behaviour, these individuals have the ability to generate deceptive perceptions, resulting in a chain reaction that initiates successive market oscillations.

The act of stealing confidential information poses a significant threat, not only to individuals involved in the market, but also to the fundamental principles of market integrity. The unauthorised access to AI algorithms, which contain proprietary trading methods, sensitive client data, or confidential market insights, might grant malicious individuals a significant advantage. Instances of such breaches have the potential to undermine investor confidence, alter the balance of the market, and potentially facilitate illicit insider trading activities. The mitigation of these vulnerabilities requires a comprehensive strategy that balances the requirement for security with the demands of flexibility. Enhancing the security of artificial intelligence (AI)-powered systems necessitates the implementation of resilient encryption mechanisms, stringent access rules, and ongoing surveillance. It is imperative for institutions and regulatory agencies to engage in collaborative efforts aimed at establishing robust cybersecurity standards that encompass algorithmic processes, data transmission, and trading platforms. Nevertheless, the task at hand involves achieving a delicate equilibrium, one that harmonises security protocols with the natural agility of algorithmic trading. Excessive security measures have the potential to unintentionally impede the effectiveness and velocity that algorithms contribute to financial markets. The ability of algorithms to make prompt decisions should not be jeopardised by burdensome security protocols.

In conclusion, it is imperative to prioritise the protection of the cybersecurity landscape and address technological vulnerabilities inside AI-driven financial markets. This necessitates a steadfast dedication to safeguarding the ecosystem, while simultaneously embracing the revolutionary capabilities offered by algorithms. It is imperative to establish a delicate balance, wherein rigorous security measures are harmoniously integrated with the agility that characterises algorithmic trading. By engaging in this endeavour bolstered by cooperation, originality, and attentiveness, individuals with vested interests can establish a fortified defence against cyber risks while also ensuring that artificial intelligence algorithms continue to facilitate the advancement of financial markets towards enhanced efficiency, adaptability, and ethical advancement.

5. Regulatory and Compliance Complexities

The expeditious advancement of artificial intelligence algorithms sometimes surpasses the progress made in establishing regulatory frameworks. Consequently, organisations and regulatory bodies encounter difficulties in formulating efficient supervision and governance procedures. Achieving an optimal equilibrium between promoting innovation and upholding market integrity necessitates regulatory adaptability and a comprehensive comprehension of artificial intelligence (AI) technology. It is imperative for regulators to maintain alignment with the rapid breakthroughs in artificial intelligence (AI) in order to take proactive measures in addressing potential risks and mitigating the occurrence of regulatory arbitrage Within the dynamic convergence of artificial intelligence algorithms and financial markets, the rapid pace of technology progress frequently encounters a persistent challenge from the deliberate pace of regulatory frameworks. The outcome reveals a complex dilemma that institutions and regulatory bodies must carefully manage with precision and foresight: a scenario in which the rapid evolution of AI algorithms surpasses the development of appropriate legislation.

The intrinsic intricacy of AI algorithms, characterised by their sophisticated decision-making processes and complex interplay, necessitates the implementation of regulatory monitoring that is similarly detailed and subtle. Nonetheless, the disparity between the advancement of innovation and the implementation of regulatory measures might result in deficiencies in supervision, hence creating opportunities for possible dangers to arise without proper monitoring. Achieving a careful balance between promoting innovation and maintaining market integrity is the fundamental aspect of this challenge, necessitating a transformation in regulatory flexibility and expertise. The convergence of AI-driven financial markets and the pursuit of innovation necessitates the establishment of a cohesive framework for effective governance. Regulatory agencies are required to develop a comprehensive comprehension of artificial intelligence (AI) technologies, by thoroughly exploring the intricate technological aspects that form the foundation of algorithmic decision-making. The understanding of this matter is crucial not just for efficient supervision, but also to proactively mitigate any hazards that may arise as algorithms get more complex.

One aspect of this difficulty pertains to the necessity of being able to change in real-time. The dynamic nature of technology evolution necessitates the development of legal frameworks that can adapt swiftly to include emerging developments in artificial intelligence. Regulatory bodies are required to actively participate in continuous communication with specialists in the field of technology, ensuring they remain well-informed about the latest advancements and proactively anticipate any potential hazards that may emerge. The presence of regulatory arbitrage, which refers to the exploitation of regulatory loopholes by market participants for their own benefit, introduces an additional level of intricacy. In order to counteract this issue, it is imperative for regulatory entities to engage in collaborative efforts spanning several countries, with the aim of establishing a unified and consistent global framework for regulating artificial intelligence. The necessity of international collaboration, combined with a dedication to maintaining technological advancement, is crucial in order to prevent the exploitation of regulatory loopholes.

In summary, the intricate legal and compliance challenges in AI-powered financial markets require a delicate balance between fostering innovation and implementing effective oversight. Regulatory authorities are required to move beyond traditional frameworks and adopt a comprehensive understanding of artificial intelligence (AI) technology, while also demonstrating a proactive and future-oriented mindset. By cultivating a mutually beneficial association between innovation and governance, stakeholders have the ability to establish a trajectory towards a financial ecosystem in which AI algorithms flourish, while being closely monitored by comprehensive and flexible regulatory frameworks. By implementing proactive strategies, fostering collaboration, and demonstrating a steadfast dedication to maintaining balance, the domain of AI-powered financial markets has the potential to emerge as a model of responsible innovation. In this envisioned future, the agility of algorithms will be effectively synchronised with the robustness of regulatory supervision. Although AI-driven financial markets offer significant potential, they are not without their share of obstacles. The dynamic nature of the current environment necessitates the adoption of a comprehensive strategy that entails cooperation among many entities such as institutions, regulatory agencies, technological specialists, and market stakeholders. By taking proactive measures to tackle these problems, which may arise from algorithmic complexity, systemic stability, bias mitigation, cybersecurity, or regulatory intricacies, stakeholders can collaboratively leverage the promise of artificial intelligence to drive the advancement of financial markets, while also ensuring protection against any drawbacks. The ongoing transformation of finance by AI necessitates a thorough comprehension of the associated risks. This understanding serves as a crucial tool in navigating the path of AI-driven financial markets, ensuring their progression towards a future marked by innovation, resilience, and responsible expansion.

Chapter 19: AI and International Trade

The incorporation of artificial intelligence (AI) into the framework of global trade has become a significant influence in influencing patterns, policies, and the dynamics of the global economy during a period characterised by remarkable technical advancements. The integration of artificial intelligence (AI) and trade is a critical point where advancements in technology interact with commercial activities, resulting in a paradigm shift that surpasses national boundaries and spans several sectors. This chapter initiates an exploration of the complex landscape of artificial intelligence (AI) and its intersection with international trade. It aims to analyse the significant influence of AI on trade patterns and competitiveness, examine the crucial role of institutions in shaping trade policies and regulations related to AI, and investigate the potential consequences for global economic governance and cooperation.

The Impact of AI on International Trade Patterns and Competitiveness

The convergence of artificial intelligence (AI) and international trade has brought about a fundamental transformation, reshaping the parameters of worldwide business transactions. AI-driven technologies, like as machine learning and data analytics, contribute to a paradigm shift in the trade domain by enabling enhanced efficiency, accuracy, and creativity. The intricate relationship between artificial intelligence (AI) and trade patterns reveals a complex web of changes and developments.

The impact of artificial intelligence (AI) on supply chains is significant, as it effectively optimises logistical operations, improves inventory management processes, and facilitates the implementation of predictive maintenance strategies. The emergence of intelligent factories driven by artificial intelligence (AI) facilitates a novel era of manufacturing characterised by enhanced customization and accelerated production capabilities. Furthermore, the capacity of artificial intelligence (AI) to analyse extensive information results in a detailed comprehension of customer preferences, empowering firms to customise their products with exceptional accuracy. Consequently, this process generates novel opportunities for trade and investment. However, the integration of artificial intelligence (AI) into several industries not only enhances trade prospects but also gives rise to competitive dynamics. Countries and sectors that adopt artificial intelligence (AI) technology enjoy a competitive advantage, reinforcing their status as prominent players in global trade. Nevertheless, the rise of companies driven by artificial intelligence (AI) can potentially result in economic displacement, hence requiring the development of new skills and tactics to maintain equitable trade patterns and foster inclusive economic growth.

The Role of Institutions in Shaping AI-Related Trade Policies and Regulations

The increasing intersection of artificial intelligence and trade has led to institutions assuming a pivotal role in shaping the future of the trade landscape. The regulatory framework that governs trade policy connected to artificial intelligence (AI) plays a crucial role in promoting a trade ecosystem that is characterised by fairness, security, and a focus on supporting innovation. In order to effectively navigate the landscape of institutional operations, it is imperative for organisations to confront the complexities associated with the synchronisation of standards, the resolution of data privacy apprehensions, and the safeguarding of intellectual property rights.

The formulation of trade policies and regulations necessitates the careful calibration of fostering AI-driven economic expansion while simultaneously mitigating potential risks and challenges. When formulating policy, it is imperative for institutions to consider the facilitation of cross-border data flow, promotion of technology transfer, and establishment of fair competition that enables both established and developing economies to effectively utilise the potential of artificial intelligence.

Potential Implications for Global Economic Governance and Cooperation in the AI Era

The proliferation of artificial intelligence (AI) in the realm of international trade has far-reaching implications that extend beyond state boundaries, hence necessitating a reassessment of global economic governance. The collaborative aspect of artificial intelligence (AI), which emphasises the need of international cooperation and data-sharing, requires the development of novel methods of interaction across nations. The establishment of cross-border partnerships to develop frameworks for data exchange, address ethical considerations, and align regulatory approaches becomes crucial.

Additionally, the emergence of artificial intelligence necessitates a need to reassess and adjust trade agreements. The inclusion of AI-related provisions in trade agreements, with a specific emphasis on data flows, technology transfer, and standards harmonisation, is indicative of the emerging digital trade landscape. The advent of artificial intelligence (AI) necessitates a reimagining of trade diplomacy, characterised by agility, flexibility, and a collective aspiration for economic well-being.

The exploration of artificial intelligence and its impact on international trade is a profound endeavour characterised by the pursuit of novel ideas, formidable obstacles, and significant potential. The interdependence between artificial intelligence (AI) and trade patterns creates a framework in which enterprises thrive, national boundaries become less distinct, and numerous opportunities arise. In the realm of AI-related trade, institutions play a crucial role as central pillars, formulating regulations that shape the parameters of this field. Consequently, they create an environment where both competition and inclusivity can coexist harmoniously. As the global landscape of economic governance continues to develop, the notion of collaboration emerges as a fundamental aspect, emphasising the necessity of collaborative frameworks that effectively traverse the trade landscape improved by artificial intelligence. In the current era characterised by vast opportunities, the integration of artificial intelligence (AI) with global trade sets the stage for a forthcoming period in which technology drives trade, trade fosters economic expansion, and the collective endeavour for wealth serves as a unifying force among nations, industries, and aspirations.

The impact of AI on international trade patterns and competitiveness

The integration of artificial intelligence (AI) with the complex network of global trade has ushered in a new era marked by significant and extensive changes. The use of sophisticated algorithms, data analytics, and automation technologies has led to the widespread integration of these tools in various aspects of trade. This integration has resulted in a ripple effect that transcends industry boundaries and geographical constraints. The implications of this revolutionary synergy have manifested as a multifaceted phenomenon that not only redefines patterns of commerce but also revitalises global competitiveness.

The profound impact of artificial intelligence (AI) is readily apparent in the complex network of supply chains and manufacturing procedures, where the integration of AI-powered technology resembles the harmonious coordination of a highly efficient and accurate symphony. The fields of logistics, inventory management, and predictive maintenance have seen a significant transformation, resulting in the development of supply chains that exhibit exceptional agility, responsiveness, and sensitivity to dynamic shifts in demand and unforeseen disturbances. The emergence of intelligent factories, driven by artificial intelligence (AI), signifies a shift away from conventional mass production methods, leading to the emergence of a domain characterised by flexible and customised manufacturing processes. The current transformation of supply chain dynamics is driving nations to strategically establish themselves as specialised centres, focusing on the mastery of producing specific components or creating niche goods that resonate with global markets.

In addition to its applications in production, artificial intelligence (AI) has demonstrated remarkable capabilities in the processing and analysis of extensive information. This has resulted in an unparalleled depth of understanding of consumer behaviours, market trends, and estimates of demand. With the utilisation of advanced cognitive abilities, businesses are now capable of deciphering complex client preferences, predicting market fluctuations, and customising their products or services with exceptional accuracy. This comprehensive comprehension drives the growth of international e-commerce and promotes the advancement of digital trade to unprecedented levels. Countries that skillfully adopt artificial intelligence (AI) are able to gain a competitive edge by refining their export strategies with precision. They are able to align their range of products and services with the ever-changing patterns of global demand.

The pervasive impact of artificial intelligence (AI) is not limited to physical goods, but also extends to the domain of services. In this context, digital platforms and AI-powered services are revolutionising the established norms of cross-border transactions and global value chains. The proliferation of artificial intelligence (AI) platforms enables the efficient delivery of services across international boundaries, leading to a shift in which knowledge-intensive services gain a competitive advantage. The concept of comparative advantage, which was formerly limited to established industries, has now being reinterpreted as nations leverage their intellectual skills and utilise AI-driven technologies to explore novel avenues of economic specialisation and trade. Nevertheless, the advent of artificial intelligence (AI) ushers in a period of extraordinary possibilities. However, this revolutionary wave also presents a set of complex issues that require skillful handling. The widespread adoption of artificial intelligence (AI) technology poses a potential risk of further widening the current inequities among nations and industries, hence potentially leading to economic displacement. The swift progression of automation, which entails the substitution of human labour in specific industries, underscores the imperative need for a steadfast dedication to re-skilling and upskilling the workforce. This commitment is crucial to guaranteeing that the benefits of trade driven by artificial intelligence are equitably shared among all individuals.

In summary, the integration of artificial intelligence (AI) with international trade coordination represents a significant transformation, characterised by the emergence of efficiency, responsiveness, and specialisation as prominent themes. The international trade arena is characterised by governments and companies that skillfully utilise the transformative power of artificial intelligence, hence enhancing trade patterns and altering comparative advantages. The symphony's composition, nonetheless, establishes a collective responsibility to confront the difficulties arising from economic upheaval. The advancement of artificial intelligence (AI) is driving international trade to unprecedented levels. In this context, there is a collective endeavour to guarantee inclusivity and fair distribution of gains. This commitment forms the basis for a future where AI serves not only as a facilitator of trade but also as a catalyst for enhanced global competitiveness.

The role of institutions in shaping AI-related trade policies and regulations

In an era characterised by the amalgamation of artificial intelligence (AI) and global trade, institutions assume a crucial role as creators of the regulatory structure that oversees this dynamic convergence. The utilisation of AI technologies in the field of trade has led institutions to assume a prominent position, as they grapple with a multifaceted landscape that necessitates a careful balance between promoting innovation and ensuring the stability of global trade. In addition to their traditional policy-making functions, institutions have a broader role in the AI era. They assume the responsibility of safeguarding ethical considerations, ensuring fair competition, and promoting harmonised trade practises.

Policies and laws pertaining to AI in commerce hold significant influence over the direction of global trade, since they have the capacity to either enhance or restrict the opportunities associated with AI. Various institutions, ranging from national governments to international organisations, face complex issues as they shape the regulatory framework. One of the primary factors to be taken into account is the need to achieve a harmonious equilibrium between fostering advancements in artificial intelligence and mitigating any drawbacks. The lack of clearly defined regulations can give rise to a state of ambiguity, which can hinder the movement of data across borders and the transfer of technology. On the contrary, too stringent laws have the potential to impede innovation and establish obstacles that inhibit the involvement of smaller economies in the AI-driven trade ecosystem.

Data governance plays a crucial role in the context of AI-driven commerce, requiring organisations to develop policies that enable the smooth exchange of data across borders, while also safeguarding data privacy and security. The smooth transfer of data plays a crucial role in the training of artificial intelligence systems, since it improves their effectiveness and pertinence. Institutions bear the responsibility of cultivating global standards that strike a delicate equilibrium between facilitating data accessible and safeguarding data, so mitigating the risk of data localization mandates that may lead to the fragmentation of global trade. Simultaneously, it is imperative for individuals to remain cautious in protecting data from unauthorised access, thereby establishing the requisite level of trust required for the widespread adoption of AI-powered commerce.

In addition, institutions are faced with the complex challenge of handling intellectual property rights (IPR) inside the realm of artificial intelligence (AI). The introduction of AI's ability to produce novel solutions presents challenges in identifying ownership and rights. The evolving nature of AI-generated outputs necessitates a reevaluation of patent and copyright frameworks by institutions. This reassessment is crucial to maintain fair protection for authors, while also avoiding excessive restrictions that could impede technological progress. The integration of artificial intelligence (AI) technologies in trade necessitates institutions to harmonise trade policy with national security concerns. The transfer of artificial intelligence (AI) technology across national borders has generated apprehensions regarding the possible use of these technologies for both civilian and military purposes, as well as the protection of essential technologies. It is vital for institutions to achieve a harmonious equilibrium that facilitates the dissemination of information while simultaneously upholding national security imperatives.

The era of artificial intelligence is characterised by a significant degree of interconnectedness, hence emphasising the utmost importance of international cooperation. Institutions play a crucial role in facilitating international collaboration, facilitating discussions aimed at aligning trade policies and standards pertaining to artificial intelligence (AI). The importance of collaborative endeavours cannot be overstated when it comes to tackling gaps among nations with differing levels of artificial intelligence (AI) preparedness. Such collaborations are crucial in order to prevent the emergence of digital trade divides that have the potential to damage the global trade ecosystem. Furthermore, it is the responsibility of institutions to incorporate ethical issues into trade policy pertaining to artificial intelligence. The establishment of ethical norms by institutions is necessary to ensure responsible utilisation of AI technology, while avoiding the perpetuation of discriminatory practises and infringement upon human rights. It is imperative that these guidelines achieve a nuanced equilibrium between fostering innovation and mitigating the potential for AI technology to be utilised as tools of detriment.

In summary, it is evident that institutions play a crucial role in influencing the development of AI-related trade rules and regulations, which will ultimately determine the parameters of international trade in the era of artificial intelligence. The diverse range of duties they undertake includes the promotion of innovation, the establishment of data governance protocols, the protection of intellectual property, the management of national security issues, the facilitation of international collaboration, and the adherence to ethical principles. As institutions traverse this complex trajectory, they establish a regulatory framework that not only fosters the expansion of AI-powered commerce but also maintains the values of equity, inclusiveness, and responsible technological progress. This guarantees that the prospective advantages of AI are actualized for all nations and participants within the global trade ecosystem.

Potential implications for global economic governance and cooperation in the AI era

The integration of artificial intelligence (AI) into economies worldwide has significant and diverse ramifications for global economic governance and collaboration. The rise of artificial intelligence (AI) as a disruptive phenomenon necessitates a critical moment for states and international organisations to reevaluate established conventions, reframe their responsibilities, and establish novel forms of cooperation in order to effectively address the complexities and prospects associated with the AI era.

The rapid advancement of artificial intelligence (AI) presents a wide range of potential ramifications for global economic administration. The primary concern is the requirement for an adjusted regulatory structure that goes beyond national boundaries, guaranteeing that advancements driven by artificial intelligence conform to ethical, societal, and economic necessities. The multifaceted and cross-disciplinary characteristics of artificial intelligence (AI) require a comprehensive strategy that incorporates several aspects such as trade, intellectual property, labour, and competition regulations. In order to address AI-related concerns effectively, institutions such as the World Trade Organisation (WTO) and the International Labour Organisation (ILO) need to modify their missions. This adaptation is necessary to provide a regulatory environment that promotes both innovation and the protection of society welfare, thereby ensuring a harmonised approach.

Moreover, the emergence of artificial intelligence (AI) gives rise to inquiries concerning conventional economic indicators and measuring procedures. The increasing prevalence of digital services, automation, and AI-driven industrial processes presents a significant challenge to traditional measurements such as GDP. Consequently, there is a pressing requirement for the development of new economic indicators that can effectively capture the complexities of the AI-driven economy. In order to obtain a thorough comprehension of economic growth and wellbeing in the era of artificial intelligence (AI), it is imperative for institutions responsible for global economic governance to engage in joint efforts aimed at redefining these metrics. The necessity of cooperation is heightened in the era of artificial intelligence (AI), given the interdependencies and interconnection of AI's worldwide influence. Consequently, collaborative endeavours are required to effectively tackle common difficulties. It is imperative for nations to surpass competing mentalities and foster a milieu that promotes the exchange of knowledge, transfer of technology, and development of capabilities. Collaborative research endeavours and the utilisation of open-source frameworks have the potential to facilitate the communal harnessing of AI discoveries, so safeguarding against any exclusion of nations or groups during this transformative period.

In addition, it is imperative for global economic governance to confront the possibility of labour market disruptions caused by artificial intelligence. In light of the transformative impact of automation and AI technologies on job responsibilities, it is imperative for institutions to engage in collaborative efforts aimed at formulating policies that facilitate the reskilling and upskilling of the workforce. There is a need to reorganise international labour norms and laws in order to ensure the equitable distribution of benefits arising from AI-driven economic growth, hence limiting the amplification of existing inequities. The domains of intellectual property and innovation governance are currently positioned for significant development. The rapid progression of artificial intelligence (AI) technology has resulted in a convergence of creation and automation, leading to the need for joint endeavours in order to modify intellectual property frameworks to effectively incorporate outputs generated by AI. The advent of artificial intelligence (AI) patents, copyrights, and trademarks raises intricate inquiries regarding attribution, ownership, and rights, hence demanding the establishment of unified international standards.The advent of artificial intelligence (AI) brings forth a period characterised by increased complexities in data governance. The establishment of norms and standards for cross-border data flows, data privacy, and cybersecurity is of utmost importance in promoting a favourable environment for the responsible and secure use of AI technology, necessitating international cooperation. Collaborative design is essential in establishing mechanisms for data sharing and developing cross-jurisdictional data management protocols to guarantee interoperability and uphold individual rights.

In summary, the ramifications of artificial intelligence (AI) on worldwide economic governance and collaboration are of great significance, necessitating the adoption of adaptable, collaborative, and future-oriented strategies. In order to effectively respond to the challenges posed by artificial intelligence (AI), institutions need to develop regulatory frameworks that can accommodate the various complex aspects of this technology. This includes redefining economic indicators to account for AI's impact, promoting collaborative innovation, addressing changes in the labour market, and navigating the complexities of intellectual property and data governance. The convergence of nations and institutions at the intersection of artificial intelligence (AI) and global economic dynamics will have a significant impact on the extent to which the AI era promotes inclusive prosperity and sustainable progress worldwide. The ability of these entities to establish new avenues of collaboration will play a crucial role in shaping the outcomes of this era.

Chapter 20: AI and Economic Policy-making

In a period characterised by swift technological progress, the amalgamation of artificial intelligence (AI) with the formulation of economic policies has introduced a novel framework of opportunities and prospects. As nations grapple with the intricacies of an ever-evolving global environment, there is a growing need to reconsider the conventional structures of economic governance. This reevaluation is being driven by the integration of artificial intelligence (AI), which holds the potential to offer groundbreaking perspectives and inventive approaches.

This chapter explores the intricate relationship between artificial intelligence (AI) and economic policy, analysing the ways in which AI technologies are transforming the process of policy development and decision-making. This study examines the interactive correlation between artificial intelligence (AI) and institutions, elucidating how these organisations utilise AI insights to enhance the development of policy designs that are better informed and more effective. Furthermore, we thoroughly examine the problems and ethical implications that arise when artificial intelligence intersects with economic policymaking. We specifically address concerns that stem from the integration of machine intelligence into the core of governance.

The Use of AI in Economic Policy Formulation and Decision-Making Processes

As the complexity and capacity of AI algorithms continue to advance, they present a valuable tool for economic policymakers to analyse extensive data sets, detect patterns, and simulate various scenarios. This section examines the several complex ways in which artificial intelligence (AI) enhances the process of economic policy development, facilitating well-informed decision-making and improving the accuracy of policy outcomes.

The Role of Institutions in Incorporating AI Insights into Policy Design and Evaluation

Institutions play a crucial role in facilitating the integration of AI findings into the framework of economic policy. In this study, we investigate the methods through which governments, think tanks, and international organisations utilise AI-driven analytics to enhance policy development, assess outcomes, and foster a more flexible approach to adaptive governance.

Potential Challenges and Ethical Considerations in the Intersection of AI and Economic Policymaking

The integration of artificial intelligence (AI) into economic policy presents a complex array of problems and ethical quandaries. This part explores unexplored areas, examining topics such as algorithmic bias, transparency, accountability, and the wider societal consequences of delegating policy decisions to computational intelligence.

In a global context where the intersection of artificial intelligence (AI) and economic policy holds both potential and risks, this chapter sets out on an investigative endeavour. Through an analysis of the intricate components of this influential collaboration, we aim to comprehend the intricacies of an AI-driven future, wherein economic governance is on the verge of unparalleled advancement.

As we explore the complicated relationship between artificial intelligence (AI) and economic policy-making, let us embark on an academic journey that navigates the dynamics of innovation, governance, and the intricate interplay between machine intelligence and human stewardship.

The use of AI in economic policy formulation and decision-making processes

The incorporation of artificial intelligence (AI) into the development of economic policies and decision-making procedures has brought about a significant transformation in the approach of governments and policymakers towards the intricate issues of the contemporary era. The capacity of artificial intelligence (AI) to analyse extensive quantities of data, identify patterns, and make predictions has established it as a transformative instrument in developing economic policies that are better informed, efficient, and adaptable to fluctuating market conditions.

1. Data-Driven Analysis and Forecasting

The power of artificial intelligence (AI) resides in its ability to efficiently process and analyse extensive datasets that would pose significant challenges for human analysis in isolation. This skill has the potential to revolutionise the conventional framework of economic policymaking by revealing previously concealed insights embedded within the complex network of economic data. Economic policymakers possess the ability to effectively navigate vast quantities of information at an unprecedented rate and level of precision through the utilisation of AI-driven technologies.

Artificial intelligence algorithms exhibit an exceptional capacity to identify nuanced relationships, trends, and anomalies in economic data that may evade human perception. Through the examination of several variables across different sectors, such as consumer spending patterns, manufacturing output, international trade flows, and financial market behaviour, artificial intelligence (AI) has the capability to unveil complex interdependencies that form the foundation of economic dynamics. These insights provide policymakers a holistic perspective on the intricate array of forces in operation, enabling a more profound comprehension of the determinants that impact economic performance. The role of AI in economic forecasting is considered to be one of its most notable accomplishments. Through the examination of previous data and the identification of recurring patterns, artificial intelligence (AI) algorithms possess the capability to forecast future trends with a degree of precision that conventional approaches find challenging to attain. Economic indicators, such as the increase of Gross Domestic Product (GDP), inflation rates, unemployment rates, and trade balances, are influenced by a multitude of factors that are often too intricate for conventional models to fully encompass. The utilisation of AI's data-driven methodology significantly improves the accuracy and dependability of economic projections, hence equipping policymakers with the ability to anticipate economic paths with heightened assurance.

AI-powered forecasting offers a significant advantage within the domain of policy making. This capability allows governments to proactively foresee prospective obstacles and opportunities, thereby matching policy choices with projected future scenarios. For example, in the event that artificial intelligence analysis indicates an imminent deceleration in a certain industry, governments have the opportunity to preemptively devise focused policies aimed at alleviating adverse consequences. On the other hand, in the event that artificial intelligence (AI) predictions suggest a positive trend in economic activity, governments have the opportunity to investigate strategies for leveraging this momentum to achieve sustainable growth. Moreover, the persistent and immediate nature of AI analytics provides policymakers with the flexibility required to adjust to swiftly changing economic circumstances. The use of real-time monitoring guarantees the ability to promptly adapt policy responses to evolving circumstances, so reducing the potential for policy delays and augmenting the overall efficacy of interventions.

AI-driven data analysis and forecasting significantly enhance the precision, intelligence, and adaptability of economic decisions, reaching unprecedented levels. Through the extraction of significant insights from extensive datasets and the subsequent translation of these insights into actionable suggestions, artificial intelligence (AI) enables governments to effectively navigate the complex terrain of economics with an unprecedented level of foresight and expertise that was previously unimaginable. As artificial intelligence (AI) progresses, its role in data-driven policy development will increasingly transform the attitude of nations towards economic governance, resulting in the cultivation of more robust and adaptable economies.

2. Policy Simulation and Impact Assessment

Artificial intelligence (AI) enables the development of complex economic models that simulate the probable consequences of different policy initiatives. Policymakers possess the capability to input various variables and policy scenarios into artificial intelligence systems, enabling the projection of potential impacts on important economic metrics resulting from alterations in tax rates, trade policies, or regulatory frameworks. The ability to predict outcomes enables policymakers to make informed decisions while minimising unforeseen repercussions.

Within the ever-evolving realm of economic policy formulation, the incorporation of artificial intelligence (AI) presents a paradigm shift in comprehending the possible consequences of policy actions. By developing complex economic models, artificial intelligence (AI) enables policymakers to simulate a wide range of policy scenarios, thereby offering a virtual platform for testing various courses of action. The utilisation of policy simulation, a methodological approach, has become increasingly significant in facilitating informed decision-making and evaluating the efficacy of policies within a dynamic and evolving context.

The fundamental essence of policy simulation empowered by artificial intelligence (AI) is in the complex interrelationship between variables and parameters that delineate economic behaviour. Policymakers have the ability to incorporate various aspects, like as tax rates, trade policies, fiscal incentives, and regulatory changes, into the AI-driven models. The provided inputs function as fundamental components in the development of complete simulations that accurately replicate the intricate nature of real-world economies. The full potential of policy simulation driven by artificial intelligence becomes evident as the algorithms analyse these inputs and produce a comprehensive perspective on several potential outcomes. Through the utilisation of simulations across a range of scenarios, artificial intelligence (AI) is capable of generating predictions regarding the potential effects of different policy choices on crucial economic indicators. The ability to forecast future outcomes enables policymakers to proactively foresee the potential consequences of their policies, hence offering valuable insights into various domains including GDP growth, employment rates, consumer spending, and inflation.

The utilisation of AI-driven policy simulation holds considerable merit due to its capacity to effectively address and minimise unexpected outcomes. Through the utilisation of a controlled digital environment, policymakers are able to conduct simulations of policy changes, so enabling the identification of potential side effects that may not be readily apparent. An illustration of this would be a tax reduction strategy implemented with the intention of bolstering consumer expenditure, which could potentially unveil unanticipated consequences pertaining to government revenue or the distribution of income. Equipped with these valuable insights, policymakers possess the ability to refine their strategies in order to optimise desired results while mitigating unfavourable consequences. Furthermore, the utilisation of AI-driven policy simulation is characterised by its dynamic nature, since it is capable of adapting to changing circumstances. As the economic landscape undergoes changes, the recalibration of AI models becomes possible in order to incorporate updated data inputs. This enables policymakers to enhance their comprehension of probable outcomes and make necessary adjustments to their strategy. The ability to react in real-time guarantees that policies retain their relevance and effectiveness, even when confronted with swiftly evolving conditions.

AI-enabled policy simulation goes beyond conventional policy analysis by offering policymakers a virtual laboratory to test out novel solutions and predict the consequences of their decisions. By leveraging the predictive capabilities of artificial intelligence (AI), policymakers have the opportunity to engage in a process of inquiry that ultimately results in decision-making that is better informed, adaptable, and influential. With the continuous advancement of AI, there is a potential for the field of economic policy formation to see improved precision and understanding. This might lead to a more robust and responsive approach to governance.

3.Real-Time Monitoring and Adaptive Governance

The utilisation of AI-powered analytics facilitates the real-time monitoring of economic trends and market dynamics by policymakers. Continuous monitoring plays a crucial role in facilitating prompt answers to developing difficulties, so empowering governments to swiftly execute flexible policy adjustments in reaction to unforeseen occurrences. The importance of flexibility becomes particularly obvious during periods of economic turbulence or global disruptions. In a period characterised by swift changes and exceptional instability, the integration of artificial intelligence (AI) and economic administration introduces a novel phase of continuous monitoring and adaptable reaction. By using AI-driven analytics, policymakers are able to acquire an unprecedented capacity to observe economic patterns and market dynamics in real-time. This empowers them to promptly execute flexible governance policies that may effectively tackle emergent issues and exploit unexpected chances.

The fundamental aspect of AI's impact on real-time monitoring lies in its relentless demand for data. Economic systems are complex networks that are impacted by a multitude of factors, ranging from consumer attitudes to worldwide supply chains. Artificial intelligence algorithms effectively consume and analyse these various data sources, providing a comprehensive and current overview of economic conditions. Continuous monitoring provides policymakers with timely information that provide the basis for informed decision-making. During periods characterised by economic instability or market disturbances, conventional approaches to data gathering and analysis may prove inadequate in effectively capturing the dynamic and swift nature of transformations. Artificial intelligence (AI), in contrast, functions at the rate of data processing, allowing governments to proactively anticipate and respond to changes and deviations as they occur.

The inherent capability of AI-driven real-time monitoring lies in its potential to facilitate adaptive governance. In the event of unexpected circumstances, policymakers possess the ability to promptly adjust their strategy by leveraging newly acquired insights from artificial intelligence. The presence of flexibility in governance allows for the maintenance of responsiveness and the ability to make precise adjustments to policy interventions in a timely manner, while simultaneously reducing the potential dangers associated with policy delays. Let us contemplate a hypothetical situation whereby an abrupt disturbance in the worldwide supply chains leads to a consequential impact on the accessibility of critical commodities. The real-time monitoring capabilities of artificial intelligence (AI) allow policymakers to immediately evaluate the situation, measure potential economic consequences, and develop focused responses to alleviate the impacts. Various responsive measures can encompass a spectrum of actions, including the modification of import/export policy and the promotion of domestic production, all with the objective of reinstating economic balance.

Moreover, the utilisation of artificial intelligence enables continuous monitoring in real-time, surpassing mere reactive actions. Through the identification of incipient trends and developing patterns, policymakers possess the ability to proactively predict forthcoming difficulties and strategically formulate policies to effectively tackle them. The implementation of a proactive approach serves to strengthen the stability of economic systems, hence mitigating the likelihood of cascading disruptions. The integration of artificial intelligence (AI)-enabled real-time monitoring and adaptive governance signifies a significant transformation in the field of economic policymaking. Artificial intelligence (AI) empowers policymakers by offering them a comprehensive and adaptable comprehension of economic dynamics. This data-driven approach gives governments with the necessary tools to effectively manage unpredictable circumstances and capitalise on potential opportunities. In light of the rapid evolution of economic landscapes, the implementation of AI-driven real-time monitoring has become an essential component for building resilience. This monitoring system plays a vital role in enabling governments to effectively address difficulties and guide their economies towards sustainable growth in an ever-changing global environment.

4.Identifying Policy Priorities and Targeted Interventions

Artificial intelligence (AI)-based insights play a crucial role in aiding policymakers in the identification of specific domains that necessitate policy intervention. Through the examination of data derived from a variety of sources including market trends, social sentiment, and consumer behaviour, artificial intelligence (AI) possesses the capability to identify sectors that necessitate attention or investment. This strategy aids in the optimisation of resource allocation and enables focused policy actions to achieve the greatest possible impact.

Within the complex framework of economic governance, the integration of artificial intelligence (AI) and policymaking presents a significant opportunity for recognising and tackling urgent policy concerns. The utilisation of AI-driven analysis, which incorporates data from various sources, enables policymakers to identify particular sectors and regions that require targeted strategic intervention. Through the examination of market trends, social sentiment, consumer behaviour, and other relevant factors, artificial intelligence (AI) sheds light on the most effective approach to allocating resources and enables the implementation of meticulously designed policy interventions that provide the potential for significant outcomes. The capabilities of AI in the field of data analysis surpass those of humans, allowing it to process and integrate an extensive range of information that was previously unattainable. As policymakers confront the intricate issues of guiding economies, artificial intelligence (AI) emerges as a reliable partner in unravelling intricate patterns and interdependencies that impact diverse sectors. Through the analysis of extensive datasets and the identification of nuanced indicators, artificial intelligence (AI) possesses the capability to identify areas that are primed for policy intervention, including the need for economic stimulus, regulatory modifications, or structural reforms.

In the context of sustainable energy development, let us contemplate a hypothetical situation wherein a nation endeavours to shift towards a more environmentally conscious and enduring energy paradigm. Artificial intelligence has the capability to systematically analyse data streams derived from energy consumption patterns, environmental indicators, and technology breakthroughs in order to uncover trends that may otherwise be difficult to discern. By utilising these perspectives, policymakers can identify areas where focused actions have the capacity to facilitate significant transformations, such as providing incentives for the adoption of renewable energy, improving energy efficiency regulations, or supporting the growth of emergent clean technology sectors.

Furthermore, the distinctive ability of artificial intelligence (AI) to assess social mood and consumer behaviour introduces a human element into the process of policy formulation. Through the examination of sentiments conveyed through various online platforms, such as social media and public discourse, artificial intelligence (AI) has the capability to assess and comprehend public viewpoints and concerns. Subsequently, policymakers have the opportunity to synchronise their actions with the prevailing societal demands and ambitions, thereby establishing a more profound correlation between governance and the overall welfare of citizens.

The utilisation of artificial intelligence in the identification of policy priorities also include the optimisation of resources. The allocation of limited resources necessitates strategic decision-making, and the capacity of artificial intelligence (AI) to identify sectors with the highest potential for investment returns enables governments to effectively allocate resources to areas of most need. Policymakers can enhance the effectiveness and influence of their actions by directing their attention towards sectors that possess unexplored potential or are in alignment with the objectives of national development.

The integration of artificial intelligence (AI) insights with policy making ultimately empowers governments to sail a trajectory characterised by precision. The outcome is a complex network of policy interventions that are carefully adjusted, adaptable, and attuned to the intricate requirements of a constantly changing economy. As the capabilities of artificial intelligence (AI) continue to advance, there is a growing potential for the integration of data-driven insights and policy decisions to significantly transform the field of economic governance. This convergence has the potential to bring about a new era where the traditional process of policymaking is enhanced by the application of scientific principles and machine intelligence.

5. Enhancing Trade and Investment Decisions

The utilisation of AI-powered analytics plays a crucial role in assisting policymakers in making well-informed decisions pertaining to international trade agreements and investment initiatives. Through the analysis of past trade trends, identification of competitive advantages, and evaluation of potential hazards, artificial intelligence (AI) plays a crucial role in assisting governments in negotiating trade agreements that are favourable and in establishing investment environments that foster economic growth. Within the complex realm of global economics, the convergence of artificial intelligence (AI) and the formulation of policies arises as a formidable influence in moulding trade and investment determinations. The analytical capabilities of AI provide policymakers with a comprehensive set of tools to analyse historical trade trends, understand competitive advantages, and evaluate future dangers. By adopting a data-driven approach, governments are able to enhance their ability to engage in effective trade negotiations and develop investment programmes that foster favourable conditions for strong economic growth.

The importance of artificial intelligence (AI) in enhancing trade decisions is manifested through its capacity to analyse complex trade patterns and historical data. Through the examination of historical trade patterns, artificial intelligence (AI) is able to reveal intricate and detailed observations regarding commodities, markets, and geographic regions that demonstrate promising prospects for expansion. This enables policymakers to discern unexplored trade opportunities and strategically position their country's export goods in accordance with global demand. In addition, artificial intelligence enhances policymakers' comprehension of competitive advantages through the analysis of extensive datasets. This analysis examines various elements, including technological capacities, efficiency in production, and levels of innovation, in order to evaluate a country's standing within the international market. With the acquisition of these valuable insights, governmental bodies are able to develop trade strategies that effectively utilise their strengths, exploit distinctive resources, and establish specialised market positions that guarantee a competitive advantage in the realm of international commerce.

The real-time data processing capabilities of AI also enable policymakers to evaluate trade risks and anticipated market swings. Through the monitoring of variables such as exchange rates, geopolitical developments, and supply chain interruptions, artificial intelligence (AI) possesses the capability to offer timely alerts and predictive assessments that serve to influence trade decisions. This proactive strategy enables governments to effectively handle possible problems and capitalise on opportunities that are in line with the changing dynamics of the market. Within the domain of investment decisions, artificial intelligence (AI) presents a comparable array of benefits. Through the examination of extensive datasets that encompass many industries, markets, and economic indicators, artificial intelligence (AI) possesses the capability to assist policymakers in the identification of sectors exhibiting significant development prospects and in the cultivation of an environment that promotes investment. This encompasses the formulation of policies aimed at attracting foreign direct investment, supporting the growth of domestic innovation centres, and establishing regulatory frameworks that both safeguard the interests of investors and promote economic dynamism.

Let us contemplate a hypothetical situation in which a governmental entity endeavours to allure international capital into its rapidly expanding technology industry. Artificial intelligence (AI)-enabled studies provide the capability to systematically analyse and examine worldwide investment trends, thoroughly evaluate clusters of innovation, and review the regulatory landscapes in order to provide suggestions that are grounded in empirical data.

These observations empower policymakers to develop incentives that attract investors while fostering an environment that expedites technical progress and promotes economic variety.

AI-driven studies serve as a navigational tool that assists policymakers in navigating the complex landscape of global trade and investment. Through the extraction of insights from data, the analysis of market trends, and the prediction of shifts, artificial intelligence (AI) enables governments to engage in astute negotiations for trade agreements and establish investment climates that foster economic development. As the capabilities of artificial intelligence (AI) progress, its impact on trade and investment decisions will persistently reshape the economic diplomacy landscape, establishing avenues for sustainable growth and global competitiveness.

6.Reducing Decision Bias and Enhancing Transparency

The impartiality of AI serves to reduce the potential impact of human biases on policy decisions. Algorithms facilitate the processing of information in an unbiased manner, hence enhancing the development of policy formulations that are more impartial in nature. Moreover, the transparent decision-making process of artificial intelligence (AI) enables stakeholders to have a deeper comprehension of the underlying reasoning behind policy choices, hence promoting enhanced public trust and involvement.

Within the domain of economic governance, the incorporation of artificial intelligence (AI) represents a paradigm shift in decision-making characterised by impartiality and openness. The capacity of AI to minimise inherent biases in human-driven policy decisions is considered to be one of its most important achievements. Through the objective analysis of information without any preexisting biases, artificial intelligence (AI) facilitates a policy formulation process that is more unbiased. Additionally, the transparent decision-making mechanism employed by AI provides insight into the reasoning behind the choices made, so promoting an atmosphere characterised by increased public trust and engagement.

The presence of cognitive biases in human decision-making processes can have unintended consequences on policy choices, leading to a distortion of the fundamental principles underlying informed decision-making. Artificial intelligence (AI), due to its inherent objectivity and neutrality, surpasses these biases. The system utilises algorithms to analyse data by identifying patterns, establishing connections, and determining statistical significance, so enabling objective decision-making devoid of subjective biases. The presence of impartiality in policy formulations guarantees that decisions are based on data-driven insights rather than unconscious biases, leading to outcomes that are more closely aligned with the overall objectives of economic governance. Transparency is a fundamental principle of democratic governance, creating an atmosphere in which individuals are well-informed and actively engaged in the formulation of policies. The transparent decision-making mechanism of AI provides a distinctive benefit in this context. Algorithms adhere to a methodical approach, wherein they manipulate data by employing predetermined rules and logical operations. The traceable decision pathway facilitates the understanding of stakeholders, including policymakers, specialists, and the general public, regarding the process by which decisions were arrived at.

Consider a hypothetical situation when a governmental body is formulating a climate strategy with the objective of mitigating carbon emissions. By leveraging AI-driven analysis, policymakers can effectively ensure that policy solutions are evaluated in an impartial manner, devoid of personal biases or political factors. The transparent decision-making process of artificial intelligence (AI) enables stakeholders to comprehend the manner in which diverse aspects, ranging from economic implications to environmental outcomes, were assessed and harmonised in order to reach the ultimate policy conclusion. Furthermore, the transparency of AI also facilitates significant public interaction. A more informed dialogue arises when stakeholders possess knowledge regarding the data-driven foundations of policy decisions. The aforementioned practises promote the provision of constructive criticism, foster a sense of responsibility, and cultivate a robust sense of trust between governing bodies and the general populace. In an era characterised by growing expectations for transparency, the role of artificial intelligence (AI) in illuminating the processes of policy making emerges as a vital resource.

Fundamentally, the combination of artificial intelligence's impartiality and clear decision-making brings forth a period of policy development distinguished by precise analysis of facts and transparent administration. AI plays a crucial role in promoting honesty, equity, and accountability within economic governance by mitigating decision biases and providing a clear justification for the choices taken. As the importance of artificial intelligence (AI) on policy-making intensifies, its capacity to enhance transparency emerges as a guiding principle for governments, leading them towards more inclusive and efficient decision-making procedures.

7. Resource Optimization and Budget Allocation

Artificial intelligence (AI) possesses the capability to analyse budgetary data in order to enhance resource allocation efficiency across several sectors. AI-guided recommendations play a significant role in promoting resource efficiency and focused investment in key areas of economic development, taking into account economic priorities, social requirements, and fiscal limitations.

Within the complex realm of economic management, the integration of artificial intelligence (AI) offers a revolutionary aspect to the optimisation of resources and allocation of budgets. The advanced analytical capabilities of artificial intelligence enable policymakers to effectively navigate the intricate landscape of fiscal decision-making, beyond the limitations of traditional methods. Through the analysis of budgetary data from the perspectives of economic priorities, social imperatives, and fiscal constraints, AI-driven suggestions assist governments in effectively distributing resources. These recommendations strategically direct investments towards sectors that are crucial for fostering sustainable economic development. The foundation of resource optimisation powered by artificial intelligence (AI) is rooted in its capacity to deconstruct and examine complex collections of budgetary data. Artificial intelligence algorithms explore the complexities of revenue streams, spending trends, and economic indicators in order to develop a thorough comprehension of a country's financial environment. By means of this intricate analysis, artificial intelligence (AI) is capable of detecting possible inefficiencies, overlaps, and areas of opportunity that may elude human observation.

Economic priorities play a crucial role in shaping policy formulation by directing the allocation of resources towards activities that promote both economic growth and societal well-being. The role of artificial intelligence in this field is highly transformative. Through the analysis of extensive economic data and the examination of various criteria, such as the contributions of different sectors to the Gross Domestic Product (GDP), the potential for job creation, and the capacity for innovation, artificial intelligence (AI) has the capability to offer valuable insights that inform resource allocation methods in accordance with broader economic goals. Social demands are a crucial aspect of resource allocation, which signifies a government's dedication to the well-being of its citizens. The utilisation of artificial intelligence enables policymakers to effectively identify certain sectors that necessitate focused investment by analysing a wide range of social data, including but not limited to demographics, health indicators, and education levels. For example, when AI analysis identifies a demand for improved healthcare services in particular areas, governments have the ability to direct resources towards addressing these deficiencies and enhancing the overall well-being of society. Fiscal limitations are an intrinsic aspect of economic governance, necessitating the careful allocation of scarce resources. The data-driven methodology employed by AI enables the optimisation of the delicate equilibrium between investments and available money through the evaluation of prospective impacts. Through the utilisation of artificial intelligence, policymakers can be guided in the development of budgets that optimise returns on investment and minimise inefficiencies, while simultaneously upholding fiscal responsibility, by simulating diverse scenarios of budget distribution.

Let us contemplate a hypothetical situation in which a governing body endeavours to rejuvenate its manufacturing industry. Artificial intelligence (AI) possesses the capability to examine historical data pertaining to the performance of various sectors, assess the dynamics of supply chains, and estimate the potential for employment creation. This analysis provides guidance to policymakers in the allocation of resources towards measures aimed at strengthening domestic manufacturing, promoting innovation, and generating sustainable employment prospects. Moreover, the significance of artificial intelligence (AI) to resource optimisation goes beyond the scope of immediate budgetary cycles. Through the process of finding and analysing long-term trends, artificial intelligence (AI) plays a crucial role in aiding governments to adopt a proactive and future-oriented strategy when allocating budgets. The adoption of this dynamic perspective guarantees that current investments align with the future demands and opportunities within the economic landscape.

In brief, the incorporation of artificial intelligence (AI) into the processes of resource optimisation and budget allocation represents a significant paradigm shift in the realm of economic governance. Through the examination of data from the perspectives of economic priorities, social imperatives, and fiscal restrictions, artificial intelligence (AI) enables governments to strategically distribute resources, thereby promoting economic growth, societal well-being, and fiscal sustainability. With the continuous advancement of AI capabilities, there is a growing potential for AI to play a significant role in efficiently allocating resources. This has the potential to greatly influence the trajectory of economic development, leading to a future characterised by responsible and influential fiscal choices. The expanding capabilities of AI are expected to contribute to the continued expansion of its involvement in economic policy formulation and decision-making. Nevertheless, despite the vast promise that AI has, its incorporation necessitates a thorough comprehension of its constraints, potential predispositions, and ethical implications. Achieving a harmonious equilibrium between innovation and accountability will play a crucial role as artificial intelligence revolutionises the realm of economic governance.

The role of institutions in incorporating AI insights into policy design and evaluation

The integration of artificial intelligence (AI) insights into the process of policy planning and evaluation signifies a significant transformation in the way institutions approach the complexities of economic governance. As artificial intelligence (AI) technologies continue to advance and exhibit their ability to analyse extensive datasets and produce insights based on data, organisations are faced with the challenge of incorporating AI into the process of policy development while balancing the need for innovation with existing practises and conventions. The diverse and dynamic nature of institutions is key to their function in this process. Institutions fulfil the role of guardians for data, collecting a wide range of information from several sources, which can then be subjected to processing and analysis by artificial intelligence. The function of data collecting is crucial in ensuring the accuracy and relevance of AI insights, as the quality and scope of the data supplied directly impact these factors.

Nevertheless, it is important to note that AI-generated ideas are not developed in isolation. Institutions play a pivotal role by providing a vital layer of expertise that situates these findings within the wider framework of economic realities and societal requirements. The establishment of a contextual understanding serves to bridge the divide between unprocessed data and policy recommendations that hold significance, so guaranteeing that the insights derived through artificial intelligence are in line with the broader objectives of economic administration. In addition to their other roles, institutions also play a significant role in the advancement and fine-tuning of artificial intelligence algorithms that are specifically designed for particular policy domains. The convergence of data scientists, economists, and policy specialists in collaborative endeavours yields algorithms that effectively capture the intricacies inherent in economic relationships and policy processes. The collective endeavour of developing and calibrating these algorithms is an iterative process that relies on institutional knowledge and technological expertise.

In addition, institutions play a crucial role in the integration of AI insights into the process of formulating policies. The AI-generated insights are translated into policy solutions that are executable and align with established legal frameworks, institutional capacities, and political imperatives. The successful execution of this procedure necessitates a careful equilibrium between harnessing the predictive powers of artificial intelligence and guaranteeing that policy proposals maintain a practical and feasible nature. Institutions are responsible for both stakeholder involvement and accountability. In the context of policy decision-making, the influence of AI insights prompts institutions to actively foster discussions among policymakers, technologists, and the general public. This study focuses on the issues surrounding algorithmic bias, ethical considerations, and possible unexpected outcomes, with the aim of promoting transparency, credibility, and public confidence in policies influenced by artificial intelligence.

Institutions cultivate an environment that promotes ongoing education, providing specialists with the necessary competencies to traverse the dynamic realm of artificial intelligence and data analytics. The organisation actively engages in enhancing the skills and knowledge of its employees to successfully interpret and utilise insights offered by artificial intelligence. The continuous nature of this learning process guarantees that institutions maintain flexibility in their interaction with AI technologies. In the final analysis, it is incumbent upon institutions to assume the responsibility of assessing the ramifications of policies derived from artificial intelligence (AI) discoveries. A variety of evaluation approaches are utilised to assess the efficacy of interventions, hence offering valuable feedback that aids in the continuous improvement and advancement of AI models. The aforementioned feedback loop highlights the iterative characteristic of the interplay between institutions and artificial intelligence.

In conclusion, the incorporation of AI insights into policy creation and evaluation by institutions is marked by a dynamic interaction among technology, expertise, and governance. The expanding role of artificial intelligence (AI) in economic policy-making necessitates the presence of institutions as a crucial component in managing this revolutionary process. These institutions play a vital role in ensuring that the potential of AI is effectively utilised to promote well-informed, efficient, and responsible economic governance.

Potential challenges and ethical considerations in the intersection of AI and economic policymaking

Within the current context of economic governance, there is a notable focus and discussion surrounding the intersection between artificial intelligence (AI) with the formulation of policies. The capacity of artificial intelligence (AI) to fundamentally transform economic policymaking through the provision of data-based insights and predictive analysis is simultaneously captivating and formidable. The incorporation of artificial intelligence (AI) presents potential benefits in terms of improved decision-making, allocation of resources, and economic development. However, it also introduces a wide range of problems and ethical concerns that necessitate careful scrutiny. This study examines the intricate relationship between artificial intelligence (AI) and the formulation of economic policies, analysing the possible challenges and ethical quandaries that necessitate attention as we negotiate this convergence.

Challenges in AI-Driven Economic Policymaking

1. The effectiveness of AI-driven policymaking is contingent upon the high quality and diverse nature of the data utilised. However, it is important to acknowledge that data frequently contains biases that result from historical prejudices and systematic imbalances. The presence of biases can be further amplified when artificial intelligence (AI) systems are trained using datasets that are already skewed, resulting in predictions that are inaccurate and policy recommendations that are unjust. Policymakers encounter the formidable task of procuring extensive and impartial data in order to guarantee that the insights generated by artificial intelligence do not perpetuate or exacerbate pre-existing inequalities.

2. The issue of complexity and interpretability arises in the context of AI algorithms, particularly deep learning models, which sometimes exhibit characteristics of "black boxes," rendering it difficult to ascertain the underlying processes that lead to specific results. In the realm of economic policymaking, the significance of transparency cannot be overstated. However, the lack of clarity and transparency associated with artificial intelligence (AI) has the potential to erode accountability and weaken the trust of stakeholders. The challenge lies in finding a middle ground between the intricacy of artificial intelligence algorithms and the imperative for policy outputs that are transparent and comprehensible.

3. Unintended Consequences: Although artificial intelligence (AI) has promise in forecasting the effects of different policy interventions, it may fall short in comprehending the intricate and unpredictable dynamics inherent in complex economic systems. The exclusive reliance on AI-generated insights, without the inclusion of human judgement, can result in unanticipated outcomes that undermine the desired policy aims. It is imperative for policymakers to exercise prudence and carefully deliberate upon the constraints inherent in the forecasting capabilities of artificial intelligence (AI).

4. The Potential Consequences of Relying on Algorithms: An excessive dependence on insights created by artificial intelligence may result in a reduced significance of human expertise and judgement. Policymakers may potentially rely on AI advice without possessing a complete understanding of the underlying rationale. These circumstances give rise to apprehensions over decision-making accountability and the ethical ramifications associated with granting algorithms the authority to determine policy directions.

Ethical Considerations in AI-Driven Economic Policymaking

1. The issue of algorithmic bias and fairness is a significant ethical dilemma that arises from the presence of biassed training data. The implementation of policies driven by artificial intelligence (AI) that either perpetuate or worsen pre-existing disparities has the potential to damage both social cohesiveness and economic justice. It is imperative for policymakers to proactively confront the issue of bias in AI algorithms, adopt tactics that promote justice, and guarantee that policies powered by AI are equitable across all societal segments.
2. The lack of openness in AI algorithms poses a threat to the concepts of transparency and accountability within governance. As artificial intelligence (AI) becomes a prominent position in influencing economic policies, several stakeholders, including individuals, industries, and civil society, express a need for elucidation regarding the rationales behind the decisions undertaken. It is imperative for policymakers to devise strategies that facilitate the provision of comprehensible justifications for suggestions generated by artificial intelligence (AI), thereby promoting accountability and engendering trust.
3. The Considerations of Privacy and Data Security: The utilisation of artificial intelligence in economic analysis frequently necessitates substantial quantities of personal and sensitive data. The ethical quandary arises from the need to strike a balance between the advantages derived from data-driven insights and the associated privacy problems and risks of data breaches. It is imperative for policymakers to develop comprehensive data protection laws that effectively uphold the rights of individuals, while simultaneously harnessing the potential benefits of artificial intelligence (AI).
4. The implementation of AI-driven policies aimed at improving efficiency and production can result in employment displacement within specific industries, hence causing social implications. It is imperative for policymakers to carefully evaluate the ethical ramifications of technological progress on both employment and societal welfare. This entails the development of policies aimed at facilitating reskilling and retraining initiatives, with the objective of alleviating adverse consequences for the workforce.

Global Implications and Case Studies

The challenges and ethical considerations associated with AI-driven economic governance transcend national borders. In the context of an increasingly linked global landscape, the act of sharing data across national borders, the presence of international trade agreements, and the interdependence of economies offer a range of extra challenges. The General Data Protection Regulation (GDPR) implemented by the European Union exemplifies a significant instance of emphasising the need of data privacy and security within AI-driven governance. China's artificial intelligence (AI) projects serve as a prime example of the potential socio-economic ramifications resulting from the swift adoption of AI technology. This underscores the significance of effectively addressing ethical considerations in order to establish a healthy equilibrium between technical advancement and the well-being of society.

Mitigation Strategies and Future Directions

Addressing the challenges and ethical considerations in AI-driven economic policymaking requires a comprehensive and proactive approach. Policymakers and institutions must adopt a multidisciplinary strategy that integrates economics, data science, ethics, law, and public policy. The following strategies offer a roadmap for navigating these challenges:

1. The importance of data quality and bias mitigation: Policymakers are advised to engage in collaborative efforts with experts in order to devise and execute data validation procedures that effectively identify and rectify biases present within training datasets. Efforts aimed at fostering open data, boosting diversity in data gathering, and conducting external audits have the potential to enhance the quality of data and alleviate biases.
2. The promotion of algorithmic transparency and accountability is recommended for policymakers, who should actively support the advancement of explainable artificial intelligence models that offer comprehensible insights. The implementation of monitoring tools, such as the incorporation of independent audits, serves to promote algorithmic accountability and foster public confidence.
3. Ethical effect Assessments: Analogous to the practise of conducting environmental effect assessments, it is proposed that legislators should require the implementation of ethical impact assessments for policies driven by artificial intelligence. These analyses would aim to examine the potential social and economic implications, so promoting informed decision-making and ethical governance.
4. Public Engagement and Education: Policymakers are required to actively include the public and relevant stakeholders in order to guarantee that policies driven by artificial intelligence are in accordance with society values and goals. popular education projects have the potential to narrow the divide between popular perception and technical comprehension, so facilitating more well-informed policy deliberations.

The convergence of artificial intelligence (AI) and economic policymaking presents significant opportunities for the development of data-driven, streamlined, and fair governance. Nonetheless, the utilisation of this technology also poses significant obstacles and ethical quandaries that necessitate careful consideration and forward-thinking approaches. As governmental bodies and organisations increasingly adopt and incorporate the capabilities of artificial intelligence (AI), it becomes imperative for them to carefully navigate the intersection between technological progress and ethical obligations. Achieving a harmonious integration of AI's capabilities with human intelligence necessitates a resolute commitment to proactive measures for risk reduction, transparent processes for decision-making, and an unwavering determination to promoting the overall welfare of society. Through a comprehensive understanding of the intricacies of issues and ethical considerations, society has the potential to effectively utilise the revolutionary capabilities of artificial intelligence (AI) in order to facilitate the development of an inclusive, accountable, and sustainable framework for economic governance in the future.

Chapter 21: AI and Capitalist Market Dynamics

Within the dynamic realm of capitalism, a significant transformation is currently taking place, characterised by the integration of artificial intelligence (AI). This technological revolution holds far-reaching consequences for market dynamics. This chapter examines the complex relationship between artificial intelligence (AI) and capitalist market dynamics, investigating the ways in which sophisticated computing systems are transforming the fundamental aspects of supply, demand, competition, and innovation. The rapid evolution of AI technology has brought forth a new era of economic interactions, which in turn has led to the transformation of existing market paradigms. This development has presented a range of unprecedented opportunities as well as intricate obstacles.

The rise of artificial intelligence (AI) is driving capitalism into unexplored domains, reshaping the principles of interaction and modifying the dynamics of economic exchanges. The integration of artificial intelligence (AI) with market dynamics introduces a collaborative effect in which algorithms and data analytics assume crucial roles in generating and facilitating value generation and exchange. This chapter delves into an exploration of the intricate aspects of this shift, providing insights into how artificial intelligence enhances, disrupts, and enhances the dynamics of capitalist markets. The progress of artificial intelligence (AI) has been truly revolutionary, starting from its origins in automation and machine learning to its advancements in deep learning and neural networks. The capacity of artificial intelligence (AI) to effectively handle extensive datasets, identify complex patterns, and provide highly accurate forecasts has positioned it as a powerful instrument for organisations aiming to optimise their operations and improve decision-making processes. The symbiotic association between artificial intelligence (AI) and capitalism highlights a significant transformation, wherein data assumes the role of a novel kind of currency, and the valuable assets derived from AI-generated studies are indispensable tools for effectively navigating the competitive landscape of the market.

This chapter goes beyond a simple presentation of technology, exploring the societal, ethical, and economic consequences that arise from the incorporation of artificial intelligence (AI) into capitalist markets. The increasing reliance on algorithms to determine pricing strategies, execute personalised marketing efforts, and forecast demand has brought out significant concerns around fairness, transparency, and the potential for market manipulation. The prominence of responsible deployment of AI and the need to mitigate bias become increasingly significant as the consequences of AI-driven market interactions escalate. Furthermore, the dynamics of competitiveness and innovation are seeing a transformation as a result of the impact of artificial intelligence (AI). Both start-ups and established organisations are currently engaged in a competitive environment where the utilisation of AI-powered advancements is reshaping industry norms and influencing client demands. This chapter examines the role of artificial intelligence (AI) as a catalyst for disruptive innovation and as a facilitator of incremental advancements. It focuses on the strategic manoeuvres that firms need to perform in order to navigate this continuously developing competitive ecosystem.

The integration of artificial intelligence (AI) into capitalist market dynamics necessitates a close examination of the interconnectedness between technology and ethics. This chapter elucidates the ethical problems that emerge as a result of the impact of artificial intelligence (AI) on market dynamics. These considerations encompass a wide range of concerns, including matters of privacy and data protection, as well as the socio-economic ramifications associated with the displacement of jobs. To effectively navigate the ethical landscape of artificial intelligence (AI), it is imperative to possess a thorough comprehension of both the potential and limitations of AI. Additionally, it is crucial to demonstrate a steadfast dedication to promoting fair and sustainable results within the market.

This chapter initiates an investigative journey into the interaction between artificial intelligence (AI) and the dynamics of capitalist markets. The chapter explores several aspects including innovation, competition, ethical duty, and societal influence. Given the ongoing rise of artificial intelligence (AI), which is profoundly impacting markets and altering the fundamental structure of capitalism, there is a pressing need to thoroughly analyse its implications in a comprehensive manner. This chapter endeavours to shed light on the interplay between artificial intelligence (AI) and market dynamics, with the objective of identifying a viable trajectory that leverages the potential of AI to promote economic growth, inclusiveness, and ethical capitalism.

The chapter delves into the profound effects of artificial intelligence (AI) on capitalist markets, exploring three fundamental themes:

1. The chapter explores the effects of AI on market dynamics, specifically examining its ability to disrupt traditional market structures and redefine concepts such as competition, market concentration, and power dynamics. This study examines the impact of AI-driven automation and data analytics on pricing strategies, consumer experiences, and market entry obstacles.

2. The examination focuses on the role of institutions in responding to the impact of artificial intelligence on markets within the regulatory framework. The chapter elucidates the efforts made by institutions to achieve a harmonious equilibrium between innovation and equitable competition, thereby exemplifying a range of regulatory strategies and policy interventions.

3. The paper examines the consequences of artificial intelligence on the efficiency and resilience of capitalism. The discourse encompasses the possibility of employment displacement resulting from automation, the significance of acquiring new skills, and the societal ramifications arising from the impact of artificial intelligence on market dynamics.

In brief, this chapter provides an analysis of the various ways in which artificial intelligence (AI) influences the dynamics of capitalist markets. These impacts encompass both immediate disruptions and the responses of institutions, as well as the wider implications for economic systems.

The impact of AI on capitalist market dynamics, including competition, market concentration, and market power

The advent of Artificial Intelligence (AI) has had a profound impact on the dynamics of capitalist markets, leading to a reconfiguration of established notions around competition, market concentration, and market influence. The convergence of artificial intelligence (AI) and market interactions has resulted in a wide range of transformations, presenting several prospects and obstacles that have significant implications across multiple sectors of the economy. This discourse explores the intricate effects of artificial intelligence (AI) on these crucial aspects of capitalist markets, examining the complexities of disruption, concentration, and power relations.

1. Redefining Competition

The advent of AI technology is instigating a significant paradigm shift in the landscape of competitive dynamics inside capitalist markets. In addition to its role in improving operational efficiency, artificial intelligence (AI) is fundamentally transforming the processes of innovation, adaptation, and the delivery of personalised offers inside enterprises. This transformation gives rise to a complex interplay of several forces that are changing the fundamental nature of competition.

Enhanced Consumer-Centricity and Personalization

The core of artificial intelligence's influence on competition resides in its exceptional capacity to decipher and understand extensive and intricate datasets. The proliferation of data has significantly contributed to the advancement of machine learning algorithms, enabling businesses to gain unparalleled understanding of consumer preferences, behaviours, and trends. The enhanced comprehension achieved enables the development of customised products and services that effectively address the specific requirements of particular consumers. Through the strategic development of products and services that elicit a strong personal response, businesses are able to surpass conventional market segmentation practises and cultivate a more profound and meaningful bond with their customers. The increased focus on consumers not only enhances their enjoyment but also fosters loyalty and affinity towards the company. By utilising artificial intelligence, businesses are able to interpret subtle cues from consumers, so obtaining a competitive advantage through the establishment of emotional connections that surpass mere transactional interactions.

Agility and Responsiveness to Dynamic Markets

The integration of AI empowers companies to surpass the limitations of reactive decision-making. The ability to collect and analyse data in real-time enables organisations to quickly adjust to evolving market conditions, so making traditional strategic planning obsolete. AI algorithms have the capability to identify changes in consumer preferences and new trends. This enables businesses to take proactive measures in adapting their plans to better line with the developing dynamics of the market. The adaptability described above is notably apparent within the retail industry, where the utilisation of artificial intelligence (AI) for demand forecasting significantly enhances the optimisation of inventory management. Businesses optimise their supply chain operations and prevent stockouts or surplus inventory by proactively anticipating demand swings. This approach not only optimises operational processes but also guarantees a consistent availability of desired products for consumers, thereby cultivating a competitive advantage rooted in enhanced efficiency and consumer contentment.

Dynamic Pricing and Competitive Edge

The integration of AI empowers companies to surpass the limitations of reactive decision-making. The ability to collect and analyse data in real-time enables organisations to quickly adjust to evolving market conditions, so making traditional strategic planning obsolete. AI algorithms have the capability to identify changes in consumer preferences and new trends. This enables businesses to take proactive measures in adapting their plans to better line with the developing dynamics of the market. The adaptability described above is notably apparent within the retail industry, where the utilisation of artificial intelligence (AI) for demand forecasting significantly enhances the optimisation of inventory management. Businesses optimise their supply chain operations and prevent stockouts or surplus inventory by proactively anticipating demand swings. This approach not only optimises operational processes but also guarantees a consistent availability of desired products for consumers, thereby cultivating a competitive advantage rooted in enhanced efficiency and consumer contentment.

Balancing Efficiency with Ethical Considerations

In the context of emerging AI-driven competitiveness, enterprises are faced with the challenge of effectively managing the intricate interplay between operational efficiency and ethical issues. The use of dynamic pricing, which aims to maximise profitability, necessitates a careful approach to prevent the occurrence of discriminatory practises that disproportionately affect consumer groups who are more susceptible to harm. Achieving this equilibrium requires the implementation of comprehensive regulatory frameworks that guarantee transparency, equity, and safeguarding of consumers in the context of market competition driven by artificial intelligence. The impact of AI on competition dynamics extends beyond operational improvements, affecting the fundamental ways in which businesses interact with consumers and respond to changes in the market. The complex influence of AI is characterised by enhanced consumer-centricity, agility, and dynamic pricing, which have propelled capitalism market rivalry into an era of unequalled dynamism. As artificial intelligence (AI) continues to alter various domains, it is imperative for businesses and politicians to engage in joint efforts to effectively navigate the dynamic landscape. This entails exploiting the immense promise offered by AI while also proactively addressing and mitigating the hazards and ethical concerns that may arise.

Evolving Market Concentration

The impact of artificial intelligence (AI) on market concentration is a complex interaction between two opposing forces, each with substantial consequences for the competitive environment. This section examines the intricate implications of artificial intelligence (AI) on market concentration, assessing both its potential for promoting diversification and the associated hazards of consolidation.

Empowering Diversification through Innovation

The democratising potential of artificial intelligence (AI) is in its ability to provide smaller entities with advanced tools and valuable insights that were previously predominantly available to larger corporations. The integration of technical capabilities possesses the capacity to equalise the competitive landscape, empowering nascent enterprises and new ventures to contest existing industry leaders. Through the use of AI-driven insights, smaller organisations have the ability to swiftly engage in innovation, enhance operational efficiency, and introduce unique products and services that effectively secure a portion of the market. Startups equipped with predictive analytics powered by artificial intelligence have the ability to discern specific market possibilities, exploit nascent trends, and establish a unique market position by satisfying distinct consumer needs. The introduction of a wide range of various products and services enhances the dynamics of the market, promoting a state of healthy competition and mitigating the risk of market monopolisation. Furthermore, with the decreasing cost of AI adoption, startups have the potential to capitalise on chances to disrupt established businesses, hence enhancing market diversity and cultivating competition driven by innovation.

Consolidation Risks and Dominant Firm Advantage

On the contrary, the potential of artificial intelligence (AI) to effectively handle and evaluate extensive datasets may paradoxically contribute to the reinforcement of larger firms' dominance. The allocation of significant resources towards AI research, development, and integration may create obstacles for smaller entities, thereby providing established companies with a notable competitive edge. As artificial intelligence (AI) increasingly becomes an essential component of corporate strategies, established companies possess the necessary financial and operational capabilities to invest in and implement sophisticated AI systems, thereby strengthening their position within the market. The utilisation of AI enables the augmentation of network effects, which in turn, confers advantages to huge enterprises. As these companies amass a greater volume of data, their artificial intelligence (AI) systems become increasingly advanced and efficient, creating a self-reinforcing cycle that maintains their competitive advantage. This phenomena has the potential to result in the consolidation of market power, whereby dominant entities utilise AI technology not only to sustain their existing dominance but also to further extend it, thereby impeding competitive dynamics and hindering the progress of innovation.

Navigating the Balance

Achieving a balance between the opportunities for diversification and the associated hazards of consolidation necessitates the adoption of a nuanced strategy. Policymakers and regulatory agencies assume a crucial role in establishing an atmosphere that cultivates robust competition while mitigating the risks associated with excessive consolidation. Achieving this equilibrium necessitates the resolution of obstacles hindering market participation, the advancement of artificial intelligence (AI) education and inclusivity, and the enforcement of antitrust policies to mitigate monopolistic inclinations. The dynamic changes in market concentration within the AI era highlight the necessity for proactive interventions that guide competition towards a stable equilibrium. By using the potential of artificial intelligence (AI), startups may be empowered and diversity can be strengthened, while simultaneously tackling the obstacles posed by entrenched market domination. This approach allows for the shaping of market dynamics in a manner that promotes the flourishing of innovation and equitable competition within a fast expanding technological environment.

3. Shifting Market Power Dynamics

The impact of artificial intelligence on market power dynamics extends beyond the conventional concepts of monopolies and oligopolies. The concept being introduced is that of "data-driven market power," wherein companies possessing extensive datasets and utilising AI-driven insights are able to exert substantial influence. Organisations equipped with extensive data repositories are capable of making better informed decisions, enhancing operational efficiency, and accurately predicting consumer preferences. The presence of market power driven by data raises issues over the existence of information asymmetry and the potential for competitive advantages. Companies that have access to larger and more sophisticated datasets have the ability to engage in market manipulation, thereby exerting influence over customer behaviour and overall market results. The AI era presents a significant challenge in finding a delicate equilibrium between promoting innovation and mitigating the consolidation of market power driven by data.

The influence of artificial intelligence (AI) on the dynamics of capitalist markets is a multifaceted interaction involving disruption, diversification, and consolidation. Artificial intelligence (AI) presents potential avenues for heightened competition, although it also presents obstacles pertaining to market concentration and power dynamics. As businesses increasingly utilise the capabilities of artificial intelligence (AI) to gain a competitive advantage in the marketplace, it becomes imperative for regulators and policymakers to effectively navigate this dynamic and growing landscape. Their primary objective should be to maintain the preservation of competitive markets while simultaneously safeguarding the interests of consumers, ensuring they continue to benefit from ongoing innovation and a wide range of choices. The primary problem in fully exploiting the benefits of AI-driven capitalist economies lies in striking a balance between the revolutionary potential of AI and the imperative for fair and open markets.

The role of institutions in ensuring fair and competitive markets in the AI era

The increasing prevalence of artificial intelligence (AI) in economies and businesses necessitates the crucial involvement of institutions in structuring equitable and competitive markets. Institutions play a crucial role in upholding market integrity by safeguarding against potential imbalances or distortions that may arise from the swift integration of AI technology. This is done to prevent any adverse effects on competition, innovation, or consumer welfare. This discourse explores the many and intricate duties of institutions in ensuring the integrity of equitable and competitive markets in the era of artificial intelligence (AI). It provides comprehensive insights and analysis into the roles and difficulties faced by these institutions.

1. Regulatory Frameworks for AI Ethics and Accountability

Institutions bear the responsibility of formulating and executing regulatory frameworks that oversee the development and use of artificial intelligence. These frameworks create the ethical parameters within which AI technologies function, guaranteeing that firms utilise AI in manners that prioritise equity, openness, and responsibility. As artificial intelligence (AI) systems continue to gain autonomy and decision-making processes get more intricate, it is imperative for institutions to establish standards in order to mitigate discriminatory practises, biassed algorithms, and unfair market advantages. One of the key obstacles involves the task of achieving a harmonious equilibrium between promoting innovation and mitigating the risk of potential misconduct. Institutions are confronted with complex ethical problems, including the issue of algorithmic prejudice and the possibility of artificial intelligence exacerbating pre-existing inequities. Institutions can facilitate equitable competition in an AI-driven marketplace by establishing comprehensive regulatory frameworks that mandate transparency in AI decision-making, data utilisation, and disclosure.

2. Antitrust and Competition Policy in the Digital Age

The emergence of artificial intelligence (AI) presents new and unique challenges to conventional antitrust and competition policies. It is imperative for institutions to readjust their policies in order to effectively tackle the challenges posed by digital markets, wherein network effects and data-driven advantages might give rise to monopolistic tendencies. In addition to their reactive efforts in preserving competition, institutions are tasked with the proactive responsibility of anticipating and addressing new anticompetitive behaviours that are enabled by artificial intelligence (AI). It is imperative for institutions to thoroughly examine mergers, acquisitions, and collaborations involving enterprises driven by artificial intelligence (AI) in order to mitigate the potential formation of dominant entities that may wield excessive market influence. Furthermore, it is imperative to take into account emerging types of rivalry that may be facilitated by artificial intelligence, like customised pricing tactics and data-centric competitive edge. In light of the dynamic nature of the current landscape, it is imperative for institutions to demonstrate flexibility in their ability to modify antitrust regulations. This is crucial in order to foster and sustain competitive markets that can effectively navigate the challenges and opportunities presented by the era of artificial intelligence.

3. Data Access, Privacy, and Consumer Protection

As AI-driven business models continue to expand, institutions assume a crucial role in protecting consumer rights and ensuring data privacy. The regulatory bodies set guidelines and protocols that control the processes of collecting, storing, and utilising consumer data. The significance of this matter is amplified due to the substantial dependence of AI on data for the generation of insights and the execution of decision-making procedures. It is imperative for institutions to prioritise the prevention of consumer exploitation and the safeguarding of privacy by enterprises. Moreover, it is imperative for institutions to promote competition by establishing mechanisms that guarantee fair and equal access to data, so preventing the concentration of vital information in the hands of monopolistic entities. The implementation of open data programmes and the enforcement of data-sharing regulations have the potential to facilitate equal access to artificial intelligence (AI) resources. This can empower startups and smaller entities to effectively compete with larger firms, which have accumulated substantial datasets. The active involvement of institutions in safeguarding data privacy and promoting equitable access serves to enhance the fundamental principles of fair and competitive markets.

4. Promoting AI Literacy and Accessibility

It is incumbent upon institutions to assume the role of fostering AI literacy and ensuring accessible for enterprises of varying scales. The organisation offers instructional resources, aids in research endeavours, and facilitates the distribution of knowledge to guarantee that the advantages of artificial intelligence are available to a diverse array of individuals involved in the market. By equitably distributing AI knowledge and capabilities, institutions enable firms to effectively compete in an economy driven by artificial intelligence. The primary obstacle involves the task of closing the gap in AI understanding, particularly for smaller firms that possess restricted resources. In order to empower businesses to effectively utilise the potential of artificial intelligence (AI), it is imperative for institutions to engage in collaborative efforts with academia, industry groups, and technological specialists. These collaborations should aim to provide comprehensive training programmes, seminars, and materials that serve to demystify AI and equip businesses with the necessary tools for harnessing its capabilities. The use of this inclusive strategy fosters a competitive environment wherein the concentration of innovation within a limited group is mitigated, allowing for a broader range of players to engage in the process.

5. International Cooperation and Standardization

In the context of a globalised economy, institutions assume a crucial role in promoting international collaboration and the establishment of standardised legislation pertaining to artificial intelligence (AI). As artificial intelligence (AI) technologies continue to surpass national boundaries, it becomes imperative for institutions to engage in collaborative efforts with their counterparts in different jurisdictions. This collaboration is necessary to set rules that are harmonised across borders, with the aim of fostering fair and competitive marketplaces on a global scale. The use of this collaborative strategy serves to mitigate regulatory arbitrage and guarantees that enterprises adhere to uniform regulations, irrespective of their geographical placement.

International cooperation also encompasses the resolution of issues related to cross-border data transfers, privacy considerations, and jurisdictional complexities. Through the process of standardisation, institutions aim to minimise obstacles for enterprises that wish to operate in numerous markets, thus creating a worldwide environment that promotes competition by removing excessive regulatory barriers. The significance and complexity of institutions in guaranteeing equitable and competitive marketplaces in the era of artificial intelligence (AI) cannot be overstated. Institutions play a crucial role in safeguarding market integrity through various measures, such as formulating ethical standards for artificial intelligence (AI), reevaluating antitrust legislation, advocating for data protection, developing AI literacy, and facilitating international collaboration. The proactive endeavours of individuals are crucial in effectively managing the intricacies and difficulties posed by artificial intelligence (AI), steering the development of markets towards a future characterised by a harmonious equilibrium between innovation, competition, and the well-being of consumers.

Potential implications for capitalism's efficiency and resilience in the face of AI advancements

The emergence of artificial intelligence (AI) has catalysed a series of profound changes in multiple domains of society, encompassing economic structures. The impact of AI breakthroughs on sectors, markets, and labour dynamics raises important considerations regarding the efficiency and resilience of capitalism. This comprehensive analysis examines the complex implications of artificial intelligence (AI) on the capitalist system, examining both the potential advantages and obstacles it presents in improving the effectiveness and adaptability of capitalist economies.

1. Enhanced Efficiency through Automation

The capacity of artificial intelligence (AI) to automate various jobs and processes holds significant potential for transforming the efficiency of capitalism. This has the potential to bring about a new era characterised by streamlined operations and enhanced utilisation of resources. Through the seamless integration of AI-driven technology across diverse industries, capitalism has the potential to achieve significant benefits in terms of productivity and operational efficiency. The utilisation of artificial intelligence (AI) in automation surpasses the limitations of conventional labor-intensive activities, presenting a transformative change that extends beyond mundane operations. In addition to the concrete advantages of mitigating human error and expediting operations, automation presents the potential to discover new pathways for innovation. As artificial intelligence (AI) assumes repetitive and tedious functions, it enables human workers to redirect their cognitive capacities towards jobs of greater value that necessitate creativity, critical thinking, and emotional intelligence.

The manufacturing sector is characterised by the utilisation of AI-powered robots to coordinate complex assembly processes with exceptional accuracy and uniformity. The advanced technological capabilities result in reduced instances of manufacturing delays and errors, leading to a chain reaction of improved operational efficiency. The advantages permeate across the complete production cycle, encompassing supply chain optimisation and just-in-time manufacturing, ultimately resulting in cost reduction and expedited product time-to-market. Furthermore, this recently acquired efficiency creates a cascading impact throughout the capitalist domain. By relieving businesses of routine activities, they are able to redistribute their resources and skilled personnel towards strategic initiatives that drive growth and enhance their competitive advantage. The advancement of artificial intelligence (AI)-driven automation has facilitated the flourishing of innovation. This is mostly due to the liberation of intellectual capital, which enables individuals with creative abilities to conceive pioneering solutions, venture into unexplored areas, and predict the demands of consumers.

In the context of economic resiliency, the significance of AI-powered automation is heightened. Through the optimisation of resource utilisation and the minimization of operational inefficiencies, capitalism inherently enhances its resilience in the presence of disturbances. The utilisation of artificial intelligence (AI) enables capitalism to enhance its ability to withstand uncertainties and emerge stronger from adversity by promptly adjusting to changes in customer demand and successfully managing supply chain complexities.

In summary, the incorporation of artificial intelligence-driven automation has the capacity to facilitate a paradigm shift towards enhanced efficiency inside the capitalist system. In addition to the immediate advantages of enhanced operational efficiency and decreased error rates, the implementation of automation enables organisations to actively adopt innovative practises, enhance their competitive edge, and strengthen their economic resilience. The evolving nature of artificial intelligence (AI) plays a pivotal role in promoting increased efficiency, hence significantly influencing the future landscape of capitalism.

2. Resilience through Predictive Insights

Within the dynamic realm of capitalism, the predictive capabilities of artificial intelligence (AI) have emerged as a crucial element that bolsters resilience through the augmentation of decision-making processes with enhanced foresight and adaptability. The incorporation of data insights driven by artificial intelligence not only enables firms to effectively traverse risks but also enhances capitalism's capacity to predict, strategize, and proactively address dynamic market conditions. The core of this potential to enhance resilience is rooted in the unique ability of artificial intelligence (AI) to analyse large datasets, effectively identifying significant trends, patterns, and anomalies that may be overlooked by human study. This highly significant resource empowers enterprises and governments to surpass the constraints of retrospective decision-making and, instead, utilise predictive insights to guide a proactive and strategically intelligent approach.

The utilisation of artificial intelligence (AI)-powered predictive insights encompasses a wide range of essential activities within the capitalist system. Within the field of risk assessment, artificial intelligence (AI) algorithms are employed to thoroughly analyse complex data streams in order to detect developing patterns, market fluctuations, and possible disruptions. The ability to anticipate future events and outcomes enables individuals in positions of authority to make informed decisions regarding the allocation of resources, effectively identify areas of weakness or susceptibility, and develop alternative strategies that effectively reduce the impact of potential dangers before they escalate into significant and unmanageable emergencies. The predictive capabilities of artificial intelligence (AI) serve to enhance supply chain management, which is a fundamental aspect of resilient capitalism. Through the examination of a multitude of factors, including geopolitical factors and limitations in transportation, artificial intelligence algorithms provide organisations with the ability to promptly identify potential disruptions in their supply chains. The outcome yields a strategic advantage that facilitates nimble decision-making, flexible procurement methods, and enhanced inventory management.

An illustrative instance can be found in the capacity of artificial intelligence (AI) to forecast supply chain interruptions arising from external causes such as weather patterns and geopolitical conflicts. By extracting valuable information from various data sources, artificial intelligence (AI) provides advance notice to organisations regarding potential disruptions. This allows firms to adjust their sourcing strategy, broaden their supplier base, and strengthen their supply chains to mitigate risks. The use of a proactive approach serves to mitigate the repercussions of unexpected occurrences, so assuring the uninterrupted functioning of capitalist systems in the midst of challenging circumstances. Furthermore, the contribution of artificial intelligence (AI) in bolstering the durability of capitalism beyond its direct operational influence. Artificial intelligence (AI) enhances investor confidence and promotes economic stability by equipping businesses with the ability to foresee market shifts and quickly adjust to them. The capacity to effectively manage ambiguous situations and proactively address obstacles fosters a resilient culture that permeates all sectors, bolstering long-term growth and progress.

The integration of artificial intelligence (AI) powered predictive insights enhances the capitalist system by providing it with a transformative ability to anticipate, strategize, and strengthen itself against unexpected threats. Through surpassing conventional decision-making paradigms and offering sophisticated foresight, artificial intelligence (AI) augments the capacity of capitalism to adjust, optimise, and flourish within a swiftly changing global landscape. In light of the ongoing intricacies of the global economy, the incorporation of artificial intelligence's predictive capabilities emerges as a symbol of adaptability, shedding light on the trajectory towards a future characterised by well-informed and flexible capitalism.

3. Unlocking Innovation and Entrepreneurship

The convergence of artificial intelligence (AI) and capitalism arises as a significant factor that not only facilitates the emergence of innovation and entrepreneurship but also propels them to the forefront of economic dynamics. Within this symbiotic association, artificial intelligence surpasses its conventional function as a technological instrument, acquiring the responsibility of a catalyst for innovation that fundamentally transforms the framework of capitalism and enhances its potential for enduring expansion and rejuvenation. The fundamental essence of artificial intelligence (AI) is in its capacity to democratise innovation, hence yielding transformative effects. Throughout history, the realm of invention has frequently been controlled by established entities that possess substantial resources and considerable research and development capacities. Nevertheless, the increased availability of artificial intelligence (AI) tools and resources effectively eliminates these obstacles, leading to a period in which emerging companies and smaller entities can utilise innovation as a powerful advantage.

The process of democratising invention introduces a renewed dynamism into the capitalist system, reinvigorating its entrepreneurial drive and stimulating market rivalry. The symbiotic relationship between artificial intelligence (AI) and entrepreneurship cultivates a conducive environment for the emergence of innovative concepts that upset established norms, compelling established entities to either adjust their strategies or face the possibility of becoming outdated.

In this particular context, entrepreneurs are seen as pioneers of innovation facilitated by artificial intelligence (AI), leveraging AI-generated insights to identify hidden market demands and develop creative solutions. AI algorithms play a crucial role in providing guidance to entrepreneurs, assisting them in exploring unexplored domains and revealing hidden market segments that could have otherwise remained undiscovered. The exceptional analytical abilities facilitate the rapid advancement of novel products and services, allowing companies to quickly refine prototypes and position their inventions for entry into the market. The utilisation of AI-derived insights provides startups with the ability to disrupt conventional sectors, leading to the revision of established paradigms and rendering long-standing business models irrelevant. Larger organisations, under the influence of transformative factors, are pushed to react and adjust in order to address these disruptive pressures. The catalytic phenomenon described below engenders a perpetual cycle of creative destruction, wherein the fluctuation and progression of innovative endeavours sustain a dynamic and adaptable capitalist ecology.

Furthermore, the influence of AI on innovation extends beyond the confines of individual enterprises, establishing a more extensive culture of experimentation and embracing risk. The increasing prevalence of successful endeavours facilitated by artificial intelligence (AI) serves as a source of inspiration for prospective entrepreneurs, who are now more confident in their ability to leverage AI to enhance their innovative initiatives. The alteration in collective perspective results in a paradigm change within capitalism, leading to its transformation into a mechanism driven by innovation. Consequently, the endeavour to generate new and original concepts becomes intrinsically linked to the advancement of the economy. Within the broader context of capitalism's historical development, the incorporation of artificial intelligence (AI) emerges as a crucial phase that facilitates the emergence of novel ideas and business ventures, presenting unparalleled possibilities for growth and advancement. As artificial intelligence becomes more accessible to a wider range of individuals and organisations, the emergence of startups as catalysts for disruptive change is facilitating the advent of a novel era characterised by dynamic and fiercely competitive markets. The symbiotic relationship between artificial intelligence (AI) and entrepreneurship serves to reinvigorate the fundamental principles of capitalism, while simultaneously safeguarding innovation as the cornerstone of its lasting impact.

4. Challenges to Labor Dynamics

The incorporation of artificial intelligence (AI) into the capitalist system gives rise to a paradoxical relationship, characterised by heightened efficiency on one hand, and the potential disruption of labour dynamics on the other. The advent of AI technologies has led to the optimisation of operations and the streamlining of processes. However, an unexpected consequence of this development is the emergence of challenges to labour and employment within the capitalist framework. The value proposition of artificial intelligence (AI) lies in its capacity to automate various processes, which may unintentionally result in the displacement of jobs, especially in industries that are highly suitable for automation. The increasing integration of AI-driven technology in various industries raises concerns about potential job shrinkage in some sectors. The aforementioned issue poses a significant problem for individuals who have been displaced from their jobs, as they must now navigate a dynamic job market in order to seek alternative channels for employment. In light of these problems, the significance of worker adaptation and upskilling becomes evident. The advent of AI-driven economies needs a fundamental adjustment in the mindset individuals adopt towards their professional advancement. The implementation of reskilling and upskilling programmes has become more important in order to provide the workforce with the necessary skills and knowledge to succeed in the era of artificial intelligence.

Moreover, the emergence of artificial intelligence (AI) technology gives rise to apprehensions pertaining to the disparity in income distribution and the concentration of wealth. The possibility of AI-driven enterprises and technology behemoths accumulating a substantial portion of the economic advantages has the potential to worsen preexisting inequalities in society. This inequality encompasses not only disparities in salaries, but also encompasses disparities in access to AI-generated opportunities, education, and resources. In order to effectively tackle these complex difficulties, capitalism necessitates the implementation of proactive regulations that place emphasis on ensuring fair and equal access to the benefits and opportunities presented by artificial intelligence (AI). The implementation of comprehensive social safety nets plays a pivotal role in ensuring the protection and welfare of individuals who have been displaced from their jobs. Safety nets serve as a protective measure during periods of transition, allowing individuals to engage in upskilling endeavours without being encumbered by immediate financial constraints. Moreover, it is crucial to implement inclusive policies that promote the engagement of all sectors of society in the economy driven by artificial intelligence (AI) to prevent the concentration of advantages only among a privileged minority. Through the active promotion of diversity, equity, and inclusion, capitalism has the capacity to effectively leverage artificial intelligence (AI) in order to improve marginalised communities and mitigate prevailing socioeconomic disparities.

In conclusion, the incorporation of artificial intelligence (AI) into the framework of capitalism presents intricate complexities pertaining to labour dynamics, job patterns, and disparities in income distribution. The potential for increased prosperity lies in the efficiency benefits of artificial intelligence (AI). However, it is imperative for capitalism to approach these difficulties with careful consideration and a compassionate mindset. By advocating for the development of new skills, enhancing existing skills, implementing inclusive policies, and establishing social safety nets, capitalism has the potential to achieve a harmonious equilibrium between the drive for technical progress and the maintenance of fair and robust labour dynamics.

5. Ethical and Regulatory Considerations

The convergence of capitalism and artificial intelligence (AI) gives rise to a complex dynamic that involves balancing the need for efficiency with the need to protect ethical principles and societal welfare. The incorporation of artificial intelligence (AI) into capitalist systems requires a thorough analysis of ethical and regulatory factors to guarantee that advancements are in line with values of fairness, accountability, and resilience. The ethical concern around AI's ability to amplify and perpetuate biases is of utmost importance and requires proactive measures to address. If not properly regulated, artificial intelligence (AI) algorithms have the potential to unintentionally include societal prejudices that exist within the data used for training, hence perpetuating discrimination across many economic aspects. In order to address this issue, institutions assume a critical role in the establishment and implementation of stringent ethical norms that require the implementation of thorough systems for detecting and mitigating biases. By adhering to stringent ethical norms in the implementation of AI technologies, capitalism enhances its ability to withstand the erosion of public trust and the persistence of systemic inequalities.

Privacy assumes a significant role as an additional fundamental aspect of ethical deliberation within the context of the AI-powered economic environment. The complex network of data gathering, examination, and application inherent in artificial intelligence (AI) technology requires careful measures to ensure the preservation of individual privacy rights. Institutions have the responsibility of establishing regulatory frameworks that mandate rigorous data protection procedures, with the aim of safeguarding personal information and enabling individuals to maintain authority over their digital footprints. The act of preserving privacy not only conforms to ethical principles but also fosters a fundamental basis of trust that is crucial for the continued viability of capitalism. The regulatory dimension of this ethical question is rooted in the delicate balance between promoting innovation and mitigating the risks of potential abuses associated with artificial intelligence. Capitalism relies heavily on the promotion of innovation; nonetheless, it is crucial to establish reasonable regulatory frameworks in order to effectively mitigate possible abuses of power associated with artificial intelligence. Institutions bear the responsibility of formulating legislation that enable enterprises to effectively utilise the potential of artificial intelligence (AI) for progress, while concurrently implementing measures to prevent monopolistic practises, excessive concentration of power, and detrimental external consequences. The delicate equilibrium maintains the fundamental principles of capitalism while facilitating a period characterised by conscientious and sustainable advancements in technology.

Ethical frameworks for artificial intelligence (AI) serve as protective measures against the unforeseen repercussions that may arise from the incorporation of AI technology. By promoting transparency, accountability, and equity, these frameworks guarantee that the revolutionary potential of AI is directed towards enhancing societal well-being and strengthening the resilience of capitalism. The harmonious balance between regulatory procedures and ethical requirements plays a crucial role in advancing efficiency while ensuring the long-term sustainability of capitalism's base.The ethical and regulatory considerations pertaining to the incorporation of artificial intelligence (AI) into capitalist systems have great importance in determining the course of economic advancement. As organisations traverse this intricate landscape, they establish a trajectory that combines inventive approaches with moral accountability, openness with effectiveness, and the welfare of society with economic durability. Through the adherence to ethical principles and the careful balance of regulatory measures, capitalism emerges as a resilient and morally congruent framework that can effectively harness the potential of artificial intelligence for the overall improvement of society.

In conclusion, the ramifications of artificial intelligence on the efficiency and resilience of capitalism are intricate and diverse in nature. Artificial intelligence (AI) presents significant opportunities for improving productivity, enabling proactive decision-making, fostering innovation, and promoting entrepreneurship. However, it also presents some issues pertaining to labour dynamics, income inequality, and ethical concerns. Effectively addressing these repercussions necessitates a synergistic endeavour involving enterprises, policymakers, establishments, and the broader societal framework. By effectively using the promise of artificial intelligence (AI) while simultaneously tackling the associated obstacles, capitalism has the capacity to undergo a transformative process, resulting in an economic system that is more efficient, adaptable, and equitable in light of breakthroughs in AI technology.

Chapter 22: AI and Capital Allocation

The advent of Artificial Intelligence (AI) has introduced a multifaceted and captivating narrative inside the intricate fabric of capitalist economies, particularly in the domain of capital allocation. This chapter explores the intricate relationship between artificial intelligence (AI) and the allocation of capital, emphasizing three key elements: the significant impact of AI on the dynamics of capital allocation in capitalist economies, the crucial role of institutions in enabling efficient capital allocation in AI-driven sectors, and the careful analysis of potential challenges and considerations necessary for maintaining a well-balanced and sustainable capital allocation system. Capital allocation, a crucial aspect of capitalist economic systems, has conventionally depended on the exercise of human judgment, market analysis, and financial skill. Nevertheless, the revolutionary capabilities of artificial intelligence (AI) have initiated a new era in which the allocation of resources is being guided towards unexplored domains through the utilization of data-driven accuracy and predictive capacities.

The commencement of our investigation entails a comprehensive examination of the profound impact of artificial intelligence on the framework of capital allocation within capitalist countries. The integration of artificial intelligence (AI) within financial markets has facilitated widespread access to sophisticated investing methods, thereby disrupting traditional conventions and presenting novel prospects for both institutional and individual investors. Artificial intelligence (AI)-powered algorithms possess the capability to evaluate vast information in real-time, thereby revealing complex patterns, trends, and anomalies that human decision-makers may fail to recognize. The emergence of this recent capability is fundamentally altering the methods by which investments are conducted, encompassing algorithmic trading and portfolio optimization. Consequently, it is sparking a significant and far-reaching shift in the fundamental mechanisms that govern the allocation of economic resources.

However, the intricate nature of the symbiotic association between artificial intelligence (AI) and the distribution of capital cannot be overlooked. Our narrative expands to examine the crucial role that institutions play in promoting effective capital allocation in sectors powered by artificial intelligence. Financial institutions, regulatory organizations, and market overseers play a crucial role in assuring the responsible utilization of AI and its connection with broader societal and economic objectives. The implementation of a comprehensive regulatory framework is crucial in order to protect against market manipulation, ethical issues, and algorithmic prejudice, hence upholding the integrity of mechanisms for allocating money. Nevertheless, while we traverse this uncharted territory, it is crucial to take a little break and thoroughly examine the possible obstacles and factors that await us. In order to ensure a balanced and sustainable capital allocation system in the era of artificial intelligence (AI), it is imperative to establish a careful equilibrium between fostering innovation and implementing effective supervision mechanisms. The issues of transparency, accountability, and the societal consequences of AI-powered resource allocation are subjects that we are now grappling with. Moreover, it is imperative to conduct a comprehensive analysis of the influence of artificial intelligence (AI) on employment in financial sectors to safeguard against potential negative consequences such as job displacement resulting from technological advancements.

In summary, this chapter provides a thorough examination of the intricate connection between artificial intelligence and the distribution of capital in capitalist economies. This study examines the impact of artificial intelligence (AI) on the distribution of resources, emphasizes the crucial role of institutions in upholding efficiency and ethical standards, and highlights the significant implications for achieving a harmonious and sustainable future. Whether you are an individual with investment interests aiming to navigate the ever-changing environment, a policymaker responsible for establishing the regulatory framework, or simply an interested observer of the profound impact of artificial intelligence on capitalism, our exploration guarantees to shed light on the complex processes at work in this era of digitalization. We invite you to partake in a scholarly journey as we delve into the profound and intellectually stimulating exploration of AI-powered capital allocation.

The influence of AI on the allocation of capital in capitalist economies

Undoubtedly, the advent of Artificial Intelligence (AI) has brought about a significant and transformational upheaval in the distribution of capital within capitalist economies. The significant transformation discussed herein carries profound implications that reverberate throughout various sectors and industries. It not only redefines resource allocation but also fundamentally alters decision-making processes, accessibility to investment opportunities, and the challenges that emerge within this swiftly evolving environment.

Enhanced Efficiency and Accuracy

The profound influence of artificial intelligence (AI) on the allocation of capital is mostly attributed to its notable advancements in efficiency and accuracy, which have had far-reaching effects on the financial domain. The aforementioned change is particularly notable when comparing it to conventional approaches that heavily depend on subjective human assessment, a component of decision-making that is prone to cognitive biases and limits. In sharp contrast, artificial intelligence (AI) leverages its exceptional ability to swiftly analyze extensive and complex datasets, dissecting them in manners that frequently elude human analysts. The adoption of a data-centric strategy significantly enhances the accuracy of investment decisions, hence reducing the inherent risks associated with the misallocation of capital. The potential for continual learning and adaptation is a notable quality of artificial intelligence (AI) that enhances its efficacy in the allocation of capital. In contrast to stationary human decision-makers, artificial intelligence (AI) systems possess the capacity to iteratively enhance and optimize their allocation techniques throughout the course of their operation. By engaging in an iterative process of examining market trends, economic indicators, and various real-time data sources, artificial intelligence consistently refines its ability to make informed decisions. The dynamic evolution of this system not only strengthens its efficiency, but also improves its ability to respond to changing market conditions and unforeseen disruptions. As a result, it becomes a powerful instrument for investors and fund managers who are looking to implement effective methods for allocating capital.

Data-Driven Decision-Making

The genuine potential of artificial intelligence (AI) becomes evident when considering its ability to facilitate decision-making based on data, especially in the intricate realm of financial markets. AI algorithms demonstrate an impressive capacity to assess and scrutinize a wide range of data sources, including real-time market data, historical patterns, economic indicators, and even the subtle sentiments conveyed through social media platforms. These algorithms are highly proficient at interpreting data, offering investors and fund managers a wealth of factual insights that were previously thought to be unimaginable. The adoption of this data-centric strategy represents a notable break from conventional decision-making paradigms, which frequently relied on intuition and qualitative evaluations. On the contrary, artificial intelligence enables decision-makers to make informed choices based on objective data and empirical evidence. The current trend towards evidence-based decision-making has the potential to enhance capital allocation techniques and, importantly, reduce risks in order to achieve greater returns. The aforementioned statement highlights a significant paradigm shift in investment management practices, emphasizing the emergence of artificial intelligence (AI) as a powerful tool for individuals seeking to navigate the complexities of contemporary financial markets.

Algorithmic Trading

The emergence of algorithmic trading, propelled by the impressive powers of artificial intelligence, represents a significant and disruptive milestone in the field of trading methodologies. These advanced algorithms demonstrate an exceptional capability to execute transactions at a speed and frequency that much exceeds the capabilities of human traders. The use of unconventional trading strategies has initiated a significant transformation in market dynamics, fundamentally altering the manner in which financial instruments are exchanged. The appeal of algorithmic trading mostly stems from its potential to improve liquidity and efficiency in financial markets. The aforementioned algorithms possess the capability to promptly react to market situations, enabling them to exploit favorable circumstances and make adjustments to positions in a matter of milliseconds. The increased efficiency has the potential to result in narrower bid-ask spreads, lower transaction costs, and enhanced price discovery methods, hence offering advantages to participants in the market.

Nevertheless, this advancement in technology also gives rise to noteworthy concerns that necessitate meticulous deliberation. A significant issue of worry revolves around the stability of the market, given the enormous velocity and magnitude of algorithmic trades, which have the potential to cause sudden and unanticipated market changes. The occurrence of the "flash crash" in 2010 provides a compelling illustration of the difficulties presented by algorithms utilized in high-frequency trading. Sustaining market stability among technology improvements necessitates ongoing monitoring, risk mitigation, and regulatory supervision. An other aspect of concern is to the equity of markets. The expeditious implementation of algorithmic transactions has the potential to generate inequalities in the availability of market information and opportunities, which may result in smaller market participants being at a disadvantage. This phenomenon prompts inquiries regarding the fairness of the market and the necessity for equal opportunities to utilize the advantages of algorithmic trading.

In addition, the increasing prevalence of algorithmic trading further emphasizes the necessity for strong regulatory frameworks in order to maintain transparency, accountability, and alignment with overarching economic objectives within the market. The establishment of these rules necessitates the achievement of a nuanced equilibrium between the promotion of innovation and the prevention of potential market abuses.

The advent of algorithmic trading, propelled by the advancements in artificial intelligence, has undeniably transformed trading methodologies and the functioning of financial markets. Although it presents the appeal of increased liquidity and efficiency, it also presents difficulties pertaining to market stability, fairness, and regulatory control. The ability to effectively navigate the intricacies associated with algorithmic trading is of utmost importance in order to maintain the resilience, transparency, and inclusivity of financial markets for all participants, regardless of their size.

Portfolio Optimization

Artificial intelligence (AI) has significantly expanded its impact in the field of portfolio optimization, demonstrating its proficiency as an advanced tool for evaluating a wide range of asset classes and risk characteristics. This capability provides investors with a heightened level of accuracy and understanding that was previously unachievable through traditional techniques. The utilization of artificial intelligence (AI) in portfolio optimization represents a significant transformation in investment strategy. This approach allows for the creation of investment portfolios that closely fit with specific investment goals and risk preferences, with a high level of accuracy and attention to detail. One notable characteristic of portfolio optimization driven by artificial intelligence (AI) is its capacity to effectively manage a wide range of variables and data points concurrently. The assessment encompasses a wide range of criteria, including historical performance data, real-time market conditions, economic indicators, geopolitical events, and several other factors that have an impact on asset performance. The use of this comprehensive methodology enables investors to construct portfolios that are precisely tailored to their individual objectives, encompassing capital preservation, income creation, or capital appreciation.

One of the key advantages of artificial intelligence (AI) in this particular situation lies in its capacity to effectively facilitate diversification and risk management. Artificial intelligence algorithms have the capability to discern connections among various asset classes and assess the dynamics of these correlations as they progress through time. The utilization of this dynamic assessment facilitates the creation of portfolios that exhibit diversification, thereby mitigating the potential impact of systemic risk. The mitigation of risk associated with individual assets or asset classes is achieved by diversifying investments among a range of assets that have low correlations. Concurrently, artificial intelligence has the capability to effectively handle the efficient distribution of resources in accordance with dynamic market circumstances, so guaranteeing that the portfolio remains in line with the investor's goals. Moreover, the capacity of artificial intelligence (AI) to enhance portfolio optimization holds significant importance within the current dynamic global economic environment. The interdependence of international markets, combined with the growing intricacy of financial instruments, necessitates a degree of expertise that surpasses the capabilities of conventional investing techniques. The versatility and real-time analytical capabilities of artificial intelligence (AI) make it well-suited to effectively navigate the complex environment of financial markets and geopolitical changes. As a result, AI provides investors with a strong tool to respond to the ever-changing dynamics of these domains.

In conclusion, the significant impact of artificial intelligence on the optimization of investment portfolios signifies a crucial advancement in the field of investment strategy. This platform provides investors with an unparalleled degree of accuracy in aligning their investment portfolios with their unique objectives and tolerance for risk. By implementing efficient diversification strategies and employing dynamic risk management techniques, artificial intelligence (AI) holds the capacity to mitigate risk exposure and optimize investment returns. In an era marked by dynamic shifts in the global economic landscape, artificial intelligence (AI) has emerged as a crucial instrument for investors aiming to effectively traverse the intricate nature of contemporary financial markets and attain their investment objectives with enhanced assurance and efficiency.

Democratization of Investment

One of the significant effects of AI on capital allocation is its notable contribution to the democratization of investment. The emergence of robo-advisors serves as a prominent illustration of this paradigm shift, as they utilize artificial intelligence algorithms to deliver automated and cost-efficient financial guidance to a wider range of investors. The process of democratizing investment has a profound impact on the finance sector, bringing forth significant potential and complex issues. Robo-advisors, which are driven by artificial intelligence (AI), provide individuals with diverse degrees of financial knowledge the chance to engage in financial markets with unparalleled convenience and inclusivity. Historically, participation in financial markets was predominantly limited to individuals or institutions possessing extensive knowledge and significant financial means. AI-driven robo-advisors effectively overcome these obstacles by providing investors with a user-friendly interface that facilitates guidance throughout the investment process. The analysts assess the unique risk profiles, financial objectives, and prevailing market conditions in order to propose customized investment plans. The act of empowering citizens, irrespective of their financial expertise, signifies a significant stride towards achieving a fairer allocation of wealth within capitalist countries.

Additionally, the process of democratizing investing poses a significant challenge to the conventional structure of investment management. Robo-advisors powered by artificial intelligence (AI) are not subject to the cognitive constraints or biases that can potentially impact human financial advisors. These entities have the capability to handle extensive datasets and implement strategies with a level of precision comparable to that of machines. Consequently, the conventional investment management sector is being obliged to undergo adaptation and transformation. There is a growing trend among human advisors to engage in collaborative efforts with artificial intelligence (AI) systems. This collaboration aims to utilize the analytical powers of AI to improve the quality of their services. Consequently, wealth management practices are shifting towards a hybrid model that combines the expertise of human advisers with the computational power of AI. Nevertheless, in addition to its potential benefits, the democratization of investment raises inquiries and necessitates careful deliberation. A prominent issue of worry pertains to the possibility of excessive dependence on AI-generated guidance, which could result in investors relinquishing their financial accountability or comprehension of investment choices. Moreover, with the growing influx of participants in the market facilitated by robo-advisors, there exists the potential for heightened market volatility as these algorithmic systems respond to various events or patterns. In order to safeguard the interests of investors and maintain stability in the market, regulatory authorities are faced with the challenge of addressing these constantly changing dynamics.

The substantial development of AI's role in democratizing investing has the potential to transform not only the financial industry but also the entire socioeconomic environment, as shown. This technology enables individuals to engage in capital allocation procedures with unparalleled accessibility and efficiency. Concurrently, it presents a challenge to the conventional standards in the field of investment management. The advent of investment democratization presents novel prospects, but also calls for a deliberate examination of investor education, regulation, and market stability in order to effectively and ethically leverage its advantages. With the continuous advancement of artificial intelligence (AI), it is anticipated that its impact in the field of finance would broaden, resulting in a more equitable landscape. However, when we further explore the incorporation of artificial intelligence (AI) into the processes of allocating wealth, a complex array of problems and ethical implications becomes apparent. Artificial intelligence (AI) holds the potential for substantial advantages, although it also introduces a range of complex concerns that necessitate thorough consideration and proactive handling. These difficulties can be outlined as follows:

High-Frequency Trading and Market Stability

One of the primary issues revolves with the phenomenon of high-frequency trading, which is mostly driven by artificial intelligence algorithms. This particular trading method has the capability to rapidly execute a significant volume of trades within extremely short time intervals, leading to a market environment characterized by swift and remarkable fluctuations in dynamics. High-frequency trading (HFT) presents the advantage of enhancing market liquidity and perhaps improving market efficiency. However, it also adds the inherent danger of market volatility and the occurrence of sudden and severe market downturns, sometimes referred to as flash crashes. The aforementioned problems possess significant consequences for the stability of financial markets, hence necessitating a thorough reassessment of market regulations and systems that might effectively mitigate sudden disruptions.

Algorithmic Biases and Data Privacy

The widespread utilization of artificial intelligence (AI) in the distribution of capital gives rise to ethical problems that transcend the boundaries of the financial domain. Algorithmic biases possess the capacity to sustain or intensify preexisting socioeconomic disparities. Algorithms have the potential to unintentionally incorporate biases that exist in historical data, resulting in discriminatory consequences when making judgments on the allocation of capital. Furthermore, the acquisition and application of extensive quantities of personal and financial data for decision-making powered by artificial intelligence (AI) raise noteworthy concerns regarding data privacy. The conscientious management of data and the reduction of algorithmic biases are critical factors that require continuous ethical examination.

Workforce Adaptation and Economic Implications

In addition to the financial sector, the growing automation and dependence on artificial intelligence (AI)-driven systems raise apprehensions regarding job displacement and the changing landscape of employment. The conventional responsibilities within the financial sector are undergoing a redefinition process due to the integration of artificial intelligence (AI) systems that are capable of managing repetitive operations. The impact of artificial intelligence (AI) on capital allocation has wider societal and economic consequences, which encompass the necessity for workforce adjustment and the acquisition of new skills to fulfill the requirements of the digital era.

In order to adeptly maneuver through these intricacies and guarantee conscientious allocation of capital powered by AI, it is imperative for regulatory frameworks to progress in parallel with technical breakthroughs. It is imperative that these frameworks place utmost importance on the principles of openness, accountability, and justice within AI-driven financial markets. Transparency methods serve the purpose of providing investors and the general public with a comprehensive understanding of the algorithms and data sources that underlie the decision-making process for capital allocation. The establishment of accountability systems is crucial in delineating unambiguous lines of responsibility for outcomes produced by artificial intelligence, hence cultivating a sense of trust in the technology. Furthermore, it is imperative that these frameworks possess adaptability and responsiveness in order to effectively navigate the ever-changing terrain. They must also be equipped to tackle the systemic dangers that arise from the significant influence of artificial intelligence (AI) in determining the allocation of resources within capitalist economies.

Fundamentally, artificial intelligence (AI) offers unparalleled prospects for enhancing efficiency and accuracy in the allocation of capital. However, it also introduces a novel epoch of intricacies and ethical deliberations. In order to effectively leverage the advantages of artificial intelligence (AI) while also addressing its potential drawbacks, it is crucial for regulatory entities, industry participants, and policymakers to engage in collaborative efforts aimed at establishing a comprehensive framework that harmonizes innovation and precaution, transparency and responsibility, as well as economic advancement and societal welfare. The collective endeavor is important to guarantee that artificial intelligence (AI) remains a driving force for beneficial change in the realm of capital allocation, while also maintaining the fundamental principles of equity and stability within financial markets.

In summary, the significant impact of artificial intelligence on the distribution of financial resources within capitalist economies is fundamentally transforming the structure of the financial sector. The utilization of this technology improves operational effectiveness, facilitates evidence-based decision-making, fosters equal access to investment prospects, and enhances the management of investment portfolios. Nevertheless, technology also brings forth a novel epoch of problems and ethical deliberations. The ongoing progress of artificial intelligence (AI) is expected to have a significant influence on the allocation of capital, leading to a deeper transformation of capitalist economies and the global financial environment. The endeavor holds great potential, yet requires careful stewardship and deliberate adaptation in order to fully actualize its promises.

The role of institutions in facilitating efficient capital allocation in AI-driven sectors

The efficient allocation of capital is of utmost importance in any economy, however, it assumes a heightened level of significance in industries that are predominantly influenced by Artificial Intelligence (AI). The key function of institutions in supporting effective capital allocation is crucial in these cutting-edge industries. This discourse examines the diverse facets pertaining to the pivotal role that institutions assume in guiding investments, promoting innovation, mitigating risks, and assuring the responsible advancement of industries driven by artificial intelligence. The effective allocation of capital in sectors powered by artificial intelligence (AI) is heavily dependent on the functions performed by institutions in terms of providing guidance, regulation, and support to these rapidly evolving industries.

Investment Guidance and Prioritization

In sectors driven by artificial intelligence (AI), both public and commercial entities exert substantial influence in guiding investment decisions. Public entities, including governmental bodies and organizations, allocate financial resources towards the advancement of artificial intelligence (AI) research and development. These entities prioritize projects that have the potential to stimulate economic growth, tackle societal issues, and enhance national competitiveness. Countries such as the United States and China have allocated significant money towards artificial intelligence (AI) efforts, including a wide range of sectors including healthcare and defense. Concurrently, private entities such as venture capital firms and accelerators actively engage in the identification and provision of support to emerging artificial intelligence enterprises. In addition to providing financial resources, these entities also offer guidance and facilitate connections, so expediting the advancement and implementation of artificial intelligence solutions across several sectors.

International organizations and partnerships, such as the Horizon 2020 program of the European Union and the Global Partnership on Artificial Intelligence (GPAI), facilitate worldwide cooperation in the field of artificial intelligence (AI) research and development. These initiatives aim to ensure effective allocation of resources and maximize the widespread advantages derived from investments in AI. The collaboration between public and private entities, facilitated by international partnerships, plays a crucial role in directing investments in artificial intelligence (AI), stimulating innovation, tackling societal issues, and enhancing economic development. The ongoing development of this collaborative endeavor is characterized by the expanding influence of artificial intelligence.

Risk Management and Regulation

In the dynamic and ever-changing domain of artificial intelligence (AI), the presence of institutions, such as regulatory organizations and government agencies, is crucial for effectively managing the intricate nature of this revolutionary technology. The rapid advancement of artificial intelligence (AI) gives rise to various ambiguities, ethical quandaries, and potential risks. In order to promote responsible development and effective capital allocation, institutions are entrusted with the responsibility of tackling these difficulties. These institutions are crucial in the management of uncertainty and ethical considerations pertaining to artificial intelligence. The individuals involved actively participate in continuous dialogues with the aim of establishing ethical standards and rules. These discussions encompass several topics, including algorithmic prejudice, data privacy, and the societal consequences of automation. In addition, institutions place emphasis on ensuring safety and responsible development of artificial intelligence by implementing stringent standards that encompass the resilience of systems and the protection of data.

By effectively managing the tension between fostering innovation and maintaining ethical and legal standards, institutions establish a conducive setting for the responsible development and advancement of artificial intelligence. They provide guidance for the allocation of capital in industries driven by artificial intelligence, ensuring that investments not only contribute to economic progress but also adhere to ethical values, prioritize safety, and promote societal well-being. The aforementioned equilibrium cultivates an environment conducive to the flourishing of innovation, all the while upholding ethical principles and providing protection against any hazards. Consequently, artificial intelligence emerges as a catalyst for constructive change.

Research and Development

In the domain of artificial intelligence (AI), the pursuit of research and development is primarily led by public institutions, which assume a crucial role in driving technological progress and the expansion of knowledge. These establishments, by means of financial backing and provision of necessary resources, cultivate ingenuity that spans from foundational investigations to pragmatic resolutions for industrial predicaments. Public organizations dedicate significant resources to the research and development of artificial intelligence (AI), acknowledging its potential to stimulate economic growth and promote societal progress. These investments encompass a wide range of sectors, including healthcare, transportation, and education. An example of a program that allocates substantial financial resources to artificial intelligence (AI)-related endeavors with the objective of tackling urgent issues and fostering innovative advancements is the Horizon 2020 initiative of the European Union. Significantly, these establishments play a vital role in fostering partnerships among universities, research institutions, as well as public and commercial sectors. These collaborations foster a dynamic ecosystem of innovation, wherein artificial intelligence technology and knowledge undergo continuous evolution. Universities and research institutes play a crucial role in providing specialized knowledge and conducting advanced research, whilst private sector involvement serves as a means to connect academic discoveries with real-world applications.

In brief, public institutions play a crucial role in driving AI research and development, advancing technological progress, and tackling practical problems. The synergy among academia, research institutions, and industry fosters a dynamic ecosystem that cultivates AI innovation, hence influencing the allocation of capital towards endeavors that possess the capacity to transform both sectors and societies.

Intellectual Property Protection

Within the realm of artificial intelligence (AI), entities that are dedicated to the preservation of intellectual property rights, such as patent offices and legal institutions, assume a crucial function in promoting innovation. These entities ensure that the rights of AI innovators are protected, hence facilitating the advancement of AI technology. The aforementioned safeguard functions as a crucial motivator for the allocation of funds towards the pursuit of research and development in the field of artificial intelligence. The primary objective of this position revolves around safeguarding intellectual property rights, so enabling individuals and organizations to preserve their investments in AI innovation and sustain a competitive advantage. AI inventors, whether they be individuals or organizations, are incentivized to allocate resources and financial investments towards groundbreaking AI initiatives, with the assurance that their intellectual property will receive adequate protection. The patent systems, specifically, function as a potent incentive. Inventors are provided the exclusive rights to their AI-related innovations for a specified duration. The presence of exclusivity serves as a motivating factor for invention by offering a means for innovators to profit from their creations, either through commercialization or collaborative agreements. Additionally, it cultivates an environment in which AI-related enterprises can get the requisite financial resources, assured of their capacity to safeguard and use their intellectual assets.

In summary, the presence of organizations that protect intellectual property rights in the field of artificial intelligence plays a crucial role in providing guidance for the allocation of capital. The establishment of such an environment fosters a system wherein individuals who introduce novel ideas are duly acknowledged and incentivized for their valuable contributions. Consequently, this approach ensures that investments in the field of artificial intelligence (AI) research and development continue to be appealing and advantageous. This phenomenon not only fosters continuous innovation but also enhances the groundwork for future progress in artificial intelligence (AI) technology and its various applications.

Education and Talent Development

Educational institutions play a pivotal role in maximizing the efficient allocation of capital within sectors driven by artificial intelligence. The production of a trained workforce capable of driving innovation in these dynamic industries is a critical duty fulfilled by them. These educational institutions provide programs and courses that provide individuals with the necessary information and abilities required to drive developments in the field of artificial intelligence. The program offers students a comprehensive education in artificial intelligence technologies, data science, machine learning, and associated disciplines, thereby establishing a robust knowledge base. The emphasis on education in this context guarantees a continuous supply of skilled individuals who are prepared to make valuable contributions to the advancement and expansion of industries reliant on artificial intelligence.

Furthermore, educational institutions engage in active collaborations with industry partners in order to facilitate the integration of academic research with real-world applications. These collaborations enable a smooth and efficient integration of up-and-coming individuals with the AI business, ensuring that their skills and knowledge are well-matched with the industry's present demands and obstacles. Through the cultivation of a symbiotic relationship between academics and industry, educational institutions facilitate the development of a labor force capable of effectively using AI expertise in practical contexts.

In summary, educational institutions play a crucial role in facilitating effective capital allocation within AI-driven sectors. They are responsible for generating the proficient professionals and innovators necessary for the progression of AI technologies. By engaging in collaborative efforts with the industry, the aim is to ensure that the pool of talent remains well-aligned with the demands of the sector. This, in turn, facilitates innovation and helps sustain the competitive advantage of industries driven by artificial intelligence.

Industry Standards and Best Practices

Professional organizations and industry groups have a significant impact on determining the effective distribution of resources in industries driven by artificial intelligence. They play a crucial role in developing and maintaining industry standards and best practices, which serve as essential guidelines for the development and deployment of artificial intelligence (AI) technology.

The purpose of these standards is to guarantee interoperability, safety, and quality within industries that are driven by artificial intelligence. They enable the smooth incorporation of artificial intelligence (AI) technologies into diverse sectors and applications. Industry standards play a crucial role in fostering confidence among investors, stakeholders, and the wider public by ensuring uniformity and dependability. Moreover, these criteria offer a robust framework for assessing and contrasting artificial intelligence (AI) initiatives and enterprises. Investors possess the ability to make well-informed decisions by evaluating the extent to which AI efforts adhere to recognized best practices. This evaluation process serves to stimulate the flow of capital towards projects that exhibit a strong dedication to upholding standards of quality, safety, and ethical considerations.

Professional bodies and industry associations play a crucial role in facilitating effective capital allocation by establishing a structured framework that promotes confidence and dependability in ventures driven by artificial intelligence. The individual's responsibility is directing investments towards projects and endeavors that adhere to established industry standards, thereby fostering innovation while mitigating potential risks.

Ethical and Societal Considerations

In addition to considering economic issues, institutions use a proactive approach in tackling the ethical and societal dimensions associated with artificial intelligence (AI). Ethical review boards, think tanks, and public policy institutes partake in extensive deliberations concerning the larger societal consequences of artificial intelligence, encompassing areas such as privacy and ethical standards. The aforementioned discussions have a substantial impact on investment choices as they direct the distribution of funds towards artificial intelligence (AI) initiatives that emphasize responsible advancement and adhere to ethical values and the betterment of society. In order to demonstrate a dedication to ethical issues and minimize potential dangers and societal harm, institutions guarantee that investments in areas powered by artificial intelligence are carefully managed.

Institutions play an active role in influencing the trajectory of AI investments by engaging in conversations and providing policy suggestions. Their aim is to guide the allocation of capital towards projects that not only demonstrate economic potential but also uphold ethical principles and privacy requirements. The establishment of a correlation between investments and ethical standards serves to cultivate confidence among stakeholders and the wider public, so strengthening the responsible advancement of artificial intelligence. So, organizations that prioritize ethical and societal factors ensure that the allocation of resources in areas driven by artificial intelligence extends beyond mere economic benefits. Their contribution lies in directing investments towards projects that prioritize ethical principles and societal well-being, thereby promoting a more equitable and ethical landscape for artificial intelligence (AI) technology.

Fundamentally, institutions play a pivotal role in establishing the fundamental framework for effective allocation of capital in industries driven by artificial intelligence. The diverse responsibilities undertaken by individuals in this profession include providing advice on investment strategies, managing risks, ensuring compliance with regulations, supporting research and development initiatives, safeguarding intellectual property, fostering talent development, establishing industry standards, and addressing ethical concerns. Institutions play a crucial role in facilitating responsible growth within AI-driven sectors by effectively performing these duties. Their contributions involve ensuring efficient allocation of resources and addressing potential hazards and ethical problems. By engaging in such activities, individuals assume a crucial role in influencing the trajectory of economies and societies that are driven by artificial intelligence.

Potential challenges and considerations for maintaining a balanced and sustainable capital allocation system

The task of managing the allocation of capital in the dynamic and evolving context of contemporary economies is a complicated and multidimensional undertaking. The distribution of capital has a crucial role in driving economic growth, fostering innovation, and promoting prosperity. However, this process is not devoid of complexities and possible challenges. This discourse explores the numerous obstacles and factors that form the basis of the pursuit of upholding a harmonious and enduring capital allocation system, an undertaking that intersects the fields of economics, finance, ethics, and society welfare. The allocation of capital plays a crucial role in stimulating economic activity by directing resources towards projects, industries, and endeavors that have the potential to generate growth and create value. In capitalist economies, the distribution of resources is influenced by market forces, investor emotion, and the drive for financial gain. However, the contemporary economic environment is characterized by a rapidly increasing rate of transformation, a dynamic revolution in digital technology, and the advent of innovative technologies such as Artificial Intelligence (AI) and blockchain. The aforementioned transformative factors bring about additional layers of intricacy to the equation of capital allocation, necessitating a careful evaluation of their consequences.

One of the primary problems in this endeavor is attaining equilibrium. Achieving a delicate balance between risk and reward, immediate profits and long-term sustainability, and economic growth and societal well-being poses a complex challenge. The adaptation of capital allocation systems is necessary in response to the dynamic nature of economic situations, technological shocks, and global issues such as climate change and pandemics. The concept of achieving equilibrium involves a wide range of factors, including ethical inquiries on conscientious investment practices and the necessity of regulatory structures that guarantee impartiality and openness in the distribution procedure.

Furthermore, the advent of the digital era has brought about a period characterized by the continuous flow of information, rapid market operations, and the blurring of conventional industry boundaries. The interconnectivity observed in global markets amplifies the significance of capital allocation, as choices made in a particular region can yield far-reaching consequences in international markets. This highlights the necessity for comprehensive risk management strategies, enhanced cybersecurity protocols, and a deeper comprehension of the interconnectedness of global factors that influence the distribution landscape. Sustainability represents a fundamental aspect within contemporary discussions surrounding capital allocation. In light of the challenges posed by climate change and resource constraint, the distribution of capital assumes a heightened significance for society. Sustainable investing, impact investing, and the utilization of environmental, social, and governance (ESG) criteria have emerged as significant factors that direct money towards firms and initiatives that not only offer financial returns but also contribute to the advancement of a more sustainable and equitable global society.

The notion of sustainability covers not just ecological considerations but also social and governance dimensions. The subject matter prompts inquiries on the ethical aspects of allocating capital, underscoring the necessity of taking into account the wider societal consequences of investment choices. The ethical dimensions of sustainability are closely connected to various aspects, including the distribution of financial resources and the reputational and social obligations of institutions engaged in sustainable practices. Technology also plays a key role within this vast terrain. The utilization of AI and machine learning algorithms in capital allocation has become more prevalent, facilitating the examination of extensive datasets and the forecasting of market trends. Although these technologies possess the capacity to improve efficiency and decision-making, they also raise apprehensions over algorithmic biases, transparency, and accountability in the allocation process.

The endeavor to establish a well-balanced and sustainable system for allocating wealth in the contemporary day is a complex endeavor. This encompasses not solely economic factors, but also ethical, social, and technological aspects. Achieving a harmonious balance between financial gain and societal impact, effectively responding to the fast-paced nature of transformations, and effectively managing interconnectedness on a worldwide scale are some of the significant obstacles that constitute the foundation of this undertaking. In the face of the challenges posed by the digital era, environmental issues, and the pursuit of ethical investments, the allocation of capital emerges as a critical arena in which the future of economies and society is shaped. This discourse delves into the various dimensions of the terrain under scrutiny, analyzing the obstacles and factors that necessitate careful consideration as we navigate a path towards a capital allocation system that is both equitable and environmentally sustainable.

Chapter 23: AI and Entrepreneurial Capitalism

The convergence of Artificial Intelligence (AI) with Entrepreneurial Capitalism is a pivotal milestone in the history of economic development. This chapter delves into the complex interaction between two dynamic forces, namely artificial intelligence (AI) and entrepreneurial capitalism. It aims to examine the various opportunities and problems that arise from the integration of AI inside the realm of entrepreneurial capitalism. Central to this discourse is a deep analysis of the interdependent connection between entrepreneurship fueled by innovation and the revolutionary capacities of artificial intelligence technology.

In the course of examining the many aspects of this chapter, we aim to provide light on the trajectory followed by entrepreneurial capitalism in a time characterized by the widespread presence of artificial intelligence (AI). This study aims to explore the diverse range of opportunities that artificial intelligence (AI) presents for forward-thinking businesses. These prospects encompass the democratization of innovation as well as the unparalleled potential for market expansion. Concurrently, we will address the various issues posed by this emerging paradigm, encompassing ethical considerations, labor displacement concerns, and the continuously developing role of human creativity within an AI-enhanced environment. The central focus of this investigation revolves around the function of institutions. Public and commercial organizations have a significant impact on promoting innovation, entrepreneurship, and startups in the era of artificial intelligence (AI). They exert their influence by means of legislation, financial support, regulatory structures, and cooperative networks that define the ecology in which entrepreneurial capitalism flourishes. The acts undertaken by these individuals have laid the foundation for the rise of companies that utilize artificial intelligence, hence facilitating the conversion of abstract concepts into practical solutions that reshape various sectors and question established norms. Moreover, we will direct our attention towards the future and reflect upon probable transformations in the fundamental characteristics and mechanisms of entrepreneurial capitalism as it experiences a profound change due to breakthroughs in artificial intelligence. This study aims to analyze the evolution of business models, the restructuring of value chains, and the introduction of novel competitive strategies in a contemporary context where data holds significant value and algorithms play a dominant role.

In conclusion, the integration of artificial intelligence (AI) and entrepreneurial capitalism marks a significant era characterized by the convergence of innovation, entrepreneurship, and the immense potential of human creativity in ways that have not been witnessed before. The range of options is extensive, the complexities of the issues are significant, and the potential consequences are of great importance. Please join us in this academic inquiry as we navigate the domain of artificial intelligence and entrepreneurial capitalism, a sphere in which the trajectory of the future is influenced by the collaborative interplay between human creativity and machine intelligence, and where the entrepreneurial drive remains the catalyst for advancement.

The opportunities and challenges AI presents for entrepreneurial capitalism

The convergence of Artificial Intelligence (AI) with entrepreneurial capitalism has initiated a period characterized by unparalleled prospects and complexities. The interplay between entrepreneurship fueled by innovation and the transformative capabilities of artificial intelligence (AI) is fundamentally altering several sectors, economies, and the fundamental structure of capitalism. This investigation involves a comprehensive analysis of the complex terrain, emphasizing the remarkable opportunities that artificial intelligence (AI) presents for entrepreneurs, while concurrently addressing the significant obstacles it presents.

Opportunities

1. Democratization of Innovation

The involvement of artificial intelligence (AI) in the democratization of innovation goes beyond mere accessibility, as it also encompasses the fundamental essence of entrepreneurship. Start-up companies are currently able to utilize artificial intelligence (AI)-based tools and platforms, which enable them to not only compete with well-established entities but also to potentially cause significant disruptions within whole industries. The increased availability of cloud-based artificial intelligence (AI) services, open-source libraries, and easily accessible machine learning frameworks has significantly reduced the obstacles for individuals to engage in these fields. This implies that individuals with innovative concepts and strong resolve have the ability to actualize their ideals without necessitating excessive research and development funding or substantial technical proficiency.

Moreover, the democratization of innovation facilitated by artificial intelligence (AI) encompasses a wide range of industries. In the field of healthcare, entrepreneurs have the potential to leverage artificial intelligence (AI) in many applications such as drug discovery, disease diagnostics, and the development of individualized treatment plans. AI-powered drones and sensors offer precision farming capabilities to small-scale growers within the agricultural sector. In some fields, the accessibility of AI tools facilitates a climate of entrepreneurship wherein innovation can emerge from unanticipated origins. The outcome entails a more prosperous and fiercely competitive entrepreneurial environment that consistently pushes the limits of what can be achieved.

2. Market Expansion and Personalization

The revolutionary nature of AI is seen in its impact on market expansion and customisation. In contemporary times, startups have transcended geographical boundaries, expanding their reach beyond local or national marketplaces to readily engage with a worldwide audience. The global reach of many technological advancements such as AI-driven recommendation algorithms, chatbots, and predictive analytics can be attributed to their significant impact and influence. These technologies facilitate entrepreneurs in comprehending the specific preferences of individual customers at a detailed level, allowing them to customize their products, services, and marketing campaigns accordingly.

For example, e-commerce businesses utilize recommendation engines powered by artificial intelligence to propose things to clients by analyzing their previous actions and interests. Content streaming services leverage artificial intelligence (AI) algorithms to compile customized playlists and provide tailored content recommendations, hence enhancing user engagement and prolonging their interaction with the platforms. The implementation of such a high degree of personalisation facilitates the development of consumer loyalty and augments the market share, thereby generating a competitive edge that can be effectively utilized by startups to achieve quick growth in both well-established and growing markets.

3. Enhanced Decision-Making

The enhancement of decision-making facilitated by AI is a fundamental aspect of its value proposition for entrepreneurs. Start-up companies have the ability to leverage artificial intelligence (AI) technologies in order to efficiently handle and analyze large datasets. The capacity for analysis spans a wide range of topics, encompassing activities such as optimizing supply chains, analyzing market trends, and assessing risks. Entrepreneurs are able to make well-informed decisions that aim to avoid risks and optimize profits by utilizing insights generated through the application of artificial intelligence.

For example, an enterprise in the logistics industry can leverage artificial intelligence (AI) technology to enhance the efficiency of delivery routes, thereby diminishing transportation expenses and enhancing delivery timelines. AI-driven predictive analytics play a crucial role in the financial sector by assisting startups in the identification of prospective investment possibilities and potential hazards. Furthermore, the utilization of AI-driven chatbots aids firms in delivering streamlined customer support services and immediately addressing concerns. The utilization of data-driven decisions enhances the ability of startups to withstand and adjust to the dynamic nature of the business environment, enabling them to effectively address market fluctuations and changing customer preferences.

4. Cost Efficiency

The implementation of artificial intelligence (AI) in startups has the potential to significantly enhance cost efficiency, hence revolutionizing their operations. The implementation of artificial intelligence (AI) in automation processes facilitates the optimization of operations, leading to a decrease in labor expenses and an enhancement of overall efficiency. Startups have the capability to implement automation in a wide range of services, encompassing customer service, data entry, and data analysis, among others, in order to streamline and expedite routine and repetitive tasks. The implementation of automation reduces the necessity for a substantial increase in the size of the personnel as the business experiences growth.

In the field of manufacturing, artificial intelligence (AI)-powered robots and systems are employed to execute repetitive operations with a high level of accuracy, hence diminishing the necessity for considerable manual work. Within the domain of customer service, chatbots are responsible for managing ordinary queries, so allowing human agents to allocate their attention towards resolving more intricate matters. Furthermore, the utilization of AI-driven data analytics technologies empowers companies to get valuable insights from extensive datasets, eliminating the necessity for a substantial workforce of data analysts.

The cost effectiveness of this approach is particularly advantageous for nascent businesses with constrained resources, enabling them to carefully focus their cash towards expansion and innovation, rather than being burdened by excessive operational expenditures. Moreover, it enables startups to achieve rapid growth and effectively compete with well-established entities inside their respective sectors.

5. Innovative Business Models

The transformative potential of AI in the context of entrepreneurial capitalism encompasses the ability to generate innovative and disruptive business models that reshape the entrepreneurial environment. Start-up enterprises are utilizing artificial intelligence (AI) to not only foster innovation, but also to fundamentally transform conventional sectors by accessing markets that were previously unexplored.

Subscription-based services exemplify the transformative impact of artificial intelligence on business paradigms. By utilizing artificial intelligence algorithms, startups have the ability to curate content, recommendations, and experiences that are tailored to individual users. Streaming platforms utilize artificial intelligence (AI) algorithms to evaluate the viewing patterns and preferences of their subscribers, enabling them to provide personalized content recommendations. This not only improves customer satisfaction but also generates regular revenue, offering financial stability and predictability that conventional pay-per-product models cannot achieve. The presence of stability enables entrepreneurs to concentrate on improving their products and services and increasing their customer base, so facilitating long-term and sustainable development. The emergence of AI-driven sharing economies has caused a significant disruption in traditional paradigms by facilitating the connection between persons possessing underutilized assets or skills. These platforms, frequently utilizing AI algorithms, effectively facilitate the alignment of supply and demand. Ride-sharing enterprises employ artificial intelligence (AI) to dynamically optimize routes and pricing, thereby enhancing the accessibility and cost-efficiency of transportation services. In the context of the sharing economy, network effects frequently manifest, wherein the value of the platform escalates for all participants as the number of users increases.

In addition, AI-driven marketplaces have emerged as potent instruments for companies to facilitate the connection between customers and sellers. These markets employ artificial intelligence algorithms to enhance search results, price, and suggestions. E-commerce businesses employ AI-driven markets as a means to offer personalized product recommendations, hence augmenting customer engagement and stimulating sales. Moreover, the utilization of AI may be leveraged to foster trust and ensure safety inside these marketplaces by implementing functionalities such as fraud detection mechanisms and identity verification systems.

The impact of artificial intelligence on creative business strategies is significant in its entirety. Startups are utilizing these models to disrupt conventional sectors and capture unexplored markets, so establishing a dynamic and constantly evolving entrepreneurial environment that consistently challenges the limits of what can be achieved in the realm of business and trade.

Challenges

1. Ethical Considerations

The integration of artificial intelligence (AI) into the field of entrepreneurship undoubtedly brings about profound changes, but, it also gives rise to notable ethical considerations. Algorithmic bias is a highly significant concern that warrants considerable attention. The perpetuation of existing inequities or biased decision-making, which has the potential to impact underprivileged communities, can occur when AI systems are taught using biased or incomplete data. Entrepreneurs are confronted with the ethical quandary of ensuring that their artificial intelligence (AI) systems exhibit fairness, impartiality, and justice. In order to address these issues and prevent any damage to their reputation or legal consequences, it is imperative for organizations to allocate resources towards enhancing data quality and promoting openness.

Privacy violations represent a significant ethical matter of utmost importance. The management of substantial quantities of user data by entrepreneurs for the purpose of fueling AI algorithms gives rise to inquiries regarding consent, data security, and user entitlements. In order to ensure the security of sensitive information, it is imperative for startups to implement rigorous privacy policies, comply with data protection legislation, and deploy robust encryption and cybersecurity methods. Failure to comply with these ethical standards can have serious consequences, including potential legal ramifications and a significant erosion of client confidence.

The ethical examination of automation also encompasses its societal influence. Although AI-driven enterprises have the potential to improve efficiency and production, they can also result in the displacement of jobs inside conventional industries. Entrepreneurs are required to thoroughly evaluate the prospective societal and economic ramifications associated with their artificial intelligence (AI) advancements. The successful implementation of responsible AI development necessitates a dedication to various initiatives, such as reskilling and retraining those who have been displaced by AI advancements. These efforts play a crucial role in facilitating a more seamless societal transition.

2. Talent Shortages

The current supply of AI expertise falls significantly short of meeting the demand, resulting in a substantial lack of skilled professionals. This shortfall presents a tough hurdle for startups. There is a significant demand for highly skilled experts in the field of artificial intelligence (AI), encompassing roles such as data scientists, machine learning engineers, and AI researchers. Established technology companies frequently attract these professionals by offering lucrative remuneration packages and comprehensive benefits. Start-up companies, characterized by their constrained resources, may encounter difficulties in both attracting and retaining highly skilled professionals in the field of artificial intelligence.

In order to tackle this difficulty, it is imperative for entrepreneurs to embrace innovative methodologies. This encompasses the provision of equity, cultivation of an innovative culture, and facilitation of opportunities for employees to engage in pioneering projects. Engaging in partnerships with academic institutions might additionally function as a means to cultivate a pool of talented individuals. Furthermore, it is worth noting that startups have the option to allocate resources towards the investment in training and enhancing the skills of their current employees, with the aim of addressing the shortage of skilled personnel.

3. Regulatory Complexity

The regulatory framework pertaining to artificial intelligence (AI) is undergoing swift transformations, hence presenting entrepreneurs with a complex and intricate terrain of legal regulations and rules. Entrepreneurs are confronted with intricate challenges encompassing data protection, algorithmic transparency, and responsibility pertaining to occurrences involving artificial intelligence. This requires a high level of legal knowledge and access to resources in order to assure adherence to regulations and minimize any legal liabilities. Furthermore, the absence of established global regulations contributes to the intricacy of the situation. Entrepreneurs that engage in worldwide activities are faced with the challenge of navigating diverse legal frameworks across multiple nations. Remaining informed about regulatory changes, adjusting to new regulations, and establishing comprehensive compliance practices are crucial in order to prevent legal setbacks and uphold trust with consumers and partners.

4. Initial Investment

The democratization of innovation facilitated by AI is accompanied by a significant requirement for initial investment when entering the AI field. The process of establishing the essential infrastructure, acquiring data of superior quality, and conducting training for artificial intelligence models might demand significant resources. Entrepreneurs are required to get financial resources in order to support their business ventures, a task that can prove to be difficult, particularly for newly established companies with low financial assets.

In order to attract funding, entrepreneurs are required to effectively communicate a persuasive business rationale for their businesses centered around artificial intelligence (AI), emphasizing the possibilities for innovation, expansion, and market upheaval. Forming collaborations with investors who possess expertise and specialization in the fields of artificial intelligence (AI) and technology can facilitate the acquisition of essential resources and knowledge. Moreover, sources of initial funding such as grants, accelerators, and government initiatives that are specifically designed to promote AI innovation might be quite helpful.

5. Disruption and Job Displacement

The potential for automation in artificial intelligence has the capacity to significantly disrupt conventional industries, resulting in the displacement of jobs. Entrepreneurs embarking on AI-driven enterprises must carefully contemplate the societal and economic ramifications of their discoveries. This entails the formulation of plans aimed at providing displaced workers with the necessary skills and training, so facilitating a fair and equitable transition. Entrepreneurs are need to actively interact with many stakeholders, such as labor unions and lawmakers, in order to effectively tackle apprehensions over employment reduction and foster cooperative approaches that harmonize the advantages of artificial intelligence (AI) with societal equilibrium. Entrepreneurs may encounter a substantial obstacle in the form of resistance from stakeholders who harbor concerns around potential job displacement. In order to address this difficulty, it is imperative for startups to engage in honest communication regarding their objectives and the possible advantages of their AI-driven initiatives. This approach is crucial for alleviating concerns and gaining the necessary support.

6. Data Privacy and Security

The dependence of artificial intelligence (AI) on data underscores the critical importance of safeguarding data privacy and security, particularly for emerging startups. The occurrence of data breaches and its subsequent exploitation can lead to adverse repercussions like as reputational harm, legal ramifications, and erosion of customer confidence. It is imperative for entrepreneurs to give utmost importance to implementing comprehensive cybersecurity protocols, which encompass encryption, access controls, and periodic security audits. These measures are crucial in ensuring the protection of user data and adhering to data protection legislation.

Furthermore, the establishment of transparency pertaining to the utilization of data and policies concerning privacy is of utmost importance in fostering a sense of confidence among clientele. It is imperative for entrepreneurs to exhibit proactive behavior in effectively conveying their dedication to safeguarding data privacy, so enabling consumers to make well-informed choices regarding the disclosure of their personal information. The practice of openness not only serves to bolster the ethical position of the startup, but also aids in effectively navigating the progressively intricate legislative framework pertaining to data privacy.

In summary, artificial intelligence (AI) presents a complex and contradictory terrain for entrepreneurial capitalism, characterized by a multitude of prospects and obstacles. Entrepreneurs that effectively navigate this domain by employing innovative strategies, demonstrating ethical awareness, adhering to legal requirements, and prioritizing societal welfare are well-positioned to leverage the revolutionary potential of artificial intelligence (AI) in order to redefine various industries, generate value, and influence the trajectory of capitalism in the future.

The role of institutions in fostering innovation, entrepreneurship, and startups in the AI era

The dependence of artificial intelligence (AI) on data underscores the critical importance of safeguarding data privacy and security, particularly for emerging startups. The occurrence of data breaches and its subsequent exploitation can lead to adverse repercussions like as reputational harm, legal ramifications, and erosion of customer confidence. It is imperative for entrepreneurs to give utmost importance to implementing comprehensive cybersecurity protocols, which encompass encryption, access controls, and periodic security audits. These measures are crucial in ensuring the protection of user data and adhering to data protection legislation.

Furthermore, the establishment of transparency pertaining to the utilization of data and policies concerning privacy is of utmost importance in fostering a sense of confidence among clientele. It is imperative for entrepreneurs to exhibit proactive behavior in effectively conveying their dedication to safeguarding data privacy, so enabling consumers to make well-informed choices regarding the disclosure of their personal information. The practice of openness not only serves to bolster the ethical position of the startup, but also aids in effectively navigating the progressively intricate legislative framework pertaining to data privacy.

In summary, artificial intelligence (AI) presents a complex and contradictory terrain for entrepreneurial capitalism, characterized by a multitude of prospects and obstacles. Entrepreneurs that effectively navigate this domain by employing innovative strategies, demonstrating ethical awareness, adhering to legal requirements, and prioritizing societal welfare are well-positioned to leverage the revolutionary potential of artificial intelligence (AI) in order to redefine various industries, generate value, and influence the trajectory of capitalism in the future.

Democratization of Innovation

The era of artificial intelligence (AI) is commonly associated with the democratization of innovation. In contrast to preceding periods, contemporary enterprises are no longer necessitated to possess substantial expenditures for research and development in order to avail themselves of the revolutionary potential of artificial intelligence. Cloud-based artificial intelligence (AI) services, open-source libraries, and AI-driven platforms have emerged as accessible technologies that offer cost-effective and adaptable solutions. The democratization being discussed here is a fundamental aspect of a growing period of entrepreneurial revitalization, in which institutions play a crucial role as the supportive framework for a significant surge of innovation.

Public Institutions: Catalysts of Innovation

Public institutions play a crucial role in the AI innovation ecosystem as they are driven by a vision of promoting economic growth, addressing societal issues, and improving national competitiveness. Significant resources are allocated towards the promotion of research and development in the field of artificial intelligence. Public institutions play a vital role in fostering the success of startups by providing research grants, support for pioneering projects, and the formation of innovation hubs. These investments serve as a catalyst for technological improvements, enabling entrepreneurs to establish themselves at the forefront of innovation.

Private Institutions: Nurturing Entrepreneurship

Private institutions, which encompass venture capital firms and technology accelerators, play a crucial role in the identification and cultivation of new artificial intelligence (AI) startups. In addition to providing necessary financial resources, they also provide mentorship, direction, and access to a network of business connections. The establishment of a collaborative alliance between public and private organizations engenders a mutually beneficial environment conducive to the proliferation of innovation and entrepreneurship. Start-up enterprises are provided with both financial support and specialized knowledge necessary to effectively navigate the intricate landscape of entrepreneurship.

Ethical Considerations: Shaping the Boundaries of AI Entrepreneurship

The era of artificial intelligence is not lacking in ethical challenges. The increasing integration of AI applications across several industries has brought out significant concerns over algorithmic bias, data privacy, and the broader societal implications. Institutions bear the responsibility of formulating rules, norms, and codes of conduct that establish the ethical parameters of AI entrepreneurship. Regulatory organizations play a crucial role in this process by implementing and enforcing legislation that strikes a balance between fostering innovation and ensuring appropriate utilization. These restrictions serve as a protective measure against the potential misuse of AI, thereby contributing to the establishment of trust among various stakeholders such as entrepreneurs, investors, and the general public. Ensuring the sustainable expansion of AI businesses and limiting the risks associated with unregulated technological advancement are crucial factors.

Educational Institutions: Nurturing AI Talent

In addition to fostering AI-driven innovation, institutions also play a crucial role in cultivating the people responsible for driving such advancements. Educational institutions play a crucial role in this context by providing specialized programs and courses that are in line with the requirements of the artificial intelligence era. These educational endeavors provide individuals with the requisite information and skills to effectively utilize the transformational capabilities of artificial intelligence. Collaborative efforts between the academic and industrial sectors serve to bridge the divide between theoretical research and practical implementation, so facilitating the continuous flow of skilled individuals capable of propelling innovation.

Standards and Best Practices: Ensuring Quality and Safety

In order to expand their impact, institutions exert their influence through defining industry standards and best practices within areas powered by artificial intelligence (AI). Frameworks are established by professional organisations and industry associations to guarantee the compatibility, security, and excellence of artificial intelligence (AI) applications. The aforementioned criteria establish a fundamental basis of uniformity and dependability, fostering assurance among investors and stakeholders. Startups may depend on these established principles for the creation and implementation of their products, which can facilitate a more seamless introduction into the market. Institutions play a crucial role in fostering a more predictable and stable entrepreneurial environment by mitigating uncertainties connected with AI entrepreneurship.

Ethical and Societal Considerations: Beyond Economic Impact

In the era of artificial intelligence, institutions are also confronted with the ethical and societal aspects of this technology. Ethical review boards, think tanks, and public policy institutes actively participate in extensive deliberations concerning the societal, privacy, and ethical implications of artificial intelligence (AI). These discussions go beyond economic factors and impact investment choices by directing the distribution of funds towards the responsible development of artificial intelligence and solutions that are in line with ethical standards and the overall welfare of society.

AI in Established Industries

The advent of artificial intelligence (AI) has not only caused significant disruptions in existing businesses, but it has also brought about a revitalization of established sectors. Institutions have a crucial role in facilitating innovation within these specific areas. Healthcare facilities play a crucial role in promoting the implementation of artificial intelligence (AI)-based diagnostic tools and treatment planning, hence improving the quality of patient care. In a similar vein, educational establishments utilize artificial intelligence (AI) to augment the process of learning by means of tailored instruction and anticipatory data analysis. These institutions serve as trailblazers, incorporating artificial intelligence to foster innovation and enhance efficiency in their respective fields.

Government Initiatives: A Catalyst for AI Startups

Governments across the globe are increasingly acknowledging the profound impact that artificial intelligence (AI) can have and are proactively implementing initiatives aimed at fostering the growth of AI firms. These programs comprise financial incentives, innovation centres, and policy frameworks with the objective of fostering AI entrepreneurship. Governments are increasingly playing a pivotal role in influencing the AI entrepreneurial ecosystem through the provision of essential resources, infrastructure, and regulatory assistance that are crucial for the success of businesses.

AI Incubators and Accelerators: Fostering Startup Growth

AI incubators and accelerators have emerged as crucial establishments committed to fostering the growth and development of AI enterprises. The organization provides a holistic ecosystem that encompasses several elements such as financial support, mentorship, technical resources, and networking opportunities for businesses. These institutions expedite the development of AI companies, guaranteeing their acquisition of the required skills and direction for achieving success in the highly competitive AI industry.

Investor Networks: Fostering Growth

Investor networks have emerged as essential entities inside the AI startup ecosystem. Angel investors, venture capitalists, and corporate investment arms proactively engage in the pursuit of prospective artificial intelligence (AI) firms. In addition to providing financial resources, their engagement encompasses strategic counsel, industry networking, and validation. This consortium of establishments ensures that emerging businesses obtain the necessary financial and intellectual assets to thrive.

Collaborative Innovation: Institutions as Catalysts

In order to promote collaborative innovation, institutions facilitate the convergence of various stakeholders. Incubators, accelerators, and industry-specific organizations serve as facilitators, fostering collaboration between startups, existing firms, research institutions, and other startups. These collaborative efforts enable the exchange of knowledge, the advancement of innovative solutions, and the expeditious entry of entrepreneurs into the market.

Scaling Up: Bridging the Growth Gap

In the context of AI startups, institutions play a crucial role in facilitating the bridging of the growth gap. These entities offer opportunities to access various resources that facilitate the expansion of activities, encompassing marketing strategies, worldwide growth, and entry into novel markets. These establishments ensure that emerging businesses receive the necessary assistance to progress from the initial stages of invention to achieving long-term viability and expansion.

International Collaboration: A Global Ecosystem

In the context of the worldwide artificial intelligence (AI) landscape, institutions assume a crucial role in promoting and enabling international collaboration. The establishment of cross-border collaborations, research endeavors, and avenues for financial support engenders a worldwide framework wherein artificial intelligence (AI) companies can avail themselves of diverse resources, markets, and specialized knowledge on an international level. These collaborative institutions facilitate the development of a more integrated and resilient AI entrepreneurship ecosystem.

Cybersecurity and Data Protection

In the current era characterized by a strong reliance on data, institutions are assuming a leading role in safeguarding cybersecurity and data protection for artificial intelligence (AI) businesses. These guidelines offer recommendations for optimal approaches to data security, aiding beginning companies in protecting confidential data. Ensuring the safeguarding of intellectual property is of utmost importance, as it serves not only to secure proprietary knowledge but also to uphold the confidence and reliance of customers.

AI in Emerging Markets: Inclusivity Through Institutions

In order to ensure that the advantages of AI entrepreneurship are extended to emerging markets, institutions play a crucial role. Institutions play a significant role in fostering inclusive growth by supporting entrepreneurs in regions that have traditionally been marginalized in the realm of technological innovation. This is achieved through various initiatives that offer valuable resources, comprehensive training programs, and facilitated access to artificial intelligence (AI) tools.

AI for Social Good: Institutions as Catalysts of Change

Institutions actively advocate for the utilization of artificial intelligence (AI) with the intention of benefiting society. Ethical review boards and public policy organizations are essential in providing guidance to AI startups in their pursuit of initiatives that effectively tackle significant societal concerns, such as healthcare inequities and environmental sustainability. These establishments ensure that AI entrepreneurship is in accordance with the wider objectives of social responsibility.

Challenges and Adaptation: The Evolving Role of Institutions

The ever-evolving nature of the artificial intelligence era requires institutions to continuously adapt. Organizations are required to maintain their agility and responsiveness in order to effectively adapt to changing technology, address ethical considerations, and comply with regulatory changes. In the context of the swiftly advancing field of artificial intelligence, institutions have the task of effectively managing the delicate equilibrium between promoting innovative practices and upholding ethical obligations.

Conclusion

In the context of the AI-powered entrepreneurial landscape, institutions play a proactive role rather than a passive one, actively contributing to its formation and development. Academic institutions have a crucial role in fostering innovation, providing essential resources, defining ethical parameters, and creating an environment conducive to the cultivation of talent. In the current epoch of artificial intelligence, it is imperative for institutions to play a crucial role in fostering an environment where entrepreneurship can flourish while upholding principles of ethics, promoting innovation, and safeguarding public welfare. As the field of artificial intelligence (AI) progresses, the importance of AI in various domains will increase, highlighting their role as guardians of a future in which emerging companies utilize the revolutionary capabilities of AI to redefine sectors, generate worth, and influence the trajectory of innovation.

Potential shifts in the nature and dynamics of entrepreneurial capitalism due to AI advancements

The emergence of Artificial Intelligence (AI) has brought forth a considerable amount of transformational potential, not solely limited to the technology domain but also impacting the dynamics of entrepreneurial capitalism. The remarkable capacity of artificial intelligence (AI) to efficiently handle extensive information, perform predictive analyses, and automate intricate operations has given rise to new prospects and obstacles. This discourse aims to delve into the potential transformations in the characteristics and mechanisms of entrepreneurial capitalism driven by breakthroughs in artificial intelligence (AI).

AI as the Catalyst for Entrepreneurial Capitalism

The impact of AI on entrepreneurial capitalism is not limited to industry transformation, but extends to a fundamental revolutionization of the concept of entrepreneurship. The democratization of innovation is facilitated by the utilization of artificial intelligence (AI), which possesses the ability to offer solutions that are both accessible and scalable. It is noteworthy to mention that this accessibility encompasses more than simply the technological aspect. AI-driven platforms, cloud-based services, and open-source libraries have emerged as essential tools for companies. These resources not only alleviate the financial load but also expedite the process of development. Start-up companies have the opportunity to leverage the capabilities of artificial intelligence (AI) without the need for substantial investment in internal research and development (R&D). This allows them to allocate their resources in a more strategic manner.

Additionally, the democratization of artificial intelligence cultivates a dynamic entrepreneurial environment in which agility and creativity flourish. Throughout history, smaller organizations have frequently encountered challenges in their ability to compete with larger established companies as a result of limitations in resources. Nevertheless, artificial intelligence (AI) equalizes the opportunities for all participants. Start-up enterprises are currently able to utilize artificial intelligence (AI) technology in order to create novel solutions that challenge established markets, thereby attaining a competitive advantage. The transformation occurring in the entrepreneurial sphere is radically reshaping the strategies employed by startups in their pursuit of innovation. This change places significant emphasis on the principles of rapid iteration, experimentation, and a strong focus on meeting the needs and preferences of customers.

Furthermore, artificial intelligence provides entrepreneurs with the tools necessary to develop business models that are based on data analysis. The proliferation of data accessible in the era of digital technology can be effectively utilized to facilitate the process of making well-informed judgments. Artificial intelligence (AI) algorithms are utilized to evaluate data in order to reveal valuable insights that assist firms in refining their plans, comprehending customer habits, and enhancing their operational processes. The utilization of a data-centric strategy in entrepreneurial decision-making has been found to significantly improve precision and mitigate risks that arise from uncertainties.

AI can be understood as more than a mere technological instrument; rather, it possesses the capacity to bring about significant changes by enabling entrepreneurs to envision new possibilities inside industries, rethink established business models, and undertake projects that have exceptional prospects for achievement. The ongoing progress and increasing availability of artificial intelligence (AI) are poised to significantly enhance its function as a catalyst for entrepreneurial capitalism, thereby stimulating additional advancements, competition, and economic expansion

.

Market Disruption and Hyper-Personalization

One of the most significant transformations observed is the tremendous influence of artificial intelligence (AI) on markets and the experiences of customers. Artificial intelligence (AI) facilitates the ability of startups to disrupt conventional sectors through the introduction of novel solutions and the questioning of current business models. Concurrently, artificial intelligence (AI) facilitates the implementation of hyper-personalization in many products and services by means of recommendation algorithms, chatbots, and predictive analytics. Entrepreneurs possess the ability to customize their products or services according to the specific preferences of particular customers, hence augmenting consumer loyalty and expanding their market share.

The significant influence of artificial intelligence (AI) on market disruption and hyper-personalization is of utmost importance and should not be underestimated. Startups acquire a distinctive competitive edge in terms of innovation and market penetration when they leverage artificial intelligence (AI) technology. Historically, well-established sectors have heavily relied on conventional procedures and established business strategies. Artificial intelligence (AI) enables startups to disrupt established norms by delivering novel and inventive solutions. Disruption lies at the heart of this shift. Artificial intelligence (AI)-powered companies possess the capability to detect inefficiencies or unaddressed demands inside well-established sectors and develop innovative solutions that bring about significant disruptions. AI-powered fintech businesses have significantly transformed the financial sector through the provision of efficient and user-centric services, hence posing a formidable challenge to conventional banking practices. The scope of this disruption is not confined to a singular industry, but rather encompasses various areas, ranging from healthcare to e-commerce.

Simultaneously, artificial intelligence plays a role in enabling hyper-personalization in various products and services. Entrepreneurs have the ability to utilize recommendation algorithms that employ user data analysis in order to offer personalized advice. The implementation of this degree of personalisation significantly improves client experiences, cultivates customer loyalty, and contributes to the expansion of market share. For example, electronic commerce platforms employ artificial intelligence (AI) to examine and interpret client behavior and preferences, thereby facilitating the provision of personalized product recommendations that align with the unique interests of individual customers. Artificial intelligence (AI)-driven chatbots offer tailored customer care, effectively resolving enquiries and concerns in a timely manner.

The outcome is a market environment distinguished by vibrant competition and a focus on consumer needs and preferences. Start-up companies are not solely engaged in the task of confronting well-established industry participants, but they are also actively influencing and molding the expectations of customers. The ongoing advancement of AI technology presents significant opportunities for continued disruption and the realization of hyper-personalization. Entrepreneurs are positioned to persistently redefine markets and enhance customer experiences, thereby establishing this transition as a fundamental aspect of entrepreneurial capitalism during the era of artificial intelligence.

Data-Driven Decision-Making

Artificial intelligence (AI) enables entrepreneurs to enhance their decision-making capabilities by leveraging data-driven approaches. Start-up companies have the ability to utilize artificial intelligence (AI) algorithms in order to efficiently analyze large datasets, thereby acquiring valuable insights that inform strategic decision-making. AI-driven analytics play a crucial role in aiding companies in making well-informed decisions that aim to reduce risks and optimize revenues, including various aspects such as streamlining supply chains and assessing market trends. The adoption of a data-centric approach significantly alters the manner in which entrepreneurs approach market strategies and risk management.

The significance of artificial intelligence (AI) in facilitating data-driven decision-making signifies a significant paradigm shift in the realm of entrepreneurship. This change exhibits various crucial aspects that underscore its significance. To begin with, the velocity and magnitude at which artificial intelligence (AI) conducts data processing are unsurpassed. Start-up companies possess the capability to efficiently process and examine extensive volumes of data in real-time, so enabling the acquisition of valuable insights that were previously unachievable. This enables entrepreneurs to make agile and well-informed decisions. In the domain of e-commerce, companies have the ability to employ artificial intelligence (AI) for real-time analysis of customer behavior. This enables them to dynamically adapt pricing, marketing methods, and product recommendations in accordance with evolving trends and consumer preferences. Furthermore, artificial intelligence enables a detailed comprehension of markets and client behavior. Start-up companies have the ability to utilize artificial intelligence (AI) in order to accurately segment their target audience, thereby uncovering certain niches and subgroups that may have been disregarded using conventional methodologies. The degree of understanding achieved enables the implementation of precise marketing initiatives, product advancement, and tactics for engaging with customers.

Furthermore, the utilization of artificial intelligence in data analysis extends beyond simple observation, since it provides prediction capabilities. Start-up companies have the capacity to utilize artificial intelligence (AI) in order to predict and anticipate market trends, patterns of demand, as well as potential hazards. The ability to make accurate predictions boosts the effectiveness of risk management strategies and enables businesses to proactively address market fluctuations. In the transportation sector, artificial intelligence (AI) has the capability to anticipate maintenance requirements for vehicles, thereby assisting startups in mitigating the financial burden associated with breakdowns and operational interruptions.

Fundamentally, the utilization of artificial intelligence (AI) enables entrepreneurs to reinvent their approach to market strategies and risk management through data-driven decision-making. The aforementioned attributes, including agility, precision, and foresight, serve to enhance the competitive advantage of startups. The ongoing progress and increasing availability of AI technologies will continue to uphold data-driven decision-making as a fundamental aspect of entrepreneurial capitalism, leading to the transformation of various industries and the promotion of innovation.

Cost Efficiency and Automation

The automation potential of AI brings about a profound transformation in the operational dynamics of companies. The automation of routine and time-consuming processes has the potential to save personnel expenses and enhance operational effectiveness. The cost-effectiveness of this approach provides significant benefits for startups, enabling them to optimize resource allocation and achieve rapid scalability without the requirement of significant labor increase. Consequently, startups have the potential to attain enhanced competitiveness and adaptability inside the market.

The importance of artificial intelligence (AI) in enhancing cost efficiency and enabling automation signifies a transformative and revolutionary shift in the paradigm for startups. This revolution comprises various crucial elements that are redefining the landscape of entrepreneurial capitalism. First and foremost, the implementation of artificial intelligence (AI) in automation optimizes operational processes by minimizing the need for manual engagement in repetitive and time-consuming tasks. One example of how artificial intelligence (AI) can be utilized is through the implementation of chatbots, which are capable of addressing consumer enquiries and providing help. This application of AI technology can effectively minimize the requirement for large customer service personnel. In the field of manufacturing, artificial intelligence (AI) can be integrated into robotic systems to facilitate the execution of complex tasks, thereby guaranteeing a high level of consistency in terms of both quality and efficiency.

The outcome encompasses not only financial savings but also improved operational effectiveness. Start-up enterprises possess the ability to strategically deploy resources, with a particular emphasis on domains necessitating human creativity, problem-solving capabilities, and innovative approaches. The reallocation of resources facilitates the development of a streamlined and adaptable organizational framework, which confers notable benefits on startups operating under resource constraints. Furthermore, the utilization of AI-driven automation allows businesses to achieve quick scalability without the conventional requirement of significant personnel augmentation. Scalability plays a crucial role in the contemporary corporate environment characterized by rapid changes and high speed. For example, e-commerce firms have the ability to effectively manage a significant increase in orders during peak seasons by employing inventory management and order processing systems that are powered by artificial intelligence (AI). The capacity to effectively adjust to market needs significantly boosts an organization's competitiveness and responsiveness.

The use of artificial intelligence (AI) in enhancing cost efficiency and automation is a fundamental aspect of entrepreneurial capitalism in the current AI era. Start-up enterprises have the capacity to accomplish bigger outcomes while utilizing little resources, exhibit enhanced flexibility in their operations, and effectively contend in rapidly evolving markets. The ongoing advancement and increasing availability of AI technologies are anticipated to have a profound effect on cost effectiveness and the automation of processes, hence exerting a greater influence on the entrepreneurial capitalist environment.

Innovative Business Models

The impact of artificial intelligence extends to the development of novel business models. Entrepreneurs now have access to subscription-based services, sharing economies, and AI-driven marketplaces. These innovative models have the potential to disrupt established sectors, hence allowing startups to penetrate markets that were previously unexplored. The phenomenon of entrepreneurial capitalism is undergoing a transformation as emerging entrepreneurs use the power of artificial intelligence (AI) to revolutionize many sectors and reinvent the processes by which value is generated and traded.

The impact of artificial intelligence (AI) on novel business models is a fundamental aspect of the evolutionary trajectory of entrepreneurial capitalism. The aforementioned change is supported by various crucial components that emphasize the significance of artificial intelligence (AI) in restructuring industries and business strategies. First and foremost, artificial intelligence (AI) facilitates the development of innovative business models that were previously unachievable. Subscription-based services utilize artificial intelligence algorithms to tailor their offerings, hence enhancing their attractiveness to clients. Start-up enterprises have the capacity to provide customized subscription services across diverse sectors, encompassing areas such as entertainment and individualized healthcare programs. The outcome entails the generation of recurring revenue and the cultivation of stronger client loyalty, so fundamentally transforming conventional revenue models.

Additionally, artificial intelligence (AI) plays a crucial role in enabling the development of sharing economies, wherein there is an efficient allocation of unused assets to meet the existing demand. AI-driven peer-to-peer platforms facilitate the connection between users, enabling various services such as ride-sharing, lodging sharing, and equipment rental. These platforms have the potential to disrupt well-established sectors, hence providing opportunities for startups to enter and exploit previously unexplored areas. The expansion of the sharing economy can be attributed to the smooth matching of supply and demand facilitated by artificial intelligence, which also plays a crucial role in assuring trust and safety.

Furthermore, marketplaces powered by artificial intelligence (AI) are reshaping the processes through which value is generated and traded. Online marketplaces that are equipped with artificial intelligence (AI) algorithms have the capability to offer individualized product recommendations, hence boosting the overall user experience. These platforms facilitate the empowerment of startups by enabling them to effectively access a worldwide audience and swiftly build their market presence. For example, e-commerce firms have the opportunity to utilize AI-driven marketplaces in order to establish connections with potential customers on a global scale. This enables them to provide a wide array of products that are specifically customized to meet the individual preferences of consumers.

The impact of artificial intelligence on creative company models is fundamentally reshaping the landscape of entrepreneurial capitalism. Startups equipped with artificial intelligence (AI) capabilities are causing significant disruptions in various industries, as they successfully penetrate new markets and revolutionize the processes of value creation and exchange. This change highlights the ever-changing character of entrepreneurial capitalism in the era of artificial intelligence, wherein cutting-edge technologies and innovative business models drive the process of innovation and value generation. The ongoing progress of artificial intelligence (AI) presents significant opportunities for substantial disruption and innovation within business paradigms.

Challenges to Entrepreneurial Capitalism

The various challenges presented by artificial intelligence (AI) to the framework of entrepreneurial capitalism necessitate a more in-depth analysis. The obstacles associated with artificial intelligence (AI), however substantial, are closely connected to the potential opportunities it offers. This underscores the imperative for entrepreneurs to effectively negotiate the intricate terrain of AI with agility and accountability.

First and foremost, ethical questions play a significant role in the era of artificial intelligence. The utilization of artificial intelligence (AI) inside the realm of entrepreneurship gives rise to inquiries pertaining to algorithmic prejudice, safeguarding data privacy, and the wider societal ramifications associated with automation. Entrepreneurs are confronted with ethical quandaries in their pursuit of AI-driven advancements. The paramount need of developing and utilizing AI technologies responsibly is heightened, particularly in light of increasing public scrutiny.

Furthermore, the presence of talent shortages within the field of artificial intelligence presents a substantial obstacle for entrepreneurs. The demand for specialists in the field of artificial intelligence (AI) frequently exceeds the available supply, resulting in intense competition for individuals possessing the necessary expertise. Start-up enterprises may encounter challenges in the recruitment and retention of proficient professionals in the field of artificial intelligence (AI), hence impeding their capacity to effectively leverage the full potential of AI. This challenge highlights the significance of allocating resources towards the enhancement of talent development and cultivating partnerships with academic institutions.

Moreover, the dynamic and swiftly changing regulatory environment pertaining to artificial intelligence introduces an additional level of intricacy. Entrepreneurs are faced with the challenge of navigating the uncertainties around data privacy legislation, the transparency of algorithms, and the issue of liability in accidents related to artificial intelligence. The complex regulatory landscape requires companies to possess legal knowledge and allocate resources, resulting in higher operational costs.

The financial commitment necessary to venture into the field of artificial intelligence can be significant. Although artificial intelligence (AI) has the potential to democratize innovation, it is important to acknowledge that startups still require adequate resources to support their infrastructure, facilitate data collecting, and enable AI training. Obtaining these resources might pose difficulties, especially for nascent enterprises in their first stages with constrained financial resources. The potential for automation in AI also gives rise to concerns regarding the displacement of jobs. Entrepreneurs are need to take into account the societal and economic ramifications of their initiatives that are powered by artificial intelligence (AI). The presence of opposition from stakeholders who express concerns regarding potential job losses might provide a significant obstacle that must be addressed. Finally, it is imperative to prioritize data privacy and security concerns. It is imperative for startups to give utmost importance to the implementation of comprehensive cybersecurity protocols, since the effective functioning of artificial intelligence (AI) is significantly reliant on the integrity and security of data. The occurrence of data breaches and instances of data misuse can result in negative impacts on an organization's reputation and legal ramifications, hence emphasizing the significance of practicing responsible data management.

In summary, the utilization of artificial intelligence (AI) holds considerable potential for driving significant changes in the realm of entrepreneurial capitalism. However, it also introduces a multifaceted array of obstacles and difficulties. The obstacles cover a range of factors including ethical considerations, talent-related issues, regulatory concerns, financial implications, societal impacts, and data privacy considerations. Entrepreneurs are required to effectively manage the aforementioned challenges, all the while leveraging the advantages offered by artificial intelligence. It is crucial to underscore the importance of adaptability, responsible innovation, and a proactive stance in order to effectively tackle these challenges within the context of the entrepreneurial landscape in the era of AI.

Conclusion

The breakthroughs of artificial intelligence are facilitating the emergence of a novel era for entrepreneurial capitalism. Startups equipped with artificial intelligence (AI) capabilities are causing significant disruptions in various markets by customizing user experiences, employing data-driven decision-making processes, and functioning with exceptional efficiency. Nevertheless, this conversion is not devoid of its obstacles. Entrepreneurs are faced with the imperative of striking a delicate equilibrium between the prospective advantages of artificial intelligence (AI) and the ethical, regulatory, and societal factors that come into play. The ongoing evolution of artificial intelligence (AI) will inevitably bring about changes in the dynamics of entrepreneurial capitalism. This shifting landscape will present a range of prospects and obstacles for innovative businesses operating within the AI era.

Chapter 24: AI and Market Disruption

In the field of contemporary economics, the emergence of Artificial Intelligence (AI) represents a significant and transformative milestone. The impact of artificial intelligence extends well beyond its ability to enhance efficiency and enhance human capabilities. It has emerged as a powerful catalyst for market disruption, posing challenges to conventional frameworks and fundamentally transforming the business environment. As we commence our exploration of this chapter, we delve into the tremendous capacity of artificial intelligence (AI) to bring about transformation in current market systems and established corporations. This study investigates the manner in which institutions exert their influence in effectively managing these disruptions, so promoting seamless transitions in the era of artificial intelligence. Additionally, we critically examine the potential consequences for capitalist economies. Furthermore, an analysis is conducted on the various approaches that individuals, corporations, and governments might utilize in order to adjust and prosper in a society characterized by market disruptions driven by artificial intelligence.

The notion of market disruption has long been a prominent topic in the fields of economics and business, spanning numerous decades. Throughout history, significant advancements such as the steam engine, assembly line, and internet have instigated profound transformations, resulting in the emergence of both beneficiaries and those adversely affected by these developments. Artificial intelligence (AI) has revolutionized market disruption by leveraging its exceptional data processing abilities, predictive capacities, and capacity to automate intricate operations. The distinguishing characteristic of artificial intelligence is in its capacity for ongoing learning and adaptation, enabling it to surpass and outperform even the most firmly established incumbents. The democratization of innovation is the core element that underlies this potential for disruption. The accessibility of AI tools and platforms has significantly reduced the obstacles faced by entrepreneurs and startups, granting them the ability to leverage the capabilities of machine learning, data analytics, and automation. The utilization of artificial intelligence (AI) is significantly transforming industries that were previously perceived as resistant to change, through the facilitation of agility and creativity. This chapter delves into the ways in which artificial intelligence (AI) enables startups to effectively compete against established industry leaders, hence promoting a dynamic competitive landscape and fundamentally altering the dynamics of various industries.

In the current epoch characterized by market disruption caused by artificial intelligence (AI), institutions assume a crucial and central position. Governments, regulatory organizations, educational institutions, and industry associations are tasked with the complex challenge of managing the interplay between promoting innovation and safeguarding public interests. Academic institutions and researchers are responsible for formulating policies, regulations, and ethical frameworks that establish the parameters in which artificial intelligence (AI) functions. In this transformative process, institutions play a crucial role as active participants rather than just observers. They exert influence on the trajectory of market disruptions and strive to ensure that these disruptions take place within a framework that is both ethical and regulatory in nature.

The advent of artificial intelligence (AI) has given rise to significant market upheavals, prompting critical inquiries into the potential ramifications for capitalist economies. What strategies will established organizations employ to effectively respond to competition driven by artificial intelligence? What implications will the integration of artificial intelligence (AI) have on jobs and the labor market? Can traditional market structures and business models effectively endure the disruptive impacts of artificial intelligence, or will they necessitate adaptation and evolution? This chapter explores the intricate nature of these concerns, offering valuable perspectives on the possible ramifications and approaches for effectively maneuvering across the evolving terrain. Finally, we examine the various approaches that individuals, corporations, and governments might adopt in order to prosper in the face of market disruptions caused by artificial intelligence. There exist various strategies that can enable individuals and organizations to not only endure but also thrive in the era of artificial intelligence. These strategies encompass activities such as retraining employees to acquire new skills, embracing technological advancements, and cultivating a flexible and adaptable organizational culture. The last section of the chapter underscores the significance of proactive measures and the pivotal role played by institutions in ensuring a seamless transition into a future that is driven by artificial intelligence (AI).

In the course of traversing the contents of this chapter, we engage in a comprehensive examination of the considerable transformative capabilities of artificial intelligence (AI) within markets, the significance of institutions in effectively addressing these disruptions, and the strategic approaches that might effectively steer individuals and nations towards a successful trajectory in the era of AI. The current state of the terrain is undergoing significant transformation, accompanied by considerable obstacles. However, amidst this dynamic upheaval, there exists the potential for novel advancements, forward movement, and unparalleled prospects.

The disruptive potential of AI on existing market structures and established firms

Artificial Intelligence (AI) represents a significant technological and economic transformation, with the potential to disrupt prevailing market systems and have profound effects on several industries. The impact of this phenomenon is of such magnitude that it is frequently denoted as the "fourth industrial revolution." This definition is appropriate, as the capabilities of artificial intelligence (AI) have extensive ramifications that encompass data analysis, automation, innovation, and personalization. These implications are causing significant changes in the corporate landscapes of many sectors. The disruptive potential of artificial intelligence (AI) arises from its unprecedented capacity to leverage data. The system possesses the capability to efficiently handle, examine, and extract practical knowledge from extensive datasets with remarkable speed. The adoption of a data-centric approach enables firms to enhance their decision-making capabilities, streamline operations, and attain a competitive advantage within their respective markets.

The disruptive impact of artificial intelligence (AI) is fundamentally rooted in the democratization of innovation. Throughout history, the realm of innovation has predominantly been occupied by established firms possessing substantial financial resources to allocate significant investments towards research and development endeavors. Artificial intelligence (AI), however, has fundamentally disrupted this conventional concept. The advent of cloud-based artificial intelligence (AI) services, open-source AI libraries, and easily available AI platforms has facilitated the utilization of AI capabilities by startups and individual entrepreneurs, eliminating the need for substantial financial resources. The equalization of opportunities has stimulated a vibrant competitive environment, wherein emerging entrepreneurs are contesting the prevailing dominance of well-established industry leaders.

In sectors characterized by a strong dependence on data analysis and decision-making processes driven by data, such as banking and healthcare, artificial intelligence (AI) is generating substantial market upheaval. Artificial intelligence (AI)-based algorithms possess the capability to analyze financial data in real-time, hence providing valuable insights for investment decisions that frequently exhibit superior performance compared to conventional tactics. Artificial intelligence (AI) is revolutionizing the field of healthcare by significantly impacting diagnostic processes and the development of individualized treatment suggestions, thereby altering traditional medical approaches. The retail industry is also undergoing a comparable change, as recommendation algorithms are being utilized to offer customers exceptionally tailored shopping experiences, hence changing prevailing marketing techniques. Hyper-personalization is an additional aspect of the disruptive influence of artificial intelligence (AI). This innovation is fundamentally transforming the manner in which firms engage with their clientele. The conventional methods of mass production and generic marketing are being substituted by the implementation of highly individualized products. Artificial intelligence (AI) employs recommendation systems, chatbots, and predictive analytics to customize products and services according to the unique tastes of each customer. The degree of customization observed in this context promotes client allegiance and poses difficulties for conventional competitors, given that individuals are progressively drawn to enterprises that cater to their distinct requirements.

For well-established companies, the disruption caused by AI poses a critical juncture where they must either adapt or risk becoming obsolete. The reluctance to embrace AI-driven transformations can result in a decline in market share and a diminished competitive edge. As a result, some well-established corporations are allocating significant resources towards the pursuit of AI research and development. Their objective is to incorporate AI technologies into their fundamental business practices, thereby preserving their market standing and venturing into novel pathways for expansion. The dynamics of competition are undergoing fast evolution as established enterprises face rising challenges from AI-driven startups. In order to succeed in the emerging AI-driven marketplace, incumbents are required to adeptly navigate the dynamic changes, effectively managing the preservation of their current market share while simultaneously embracing innovation. The current situation has led to an increase in partnerships between well-established companies and startups, as the former seeks to leverage the agility and innovative capabilities of the latter in order to maintain competitiveness.

The disruptive potential of artificial intelligence (AI) is not confined solely to the modification of market dynamics, but rather encompasses the fundamental underpinnings of business models. Subscription-based services, sharing economies, and AI-driven marketplaces have emerged as feasible alternatives for businesses. These novel models have the potential to disrupt established sectors, hence allowing startups to penetrate markets that were previously unexplored. The phenomenon of entrepreneurial capitalism is currently experiencing a significant shift, wherein startups are utilizing artificial intelligence (AI) to fundamentally alter several industries and reinvent the processes through which value is generated and transferred. Nevertheless, the disruptive potential of artificial intelligence (AI) is accompanied by a series of noteworthy problems and considerations. The debate of ethical considerations surrounding algorithmic prejudice, data privacy, and the societal implications of automation necessitates careful consideration. The presence of talent deficits in the field of artificial intelligence (AI) presents significant recruitment obstacles for both emerging startups and well-established companies. The intricate regulatory framework pertaining to artificial intelligence necessitates the presence of legal competence and adequate resources. Startups sometimes face significant challenges in terms of initial investments required for the establishment of AI infrastructure, data collection, and training. In addition, the potential for automation by AI has the capacity to disrupt conventional labor markets, hence requiring meticulous examination of the social and economic ramifications. Robust cybersecurity measures are crucial in addressing the concerns surrounding data privacy and security.

In summary, the unquestionable disruptive potential of artificial intelligence (AI) on existing market structures and established enterprises has been established. The democratization of innovation, utilization of data-driven decision-making, and implementation of hyper-personalization capabilities are already causing significant transformations within several industries, ultimately changing the dynamics of competitiveness. Artificial intelligence (AI) poses considerable problems to established entities, although it also promises transformative prospects for those who are open to adaptation and embracing the future shaped by AI. The ongoing advancement of AI technology will increasingly affect market structures and existing enterprises, hence emphasizing the importance of adaptation and innovation as crucial factors for achieving success in this developing environment. The upcoming years hold a combination of unpredictability and exceptional possibilities as artificial intelligence (AI) continues to change the parameters of the commercial landscape. This development lays the foundation for a novel period of creativity and rivalry, which will significantly influence the trajectory of various industries and economies.

The role of institutions in managing market disruptions and facilitating smooth transitions in the AI era

The emergence of Artificial Intelligence (AI) signifies a significant paradigm shift in the realms of commerce and technology. The disruptive potential of AI has had a pervasive impact across various sectors, resulting in the restructuring of market dynamics, questioning long-standing conventions, and cultivating a climate conducive to innovation and competitive dynamics. In the current period characterized by rapid and transformative changes, institutions have assumed a critical role as facilitators, guiding society through the tumultuous waters of market disruption and facilitating a more seamless transition into the era of artificial intelligence. This extensive investigation delves into a thorough examination of the diverse function of institutions in the era of artificial intelligence. The aforementioned responsibilities include the crucial task of managing disruptions in the market, developing legal frameworks, fostering innovation, and ensuring fair and equal access to the benefits of artificial intelligence.

AI's Disruptive Influence on Markets

The extensive impact of artificial intelligence (AI) has resulted in a fundamental transformation of various industries and a significant reconfiguration of competitive dynamics. Established firms, which were formerly deeply entrenched in their respective markets, are already facing significant challenges posed by agile startups powered by artificial intelligence (AI). The current shift in paradigm necessitates incumbents to display adaptation and innovation in order to sustain their competitive edge. However, in the midst of this surge of technological disruption, institutions arise as stabilizing forces, offering direction and assistance in navigating these ever-changing market dynamics.

In tackling the various difficulties provided by market disruptions produced by artificial intelligence (AI), institutions assume a central role. Ethical considerations have emerged as a prominent focal point, as issues surrounding algorithmic prejudice, privacy violations, and the societal implications of automation have gained significant attention. Institutions play a crucial role in upholding ethical frameworks, thereby ensuring the responsible and transparent development and deployment of artificial intelligence (AI)

•

Regulatory Frameworks for Ethical AI

The regulatory environment is experiencing a significant shift in reaction to the rapid progress of artificial intelligence. In the realm of artificial intelligence (AI), several entities such as governmental bodies and specialized regulatory agencies bear the responsibility of formulating the regulations that regulate the utilization of AI. The scope of these legislation encompasses a diverse range of issues, including the protection of data privacy, the promotion of algorithmic openness, and the establishment of liability in situations involving mishaps connected to artificial intelligence. The appropriate and ethical utilization of AI requires the experience of legal professionals, adequate resources, and careful supervision, all of which are provided by institutions to effectively navigate this complex landscape.

In the era of artificial intelligence (AI), institutions play a crucial role as catalysts for innovation. They are essential in facilitating successful market transitions among the disruptions caused by AI. Public entities frequently commit significant resources to finance research and development in the field of artificial intelligence (AI), therefore advancing technological boundaries and stimulating economic expansion. The organization establishes innovation hubs, allocates funding to support pioneering research activities, and offers awards to startups that are at the forefront of AI innovation. Private entities, such as venture capital firms and technology accelerators, engage in the identification of prospective artificial intelligence (AI) businesses and provide them with the necessary financial support and mentorship to foster their development. Institutions play a dual role as both supporters and catalysts of innovation, driving the evolution of markets and industries.

Access to AI's Benefits

In the democratization of AI's benefits, institutions play a crucial role. The emergence of AI in various industries gives rise to the possibility for societal inequalities. In this context, educational and training activities are implemented by institutions with the objective of equalizing opportunities. It is widely acknowledged that in the era of artificial intelligence, providing individuals with the requisite skills is of utmost importance. An essential aspect that warrants attention is the mitigation of the digital gap. In order to promote equitable access to the benefits of artificial intelligence (AI), institutions make concerted efforts to ensure that individuals from all socioeconomic backgrounds are able to avail themselves of these advantages. By mitigating obstacles to entry, they foster inclusiveness and empower individuals from various socio-cultural backgrounds to engage in and make valuable contributions to the workforce driven by artificial intelligence.

Institutions, in partnership with both governmental and non-governmental organisations, also endeavor to establish avenues for lifelong learning. It is acknowledged that the rapid progress of artificial intelligence necessitates continuous skill development and adaptation. As a result, institutions are dedicated to offering the necessary resources and support to ensure that all individuals have an opportunity to derive advantages from the profound impact of artificial intelligence.

International Cooperation and Standards

In addition to their significant presence, institutions also assume a pivotal role in the global arena by facilitating collaboration and the development of universal benchmarks for artificial intelligence (AI). Given the absence of geographical limitations, it is imperative to foster international cooperation in order to establish regulatory consistency, tackle the challenges associated with cross-border data transfer, and establish a comprehensive framework that promotes responsible development and implementation of artificial intelligence (AI) technology. In the domain of international collaboration and standards for artificial intelligence (AI), institutions exert substantial impact. In a globally interconnected society, the significance of artificial intelligence (AI) is elevated as it surpasses geographical limitations. They function as facilitators, promoting cooperation among governments and organizations on an international scale.

In order to achieve coherence in the legislation pertaining to artificial intelligence (AI) at the international level, institutions engage in diplomatic channels and collaborative initiatives with unwavering dedication. The individuals involved acknowledge the importance of establishing a comprehensive structure to effectively handle the intricate nature of international data transfers. This framework aims to safeguard data privacy and security, while also promoting the responsible advancement and implementation of artificial intelligence technology. Furthermore, it can be argued that institutions play a pivotal role in promoting responsible development of artificial intelligence (AI) on a worldwide scale. They play a crucial role in fostering dialogues and mediations that result in the formulation and implementation of ethical principles and benchmarks. Institutions play a crucial role in establishing a comprehensive international framework that facilitates countries in effectively navigating the era of artificial intelligence (AI). This framework is characterized by a collective dedication to principles of openness, fairness, and ethical considerations. By engaging in such actions, individuals contribute to the worldwide realization of the advantages of artificial intelligence, while simultaneously addressing and minimizing any risks and problems.

Institutional Flexibility and Adaptability

In the context of a swiftly developing artificial intelligence (AI) environment, it is imperative for institutions to demonstrate a high degree of flexibility and adaptation. It is imperative that individuals maintain a state of constant vigilance in monitoring the progress of artificial intelligence (AI) and make necessary adaptations to regulatory frameworks in order to effectively accommodate the emergence of new technologies. This must be done while simultaneously ensuring that ethical issues are upheld and protected. In the context of the rapidly evolving field of artificial intelligence, academic institutions are confronted with the crucial necessity of possessing a high degree of flexibility and adaptability. They serve as the adaptable stabilizers of a continuously developing ecosystem, aware of the need to stay up to date with fast-paced technological progress.

Institutions acknowledge that the trajectory of artificial intelligence (AI) is dynamic rather than static. The continuous progression of innovation necessitates unwavering attentiveness and a proactive approach. They actively participate in continuous monitoring of breakthroughs in artificial intelligence, conscientiously keeping track of developing technologies and their possible ramifications for both society and markets. As the emergence of new AI applications takes place, institutions exercise their regulatory jurisdiction with meticulousness. They actively assume the position of facilitators, modifying regulatory frameworks to accept and support creative breakthroughs, all the while maintaining a steadfast commitment to preserving ethical issues. The capacity to adapt exhibited by artificial intelligence (AI) guarantees the responsible utilization of its transformational capabilities, while also ensuring that it remains in accordance with the changing requirements of society. In the AI era, institutions play a crucial role by serving as a guiding force for ethical and regulatory decision-making, ensuring that these decisions align with the dynamic technical landscape. The capacity to effectively reconcile innovation with responsibility is a defining characteristic that plays a crucial role in setting the trajectory of AI-driven markets and economies.

Promoting Ethical AI

Institutions advocate for the advancement of ethical artificial intelligence. The experts, organizations, and stakeholders are brought together to engage in the collaborative process of formulating rules and codes of behavior that regulate the ethical utilization of artificial intelligence. In addition, they develop methods for conducting audits and providing certifications for AI systems, thereby ensuring their adherence to the aforementioned ethical norms. The promotion of ethical artificial intelligence (AI) is a crucial objective for institutions operating in the AI era. It is acknowledged that while the possibilities of artificial intelligence are remarkable, the appropriate utilization of this technology is paramount. Institutions, in their role as custodians of ethical AI development, adopt a proactive approach to influence the moral orientation of the AI-driven environment. In order to foster collaboration and knowledge exchange, institutions leverage their ability to convene and assemble a wide array of experts, organizations, and stakeholders from many sectors. By means of collaborative endeavors, they facilitate the formulation of comprehensive standards and codes of conduct that regulate the ethical utilization of artificial intelligence. These recommendations function as guiding principles, directing AI developers and users towards responsible behaviors that stress openness, justice, and responsibility. In addition, institutions implement stringent methods to conduct audits and provide certifications for artificial intelligence (AI) systems. These methods function as gatekeepers, guaranteeing that AI applications conform to the ethical norms established. Institutions employ audits and certifications to offer a degree of confidence to users and consumers, so cultivating trust in artificial intelligence (AI) technologies and promoting responsible advancement.

Institutions have a crucial and central role in advocating for the ethical implementation of artificial intelligence. The proactive endeavors undertaken by individuals or organizations to set ethical principles and certification processes serve to foster responsible development of artificial intelligence (AI), thus facilitating a balanced cohabitation between cutting-edge technology and social values.

Mitigating Bias and Discrimination

Addressing bias and discrimination in AI systems is a paramount concern for institutions operating in the era of artificial intelligence. It is acknowledged that artificial intelligence (AI) has the potential to yield significant progress, yet it can also accidentally sustain bias and discrimination if not effectively controlled. Consequently, organizations proactively undertake endeavors to guarantee the fairness and impartiality of artificial intelligence (AI) technologies. In addressing this difficulty, institutions adopt a multifaceted strategy. They play a crucial role in the development of comprehensive protocols for addressing bias in AI systems. These standards cover various areas, including data collecting, algorithmic design, model training, and deployment. Institutions play a crucial role in enabling AI engineers to effectively mitigate bias across the whole lifecycle of the technology by offering explicit and implementable suggestions.

Transparency is an additional focal point of importance. Institutions actively support the idea of enhancing transparency in AI algorithms, so encouraging the disclosure of information regarding the data sources and decision-making procedures that underlie AI systems. The transparency of AI technology not only serves to improve accountability, but also facilitates external inspection, enabling stakeholders to evaluate the fairness of these technologies. In addition, institutions advocate for the promotion of justice in the decision-making processes of artificial intelligence. The authors place significant emphasis on the significance of achieving fair outcomes and advocate for the advancement of artificial intelligence (AI) systems that refrain from engaging in discriminatory practices against individuals or groups on the basis of race, gender, or other legally safeguarded attributes.

In summary, it may be argued that institutions play a vital role in addressing and reducing bias and discrimination within the field of artificial intelligence. The endeavors undertaken by the individuals involve the formation of guidelines, the promotion of transparency, and the advocacy for justice. These efforts are all directed towards the objective of ensuring that artificial intelligence (AI) technologies are created and used in a manner that adheres to societal values and principles of equity.

AI in Education

In the integration of artificial intelligence (AI) into education systems, institutions hold considerable sway, acknowledging the profound capacity of AI to shape the future labor force. The responsibilities of this position are diverse, include the development of educational programs, fostering partnerships, and equipping students for occupations influenced by artificial intelligence. In the initial stages, institutions proactively cultivate alliances with educational entities, encompassing schools, colleges, and universities. These collaborations serve to facilitate the integration of AI courses into educational programs at multiple levels. The curricula have been meticulously crafted to offer students a holistic comprehension of artificial intelligence principles, practical implementations, and ethical deliberations.

Institutions collaborate closely with academic establishments to ensure that students are adequately equipped for occupations that include artificial intelligence. The acknowledgement is made that the future labor force will necessitate proficiency in AI-related competencies, thereby advocating for the integration of AI education into established academic institutions. By engaging in this practice, educational institutions provide students with the necessary competencies and information required to excel in a society where artificial intelligence is becoming more prevalent. In addition, organizations place significant emphasis on the significance of artificial intelligence (AI) in promoting societal welfare. Educational institutions are encouraged to imbue pupils with the principles of ethical AI development and responsible AI utilization. This not only equips students for professions in AI but also guarantees that they engage with AI in a manner that is ethically sound, so promoting the responsible advancement and utilization of AI technology.

In essence, institutions assume a crucial role in influencing the incorporation of artificial intelligence (AI) into the field of education. The endeavors undertaken by the individuals involved go beyond the mere production of educational programs, as they also involve establishing collaborative relationships, preparing individuals for the job market, and fostering the adoption of ethical ideals in the field of artificial intelligence. By implementing these initiatives, educational institutions actively contribute to a prospective reality in which AI education becomes readily available, enabling students to acquire the necessary skills and knowledge to effectively utilize AI technology for the advancement and improvement of society.

Support for AI Startups

Institutions prioritize the support of AI startups due to their recognition of the significant role these businesses play in promoting innovation and stimulating economic growth within the AI era. Institutions play an active role in offering several sorts of assistance to foster the development and achievement of these fledgling enterprises. One of the principal means by which institutions support artificial intelligence (AI) companies is through the provision of financial possibilities. The organization allocates financial resources, grants, and funding programs that are specifically designed to provide support to companies engaged in projects linked to artificial intelligence (AI). The provision of financial support plays a vital role in sustaining startups, since it empowers them to allocate resources towards activities such as research, development, and the expansion of their creative products.

In addition to providing financial assistance, institutions often provide mentorship programs. Experienced professionals, who are frequently associated with institutions or have established connections within their networks, offer assistance and mentorship to founders of artificial intelligence (AI) startups. The mentorship program encompasses strategic guidance, assistance with business development, and valuable insights towards effectively navigating the intricate realm of AI entrepreneurship. In addition, schools offer entrepreneurs the opportunity to utilize research and development resources. This might also entail establishing collaborations with academic organizations like as universities, research institutions, or dedicated artificial intelligence laboratories. Start-up enterprises have the opportunity to utilize these resources in order to gain access to state-of-the-art research, conduct experimentation on their artificial intelligence models, and engage in collaborative endeavors focused on pioneering projects. The provision of such access expedites their progress and augments their level of competitiveness.

In summary, institutions play a crucial role in facilitating the success of AI startups. The scope of their support includes providing financial aid, mentorship, and facilitating access to significant research and development resources. Institutions play a significant role in fostering the development of AI startups, thereby enhancing the dynamism of the AI ecosystem and propelling advancements in innovation and economic well-being during the era of artificial intelligence.

Ensuring Data Privacy

In the current era of artificial intelligence (AI), institutions acknowledge the significant significance of data privacy and assume a leading role in formulating and implementing rules aimed at protecting individuals' rights pertaining to their data. The recognition of the increasing prevalence of AI necessitates the prioritization of responsible data management in order to establish confidence and guarantee adherence to stringent privacy regulations in AI applications. In order to mitigate these issues, organizations use a proactive approach by developing policies and norms pertaining to data privacy. The purpose of these legislation is to establish explicit criteria for the manner in which businesses, particularly those employing artificial intelligence, acquire, manipulate, retain, and distribute data. Frequently, these regulations encompass explicit permission requirements, data anonymization protocols, and data breach reporting obligations, alongside other significant stipulations.

Furthermore, these policies are enforced by institutions through the implementation of supervision mechanisms and regulatory organizations. These regulatory agencies are responsible for overseeing enterprises' adherence to data privacy regulations, conducting investigations into breaches, and enforcing sanctions for instances of non-compliance. The existence of these regulatory procedures acts as a disincentive against the inappropriate use of data and strengthens the significance of safeguarding data privacy. In addition, institutions also promote and advocate for transparency in the processes related to the handling of data. They urge for companies, such as AI developers and startups, to promote transparency by providing explicit elucidations regarding the utilization of data, and to empower individuals by granting them autonomy over their own data. The establishment of transparency fosters confidence among users and guarantees the ethical and responsible development and utilization of AI technologies.

In the AI era, it is evident that institutions play a crucial and central role in safeguarding data privacy. By implementing and enforcing legislation, conducting supervision, and advocating for transparency, a framework is established to safeguard individuals' data rights and ensure that AI applications adhere to rigorous privacy standards. This promotes the development of trust and the implementation of ethical data practices inside the AI ecosystem.

AI in Healthcare

In the domain of healthcare, institutions assume a pivotal role in facilitating the responsible utilization of artificial intelligence. The individuals acknowledge the considerable capacity of artificial intelligence (AI) to enhance medical diagnosis, treatment, and patient care. Simultaneously, they acknowledge the importance of protecting patient data and ensuring that AI-based medical solutions comply with rigorous regulatory standards. The construction and implementation of regulatory frameworks are regarded as crucial functions of institutions within this particular setting. These frameworks establish the criteria by which the application of AI in healthcare contexts can be evaluated. AI-driven medical solutions incorporate several components such as data privacy rules, ethical principles, and clinical validation requirements in order to guarantee the safety and effectiveness of these solutions.

In addition, organizations endeavor to develop regulatory bodies tasked with overseeing the adoption of artificial intelligence (AI) inside the healthcare sector. These entities assess the accuracy, fairness, and clinical usefulness of AI systems. AI technologies undergo thorough testing and validation procedures to guarantee their integration into clinical practice is accompanied by a rigorous approach, hence mitigating possible hazards to patients. In addition, institutions prioritize the protection of data security and the confidentiality of patient information. Regulations are formulated by regulatory bodies to provide mandatory protocols for the secure management of patient data, encompassing electronic health records. In order to safeguard sensitive patient information from breaches and unauthorized access, these requirements necessitate the implementation of encryption, access controls, and data anonymization measures. Furthermore, organizations actively foster collaboration among healthcare professionals, producers of artificial intelligence (AI), and academics. The organization promotes collaborations that assist the advancement and verification of artificial intelligence-driven medical solutions. By cultivating these partnerships, institutions guarantee that the implementation of artificial intelligence in healthcare is both pioneering and subject to rigorous examination and validation.

In essence, institutions play a crucial role in allowing the responsible utilization of artificial intelligence (AI) within the healthcare domain. The presence of robust legislative frameworks, effective oversight mechanisms, and a strong focus on data security and patient privacy inside their healthcare systems establish conducive conditions for the successful development and implementation of AI-driven medical solutions, while ensuring adherence to rigorous ethical and clinical standards. This guarantees that individuals receive high-quality and secure healthcare services, while also benefiting from the breakthroughs in artificial intelligence.

Supporting Ethical AI Research

Institutions acknowledge the urgent necessity for the ethical advancement of artificial intelligence (AI) and are actively involved in providing financial resources and assistance to research endeavors that address the ethical quandaries presented by AI. The recognition of the utmost importance of ethical considerations is evident as AI technologies progressively evolve and become increasingly integrated into diverse domains of society. In the context under consideration, institutions assume a pivotal function in the provision of resources dedicated to the pursuit of ethical artificial intelligence (AI) research. The organization offers scholarships, financing opportunities, and research fellowships to provide support for projects and initiatives that prioritize the development of ethical artificial intelligence. The provision of financial resources facilitates the exploration of intricate ethical predicaments by researchers, enabling them to devise remedies that are in accordance with ethical standards and promote the welfare of society.

In addition, academic institutions promote and facilitate interdisciplinary collaboration within the field of ethical artificial intelligence. The promotion of interdisciplinary collaboration is advocated, wherein academics from various backgrounds, encompassing ethicists, technologists, social scientists, and legal specialists, are encouraged to engage in joint efforts. The utilization of an interdisciplinary approach guarantees a thorough analysis of ethical dilemmas and fosters the creation of comprehensive solutions that take into account both technological and ethical aspects.

In addition to their primary functions, institutions also construct specialized research centers and institutes that are specifically focused on the study and development of ethical artificial intelligence. These centers function as central nodes for the purpose of performing ethical AI research, facilitating the collaboration of specialists, undertaking empirical investigations, and formulating ethical principles and optimal methodologies. They play a significant role in the establishment of a comprehensive ethical framework for artificial intelligence (AI) technology. In addition, academic institutions arrange conferences, seminars, and workshops that foster dialogues pertaining to the ethical considerations surrounding artificial intelligence. These gatherings facilitate the convergence of influential intellectuals, scholars, government officials, and professionals from various industries to partake in substantive dialogues concerning the ethical ramifications of artificial intelligence. These conferences facilitate the exchange of knowledge and the promotion of ethical perspectives among members of the AI community.

In the realm of ethical AI research, institutions have a crucial and central role in providing support. By means of financial support, fostering interdisciplinary collaboration, establishing research centers, and promoting knowledge-sharing efforts, they actively contribute to the resolution of ethical concerns posed by artificial intelligence. This approach guarantees the responsible and ethically appropriate development and use of AI technologies, hence promoting trust and social acceptance of AI progress.

Global Leadership in AI Ethics

In the realm of AI ethics, organizations hailing from prominent economies strive to establish themselves as global leaders by actively engaging in international debates and negotiations. It is widely acknowledged that the establishment of global standards in the field of AI ethics is of utmost importance in order to guarantee the responsible development and utilization of AI technology on a global level. One of the principal roles of these institutions is to actively participate in diplomatic endeavors and engage in discussions with other countries and international organizations. Their efforts are focused on the establishment of ethical norms and guidelines that can serve as a fundamental basis for the development and implementation of artificial intelligence (AI) across international boundaries. The aforementioned principles contain a diverse array of ethical considerations, which encompass but are not limited to justice, openness, privacy, and accountability within the realm of artificial intelligence systems. Moreover, prominent institutions from major economies are actively working towards the alignment of international rules pertaining to the ethical considerations of artificial intelligence. Their objective is to establish a comprehensive framework that fosters uniformity in ethical norms and behaviors on a global scale. By harmonizing legislation, any conflicts and complexity arising from divergent ethical principles across different locations are mitigated.

These institutes actively foster international cooperation and collaboration among governments and organizations as part of their endeavor to establish worldwide leadership in the field of AI ethics. International summits, conferences, and working groups are organized with the purpose of fostering discourse and promoting the exchange of knowledge regarding the ethical implications of artificial intelligence (AI). Collaborative endeavors of this nature facilitate the sharing of perspectives, exemplary methodologies, and acquired knowledge across diverse geographical areas, hence fostering the establishment of all-encompassing and widely embraced ethical norms.

Furthermore, prominent institutions in advanced economies serve as role models by integrating ethical ideas into their domestic plans and policies concerning artificial intelligence. They exhibit a dedication to upholding ethical practices in the field of artificial intelligence inside their respective jurisdictions, thereby setting a precedent for other countries and entities to emulate. In essence, institutions originating from prominent economies are actively involved in influencing the development of global artificial intelligence ethics. The objective is to construct a comprehensive set of ethical rules that govern the responsible development and utilization of artificial intelligence (AI) worldwide, achieved through diplomatic endeavors, regulatory harmonization, collaborative initiatives, and the establishment of ethical precedents. Leadership plays a crucial role in ensuring that artificial intelligence (AI) technologies are utilized in a manner that is advantageous to humanity, while simultaneously adhering to ethical standards and societal values.

In summary, institutions play a crucial role in the era of artificial intelligence (AI), exerting significant influence on the trajectory of market disruptions driven by AI. They are responsible for promoting ethical considerations, establishing regulatory frameworks, fostering innovation, and assuring fair and equal access to the benefits of AI. The adaptability, skill, and commitment of institutions will play a crucial role in promoting a future where AI is utilized as a catalyst for good societal and market transformations, as the rapid evolution of AI persists.

Potential implications for capitalist economies and strategies for adapting to AI-driven market disruptions

The emergence of Artificial Intelligence (AI) has profound ramifications for capitalist systems. The potential for market disruptions produced by artificial intelligence (AI) is significant, since it has the capacity to fundamentally redefine industries, modify the dynamics of competition, and have far-reaching effects on different aspects of economic activity. In order to effectively manage these developments, capitalist economies must implement policies that encompass the transformative capabilities of artificial intelligence (AI) while concurrently addressing the obstacles that arise from its implementation. In this discourse, we explore the prospective ramifications of artificial intelligence (AI) on capitalist economies and deliberate on approaches for adaptation.

1. **Industry Transformation**

The transformational potential of artificial intelligence (AI) spans a broad range of industries, leading to the restructuring of their core frameworks and operational processes. The aforementioned sectors, namely manufacturing, healthcare, finance, and transportation, are experiencing a significant influence due to the introduction of automation, predictive analytics, and data-driven decision-making. These advancements are causing a revolution in existing processes within these industries.

In the field of manufacturing, artificial intelligence (AI)-enabled robots and automation systems are being utilized to optimize production processes, resulting in decreased occurrences of errors and enhanced operational efficiency. The aforementioned approach not only results in a reduction of operational expenses, but also facilitates the ability to produce customized items on a large scale, thereby effectively meeting the ever-changing needs and preferences of consumers. The healthcare sector is currently experiencing the impact of artificial intelligence (AI) in the form of diagnostic AI algorithms, which are capable of analyzing medical pictures and data. This technological advancement has resulted in improved accuracy and timeliness of diagnoses. The aforementioned improvements are contributing to the enhancement of patient outcomes, the mitigation of healthcare expenditures, and the promotion of innovation in the fields of telemedicine and remote patient monitoring.

The utilization of artificial intelligence (AI) algorithms in the field of finance is revolutionizing the management of investments. Robo-advisors employ artificial intelligence (AI) to furnish tailored investment suggestions that align with an individual's risk tolerance and financial objectives. This approach facilitates the democratization of financial services and diminishes dependence on conventional financial advisors. Moreover, the transportation sector is undergoing a transformation due to the emergence of autonomous vehicles. Artificial intelligence (AI)-enabled autonomous vehicles possess the capacity to significantly transform transportation infrastructures by mitigating accidents, enhancing traffic control, and reshaping commuting patterns.

The aforementioned instances serve to demonstrate that the industry-wide transformation brought about by artificial intelligence (AI) extends beyond a singular sector, including several disciplines within the economy. In order to effectively respond to these changes, capitalist economies need proactively cultivate innovation ecosystems that promote the use of AI technologies by both startups and established firms. The allocation of resources towards research and development in the field of artificial intelligence, along with the implementation of various incentives such as tax credits and grants, has the potential to catalyze a significant shift in the industrial landscape. Furthermore, it is imperative for governments and institutions to engage in collaborative efforts with companies in order to develop comprehensive plans for the integration of artificial intelligence (AI). This proactive approach will guarantee that the resulting transformations not only have a positive impact on society at large but also foster sustainable economic advancement.

2. Labor Market Disruptions

The extensive implementation of artificial intelligence (AI) technology has the capacity to cause significant disruptions in labor markets. The implementation of automation and artificial intelligence (AI) in various processes has the potential to result in the displacement of specific occupations that primarily entail monotonous and repetitive duties. Nevertheless, it is imperative to acknowledge that artificial intelligence (AI) also generates novel employment prospects in burgeoning domains like data science, machine learning engineering, and AI ethics. It is imperative for capitalist economies to adopt preemptive measures in order to effectively manage labor market shocks, hence facilitating a seamless transition for the workforce. The first step is allocating resources towards education and workforce development initiatives that effectively equip individuals with the necessary skills demanded by the job market influenced by artificial intelligence. It is imperative that these programs are meticulously crafted to cater to the burgeoning need in specific domains, like data analysis, AI programming, and cybersecurity.

In conjunction with the facilitation of job market integration for fresh entrants, the implementation of reskilling and upskilling endeavors is imperative for the incumbent workforce. Individuals employed in positions that are vulnerable to automation have the potential to gain additional skills that would enable them to become valued assets inside sectors powered by artificial intelligence. As an illustration, a factory worker has the potential to transfer into a position where they have responsibility for supervising and upholding AI-driven technology. It is imperative for governments, educational institutions, and businesses to engage in collaborative efforts aimed at facilitating these programs. This collaboration should involve the provision of financial incentives and support to assist people in adapting to the dynamic nature of the job market. This method not only ensures the protection of people' economic welfare but also enhances the overall competitiveness of the economy. Moreover, the cultivation of a culture that promotes continuous learning throughout one's life is of utmost importance. In a constantly evolving AI-driven economy, individuals who consistently enhance their skills and knowledge will possess a competitive advantage in effectively navigating the employment market. Promoting a cognitive orientation towards adaptation and embracing change is crucial in order to maintain worker resilience amidst labor market upheavals propelled by artificial intelligence (AI) and automation.

3. Economic Growth

The influence of artificial intelligence (AI) on economic growth is considerable, as it has the capacity to generate improvements in productivity, savings in costs, and stimulate innovation across several sectors. In order to maintain competitiveness in the global arena, it is imperative for capitalist economies to place a high priority on the advancement and extensive implementation of artificial intelligence (AI) technology. One of the key contributions of artificial intelligence (AI) to economic growth lies in its ability to enhance productivity. Artificial intelligence (AI) systems provide the capability to efficiently manage jobs that are repetitive and consume significant amounts of time, surpassing the pace at which humans can perform these operations. As a result, AI systems enable the allocation of human resources towards endeavors that need strategic thinking and creativity. In the field of manufacturing, the utilization of artificial intelligence (AI)-enabled robots has the potential to optimize production processes, resulting in increased levels of output and reduced costs. Within the service industry, the utilization of chatbots and virtual assistants has the potential to enhance the efficiency of customer service by effectively managing and addressing consumer enquiries.

Furthermore, the utilization of AI-powered predictive analytics has the potential to assist enterprises in enhancing their operational efficiency through the implementation of data-informed decision-making processes. This practice facilitates the optimal distribution of resources, minimizes inefficiencies, and boosts overall operational effectiveness. Logistics organizations have the ability to employ artificial intelligence (AI) algorithms for the purpose of optimizing route planning, hence resulting in decreased fuel consumption and diminished operational expenses. In addition, artificial intelligence (AI) contributes to the advancement of innovation through its facilitation of novel product and service creation. Both startups and established companies are utilizing artificial intelligence (AI) to develop inventive solutions that cater to the changing needs of consumers. This innovation has the ability to not only attract investment, but also create new markets and produce additional revenue streams.

In order to optimize the economic growth potential of artificial intelligence (AI), it is imperative for capitalist countries to foster entrepreneurship and establish comprehensive support systems for startups operating within the AI industry. This encompasses the provision of financial possibilities, mentorship programs, and access to research and development resources. Government incentives, such as the provision of tax credits specifically targeted towards the field of artificial intelligence (AI) research, have the potential to effectively stimulate increased investment in the realm of AI-driven innovation. Furthermore, it is imperative for economies to place a high priority on the advancement and widespread adoption of artificial intelligence (AI) technology in many industries. This encompasses the allocation of resources towards the advancement of AI research and development, the facilitation of partnerships between governmental and corporate entities, and the establishment of a supportive ecosystem that promotes the widespread integration of AI technologies.

By harnessing the power of artificial intelligence (AI) to optimize productivity, minimize expenses, and cultivate creativity, capitalist economies have the potential to establish themselves as frontrunners in the international market, hence propelling continuous economic expansion and affluence.

4. Income Inequality

The utilization of AI-driven advancements in economic expansion has the ability to stimulate prosperity, though it also raises a significant apprehension about the prospective exacerbation of income inequality within capitalist economies. The equitable distribution of gains stemming from the progress in artificial intelligence necessitates careful policy deliberations in order to foster inclusive economic development. In order to effectively tackle the issue of income inequality in the era of artificial intelligence (AI), it is imperative for capitalist economies to contemplate the adoption of policies that place a strong emphasis on inclusivity. Progressive taxation is an example of a policy instrument. Governments can create cash to benefit lower-income citizens by implementing progressive tax policies that involve higher tax rates for individuals with higher earnings. This approach enables the funding of social programs and projects.

Furthermore, the implementation of social safety nets assumes paramount importance. Safety nets can serve as a means of financial support for individuals who may experience a disproportionate impact due to job displacement caused by artificial intelligence. Various social welfare programs, including but not limited to unemployment benefits, job training initiatives, and healthcare coverage, have the potential to alleviate the negative consequences arising from economic disruptions resulting from the transformative impact of artificial intelligence (AI) on the labor market. Further investigation on techniques for wealth redistribution should be undertaken. Various strategies can be employed, such as targeted wealth taxes, which specifically target the most affluent individuals or corporations. The funds collected from these taxes have the potential to be allocated towards educational initiatives, healthcare services, and workforce development programs, thereby contributing to the improvement of underprivileged communities.

Moreover, capitalist economies have the potential to foster inclusive growth through the facilitation of investments in regions that have been historically neglected or underserved. By promoting the establishment of artificial intelligence (AI) hubs and technology clusters in regions beyond large urban areas, there is potential to broaden economic growth and facilitate job creation in a more varied range of regions and communities. In addition, it is worth considering the implementation of progressive policies, such as universal basic income (UBI). Universal Basic Income (UBI) is a social welfare policy that entails the provision of a consistent and unconditional cash distribution to all individuals within a given society, hence guaranteeing a fundamental level of income for every person. Although this technique garners support and criticism, it signifies a novel method to tackle the issue of income disparity and ensure economic security amidst labor market upheavals caused by artificial intelligence.

The issue of income inequality in capitalist economies has become increasingly urgent in light of the advancements in artificial intelligence. By enacting policies that facilitate inclusive economic expansion, such as the adoption of progressive taxation, the establishment of social safety nets, the redistribution of wealth, and the allocation of investments in marginalized regions, these economies can endeavor to ensure a more equitable distribution of the advantages stemming from the prosperity driven by artificial intelligence.

5. Data Privacy and Security

The increasing integration of artificial intelligence (AI) inside capitalist economies has led to a heightened prominence of concerns pertaining to data privacy and security. The widespread use of artificial intelligence (AI) is strongly dependent on the availability of data, including personal and sensitive information. Consequently, it is crucial for governments and organizations to implement strong protective measures to uphold trust in AI-powered systems.

A crucial approach to mitigating these concerns involves the formulation and implementation of comprehensive legislation pertaining to data protection. It is imperative for capitalist economies to accord high priority to the establishment of legislative frameworks that effectively regulate the processes of collecting, storing, and utilizing personal data. Regulations such as the General Data Protection Regulation (GDPR) implemented by the European Union establish criteria for safeguarding data privacy and grant individuals authority to exercise control over their personal information. Moreover, the implementation of robust cybersecurity measures is of utmost importance in the era of artificial intelligence. In order to mitigate the risks associated with data breaches and cyberattacks, it is imperative for capitalist economies to allocate resources towards the implementation of advanced cybersecurity protocols and technology. These measures should comprise a comprehensive range of security practices, including encryption, network security, frequent security audits, and threat assessments.

The cultivation of a data ethical culture is vital, alongside the implementation of rules and cybersecurity measures. It is imperative for both public and private institutions to actively promote and uphold ethical practices in the utilization of data inside artificial intelligence (AI) applications. This encompasses the promotion of transparency in the processes of data collection and utilization, the acquisition of informed consent from individuals, and the assurance that artificial intelligence algorithms are devoid of biases that could potentially jeopardize data privacy or security.

International collaboration plays a pivotal role in effectively addressing the challenges around data privacy and security in the context of artificial intelligence (AI). The existence of data that frequently traverses international boundaries necessitates the establishment of globally standardized frameworks for safeguarding data. It is imperative for capitalist economies to actively participate in international conversations and negotiations with the aim of establishing shared rules and norms that control the movement of data across borders. This is crucial in order to uphold the significance of data privacy within a globally interconnected society.

Finally, it is imperative to emphasize the significance of ongoing research and development in the realm of artificial intelligence (AI) ethics and security. Institutions have the capacity to provide assistance for programs that are focused on enhancing comprehension of the ethical dilemmas associated with artificial intelligence (AI) and devising inventive strategies to address the potential hazards to data privacy and security. Data privacy and security have utmost importance inside the AI-driven landscape of capitalist economies. In order to effectively address these concerns and uphold trust in AI-driven systems, it is imperative to establish comprehensive legislation for data protection, implement robust cybersecurity measures, promote data ethics, create international cooperation, and make investments in research and development.

6. Ethical Considerations

The emergence of artificial intelligence (AI) inside capitalist systems presents a multitude of ethical problems that institutions must confront. These ethical difficulties pertain to concerns such as algorithmic prejudice, the ethical application of artificial intelligence (AI) in decision-making processes, and the equitable distribution of AI technology for the betterment of society. In capitalist economies, institutions play a crucial role in addressing ethical challenges. It is imperative for individuals to actively participate in ethical deliberations, fostering collaboration among experts, organizations, and stakeholders in order to formulate comprehensive standards and codes of behavior that regulate the ethical implementation of artificial intelligence (AI). These standards function as a navigational tool for organizations and entrepreneurs, guaranteeing that their AI-driven endeavors align with ethical values. The mitigation of algorithmic bias is a pivotal element in ensuring ethical artificial intelligence. In order to promote openness in AI algorithms, institutions have the capacity to advocate for corporations to conduct frequent audits and assessments of their AI systems to identify and mitigate biases. In addition, institutions have the capacity to promote the advancement of algorithms that exhibit fairness and impartiality, with the aim of achieving equity in decision-making processes facilitated by artificial intelligence.

Institutions should aggressively support the adoption of responsible practices in the field of artificial intelligence (AI). This necessitates not just abiding by ethical principles, but also contemplating the wider societal ramifications of artificial intelligence (AI) technologies. Institutions have the capacity to facilitate research pertaining to the ramifications of artificial intelligence (AI) on employment markets, as well as endeavor to develop solutions aimed at alleviating the potential displacement of jobs. Transparency serves as a fundamental principle in the realm of ethical artificial intelligence. It is imperative for institutions to actively promote the practice of corporations offering transparent elucidations regarding the decision-making processes employed by artificial intelligence (AI) systems, particularly in domains of utmost importance such as healthcare and finance. The provision of transparency not only cultivates trust but also empowers humans to enhance their comprehension and challenge decisions made by AI systems.

Furthermore, it is imperative to prioritize education and awareness activities. Incorporating AI ethics into curricula through collaboration between institutions and educational establishments can effectively equip future generations of entrepreneurs and workers with a comprehensive understanding of ethical considerations. Public awareness campaigns can additionally serve the purpose of educating individuals about the ethical ramifications of artificial intelligence (AI) and equipping them with the knowledge necessary to make well-informed decisions.

Ethical considerations play a pivotal role in the incorporation and assimilation of artificial intelligence inside capitalist systems. In order to ensure the ethical development and deployment of artificial intelligence (AI), institutions play a crucial role as custodians. They fulfill this responsibility by defining comprehensive norms, supporting openness in AI practices, pushing for the use of fair algorithms, and increasing education and awareness regarding AI ethics. By proactively confronting these ethical dilemmas, capitalist economies may guarantee that market disruptions produced by artificial intelligence are in accordance with ethical norms and contribute to the overall welfare of society.

7. International Cooperation

Given the borderless nature of artificial intelligence (AI), it is imperative for capitalist economies to acknowledge the significance of international collaboration in effectively addressing the difficulties and capitalizing on the opportunities presented by AI-induced market disruptions. International collaboration plays a crucial role in achieving regulatory harmonization, managing cross-border data flows, and establishing a framework that promotes responsible research and deployment of artificial intelligence (AI). In capitalist economies, institutions play a vital role in facilitating international collaboration. One potential course of action is for stakeholders to actively participate in diplomatic endeavors aimed at establishing universally accepted standards and norms for artificial intelligence (AI) technologies on a global scale. These standards encompass a broad range of domains, including data privacy and security, ethical development of artificial intelligence (AI), and the regulation of enterprises driven by AI.

Collaborative endeavors between capitalist economies and foreign counterparts can effectively facilitate the exchange of optimal methodologies. Through the exchange of insights and the dissemination of lessons gained, nations can expedite their comprehension of the ramifications of artificial intelligence (AI) and formulate more efficacious approaches to navigate market upheavals. These initiatives may also facilitate the harmonization of regulations, so ensuring the consistency of AI-related legislation and norms across different jurisdictions. International cooperation has a crucial role in effectively tackling the issue of cross-border data flows. Data plays a crucial role in the functioning of artificial intelligence (AI), as it serves as a vital resource. It is imperative to provide an environment where data can be exchanged securely and without restrictions across nations, since this is fundamental for the advancement and implementation of AI technologies. Collaborative efforts across institutions can be employed to facilitate the establishment of data-sharing agreements and the formulation of protocols that effectively address privacy and security considerations.

In addition, the scope of international cooperation might encompass joint endeavors in the realm of research and development. Capitalist economies have the potential to engage in collaborative partnerships with other nations, thereby combining their resources and skills to foster advancements in artificial intelligence (AI) research. These collaborative alliances have the potential to drive significant advancements in artificial intelligence (AI) technology and bolster the international competitiveness of the economies involved. International cooperation plays a pivotal role in properly addressing market disruptions induced by artificial intelligence inside capitalist economies. In the realm of promoting collaboration, institutions assume a crucial role by actively participating in diplomatic endeavors, exchanging exemplary methodologies, and engaging in joint research and development endeavors. Through collaborative efforts on an international scale, capitalist economies may effectively leverage the complete capabilities of artificial intelligence (AI) while simultaneously confronting the various difficulties it poses in a cohesive and synchronized fashion.

8. Innovation Ecosystems

In order to foster innovation ecosystems that facilitate entrepreneurship driven by artificial intelligence (AI), capitalist economies need adopt a comprehensive and diverse strategy. This entails promoting collaboration among academia, industry, and government entities in order to establish a favorable climate for the emergence and growth of AI startups. Universities have the potential to assume a crucial position in the advancement of artificial intelligence (AI) through the pursuit of innovative research and the provision of specialized educational programs that cultivate the requisite competencies for AI-driven entrepreneurship among students. The establishment of partnerships between academic institutions and industrial sectors can effectively enable the exchange of knowledge and technology, thereby empowering startups to capitalize on the most recent breakthroughs.

In addition, the provision of financial support and other resources is crucial for the cultivation and development of artificial intelligence enterprises. Governments and private institutions have the capacity to develop specialized funds and incubators for artificial intelligence (AI) startups, thereby providing financial assistance in the form of grants, venture capital investments, and angel funding. These entities not only provide financial support but also offer guidance, networking opportunities, and access to cutting-edge technologies. These resources facilitate the transformation of startups' novel concepts into commercially viable goods and services, hence promoting innovation and enhancing competitiveness within the AI industry.

It is imperative to establish regulatory frameworks that foster innovation and simultaneously uphold ethical norms in the field of artificial intelligence. It is imperative for regulatory organizations to establish comprehensive norms pertaining to the utilization of artificial intelligence (AI) in many industries, with the aim of fostering transparency in AI algorithms and the decision-making procedures associated with them. Furthermore, it is imperative to promote the adoption of ethical AI principles among startups, so guaranteeing the realization of the advantages of AI-driven entrepreneurship while safeguarding public welfare. The establishment of a conducive regulatory framework facilitates the ability of startups to effectively navigate the intricate landscape of AI ethics. This, in turn, cultivates a sense of trust among both customers and investors, thereby making a significant contribution to the long-term and sustainable expansion of AI-driven entrepreneurship within capitalist economies.

9. Resilience and Adaptability

Finally, it is imperative for capitalist economies to place a high degree of importance on the prioritization of resilience and adaptation when confronted with shocks caused by artificial intelligence. This entails the ongoing surveillance of AI breakthroughs, adaptation of legal frameworks, and maintaining flexibility in response to evolving market conditions. In order to effectively cultivate resilience, it is imperative to incorporate risk mitigation strategies that address possible issues arising from artificial intelligence.

In order to cultivate resilience and adaptation in the face of disruptions brought by artificial intelligence, it is imperative for capitalist economies to embrace a proactive and future-oriented stance. This entails the ongoing surveillance and evaluation of AI progress, remaining knowledgeable about emerging technologies, and comprehending their possible ramifications for many industries. The design of regulatory frameworks should prioritize flexibility, enabling prompt revisions in light of shifting market dynamics and technology advancements. Furthermore, it is imperative to formulate comprehensive risk mitigation strategies in order to effectively tackle any issues associated with artificial intelligence. The proposed plans should include comprehensive strategies for effectively managing labor market disruptions, safeguarding data privacy and security, addressing ethical considerations, and effectively navigating economic upheavals that may arise as a consequence of the use of artificial intelligence. Through proactive identification and preparation for potential risks, capitalist economies possess the ability to effectively navigate disruptions caused by artificial intelligence (AI). This navigation is achieved by demonstrating resilience and adaptability, ultimately allowing these economies to harness the transformative capabilities of AI for the betterment of society as a whole.

In summary, the ramifications of artificial intelligence (AI) on capitalist economies are diverse, presenting prospects for expansion and ingenuity alongside obstacles that necessitate prudent oversight. Achieving effective adjustment to market disruptions induced by artificial intelligence (AI) mandates the adoption of a proactive strategy encompassing key elements such as educational investment, innovation, ethical considerations, and international cooperation. By strategically and ethically adopting AI, capitalist economies can effectively utilize its potential to promote prosperity and enhance societal well-being during the era of artificial intelligence.

Chapter 25: AI and Capitalist Ideals

The convergence of Artificial Intelligence (AI) with capitalism is a significant catalyst for innovation and societal change in contemporary times. The core of this convergence is centered around a captivating narrative that explores both the harmonious coexistence and the conflicting dynamics between the enduring principles of capitalism and the transformative potential of artificial intelligence. This chapter initiates an intellectual exploration of the intricate connection between artificial intelligence (AI) and capitalist principles. It delves into the examination of their compatibility, the crucial involvement of institutions, and the ethical discussions that surround this dynamic intersection.

Capitalism, as a socio-economic framework, upholds the principles of individual autonomy, private ownership of assets, and economic incentives as its fundamental tenets. The underlying principle of this concept is predicated on the idea that individuals possess the freedom to actively pursue their economic self-interest, amass and safeguard private property, and partake in voluntary transactions that maximize overall satisfaction. The driving force behind capitalism is derived from the principles of competition, innovation, and entrepreneurship, which are harnessed to further societal development and economic well-being. The convergence of principles in artificial intelligence is grounded on this fundamental foundation, so establishing a framework for a comprehensive and intricate investigation.

The intricate interplay between AI and capitalist values gives rise to considerations regarding their compatibility. On one hand, artificial intelligence (AI) emerges as an unparalleled set of technologies that have the potential to enhance the fundamental principles of capitalism. The optimization of resource allocation, enhancement of productivity, and facilitation of innovation and wealth generation are key outcomes of this phenomenon. Artificial intelligence (AI) has the potential to automate repetitive jobs, optimize decision-making processes, and augment human abilities, hence presenting an opportunity to significantly boost the efficiency and competitiveness of capitalist economies. Nevertheless, the widespread adoption of AI gives rise to significant inquiries. Inquiries pertaining to the fair allocation of economic advantages, the ramifications of job displacement caused by artificial intelligence, and the possible concentration of authority among individuals who possess control over AI technologies. These inquiries intersect with and challenge the fundamental tenets of capitalism, hence necessitating a more profound exploration.

Within the complex interplay of artificial intelligence and capitalism, institutions assume a pivotal role as key actors in the overarching narrative. In the realm of social values and regulatory frameworks, institutions play a crucial role in managing the intersection of capitalism and artificial intelligence (AI). In the era of AI, individuals are tasked with the responsibility of reconciling the demands of capitalism with the principles of ethics, equality, and social welfare. The chapter explores the significant role that institutions play within this complex context, encompassing their influence on regulatory laws that promote equitable competition and protect consumer rights, as well as their contribution to the development of innovation ecosystems that stimulate economic advancement. In the context of the coexistence of artificial intelligence (AI) and capitalism, institutions play a pivotal role as the central mechanism for coordination and facilitation.

Furthermore, educational establishments are positioned at the forefront of tackling ethical problems and engaging in debates that emerge as artificial intelligence and capitalist principles become increasingly intertwined. The emergence of algorithmic prejudice, apprehensions regarding privacy violations, and the ethical ramifications of artificial intelligence (AI) across diverse sectors such as banking and healthcare highlight the necessity for ethical principles and standards. In order to uphold the integrity of capitalism amidst the ethical problems posed by artificial intelligence (AI), institutions partake in conversations, develop ethical frameworks, and establish oversight systems.

In conclusion, the complex interplay between artificial intelligence and capitalist principles carries significant ramifications for our economic, social, and ethical domains. This chapter undertakes a thorough examination of the relationship between AI and capitalism, examining the extent to which AI aligns with the fundamental principles of capitalism. It also highlights the crucial role that institutions play in upholding and reconciling these principles, and delves into the ethical considerations that underlie this transformative intersection. The increasing integration of artificial intelligence (AI) within capitalist economies has profound implications for the trajectory of our economic systems and society as a whole. Our capacity to effectively negotiate the dynamic interplay between AI and capitalism values will play a pivotal role in shaping these outcomes.

The compatibility of AI with fundamental principles of capitalism, such as individual freedom, private property rights, and economic incentives

The compatibility of artificial intelligence (AI) with fundamental principles of capitalism, including individual freedom, private property rights, and economic incentives, is a complex and multifaceted topic that has generated considerable debate. To understand this compatibility, it's essential to examine how AI intersects with these principles and the potential implications for society and the economy.

1. Individual Freedom

Enhancement of Individual Freedom:

The varied nature of AI's ability to promote individual freedom is evident. Primarily, artificial intelligence (AI) possesses the capability to automate monotonous and recurring jobs across several sectors, hence exerting a substantial influence on the day-to-day experiences of individuals. By assigning these mundane duties to artificial intelligence, individuals are able to regain significant amounts of time and cognitive resources that can be reallocated to more imaginative and purposeful endeavors. In the context of professional environments, artificial intelligence (AI)-powered automation has the potential to alleviate the workload associated with administrative duties, thereby enabling employees to dedicate their efforts towards problem-solving, innovation, and activities that necessitate human ingenuity and discernment. This not only increases job happiness but also cultivates an atmosphere where individuals are able to offer their distinct skills and talents.

Furthermore, the utilization of AI-driven technology facilitates humans in promptly and efficiently accessing extensive volumes of information. The availability of information enables individuals to make better-informed decisions across a range of domains, including healthcare, finance, and everyday consumer purchases. For example, artificial intelligence (AI)-enabled recommendation systems utilized in electronic commerce have the capability to offer individualized product recommendations by analyzing an individual's preferences and historical actions. This enhances the convenience and customization of the purchasing process. Moreover, the utilization of AI-powered data analysis has the potential to assist individuals in monitoring and effectively managing their health and well-being, hence facilitating the adoption of more informed lifestyle decisions. In conclusion, the capacity of artificial intelligence to automate chores and offer information enables individuals to attain greater autonomy and knowledge, thereby enhancing their quality of life.

Moreover, the importance of artificial intelligence in augmenting personal autonomy extends to the provision of tailored services. Artificial intelligence (AI) possesses the capability to evaluate extensive datasets in order to customize services according to individual needs and preferences, so achieving a level of personalization that was previously unattainable. Artificial intelligence (AI) has the potential to enhance healthcare by facilitating the diagnosis and treatment of medical disorders on an individualized basis, hence maximizing overall healthcare results. Within the field of education, platforms powered by artificial intelligence have the capability to customize learning materials based on individual learning styles and levels of advancement, thereby addressing the distinct requirements of students. The provision of personalized services not only serves to promote individual autonomy by enhancing the standard of services received, but also facilitates greater individual engagement in influencing their experiences and outcomes across different aspects of life.

Concerns about Surveillance and Privacy

Artificial intelligence (AI) exhibits the potential to augment personal autonomy; nonetheless, it concurrently elicits substantial apprehensions pertaining to surveillance and the safeguarding of privacy. The utilization of artificial intelligence technologies in mass surveillance has the potential to undermine individual freedoms through several means. Governments and companies have the capability to utilize artificial intelligence-based surveillance systems in order to extensively monitor the actions, conversations, and behaviors of people or employees. The pervasive nature of surveillance can cultivate an atmosphere characterized by apprehension and self-restraint, as individuals may exhibit reluctance in voicing their viewpoints or participating in actions they perceive as susceptible to scrutiny or misinterpretation.

Data profiling is a significant concern associated with the implementation of AI-powered surveillance systems. The capacity of artificial intelligence (AI) to effectively handle and examine extensive quantities of personal data has the potential to facilitate the development of comprehensive individual profiles. While the utilization of targeted marketing and personalized services can offer benefits, it can also lead to the perpetuation of discriminatory behaviors and the reinforcing of biases. For example, artificial intelligence systems have the potential to unintentionally present discriminatory content or ads to specific demographic groups, so exacerbating societal divisions and eroding individual agency.

Moreover, the storage and management of personal data within artificial intelligence (AI) systems pose a potential threat of data breaches and cyberattacks. When instances of breaches arise, there is a potential for the disclosure of sensitive personal information, which can result in identity theft, financial detriment, and various infringements upon privacy. These occurrences have the potential to significantly diminish an individual's perception of security and privacy, ultimately undermining their ability to freely interact with digital services and platforms without apprehension.

In summary, the utilization of artificial intelligence (AI) presents opportunities for augmenting human autonomy through automation, information accessibility, and tailored provisions. However, apprehensions about surveillance, data profiling, and infringements against privacy underscore the want for comprehensive regulatory measures and ethical frameworks. The task of reconciling the benefits of artificial intelligence (AI) with the preservation of individual rights is a multifaceted dilemma in the current period dominated by AI. This underscores the significance of responsible AI advancement and the protection of privacy rights within societies that adhere to capitalist principles.

2. Private Property Rights

AI as Intellectual Property

Within the context of a capitalist framework, the notion of artificial intelligence (AI) as intellectual property assumes a pivotal role in fostering innovation and facilitating investment in the field of AI research and development. The advancement of AI technology frequently relies on the formulation of exclusive algorithms, the aggregation of comprehensive information, and the construction of specialized software. The safeguarding of these components is crucial in order to incentivize organizations and individuals to allocate their resources, time, and expertise towards the progression of artificial intelligence innovations, since they represent significant intellectual assets.

Intellectual property rights, encompassing patents, copyrights, and trade secrets, serve as a means for inventors to protect their AI-related ideas and advancements. The provision of protection in the form of intellectual property rights serves as a crucial motivating factor for businesses to engage in research and development activities related to artificial intelligence. This protection ensures that businesses have the opportunity to recover their investments and perhaps gain financial returns from their innovative innovations. The establishment of a framework that acknowledges and safeguards artificial intelligence (AI) as intellectual property is a characteristic of capitalism. This framework creates a transparent system of incentives that promotes the development of innovative AI technologies, encourages competition, and ultimately enhances consumer welfare by facilitating the introduction of state-of-the-art products and services.

Furthermore, the safeguarding of artificial intelligence (AI) as intellectual property extends beyond the realm of private enterprises. This paradigm also has significant advantages for individual inventors and researchers, as it enables them to maintain ownership of their AI-related endeavors and perhaps generate financial gains from their innovations. This particular facet of capitalism fosters a wide range of innovators to participate in the field of artificial intelligence research, hence fostering a dynamic and competitive ecosystem within the AI domain.

Challenges with Data Ownership

The matter of data ownership assumes significant significance within the realm of artificial intelligence (AI) advancement. Artificial intelligence (AI) systems exhibit optimal performance when provided with abundant data, as extensive datasets are crucial for the training and enhancement of these systems. Nevertheless, inquiries emerge about the ownership and governance of the ensuing artificial intelligence models, as well as the consideration of whether individuals ought to possess a share in the accrued riches.

Individuals frequently provide their data to artificial intelligence (AI) systems, either consciously or unconsciously, via online engagements, wearable gadgets, or alternative modalities. The issue at hand pertains to the determination of whether the individuals providing the data should own a legitimate entitlement to the artificial intelligence models that are developed utilizing their data. The significance of this topic is heightened within the framework of capitalism, where the commercialization of AI models is widespread.

One contention posits that persons who provide data should be entitled to some sort of ownership or remuneration for the utilization of their data. This method is in accordance with the concepts of equity and the protection of individual property rights. Nevertheless, the use of this technology also presents challenges in terms of monitoring data submissions and establishing fair remuneration.

In contrast, advocates of the existing capitalist framework contend that data inputs are frequently anonymised and consolidated, hence presenting difficulties in clearly attributing specific AI models or profits to individual data sources. The argument put forth is that data is a communal asset, and the benefits derived from AI models should predominantly accrue to the entities that allocate resources towards AI research and development.

The reconciliation of these considerations with regards to data ownership is a serious dilemma within the realm where artificial intelligence intersects with capitalism. The matter necessitates careful examination of legal and ethical frameworks that recognize the significance of safeguarding individual data privacy while also promoting the advancement and financial support of artificial intelligence. Potential solutions to address the issue at hand may encompass enhanced levels of openness, more explicit agreements for data usage, and the establishment of procedures that uphold fair distribution of rewards for those who provide data. It is crucial to strike a balance between these measures and the promotion of innovation within capitalist frameworks, so as not to impede the potential advancements of artificial intelligence.

3. Economic Incentives

Innovation and Entrepreneurship

Within the framework of a capitalist environment, the impetus for economic growth is primarily fueled by innovation and entrepreneurship. Notably, artificial intelligence (AI) has emerged as a potent catalyst for fostering advancements in both domains. AI technologies present a multitude of options for innovation, including a spectrum of advancements such as automation, enhanced efficiency, and the emergence of novel business prospects. Automation, specifically, serves as a prominent catalyst for innovation by freeing up human resources from monotonous chores, enabling workers to redirect their creative and problem-solving abilities towards activities that provide greater value. This phenomenon not only contributes to increased levels of job satisfaction but also serves as a catalyst for the initiation and growth of entrepreneurial endeavors.

The potential of artificial intelligence (AI) to reduce operating expenses and enhance productivity carries significant ramifications for enterprises. Through the implementation of automation, organizations are able to streamline operations and procedures, resulting in enhanced productivity in the production of goods and services. Consequently, this increased efficiency can lead to reduced costs for customers. Furthermore, the use of AI-powered insights obtained through rigorous data analysis empowers organizations to make well-informed strategic choices, hence cultivating a competitive edge inside the marketplace.

Moreover, artificial intelligence (AI) technologies have the potential to generate novel markets and enterprises. The emergence of autonomous vehicles has given rise to a novel segment within the transportation sector, hence creating prospects for established enterprises as well as newly founded ventures to foster innovation and secure a portion of the market. The allure of transformative breakthroughs and the prospect of addressing intricate challenges using artificial intelligence (AI) serve as strong motivations for enterprises to make substantial investments in AI research and development. This, in turn, fosters economic expansion and technological advancement within the capitalist system.

Income Inequality

Artificial intelligence (AI) has significant opportunities for innovation and economic expansion, but concurrently presents difficulties pertaining to income inequality within the capitalist framework. There are apprehensions that occur when artificial intelligence (AI)-driven automation results in the displacement of employees from conventional employment, notably in industries such as manufacturing, retail, and customer service. The phenomenon of displacement resulting from advancements in artificial intelligence (AI) has the potential to cause job loss and pay stagnation within specific sectors of the labor force. Consequently, this could result in the concentration of wealth around a small number of dominant tech companies that hold significant influence over the AI industry.

The significance of resolving matters pertaining to fairness and equal opportunity is highlighted by the interplay between artificial intelligence (AI) and income inequality. The principle of equal opportunity is fundamental in capitalist systems, and the existence of income inequality contradicts this ideal. The possibility of artificial intelligence (AI) intensifying income inequalities underscores the need for deliberate governmental interventions, such as initiatives for retraining the workforce and implementing policies to ensure a wider distribution of AI benefits.

Furthermore, the issue of economic inequality in the era of artificial intelligence necessitates a meticulous examination of taxation policies and systems for wealth redistribution. There are proponents who argue in favor of implementing policies such as universal basic income (UBI) as a strategy to alleviate the adverse consequences of job displacement caused by artificial intelligence (AI). The objective is to provide individuals with a financial safety net throughout the transitional period while they navigate the evolving job landscape.

In summary, the influence of artificial intelligence (AI) on innovation and entrepreneurship plays a significant role in fostering economic expansion within a capitalist framework. However, it is imperative to acknowledge and confront the potential of AI to exacerbate wealth inequality. Through the implementation of strategies aimed at fostering equitable access to opportunities driven by artificial intelligence (AI), as well as the establishment of education and retraining programs, and the formulation of policies that ensure the fair distribution of AI benefits, capitalism can undergo an evolution that effectively harnesses the advantages of AI technology. This evolution would also address the challenges associated with AI in a manner that aligns with principles of fairness and equal opportunity.

4. Regulation and Ethics

Balancing Freedom and Responsibility

The extent to which AI can coexist with capitalism depends on the establishment of a careful balance between individual autonomy and effective governance. Capitalism places a significant emphasis on individual freedom as a fundamental principle of its philosophy. However, the unregulated advancement of artificial intelligence (AI) can potentially give rise to various hazards and concerns. When carefully crafted, regulation can serve as a protective measure against the inappropriate use of AI, while simultaneously upholding the principles of innovation and competition that are integral to the capitalist system.

Responsible regulation can fulfill multiple objectives within the realm of artificial intelligence. The establishment of explicit guidelines and standards for the development of artificial intelligence (AI) can effectively ensure that AI systems are created with a focus on safety, transparency, and responsibility. For example, legislation have the ability to enforce the requirement of disclosing the utilization of artificial intelligence (AI) in crucial domains such as autonomous vehicles or healthcare decision-making. This would result in individuals gaining enhanced knowledge and control over the involvement of AI in their daily existence.

In addition, regulatory measures have the capacity to effectively tackle issues pertaining to privacy and the safeguarding of data. Regulations can successfully safeguard individuals' personal information and preserve their privacy rights while allowing for the effective functioning of AI by implementing rules that control data collection, usage, and preservation.

Regulatory measures of this nature provide the potential to cultivate confidence in artificial intelligence (AI) systems, hence facilitating their broader implementation across diverse industries.

It is of utmost importance that responsible regulation achieves a delicate equilibrium that avoids impeding innovation. Capitalism flourishes through the mechanism of competition and the impetus it provides for enterprises to engage in innovation. The presence of excessive or unduly restrictive regulation has the potential to impede the progress of AI technologies and limit their capacity to contribute to societal advancements. Hence, the imperative task for policymakers lies in striking an optimal equilibrium between liberty and accountability, thereby guaranteeing the harmonious coexistence of artificial intelligence (AI) within the framework of capitalism.

Ethical Considerations

Within capitalist civilizations, economic operations are conducted within predetermined societal and ethical parameters. The integration of artificial intelligence (AI) into several domains raises a multitude of ethical problems that collide with the principles and practices of capitalism. These considerations pertain to matters with prejudices, discrimination, and accountability, and necessitate resolution through suitable regulation and conscientious business practices.

One of the key ethical considerations revolves around the issue of bias inside artificial intelligence (AI) systems. Machine learning models have the potential to unintentionally acquire biases inherent in the training data, resulting in discriminatory consequences in domains such as lending, employment, and the criminal justice system. To effectively tackle this matter, it is imperative to engage in comprehensive data preparation techniques while concurrently establishing ethical norms and regulations that foster equity in artificial intelligence systems.

Discrimination is a significant ethical challenge. It is imperative that AI systems refrain from engaging in discriminatory practices against persons on the basis of race, gender, age, or any other legally protected attributes. Capitalism, being a socio-economic system that emphasizes the need of equal opportunity, requires the implementation of responsible business practices and laws in order to effectively tackle these concerns. It is imperative for companies to proactively address and mitigate instances of discriminatory results resulting from artificial intelligence (AI) systems. Concurrently, governments play a crucial role in establishing effective oversight mechanisms and legislative frameworks that ensure corporations are held responsible for any discriminatory practices facilitated by AI.

Moreover, accountability represents a fundamental ethical consideration. In instances where AI systems exert influence on individuals through decision-making processes, it is imperative to establish unequivocal accountability for these judgments. The implementation of accountability procedures and regulatory frameworks serves to provide individuals with avenues for seeking redress in instances where AI systems inflict harm. This practice is in accordance with the values of justice and ethical responsibility that are upheld under capitalist society.

In essence, the inclusion of ethical issues in the realm of artificial intelligence is important in order to establish and maintain ethical parameters within the framework of capitalism. The resolution of these ethical difficulties is contingent upon the implementation of responsible regulation, transparent procedures, and corporate accountability measures. By adopting this approach, capitalism may effectively leverage the advantages of artificial intelligence (AI) while maintaining its dedication to principles of fairness, equality, and ethical corporate behavior.
The compatibility between artificial intelligence (AI) and the core principles of capitalism is not a dichotomous matter, but rather necessitates a judicious approach to navigation. Artificial intelligence (AI) has the potential to augment and expand individual autonomy, safeguard the rights to private property, and foster robust economic motivations for fostering innovation. Nevertheless, the proliferation of technology also presents a set of issues pertaining to privacy, ownership of data, disparities in economic distribution, and ethical considerations. In capitalist societies, it is imperative to achieve a harmonious equilibrium by enacting regulatory measures that foster conscientious development and utilization of artificial intelligence (AI), all the while facilitating ongoing economic expansion and fostering innovation. The identification of this equilibrium will be of utmost importance in guaranteeing that artificial intelligence (AI) adheres to the fundamental principles that form the basis of capitalist systems and effectively serves the wider interests of society.

The role of institutions in upholding and reconciling capitalist ideals in the context of AI-driven economic systems

The complicated and crucial role of institutions in maintaining and harmonizing capitalist principles within the framework of AI-driven economic systems cannot be overstated. In the realm of economic operations, both governmental and non-governmental institutions hold a pivotal position in the formulation of laws, regulations, and ethical frameworks. In the era of artificial intelligence, the convergence of innovation, competition, and individual liberties with ethical, equitable, and privacy-related concerns necessitates that these institutions strive to achieve a nuanced equilibrium. This equilibrium aims to secure the advantages of capitalism while effectively tackling the obstacles presented by AI.

1. Regulatory Frameworks

Government agencies play a pivotal role in formulating regulatory frameworks that control the development and use of artificial intelligence (AI) within various institutions. It is imperative to

establish rules that effectively achieve a harmonious equilibrium between fostering innovation and guaranteeing the ethical and responsible utilization of artificial intelligence. For instance, it is possible to enforce the implementation of transparency measures in the decision-making processes of artificial intelligence (AI). Additionally, it is feasible to establish the necessity of conducting risk assessments for AI systems operating in sensitive sectors such as healthcare. Moreover, sanctions can be instituted to address instances of privacy rights abuses. These restrictions serve to maintain the fundamental tenets of capitalism by ensuring fair competition among enterprises and cultivating consumer confidence.
Regulatory frameworks play a crucial role in the context of AI-driven capitalism, as they effectively manage the complex convergence of innovation and ethics within the dynamic and ever-changing technological environment. The duty for formulating laws and standards that achieve a delicate balance between promoting innovation and guaranteeing ethical and responsible development and deployment of AI technologies lies with government agencies and regulatory authorities.

The establishment of transparency is a fundamental aspect in the efficient control of artificial intelligence. In order to preserve the tenets of capitalism, it is possible for legislation to be implemented that require transparency in the decision-making processes of artificial intelligence. This stipulation necessitates that enterprises and institutions employing artificial intelligence must exhibit transparency regarding the decision-making processes employed by their algorithms. In the financial industry, it is imperative for AI-powered credit scoring systems to provide transparency by disclosing the specific variables taken into account during the assessment of an individual's creditworthiness. The provision of transparency not only serves to bolster consumer confidence but also fosters a competitive environment by empowering consumers to make well-informed decisions regarding the utilization of AI-driven services.

In fields characterized by their sensitivity, such as healthcare, rules may extend their scope to encompass the mandatory inclusion of risk assessments for artificial intelligence (AI) systems. Within this particular framework, the use of AI technology holds the potential to greatly enhance the quality of patient care and ultimately improve health outcomes. However, it is crucial to acknowledge that the presence of errors or biases within AI algorithms can lead to profound and potentially irreversible effects for individuals. Regulatory frameworks mandate the need for thorough evaluations of the potential risks associated with AI systems, hence assuring their compliance with rigorous safety criteria prior to their implementation. This method is in accordance with capitalist principles as it serves to safeguard customers from potential harm while also promoting innovation within the healthcare sector.

Furthermore, the implementation of sanctions for infringements upon privacy rights plays a key role in maintaining the integrity of capitalist ideals. It serves to guarantee that businesses prioritize the importance of data privacy and strengthens the level of confidence and reliance among consumers. Regulations have the capacity to establish specific repercussions for instances of data breaches or the inappropriate use of personal information, thereby imposing responsibility on organizations to protect individuals' data. The promotion of ethical conduct and the establishment of a fair business environment are both facilitated by adherence to privacy standards, which in turn can confer a competitive edge.

In conclusion, regulatory frameworks play a crucial role in the context of AI-driven capitalism. Responsible innovation is effectively facilitated by the promotion of transparency, the imposition of risk assessments, and the enforcement of fines for privacy infractions. These rules aim to achieve a harmonious equilibrium between the encouragement of innovation and the guarantee of ethical and responsible growth of artificial intelligence (AI). Consequently, they contribute to the cultivation of consumer trust and the preservation of the fundamental tenets of capitalism within the AI era.

2. Intellectual Property Protection

Intellectual property laws constitute a vital pillar of the capitalist system. In the realm of intellectual property, entities such as patent offices and copyright agencies play a crucial role in safeguarding the rights of inventors, encompassing those operating within the domain of artificial intelligence. The granting of exclusive rights to AI inventions for a limited term plays a vital role in motivating research and development in the field of artificial intelligence. This protective measure enables enterprises to leverage their discoveries, thereby promoting competitiveness and encouraging investment in artificial intelligence (AI).

The safeguarding of intellectual property plays a pivotal role in the framework of capitalism, and its importance is further accentuated in the setting of innovation driven by artificial intelligence. Patent offices and copyright agencies function as custodians of invention and creativity, assuming a crucial role in stimulating research and development within the field of artificial intelligence.

Intellectual property laws, under the framework of capitalist regimes, serve as a catalyst for innovation by bestowing exclusive rights upon innovators, especially those engaged in the domain of artificial intelligence. The aforementioned exclusivity encompasses AI algorithms, software, and datasets, thereby granting innovators a temporary monopoly over their creations. The establishment of a monopoly, frequently facilitated by patents or copyrights, serves as a means to compensate innovators for their endeavors and investments in the field of artificial intelligence research and development. The aforementioned compensation mechanism exhibits a strong congruence with capitalist ideals, as it effectively encourages and motivates innovation while simultaneously fostering a competitive environment wherein enterprises endeavor to surpass their rivals through superior invention.

The safeguarding of intellectual property within the realm of artificial intelligence serves as a catalyst for both research and investment in this domain. Companies demonstrate a greater inclination to allocate significant resources towards the study and development of artificial intelligence (AI) when they possess the guarantee of protecting their intellectual property rights. This cultivates a competitive atmosphere wherein enterprises endeavor to develop state-of-the-art AI technology, hence propelling economic expansion and scientific progress.

In essence, safeguarding intellectual property is a crucial element of the innovation-centric mechanism that underpins capitalism. Within the domain of artificial intelligence (AI), it serves as a catalyst for stimulating research and development activities, cultivating a competitive environment, and drawing significant investments. Institutions that are committed to safeguarding intellectual property rights serve to uphold the principles of capitalism by incentivizing innovation and fostering economic development, while also ensuring that developers of artificial intelligence can enjoy the advantages derived from their pioneering contributions.

3. Ethical Oversight

In addition to their primary functions, institutions bear the responsibility of establishing regulatory bodies and formulating ethical frameworks to govern the deployment and operation of artificial intelligence (AI) systems. These institutions, which may be either governmental or industry-specific, play a crucial role in ensuring that artificial intelligence (AI) operates in accordance with ethical norms within the context of a capitalist system. For example, someone in this role can assume responsibility for supervising the formulation of ethical rules for artificial intelligence (AI), ensuring adherence to these guidelines, and establishing mechanisms for addressing ethical transgressions. Through their actions, these institutions actively contribute to the responsible utilization of artificial intelligence (AI), thereby aligning it with the principles of capitalism that prioritize justice and transparency.

The presence of ethical oversight plays a crucial role within the context of AI-driven capitalism, functioning as a protective measure to ensure responsible innovation and the advancement of technology. In this setting, institutions, whether governmental or industry-specific, play a crucial role by creating ethical norms and overseeing adherence to ensure that artificial intelligence (AI) conforms to ethical principles while operating within the framework of capitalism.

The primary function of ethical oversight institutions is to provide supervision and regulation in the formulation and implementation of ethical norms pertaining to artificial intelligence (AI). In the context of a capitalist system, characterized by the prominence of competition and innovation, the establishment of clear and comprehensive standards becomes imperative to effectively address significant ethical considerations. As an illustration, these standards have the capacity to cover principles pertaining to equity, responsibility, openness, and the reduction of bias in artificial intelligence systems. Ethical guidelines serve as a guiding framework for corporations and researchers, enabling them to effectively navigate the intricate landscape of AI development while upholding moral principles.

Moreover, these entities provide a vital function in terms of monitoring. The monitoring of adherence to ethical principles is conducted to ensure that artificial intelligence (AI) systems comply with the mandated ethical norms. The implementation of regular audits and evaluations plays a crucial role in the identification and resolution of ethical deficiencies within artificial intelligence (AI) applications, hence bolstering the overall reliability and credibility of AI-driven services. This lack of attention adds to the proper utilization of artificial intelligence, cultivating a commercial atmosphere where ethical deliberations are not compromised in the endeavor for financial gain, a fundamental aspect of capitalism ideologies.

Furthermore, these establishments also offer channels for seeking remedy in cases of ethical transgressions. This facet of ethical supervision guarantees that persons or entities adversely affected by unethical acts in the field of artificial intelligence possess a mechanism via which they can pursue legal recourse or obtain reparation. This protective measure is in accordance with the fundamental ideals of equity and openness, which are integral to the capitalist system, as it ensures that AI creators and users are held responsible for their activities.

In essence, ethical oversight institutions fulfill the role of safeguarding ethical standards within the context of AI-driven capitalism. They play a crucial role in shaping the ethical rules for the development of artificial intelligence (AI), overseeing adherence to these guidelines, and establishing ways to rectify any ethical breaches. By engaging in such actions, individuals actively promote the responsible and ethical utilization of artificial intelligence (AI) within the context of capitalism. This serves to establish a balanced and equitable environment where innovation and competition can thrive alongside principles of justice and transparency.

4. Education and Workforce Development

In the era of artificial intelligence, institutions, such as educational organizations and workforce development agencies, assume a crucial role in sustaining the capitalist system. The primary responsibility of these entities is to equip individuals with the necessary skills to excel in economies that are heavily influenced by artificial intelligence. This encompasses not just technical proficiencies but also the capacity for critical analysis, adaptability, and aptitude in resolving complex issues. Education and training institutions play a crucial role in facilitating the engagement and advantageous involvement of individuals in economic systems powered

by artificial intelligence (AI). This involvement serves to mitigate the potential for wealth disparity and foster the promotion of individual liberties.
Education and workforce development institutions play a crucial role in facilitating the integration of capitalism with the AI era, wherein innovation and skills are of utmost importance. The responsibilities of these individuals extend beyond the mere provision of technical information. They bear the responsibility of molding the workforce to thrive in economies powered by artificial intelligence, while also complying with the values of capitalism that prioritize individual opportunity and economic freedom.

In the current era of artificial intelligence, there is a significant demand for specialized technical abilities, particularly in the fields of data science and machine learning. Nevertheless, it is imperative for institutions to surpass this requirement and foster a more comprehensive range of skills. This encompasses the cultivation of critical thinking skills, adaptability, and problem-solving capabilities. The aforementioned talents are crucial in a perpetually changing artificial intelligence (AI) environment, wherein workers are required to scrutinize, adjust to, and resolve novel issues. Educational organizations employ strategies to ensure that students possess not only technical expertise but also the ability to effectively navigate a constantly evolving job market, which is a crucial element of a capitalist system.

Furthermore, it is imperative to acknowledge the significant contribution of educational and training institutions in addressing and reducing income disparity. These institutions mitigate the potential negative consequences of job displacement and income inequities by equipping individuals with the necessary skills to engage in economic systems driven by artificial intelligence. This, consequently, corresponds with the capitalist principles of equitable opportunity and socioeconomic advancement. The provision of inclusive educational and training opportunities plays a crucial role in facilitating the engagement and utilization of artificial intelligence (AI) for individuals from various socio-economic backgrounds. This fosters economic empowerment and contributes to the mitigation of social disparities.

In addition, it is imperative for educational institutions to demonstrate flexibility in modifying their curricula to align with the changing requirements of the AI era. This entails promoting interdisciplinary education, as artificial intelligence connects with other domains. Education institutions play a crucial role in preparing students for the complex problems and opportunities that arise from the emergence of AI-driven capitalism. This is achieved by providing students with a comprehensive range of skills and information.

In essence, the presence of education and workforce development institutions plays a crucial role in sustaining capitalism within the context of the AI era. These programs aim to provide students with both technical skills and the ability to think critically and adapt, therefore enabling them to succeed in economies that are heavily influenced by artificial intelligence. These institutions are essential in mitigating income inequality and advancing individual liberties through the provision of accessible educational and training opportunities. They also contribute to cultivating a vibrant and competitive labor force within the capitalist system.

5.Data Governance and Privacy Protection

In economies powered by artificial intelligence, data holds significant value. In the context of capitalist systems, data protection and privacy are upheld by various institutions, including data protection authorities and privacy advocacy groups, who are responsible for ensuring the preservation of individual privacy rights. The establishment of norms and standards for data collection, utilization, and sharing serves the purpose of safeguarding individuals from privacy infractions, while simultaneously facilitating responsible data-driven innovation.

In AI-driven capitalist economies, the presence of data governance and privacy protection organizations is crucial in safeguarding individual rights and privacy. In the current context where data holds significant value, these establishments assume a crucial function in safeguarding privacy rights and guaranteeing that data-centric advancements are in accordance with the principles of individual liberties and economic motivations inherent in capitalism.

In economies driven by artificial intelligence, where innovation and competition are fueled by data, the establishment of norms and standards for ethical data management by data protection agencies and privacy advocacy groups is of utmost importance. The regulations address a range of data governance aspects, encompassing the collecting, storage, processing, and exchange of data. Through the establishment of well-defined norms, these organizations establish a structural framework that enables firms to effectively utilize data while also safeguarding individual privacy. This facilitates a balanced and mutually beneficial connection between capitalism and innovation driven by data.

Furthermore, these establishments serve to protect individuals from infringements on their privacy. Within a capitalist framework, individuals are afforded the liberty to actively participate in digital services and platforms, with the assurance that their personal data would not be mismanaged or subjected to unauthorized use. Data protection authorities impose stringent penalties for data breaches, thereby ensuring organizational accountability and promoting the adoption of effective data security measures. This is consistent with the principles of capitalism, which prioritize the protection of individual property rights and the utilization of economic incentives.

Moreover, these establishments play a vital role in maintaining a delicate equilibrium between fostering innovation and safeguarding privacy. While capitalism serves as a catalyst for fostering innovation inside firms, it is imperative that such endeavors are undertaken with a sense of responsibility. Data governance and privacy protection institutions play a crucial role in enabling organizations to leverage the potential of data for innovation, while simultaneously adhering to the limitations imposed by privacy legislation. The delicate equilibrium between fostering innovation and protecting privacy is crucial for upholding individual rights and ensuring that data-driven advancements are conducted in an ethical manner, aligning with the fundamental principles of fairness and openness that underpin capitalism.

In summary, the establishment of data governance and privacy protection institutions plays a crucial role in AI-driven capitalist economies. The establishment of regulations and standards is crucial in facilitating responsible data-driven innovation while simultaneously protecting the rights of individuals with regards to privacy. These establishments play a crucial role in fostering the prosperity of capitalism while upholding individual liberties and privacy, so making significant contributions to a vibrant and morally sound economic environment driven by AI technology.

6.Competition and Antitrust Regulation

Capitalism is predicated upon the utilization of competitive markets as a means to foster innovation and deter the emergence of monopolistic practices. Antitrust authorities are responsible for overseeing market competition and enforcing measures against anti-competitive acts that have the potential to impede innovation. Within the realm of artificial intelligence (AI), these establishments assume a pivotal function in mitigating the risk of excessive consolidation of AI authority and guaranteeing equitable opportunities for emerging participants to engage in competition.

Competition and antitrust regulation play a crucial role in upholding the fundamental principles of capitalism in economic systems driven by artificial intelligence (AI). These institutions are specifically structured to uphold competitive markets, which function as fertile environments for fostering innovation, deterring monopolistic practices, and facilitating fair competition among enterprises. These elements are considered fundamental tenets of capitalist principles.

Capitalism flourishes through the mechanism of competition, which serves as a catalyst for enterprises to engage in innovation, enhance their offerings, and strive for operational efficiencies. In the realm of artificial intelligence (AI), where innovation possesses the potential to bring about transformational and potentially disruptive changes, competition authorities assume the role of safeguarding the dynamic essence of capitalism. By promoting and maintaining competitive markets, there is a conducive climate for the emergence of new AI technologies, which in turn poses challenges to incumbent companies and facilitates advancement.

Furthermore, competitive institutions assume a crucial function in mitigating monopolistic conduct, which has the potential to impede innovation and curtail consumer options. In economies driven by artificial intelligence (AI), wherein the phenomenon of network effects can result in the consolidation of power within a small number of dominant technology giants, regulatory bodies specializing in antitrust matters intervene to mitigate activities that hinder competition. The primary objective is to prevent dominant AI companies from employing exclusionary strategies that impede competition or engaging in predatory pricing practices that undercut smaller competitors. By adopting this approach, organizations uphold a competitive environment that allows for the participation of various entities in fostering innovation, aligning with the fundamental tenets of capitalism.

Moreover, antitrust institutions strive to ensure that emerging players and entrepreneurial ventures are provided with equitable opportunities to engage in competition. In the context of the dynamic domain of artificial intelligence (AI), whereby limited access to data and resources might impede participation, these establishments serve to mitigate disparities and promote equitable opportunities. Through the surveillance of mergers and acquisitions and the evaluation of their prospective influence on competition, regulatory bodies aim to avoid the excessive concentration of power in the field of artificial intelligence (AI) and safeguard the emergence of new innovators.

Competition and antitrust legislation play crucial roles within the framework of AI-driven capitalism. One of the key objectives of regulations is to foster competition, discourage monopolistic practices, and facilitate the inclusion of new participants in AI-driven economic ecosystems. These institutions play a crucial role in upholding the fundamental tenets of capitalism, namely innovation, choice, and fair competition. By creating a conducive atmosphere, they facilitate the growth and development of artificial intelligence (AI) while simultaneously ensuring that society as a whole reaps the benefits.

7.International Cooperation

In the context of AI-driven capitalism, the presence of institutions that promote international cooperation and establish standards is of utmost importance. Artificial intelligence (AI) has become a pervasive worldwide phenomena, necessitating the need for international cooperation to build shared ethical and legal frameworks. In the realm of artificial intelligence (AI), entities such as the United Nations and international trade organizations assume the responsibility of aligning regulations pertaining to AI and safeguarding the adherence to capitalist principles on a global scale.

International cooperation institutions play a vital role within the framework of AI-driven capitalism, owing to the intrinsically global characteristics of artificial intelligence. These institutions play a crucial role in influencing the global AI development landscape by facilitating the establishment of universal ethical and regulatory norms, and by upholding principles of competition, innovation, and economic incentives within an international context.

The widespread presence of artificial intelligence (AI) and the transnational character of data transfers necessitate the imperative of international cooperation. International organizations such as the United Nations (UN) and global trade associations offer platforms for nations to synchronize their policies pertaining to artificial intelligence (AI). The establishment of collaborative efforts is crucial in guaranteeing the smooth integration of AI technologies into international markets while upholding standardized practices. The promotion of fairness and transparency in international trade is a key objective, as it facilitates a competitive environment that enables enterprises from many countries to engage in fair competition.

Furthermore, it is worth noting that international cooperation organizations have a significant role in establishing ethical rules for artificial intelligence (AI). The ethical standards governing artificial intelligence (AI) should not be limited to national boundaries, but rather should encompass universal ideals. Institutions such as the United Nations play a significant role in fostering the establishment of global ethical frameworks for artificial intelligence (AI), with a particular emphasis on concepts such as fairness, accountability, and transparency. This ensures that artificial intelligence technology adhere to ethical standards while complying with capitalist principles.

Moreover, the establishment of international collaboration plays a pivotal role in effectively tackling worldwide issues pertaining to artificial intelligence (AI), such as the ethical utilization of autonomous weaponry or guaranteeing equitable distribution of AI advancements for the betterment of all humankind. These institutions play a crucial role in fostering international collaboration, which in turn enables the sharing of information and best practices. This collaborative approach allows nations to collectively tackle these difficulties while maintaining the fundamental ideals of justice and equal opportunity that are inherent to the capitalist system.

International cooperation institutions play a crucial role within the framework of AI-driven capitalism, as evidenced by their significance. Global institutions play a crucial role in facilitating the adoption of shared ethical and regulatory norms, promoting the universal application of capitalist principles beyond national boundaries, and offering effective tools for tackling global issues. By engaging in such actions, individuals provide a conducive atmosphere for the flourishing of AI technologies on a worldwide level, hence yielding advantages for both personal liberties and economic expansion within a capitalist paradigm.

In summary, institutions play a fundamental role in preserving and harmonizing capitalist principles within the context of AI-driven economic systems. The establishment of laws, regulations, and ethical standards governing artificial intelligence (AI) serves to foster innovation and competitiveness, while simultaneously addressing ethical concerns, privacy issues, and the need for justice. Within this ever-changing and complex environment, these establishments hold significant importance in influencing the trajectory of AI-powered commerce and its ramifications on society. The efficacy and adaptability of capitalism will play a crucial role in determining its ability to effectively utilize the advantages of artificial intelligence while also addressing and minimizing its potential drawbacks.

Ethical considerations and debates surrounding the intersection of AI and capitalist values

The intersection of AI and capitalist values has sparked a range of ethical considerations and debates that touch upon various aspects of this complex relationship. Here, we delve into some of the prominent ethical issues and debates surrounding AI within the context of capitalist systems:

1. Bias and Discrimination

One of the primary ethical considerations revolves with the possibility of bias and discrimination inside artificial intelligence (AI) algorithms, particularly in domains such as employment, lending, and the criminal justice system. Artificial intelligence (AI) systems have the potential to unintentionally acquire biases that exist within the training data, resulting in the emergence of discriminating consequences. For example, algorithms that exhibit prejudice have the potential to unjustly discriminate against specific ethnic or gender demographics, so contradicting the fundamental tenets of capitalism that emphasize equal opportunity and justice. The focal point of the ethical discourse revolves around the methods employed to identify, forestall, and alleviate these biases. Advocates of this perspective contend that implementing more stringent rules and fostering transparency in the development of artificial intelligence are necessary measures to guarantee equity in decision-making processes influenced by AI.

The ethical concern surrounding bias and discrimination in AI algorithms is a complex topic with wide-ranging ramifications, particularly in domains directly associated with capitalist ideas, including employment, banking, and justice systems. The ethical discourse pertaining to this matter digs extensively into the methods via which biases may arise in artificial intelligence (AI) systems and the necessary measures to remedy and mitigate them.

The utilization of training data in the development of AI algorithms is a key factor contributing to bias inside these systems. When historical data exhibits societal prejudices or disparities, AI models have the potential to unintentionally perpetuate these biases while making decisions. In the context of employment, the utilization of historical data to train artificial intelligence (AI) recruitment tools that exhibit gender or racial biases might result in discriminatory consequences, so compromising the fundamental tenets of equal opportunity and fairness within a capitalist framework. Hence, the ethical discourse encompasses not alone the prejudices inherent in AI, but also the biases deeply rooted in society.

Efforts aimed at mitigating bias and discrimination in artificial intelligence (AI) cover a range of tactics. These strategies include conducting audits of AI models to identify and correct biases, reassessing the training data used to develop these models, and building algorithms that actively work to minimize biases. Ethical deliberations underscore the significance of transparency in the advancement of artificial intelligence (AI), advocating for increased disclosure on the utilized data, employed algorithms, and decision-making procedures. This emphasis on transparency aims to facilitate the identification and rectification of biases.

Furthermore, there is a contention that more stringent rules are needed in order to ensure equity in decision-making processes facilitated by artificial intelligence. Potential regulatory measures may encompass compulsory bias audits, protocols for ensuring fairness in the development of AI systems, and penalties for corporations that propagate bias in their AI applications. The ethical problem lies in effectively reconciling these regulatory measures with the fundamental capitalism premise of fostering innovation, competition, and entrepreneurship.

The issue of prejudice and discrimination in AI algorithms is a significant ethical concern that necessitates an examination of the underlying factors contributing to these biases. This highlights the importance of including transparency, accountability, and fairness into the creation of AI systems. The task at hand is the identification of ethical resolutions that are congruent with the principles of capitalism, specifically those pertaining to equal prospects, while simultaneously cultivating an atmosphere conducive to the sustained growth of innovation and competition. The resolution of these challenges is of utmost importance, as it serves the dual purpose of sustaining ethical norms and ensuring that AI-driven systems contribute to the overall welfare of society within the context of a capitalist framework.

2. Surveillance Capitalism

The concept of surveillance capitalism, originally introduced by researcher Shoshana Zuboff, gives rise to notable ethical considerations within the framework of capitalist systems. The term "commodification of personal data through surveillance for profit" is the process by which personal data is transformed into a marketable commodity through the utilization of surveillance techniques with the primary objective of generating financial gains. Technology corporations frequently amass huge quantities of user data, so giving rise to apprehensions pertaining to privacy and the autonomy of individuals. Critics contend that the commodification of personal information encroaches upon the rights and choices of individuals, giving rise to

ethical quandaries regarding the balance between convenience and privacy within the framework of capitalism.
The notion of surveillance capitalism provides a significant ethical dilemma within capitalist frameworks, illuminating the inherent conflict between profit-oriented advancements and the protection of individual rights, including privacy. The aforementioned concept, as introduced by Shoshana Zuboff, highlights the ethical quandaries that emerge when individuals' personal data is transformed into a marketable asset inside a capitalist environment powered by artificial intelligence.

The central focus of the ethical discourse pertaining to surveillance capitalism is in the extensive accumulation of personal data by technological corporations. These businesses collect substantial user data, frequently without complete transparency or consent, in order to support their business operations. Critics contend that the commercialization of personal information has the potential to encroach upon individuals' entitlements to privacy and autonomy, both of which are integral components of capitalist principles. The ethical concern arises from the concept that individuals are essentially commodified through the process of data harvesting and trading, resulting in a perceived degradation of their autonomy and ability to make choices.

This discourse beyond the basic acquisition of data and dives into the intricate trade-offs between convenience and privacy. The utilization of AI-driven services offers customers unparalleled convenience and personalized experiences. However, the ethical dilemma arises as to whether these advantages are obtained at the expense of compromising individual privacy. The task at hand is achieving a harmonious equilibrium between the capacity for groundbreaking advancements and financial gain within a capitalist structure, while concurrently safeguarding essential individual liberties.

Furthermore, the ethical discourse encompasses the necessity for enhanced levels of openness, consent systems, and rights pertaining to data ownership. There exists a contention that individuals need to possess greater agency over their data, encompassing the entitlement to determine its utilization and dissemination. These policies would be consistent with the capitalist values of upholding individual property rights and promoting freedom of choice.

Surveillance capitalism presents a notable ethical quandary within capitalist frameworks, wherein the pursuit of financial gain and advancement may occasionally conflict with personal privacy and autonomy. The identification of ethical resolutions within this particular framework necessitates the careful negotiation of the intricate equilibrium between convenience and privacy, the promotion of openness and consent, and the preservation of individual rights, all while ensuring that capitalism remains a catalyst for fostering innovation and competition.

3. Job Displacement and Income Inequality

The ethical implications of AI-driven automation on the labor market are a subject of intense debate. Artificial intelligence (AI) has the potential to enhance operational efficiency and increase production. However, it is important to acknowledge that AI implementation may also result in the displacement of human workers from conventional employment positions. This phenomenon gives rise to apprehensions regarding income inequality within the framework of capitalism, as certain individuals contend that the implementation of AI-driven automation will potentially result in the consolidation of wealth within a select group of technology giants, while simultaneously depriving a significant portion of the population of viable employment prospects. The focal point of the discussion revolves around the optimal equilibrium between the economic incentives associated with automation and the ethical duty to confront the potential repercussions of job displacement. Various proposals, such as the implementation of universal basic income, are garnering increasing support in this context.

The ethical considerations pertaining to the displacement of jobs and the unequal distribution of money in the era of automation driven by artificial intelligence hold significant relevance within the framework of capitalist systems. The subject matter at hand is a multifaceted and controversial matter that centers on the fundamental inquiries regarding equitable distribution of economic resources, access to opportunities, and the broader implications for society resulting from technological progress.

The utilization of AI-driven automation, despite its evident advantages in terms of enhanced efficiency and increased productivity, exerts a significant influence on the labor market. The central ethical quandary pertains to the possible displacement of human laborers from conventional occupations, particularly in industries where artificial intelligence (AI) exhibits significant efficacy. The phenomenon of displacement caused by automation has the potential to give rise to economic inequality, as certain persons may encounter difficulties in securing alternative work prospects, while others reap the advantages of cost-saving measures facilitated by automation.

The discourse surrounding job displacement and income inequality within the framework of capitalism revolves around the quest for a harmonious equilibrium between the economic motivations driving automation and the moral obligation to address its adverse effects. The challenge encompasses multiple facets. Capitalism, as an economic system, incentivizes and promotes advancements in technology and the quest for increased efficiency. This, in turn, can be facilitated by the implementation of AI-driven automation. However, it is important to note that capitalism also places significance on economic mobility and equitable opportunity. Nevertheless, these principles might be compromised when substantial portions of the populace encounter job insecurity or unemployment as a result of automation.

In light of these ethical considerations, there has been an increasing acceptance and support for initiatives such as universal basic income (UBI). Universal Basic Income (UBI) is regarded by certain individuals as a potential solution to mitigate income inequality. This approach entails the provision of a guaranteed minimum income to all members of a society, regardless of their job circumstances. Advocates contend that Universal Basic Income (UBI) has the potential to provide a more equitable distribution of the advantages brought about by automation within the confines of a capitalist system, thereby mitigating the excessive accumulation of wealth.

Nevertheless, the execution of these suggestions continues to be a topic of continuous discussion. Critics express apprehensions over the viability and long-term viability of Universal Basic Income (UBI), with its capacity to undermine job motivation. The key problem in AI-driven capitalism lies in striking a delicate equilibrium between fostering innovation through automation and fulfilling the ethical responsibility to mitigate severe wealth inequality.

In summary, the ethical concerns pertaining to the displacement of jobs and the unequal distribution of income in the era of AI automation pose an intricate and diverse dilemma within capitalist frameworks. The ongoing discussion highlights the need of harmonizing the endeavor for technological advancement with the ethical obligation to guarantee equitable distribution of its advantages, so sustaining the fundamental tenets of capitalism, including economic opportunity and fairness, at a period characterized by swift technological transformations.

4.Data Ownership and Privacy

Data ownership and privacy rights are subjects of ongoing ethical discourse. Within a capitalist framework, it is commonplace for corporations to gather and commercialize consumer data. Nevertheless, inquiries emerge over the ownership of this data and the extent to which individuals should own greater authority over it. There is a contention advocating for more robust legislation pertaining to data privacy and the implementation of mechanisms that afford individuals greater control over the utilization of their data. This perspective aligns with the fundamental tenets of capitalism, namely the recognition of property rights and the preservation of individual freedoms.

The examination of ethical considerations surrounding the ownership of data and the protection of privacy rights within the framework of capitalism involves a comprehensive analysis of the complex interplay between individual liberties, property rights, and the commodification of personal data. The discourse surrounding this topic plays a crucial role in delineating the limits between corporate interests and personal autonomy within the context of AI-driven capitalism.

Within capitalist economic systems, it is common for firms to amass and use customer data as a valuable asset in order to generate financial gains. The aforementioned practice, while fostering the advancement of innovative ideas and stimulating competitive dynamics, gives rise to significant ethical inquiries. Central to this discourse lies the inquiry of the rightful ownership of data produced by individuals. The conventional tenets of capitalism place significant importance on the inviolability of property rights. However, when it comes to personal data, the application of these principles presents a challenge to the concept of ownership. Critics contend that granting individuals greater agency in managing their data is vital, as it serves as an extension of their personal identity and actions.

The discourse surrounding data ownership and privacy is intricately linked to the overarching ethical issue of how personal information is employed. There is a contention in favor of more stringent legislation regarding data privacy, which would grant individuals the authority to determine the manner in which personal data is gathered, retained, and employed. The regulations may include several elements, including processes for obtaining consent, rights to access data, and the right to have personal information erased. The objective is to achieve a harmonious equilibrium between the financial motivations of data-centric enterprises and the ethical obligation to uphold the rights and autonomy of persons.

Proponents of methods that grant individuals enhanced control over their data match their stance with capitalist ideas pertaining to individual freedoms and property rights. The authors contend that it is imperative for individuals to assume the role of primary decision-makers with respect to their personal data, while corporations must demonstrate transparency and accountability in their handling of such data.

Nevertheless, the incorporation of comprehensive data privacy legislation inside capitalist frameworks presents certain obstacles. The task of achieving a harmonious equilibrium between safeguarding individual privacy and facilitating company innovation and competition might present intricate challenges. Furthermore, the inherent global nature of data flows presents challenges in establishing uniform privacy standards across different countries, hence giving rise to concerns regarding the worldwide harmonization of data governance in a manner that upholds the ethical principles of privacy and individual autonomy.

The ethical discourse pertaining to data ownership and privacy rights encapsulates the inherent conflict between capitalist tenets, specifically the ideals of property rights and individual liberties, and the commodification of personal data. The attainment of an ethical equilibrium necessitates the skillful negotiation of the intricate dynamics between commercial interests and individual autonomy, as well as the establishment of regulatory frameworks that promote innovation while upholding fundamental rights and choices within a capitalist environment powered by artificial intelligence.

5. Transparency and Accountability

The ethical aspect of ensuring transparency and accountability in AI systems is of utmost importance. The ideology of capitalism places significant importance on the ability of consumers to make well-informed choices. However, the presence of opaque artificial intelligence algorithms has the potential to impede this process. Ethical discussions revolve around the question of whether it is imperative for businesses and developers to enhance the level of transparency regarding the inner workings of their AI systems, as well as whether they should bear responsibility for the decisions made by AI. There is a contention among proponents that the implementation of legislation mandating transparency and accountability in artificial intelligence (AI) systems is necessary to foster confidence and ensure ethical utilization within the context of a capitalist framework.

The academic discussion over the ethical considerations related to transparency and accountability in artificial intelligence (AI) systems operating within capitalist frameworks highlights the intricate interplay between innovation, customer confidence, and well-informed decision-making. The ethical aspect plays a pivotal role in ensuring that AI technologies are in accordance with the principles of capitalism, namely those related to competition and individual choice.

In capitalist economies, the significance of educated consumer decisions is greatly emphasized due to their contribution to fostering competition and facilitating the functioning of efficient markets. Nevertheless, artificial intelligence (AI) systems are sometimes perceived as "black boxes," characterized by intricate decision-making processes that are not readily comprehensible to end-users. The absence of transparency in this context may impede humans' capacity to make well-informed decisions and gives rise to ethical considerations regarding the lack of clarity in decision-making processes powered by artificial intelligence.

A fundamental element of the ethical discourse is to the question of whether corporations and developers ought to enhance the level of transparency regarding the internal mechanisms of their artificial intelligence (AI) systems. Proponents of transparency contend that individuals possess a legitimate entitlement to be informed about the manner in which artificial intelligence (AI) algorithms exert influence over decisions that have a direct impact on their life. The concept of transparency can be seen in diverse manners, including the provision of explanations for algorithmic judgments, the disclosure of data sources, or the accessibility of the underlying code of artificial intelligence systems. Through this action, individuals can enhance their comprehension and assessment of the commodities or services they engage with, so fostering ethical decision-making within the framework of capitalism.

Accountability represents an additional crucial aspect. The ethical discourse revolves around the question of whether businesses and developers need to bear responsibility for the choices made by artificial intelligence systems. The emergence of biased or negative outcomes generated by AI systems prompts inquiries on accountability. There is a contention among certain individuals that rules ought to enforce accountability measures, which would necessitate firms to assume responsibility for the ethical utilization of their artificial intelligence (AI) technologies. This may involve the implementation of strategies to mitigate AI-related negative consequences, provision of reparation for persons impacted by AI-driven decisions, or imposition of sanctions for unethical AI behaviors.

Nevertheless, the incorporation of transparency and accountability mechanisms inside capitalist frameworks presents certain obstacles. Achieving a harmonious equilibrium between promoting innovation and safeguarding consumer interests can be a complex challenge. Furthermore, the complexities surrounding the determination of suitable levels of transparency and accountability are evident, given the vast range of applications and impacts exhibited by AI technology.

In essence, the ethical discourse pertaining to transparency and accountability in artificial intelligence (AI) systems within capitalist settings underscores the significance of well-informed consumer decision-making and conscientious corporate conduct. The attainment of an ethical equilibrium necessitates the skillful navigation of the complexities of AI transparency and accountability. This requires the formulation of regulatory frameworks that foster trust and ethical utilization of AI within the context of capitalist systems, all the while safeguarding the preservation of innovation and competition.

6. Access and Equity

The issue of uneven access to AI-driven technology raises ethical concerns regarding the distribution of gains derived from AI within a capitalist framework. There exist apprehensions over the potential for AI developments to exhibit a lopsided distribution of benefits, favoring specific socioeconomic groups while potentially neglecting others. Ethical discussions center on the imperative of guaranteeing fair and just access to artificial intelligence (AI) technologies, fostering programs aimed at narrowing the digital divide, and tackling discrepancies in the adoption of AI in a manner consistent with the ideals of equal opportunity within a capitalist framework.

The ethical discussion around the accessibility and fairness of artificial intelligence (AI) technologies within a capitalist system highlights the importance of balancing the values of equal opportunity and innovation with the possibility of uneven access and discrepancies in the distribution of advantages.

The equal distribution of chances and benefits is a fundamental premise in capitalist systems. Nevertheless, artificial intelligence (AI) technologies, due to their diverse range of uses, have the potential to unintentionally worsen pre-existing disparities. The ethical discussions within this particular setting revolve around the strategies and measures required to guarantee equitable access to the advantages offered by artificial intelligence, regardless of an individual's socioeconomic standing.

One of the primary ethical considerations pertains to the phenomenon known as the digital divide, which denotes the disparity in individuals' access to digital technologies and the internet. This disparity may result in inequitable availability of AI-powered services, particularly within marginalized or underserved areas. Ethical discourse places significant emphasis on activities aimed at bridging this difference, including the expansion of internet accessibility, implementation of digital literacy programs, and the equitable distribution of AI technologies to marginalized groups. These endeavors strive to adhere to the tenets of capitalism, specifically the notion of equal opportunity, in order to guarantee that every individual is afforded a just and equitable opportunity to reap the benefits of AI advancements.

Moreover, the existence of discrepancies in the adoption and exploitation of artificial intelligence (AI) also gives rise to ethical concerns. Certain socioeconomic strata may encounter restricted availability of AI-driven healthcare, education, or employment prospects, resulting in disparate outcomes. Ethical discussions within the framework of capitalism revolve around the formulation of approaches aimed at mitigating these discrepancies. This may entail the implementation of specific rules, subsidies, or incentives to ensure that the deployment of AI technologies is oriented towards fostering equitable access and advantages.

Nevertheless, the ethical dilemma resides in the delicate equilibrium between these endeavors and the imperative to cultivate innovation and competitiveness. Capitalism is characterized by its reliance on entrepreneurial initiatives and competitive dynamics, which can serve as catalysts for the advancement of novel AI solutions. Ethical deliberations underscore the importance of ensuring that endeavors aimed at fostering accessibility and fairness in the innovation ecosystem are mutually reinforcing rather than obstructive.

The ethical discourse pertaining to the accessibility and fairness of AI technology within capitalist systems underscores the necessity of guaranteeing universal access to the advantages offered by AI. Attaining this equilibrium necessitates navigating the intricacies associated with the digital divide, rectifying disparities in the adoption of artificial intelligence (AI), and advocating for endeavors that uphold the capitalist tenets of equal opportunity and competition, all while fostering a societal environment wherein AI technologies are utilized for the advancement and welfare of all individuals.

In summary, the convergence of artificial intelligence and capitalist principles gives rise to intricate ethical problems and engenders disputes of a multifaceted nature. These talks encompass topics such as bias, discrimination, surveillance capitalism, employment displacement, data ownership, transparency, accountability, and access to artificial intelligence (AI) technologies. The identification of ethical resolutions within capitalist frameworks frequently necessitates the establishment of a harmonious equilibrium between the drive for innovation and financial gain, and the imperative to maintain principles of equity, openness, and personal liberties. The resolution of these ethical arguments will have a significant impact on the ethical and societal consequences of artificial intelligence (AI) in capitalist countries.

Book Conclusion

Within the context of our exploration of "The Economics of Artificial Intelligence: Institutional Transformations and Implications for Capitalism," we have embarked upon a multifaceted terrain wherein technology, economics, and ethics intersect. Through the progression of each chapter, we have systematically examined the complex mechanisms by which artificial intelligence is reshaping our economic structures, institutions, and societal conventions. In conclusion, it is apparent that the influence of artificial intelligence (AI) is extensive, significant, and revolutionary.

The predominant motif that has resonated throughout this literary work pertains to the intricate dynamics between artificial intelligence and capitalism principles. The observation has been made of the significant capacity of artificial intelligence (AI) to enhance processes, stimulate innovation, and generate novel economic prospects. Concurrently, we have encountered the ethical problems and controversies that arise when artificial intelligence connects with the core tenets of capitalism, namely, the notions of individual autonomy, the rights to private property, and economic motivations.

The Balancing Act: AI and Individual Freedom

The ascendancy of artificial intelligence (AI) presents a dual impact on individual freedom, a fundamental tenet of capitalist ideology, as it simultaneously enhances and poses challenges to this principle. On the one hand, artificial intelligence (AI) provides individuals with the opportunity to free themselves from monotonous duties, therefore granting them additional time and cognitive capacity to engage in creative and purposeful pursuits. The provision of information and specialized services empowers individuals, granting them increased autonomy in the process of making decisions.

However, artificial intelligence (AI) also gives rise to apprehensions over the issues of surveillance, privacy, and algorithmic control. The potential encroachment into individual rights arises from the data-driven characteristics of AI systems in cases of mishandling or misuse. Achieving a delicate equilibrium between using the promise of artificial intelligence (AI) to promote individual freedom and mitigating the risks of its future intrusion represents a crucial ethical and regulatory dilemma.

The Nexus of Property Rights and AI

Capitalism upholds the significance of private property rights as a mechanism to stimulate innovation and encourage investment. The utilization of artificial intelligence (AI) raises significant concerns regarding the parameters and dynamics of intellectual property rights. The fundamental components of artificial intelligence, namely algorithms, databases, and software, have the potential to challenge conventional boundaries of intellectual property. In guaranteeing the rights of innovators, institutions such as patent offices and copyright agencies have a crucial position. However, it is imperative for these institutions to adapt to the ever-changing world of artificial intelligence (AI).

Concurrently, artificial intelligence (AI) prompts issues around the ownership of data. The act of individuals providing their data to AI systems raises intricate questions around the ownership and governance of the resultant AI models. The constant challenge for institutions operating within a capitalist framework is to strike a balance between the motivating influence of property rights and the imperative to tailor these rights to accommodate the distinct qualities of artificial intelligence (AI).

Economic Incentives in an AI-Driven World

Capitalism flourishes through harnessing innovation and entrepreneurial endeavors, and the advent of artificial intelligence (AI) is positioned to foster economic expansion through the automation of tasks, improved efficiency, and the emergence of novel business opportunities. The implementation of artificial intelligence (AI) has the potential to reduce expenses, enhance efficiency, and create opportunities for market expansion, hence drawing investments in the field of AI research and development.

Nevertheless, the impact of AI on economic incentives is not universally beneficial. The issue of income inequality becomes a prominent concern in instances where workers are displaced by AI-driven automation, as it has the potential to concentrate wealth within the tech industry's major corporations. This statement questions the fundamental principles of capitalism, particularly in terms of fairness and equal opportunity. It emphasizes the need for creative governmental measures to reconcile the economic advantages of artificial intelligence (AI) with the overall welfare of society.

The Intersection of Ethics and Capitalism

Throughout our investigation, the concept of ethics has consistently emerged as a prominent theme in the narrative. The field of artificial intelligence (AI) presents a multitude of ethical dilemmas, encompassing issues such as algorithmic prejudice and discrimination, apprehensions over monitoring and data privacy, as well as the need for openness. The consistent theme of achieving a harmonious equilibrium among the promotion of innovation, competition, and ethical responsibility has been observed again.

In the era of artificial intelligence, institutions have assumed a crucial role in sustaining and harmonizing the principles of capitalism. Proposals for regulatory frameworks have been put out with the aim of providing guidance for the development and utilization of artificial intelligence (AI), thereby striking a balance between fostering innovation and upholding ethical responsibility. Ethical oversight authorities, educational institutions, data governance groups, and market regulators each contribute to the development of a responsible and equitable economic landscape powered by artificial intelligence (AI).

Charting the Path Forward: Balancing Innovation and Responsibility

The exploration of "The Economics of Artificial Intelligence" has revealed the complex interplay between AI and capitalism, providing valuable perspectives on the opportunities and obstacles they collectively entail. The compatibility of artificial intelligence (AI) and capitalism is contingent upon achieving a nuanced equilibrium. This equilibrium must safeguard the flourishing of individual freedom, facilitate the adaptation of property rights, maintain inclusive economic incentives, and prioritize ethical considerations as a guiding force for progress.

In the realm of economic dynamics, institutions assume the crucial role of both safeguarding and shaping the overall landscape, thereby bearing the onus of attaining this state of equilibrium. It is imperative for regulatory frameworks to promote innovation while upholding ethical principles. It is imperative for educational and vocational institutions to provide individuals with the necessary skills and knowledge to thrive in a society increasingly influenced by artificial intelligence. The imperative for data governance entities lies in safeguarding privacy and facilitating conscientious innovation. It is imperative for market authorities to effectively promote competition and simultaneously avoid the emergence of monopolistic practices.

The unquestionable disruptive capacity of artificial intelligence (AI) is evident, and its ongoing incorporation into capitalist institutions holds significant potential. However, the fulfillment of this commitment presents significant ethical, regulatory, and economic obstacles that require our utmost focus. The navigation of these problems will be crucial in delineating the trajectory ahead, one that entails the harmonious coexistence of capitalism and AI. This trajectory will prioritize the safeguarding of individual freedom, the adaptation of property rights, the equitable distribution of economic incentives, and the upholding of ethical principles. The ongoing journey holds significant potential and promise for the future of our economic systems and society as a whole.

www.ingramcontent.com/pod-product-compliance
Lightning Source LLC
LaVergne TN
LVHW060437061126
851857LV00016B/1661